VIARTIS

MAGELLAN

Francis Guillemard
Antonio Pigafetta
Francisco Albo
Gaspar Correa

PUBLISHING DATA

TITLE : Magellan

AUTHORS : Francis Guillemard, Antonio Pigafetta, Francisco Albo, Gaspar Correa

EDITORS : Keith Bridgeman, Tahira Arsham

ISBN : 978-1-906421-00-7

PUBLISHER : Viartis (http://viartis.net/publishers)

PUBLICATION DATE : 2008

PLACE OF PUBLICATION : England

LANGUAGE : English

FORMAT : Paperback

EDITION : First

TOPICS : Biography

LIBRARY CLASSIFICATION (Dewey decimal classification) : 920

SHORT DESCRIPTION : The biography of Ferdinand Magellan (1480–1521), the commander of the first ships to sail around the world.

LONG DESCRIPTION : The biography of Ferdinand Magellan (1480-1521), the commander of the first ships to sail around the world. In 1519, Magellan set out in command of a fleet of five ships. They were the first Europeans to sail around the south of South America, and across the Pacific Ocean, and the first to sail around the world. Their epic voyage continued despite mutiny, starvation, scurvy, warfare, and treachery, that resulted in the considerable loss of lives and ships. Included are all of the first hand accounts of their journey, recorded by Antonio Pigafetta, Francisco Albo, "the unknown Portuguese", Gaspar Correa, the "Genoese pilot", and an account by Maximilian Transylvanus. Of the five ships and more than 270 men that set out on that famous first voyage around the world, only one ship was to complete it, with only eighteen of those men aboard, but Magellan was not one of them.

SIZE : 229 mm x 152 mm

PAGES : 408

ILLUSTRATIONS : 10

INTRODUCTION

This is the biography of Ferdinand Magellan (1480–1521), the commander of the first ships to attempt to sail around the world.

Ferdinand Magellan was born in Portugal in 1480. In 1517, he went to Spain to see the teenaged Spanish king, the future Holy Roman Emperor Charles V. He sought and gained his support for the first voyage around the world.

In 1519, by then Spanish, Magellan set out from Spain in command of a fleet of five ships. His aim was to sail around the southern tip of South America, even though it was then not known if there was such a route. From there he aimed to make the first ever journey across the Pacific Ocean to the tremendously lucrative Spice Islands, before completing his journey around the world by returning to Spain.

The ship's crew saw lands, seas, animals, plants, fruits and peoples never seen by Europeans before, including a "camel without humps" (possibly a llama, guanaco, vicuña, or alpaca), and a penguin, that they described as a "black goose" that had to be skinned instead of plucked. They were astonished by the appearance of a Patagonian Giant - a man of gigantic stature on the beach, who sang and danced, pouring sand upon his head in token of amity.

They were the first Europeans to sail around the south of South America, and to sail across the Pacific Ocean, which was named by them. They were also the first to sail from Europe westwards to Asia, and the first men to sail around the world. Their epic voyage continued despite mutiny, starvation (which caused them to eat rats, hides and sawdust), scurvy, warfare, and treachery, that resulted in the considerable loss of lives and ships.

Included are all of the first hand accounts of their journey, recorded by Antonio Pigafetta, Francisco Albo, "the unknown Portuguese", Gaspar Correa, the "Genoese pilot", and by Maximilian Transylvanus.

Of the five ships and more than 270 men that set out on that famous first voyage around the world, only one ship was to complete it, with only eighteen of those men aboard, but Magellan was not one of them.

CONTENTS

CONTENTS

CHAPTER 1

EARLY LIFE

Fernão de Magalhães (Ferdinand Magellan) was born about the year 1480 - we do not know the precise date - at Sabrosa, near Chaves, in the province of Tras-os-Montes, one of the wildest districts of Portugal. Separated from the tamer seaboard province of Entre Douro e Minho by the bold Serra de Marão, the country presents few features of attraction to the ordinary traveller. Its inaccessibility, and the lack of anything of interest save a certain gloomy grandeur in its scenery, do not invite a visit.

It is true that he left it in his youth, and that we hear nothing of his return; that his short life seems, after a brief period of attendance at court, to have been spent in a swift succession of intoxicating successes with sword and compass - a ceaseless medley of fighting and exploration that can have left little time for home thoughts, and none for the strengthening of home-ties and friendships. However, the influence of his childhood's surroundings was there.

As we follow his life step by step, we are not left long in doubt as to the character of the man. Its leading feature is what his enemies would term an overweening confidence in his own powers - an obstinacy without an equal. Others would name it differently. His faults, if faults they were, were those of strength. If men have been termed men of iron, Magellan may fairly be said to have been of steel. For him, difficulties were made only to be disregarded, dangers only to be despised. Through the barriers of an impossibility he passed confident and unmoved. With almost every one against him, the India House, the ambassador of the King of Portugal, and his own friend, he started upon his voyage. With a mutiny but half repressed and starvation imminent, he pressed southward till he found his long hoped for straits. With his captains' advice to the contrary ringing in his ears, he went to his death. The story of his life is full of such traits, and it is hard not to ascribe them in some measure to the influence of the country in which his boyhood was passed.

Other reasons, it may be, lay in his birth, for Magellan was of noble family - "of the oldest in the kingdom," as he himself tells us. There were at that period five grades of nobility in Portugal, to the fourth of which the family of Magalhães belonged - the "fidalgos da cota de armas e geração que tem insignias de nobreza" - a rank to which in England there is no equivalent. Of those who bore it before the great navigator we have no such clear account. Various names have been given by Antonio de Lima and other genealogists as those of his father and grandfather, but as they do not agree, we are forced to reject them and to fall hack upon surer evidence. Of this there is something, though unfortunately far less than we desire. In a receipt for his salary as "moço fidalgo" in the king's service, dated June 12, 1512, Magellan describes himself as "filho de Pedro de Magalhães" but this appears to be the sum total of our certain knowledge of his forbears.

Even of his own family we know little. His Mother was Alda de Mesquita. He seems to have had but one brother, Diogo de Sousa. We learn incidentally, from the mention of their names in his wills, of the existence of two sisters, Isabel and Thereza, who married a certain João da Silva Telles, of whom we shall hear more presently. A shadowy Ginebra figures as a third sister, but her existence, at all events in that relationship, is doubtful. His own two children dying as infants, the family of Magalhães became extinct in his father's line.

The name, however, appears frequently in the old chroniclers at the early part of the sixteenth century. A certain Martin de Magalhães accompanied the navigator in his great voyage, and the deeds of two brothers, Antonio and Pero Barreto de Magalhães, who were doubtless members of his family, are many times recorded. Both served under the first Viceroy of India, Don Francisco d'Almeida. Both fell in battle - the former in the noble defeat of Don Lourenzo by the Turks under Mir Hoseyn and Malik Jaz at Chaoul, the latter by the side of the Viceroy himself, when he and sixty-five of his men perished in a skirmish with the Kafirs of Saldanha Bay. Of yet another, Christovão de Magalhães, we hear as accompanying Alfonso d'Albuquerque in his expedition to Ormuz. However, beyond the fact that, together with many other of the Viceroy's captains, he was badly wounded in an engagement with the Persians at Lara, we know nothing.

Magellan lost his father and succeeded to the estates when still comparatively young, for in his first will, made at Belem before sailing for India under Almeida, we find him bequeathing the Sabrosa property, in which parish he owned the Quinta de Souta. He makes no mention of the Casa da Pereira, which, from a most curious and interesting document not long since brought to light, we know to have also belonged to him. In this, which is the will of Magellan's great nephew, Francisco da Silva Telles - the testator inveighs in the most vehement terms against his ancestor, ordering that thenceforward over his house in Sabrosa (the Casa da Pereira) no heir or descendant soever should restore the coat-of-arms of the family, "since I desire that it should for ever remain obliterated, as was done by order of my lord the king, as a punishment for the crime of Ferdinand Magellan, in that he entered the service of Castile to the injury of this kingdom, and went to discover new lands, where he died in the disgrace of our king."

To understand this, it is necessary to anticipate. Magellan, unable to obtain a recognition of his services at the hands of his sovereign, Dom Manoel, did what a triad of great navigators - Columbus, Cabot, and Vespucci - had already done before him, and what was at that period by no means unusual : he left his country and offered his sword to Charles V. These others have escaped with hardly a word of blame. However, owing to a combination of circumstances that will have presently to be considered, a quadruple obloquy appears to have fallen upon Magellan. The result we have partly seen. The King of Portugal, furious at the rise of Spanish influence in the Moluccas, commanded that the arms of Magellan should be erased from the gateway of his house. The effect of an order such as this in a remote village like Sabrosa may be imagined, and we can understand, even though we may not be able to forgive, the animus of Magellan's heir. We know that no man is a prophet in his own country. His fellow-townsmen forgot his years of faithful service in the East; forgot the coldness of his king; forgot that the glorious exploit in which he met his death made him one of the world's greatest men, and remembered him only as a renegade, whose heirs and their belongings were to be treated as they would have treated him. Every sort of insult was offered to Francisco da Silva; his name was execrated, and stones were thrown at him in the streets. Ultimately he was compelled to leave the country, and it was in the far-off province of Maranhão, in Brazil, that he dictated the will to which allusion has just been made.

The house, deserted by its owners, fell eventually to ruin. The family remained for long expatriated. It was not until much later - towards the end of the seventeenth century in fact - that any of its members resumed the name. About that time Dom Pedro II gave the title of Visconde de Fonte Arcada to a certain Pedro Jaques de Magalhães. However, the family appear never to have returned to Sabrosa. The old house, or rather its ruins, passed into other hands. A modern building took its place, constructed in part from the stones of the older mansion. One of these was that bearing the coat-of-arms "rasadas por ordem de El Rey." Torn from its place over the doorway, it subsequently occupied an ignoble position at the corner of the house.

Of Sabrosa and its belongings little more need be said. Upon Magellan's actual life there, history is silent. We can picture him amid his native mountains, riding the horses for which the district is still so famous, and hunting the game with which its woods abounded. We feel that in some such way his youth must have been spent, in active and vigorous exercises such as these, for, as we shall see, action and vigour were the two most marked features of his temperament. However probable the assumption, it will never pass within the domain of proof, for even Correa - most diffuse and garrulous of historians - treats us to no details of this period of his life.

Neither student nor courtier by nature, it was nevertheless Magellan's fate to become both in the course of his career. From the wilds of the Tras-os-Montes he was early transplanted to the capital. As in other courts, so in that of Portugal it was the custom at that period for the heirs of noble families to receive their education under the eye of their sovereign, their studies directed by him, and their successes rewarded by his approval. "Criose Magallanes en seruicio de la Reyna dopa Leonor" Argensola briefly tells us; and from the Anales de Aragon of Curita we learn that he was brought up as one of the pages of this queen, the widow of D. João II "the Perfect."

He did not long retain the post. In 1495 the King Dom Manoel, first of the House of Vizeu, came to the throne, and young Ferdinand Magellan passed into his service. In the whole course of the history of Portugal, no one - alone excepting Prince Henry the Navigator - had more to do with the foundation of her maritime power and the extension of her dominion than this king. His idée mère was to establish Portuguese influence in the East. In the half century immediately preceding, the aim and object of Prince Henry's work had to some extent been lost sight of. Exploration had indeed been going on, but in a more desultory manner. Bartholomew Diaz, it is true, had doubled the Cape of Good Hope, but eight long years had already elapsed when Dom Manoel came to the throne, and no action had as yet followed upon that event. Dom João II, a great geographer, a prince of the widest views upon the foreign policy of Portugal, and one of the most intellectual of her rulers, was, however, less a man of action than Dom Manoel. With the advent of the latter, the half-awakened energies of the Portuguese leapt suddenly into life. Within the short space of two decades the nation had reached the zenith of its glory, and had become the greatest maritime power of Europe.

Even at the present day, habituated as we are to the rapid march of events, and with the remembrance of the presto-like unfolding of the secrets of an almost unknown continent fresh in our memory, we find it hard to grasp the suddenness of this development of the Portuguese dominion; still harder, perhaps, to realise the boundless enthusiasm that it must have created.

Let us turn for a moment to the consideration of actual facts to a list of the expeditions despatched about this period from the shores of the mother country. Vasco da Gama, passing the Cape ten years after Bartholomew Diaz, had brought India from the shadowy regions of romance into those of vivid reality, and the Peninsula was ringing with his fame. Cabral, sailing for India in 1500, had discovered Brazil, and Gaspar Cortereal, almost at the same time, was coasting Labrador. In the following year the fleet of João da Nova discovered St. Helena, and in 1502 the second expedition of Vasco da Gama left the Tagus for India, combined with the fleet of Vicente Sodre. Two months later a second Indian expedition was despatched under Estevão da Gama. When the season was sufficiently advanced, ships were sent to the

"Terra de Bacalhaos" and Labrador to carry on the work of exploration, and to search for the missing Cortereals. In 1503 Alfonso and Francisco d'Albuquerque captained another armada for the East, and Gonzalo Coelho ventured far southwards along the unknown coasts of South America. From year to year this activity increased rather than diminished. In 1504, no less than three great expeditions were despatched. An armada of thirteen ships proceeded to India under Lopo Soarez d'Alvarenga. Dom João de Meneses headed an expedition against the Moors of Larache. Antonio de Saldanha left the kingdom a few weeks later with another Indian fleet.

Such, in a few words, is the bare list of expeditions that must have been fitted out and despatched under the very eyes of Magellan at the most impressionable period of his life. Of their coming and going, of their many victories and rare defeats, of their successful venture or disastrous loss, how much he must have heard ! The whole country was seething with excitement. The new worlds, alike of the East and of the West, held out a brilliant picture of infinite possibilities to the humblest in rank. The dockyards rang with the sound of axe and hammer. The ships were barely launched before they sailed for the lands that were to bring riches and distinction to every one - to every one, at least, who lived. One had but to be equipped with youth, and health, and ambition. Men left their country in shoals, careless of danger, heedless of death-rates, mindful only of the possible glory that awaited them. We can imagine the effect that experiences such as these must have had upon one so adventurous as Magellan. At such a time, when all around him were up and doing, it was impossible that he should remain a mere spectator. He did not hesitate for long. Applying to his sovereign for leave of absence, he bade adieu to court life. At the end of 1504 he enlisted as a volunteer in the great armada of Dom Francisco d'Almeida, at that time preparing to sail for India.

CHAPTER 2

SERVICE IN INDIA

Almeida's fleet was the largest that had hitherto set out for that promised land. Successful as other expeditions had been upon the whole, they had from time to time met with such difficulties and opposition as had served to warn Dom Manoel that a stronger hand would be advisable, and that the time had come for the appointment of a resident official who should hold the reins of government. The distance of the mother country from her Eastern possessions was indeed so great and the latter so scattered, that this had become an imperative necessity. The King's choice fell upon Francisco d'Almeida, son of the first Conde d'Abrantes, and it would have been hardly possible to make a better selection. To him, as first Viceroy of India, fell the task - Herculean in difficulty - of organising and ruling countries and peoples as yet almost unknown to their conquerors, and nobly he fulfilled it. His name extinguished by the greater glory claimed for his successor, Albuquerque is unfamiliar to many of us, but few, if any, have left the East with cleaner hands and a record more unsullied than Almeida. "Much did they love him," says Correa, "as being one blameless in his actions.....a man without a shadow of deceit." Such a man naturally attracted to him persons of like qualities, and his ships were not long in being manned. From all parts of the kingdom there flocked to him "many fidalgos and cavaliers, and people of distinction," says Correa, "many gallant men and cavaliers experienced in war," another writer tells us. Magellan could not well have begun his Indian experiences under better auspices or with better comrades.

The preparations made for Dom Francisco's fleet in the way of stores and outfit were in keeping with the importance of the expedition. Never before had things been done upon a larger scale. Of the exact number of ships of which the armada itself consisted, the historians of the period have left us in doubt. There were, however, at least twenty. Correa speaks of them as eight large ships (naos) for cargo, six of smaller size (nauetas), and six caravels. In addition wood was carried already shaped into the necessary planks and beams for two galleys and a "bargantym," which were to be constructed, on the arrival of the fleet in

India. They bore fifteen hundred men-at-arms, two hundred bombardiers, and four hundred seamen as supernumeraries for Indian commissions. Artisans of almost every kind were taken, and among them many carpenters, rope makers, and blacksmiths. The artillery and ammunition were "em muyta abastanza" in great plenty as indeed might be expected, for Vasco da Gama, in virtue of his new appointment as Admiral of India, gave to them his especial supervision. The daily presence of the King stimulated the labours of his subjects. The preparations advanced with great rapidity, and almost before the winter was over the ships were ready for sea.

In those days the departure upon an expedition such as this was looked upon as a serious matter. The most limited acquaintance with the historians of that date leaves no cause for wonder upon the subject. Sword and fever on land, and scurvy and shipwreck at sea thinned the ranks in a manner that was positively appalling. It would be interesting to know the usual percentage of survivors in these armadas. In some cases we do know it. In the final voyage of Magellan, for example, when we find that for every man who returned, six, or nearly six, perished. So we scarcely wonder at the solemnities which custom demanded of those who took part in them - at the special confession and mass, at which attendance was enjoined.

On this present occasion the ceremony was invested with a more than ordinary interest, for the standard of the Viceroy of India, after having been blessed by the bishop, was to be formally presented to Almeida by the King. Correa relates the function at some length, in words quaint and bald enough even for the days in which he wrote, but quite as powerfully descriptive, perhaps, as those from some more florid pen. We have little difficulty in realising the scene : the cathedral, filled almost to the doors with the members of the expedition alone; the king-at-arms clad in his rich habit, holding above Dom Manoel the "royal flag of white damask with Christ's cross in crimson satin bordered with gold"; Almeida kneeling at the King's feet and receiving it into his solemn care and keeping; his silent prayer before the high altar with the standard in his hand; and finally, the loud-voiced proclamation by the herald, "Dom Francisco d'Almeida, Governor, Viceroy of India for our lord the King." Upon a mind like that of

Magellan, in which religion had taken deep root, the scene must have made a strong impression, not less from the fact that it was the last day he was destined to spend upon his native soil for sometime to come for seven long years it actually proved.

Things temporal were nevertheless not entirely excluded from Magellan's mind by the pomp and ceremonial of religion, and before leaving Portugal he executed his first will to which allusion has already been made. In it he makes his sister, Doña Thereza, wife of João da Silva Telles, his sole heir, with instructions for the saying of twelve masses yearly at his altar of Our Lord Jesus in the Church of Santo Salvador at Sabrosa.

Magellan's first will of Magellan was discovered in Lisbon in 1855 by a descendant of the great navigator. It was executed at Belem on 17th December 1504, in advance of his departure with Almeida's expedition, before the notary Domingo Martins. It is in many ways more interesting than his final will. While the latter is written in Spanish and in the stilted legal phraseology that proclaims it the work of the notary-public, that executed at Belem bears evidence of being more or less the product of his own pen, and is in his native tongue. The most important clauses run as follows :

"I desire that, if I die abroad, or in this Armada in the which I am now proceeding for India in the service of my Sovereign, the Most High and Mighty King, Dom Manoel, whom may God preserve, that my funeral may be that accorded to an ordinary seaman, giving to the chaplain of the ship my clothes and arms to say three requiem masses.

I appoint as my sole heirs my sister Donna Thereza de Magalhães, her husband, João da Silva Telles, and their son, my nephew, Luiz Telles da Silva, their successors and heirs, with the understanding that the afore-said my brother-in-law shall quarter his arms with those of the family of Magalhães, which are those of my ancestors, and among the most distinguished, best, and oldest in the kingdom; founding, as I hereby found, in the male line - or in the female in default thereof - descendants of the aforesaid my sister Donna Thereza de Magalhães, and her husband, my brother-in-law, and their son, Luiz Telles da Silva, a bequest of twelve masses yearly to be said at the altar of the Lord Jesus in the Church of San Salvador in Sabrosa in connection with my property, the quinta de Souta, in the aforesaid parish of Sabrosa, that it may be a legacy in perpetuo, and that it may remain for ever as a memorial of our family, which it will be the duty of our successors to re-establish, should it through any chance or misfortune fall into desuetude, without increase or diminution in the number of the masses, or other alteration.

And everything that I thus ordain I desire may be carried out justly, and remain without alteration henceforth and for ever, should I die without legitimate offspring; but should I have such, I desire that he may succeed to all my estate, together with the same obligation of the entailed bequest, that it remain established as such, and not in any other form; in order that the barony may increase, and that it may not be deprived of the little property I own, the which I cannot better, or in any other manner bequeath."

When the blessing of the flag was over, the fleet dropped down the river to Belem, and anchored off the church for which it was then, as now, so famous - a building inseparably connected with the memories of the great Portuguese explorers. Here, in the days of Prince Henry the Navigator, and erected by him, stood a little chapel, much favoured by sailors, in which only eight years before, Vasco da Gama had prayed for his success before starting on his memorable voyage. Now the pile of florid Gothic, built in gratitude therefore, had usurped its place, white and new from the builder's hands, the last monument upon which the sailor's eye would rest on leaving his native land. Within it the bones of Vasco da Gama, of Camões who sang his successes, and of Dom Manoel who inspired them, were destined ultimately to rest. It was an ideal spot for the start of such an expedition. Next day, the 25th March 1505, the final departure took place. The King came down in state from the city and went on board the Viceroy's ship. Anchors were then weighed and the whole fleet proceeded slowly towards the bar, the King accompanying them, "going from ship to ship and speaking to the captains, taking leave of them and wishing them a prosperous voyage".

Clearing the mouth of the Tagus, the fleet proceeded southwards and touched at Port Dale on the Guinea Coast, where they took in water and lay at anchor for nine days. Here the Viceroy, finding that some of the ships were much more speedy than the others, divided the fleet into two squadrons. They crossed the line on the 29th April, and continuing their voyage, passed the Cape as far south as latitude 40° S., where they encountered severe weather and underwent great hardships. On the 20th June, Almeida, estimating that they had cleared the meridian of the Cape, shaped his course northward. In the account given by Castanheda the fleet are said to have gone to latitude 44° S, and to have passed the meridian of the Cape on the 26th June. They had already met with one misfortune, for the ship of Pero Ferreira had foundered in the equatorial calms. Now, on reaching the Indian Ocean, Lopo Sanchez was forced to run his vessel ashore, after having in vain tried to overcome a leak. The survivors, although many perished on the way, eventually reached Mozambique in safety, where they were picked up by their countrymen.

Before leaving Portugal, the fullest instructions had been given as to the disposal and action of the fleet; instructions that show how gigantic was the scale upon which the subjugation of India and Eastern Africa had been planned. Arriving at Sofala, a fortress was to be erected and garrisoned; and this done, the fleet was to sail for Quiloa without loss of time. Here the same steps were to be taken, but, in addition, two ships - a caravel and a "bargantym" - were to remain, in order to patrol the coast north and south of the port. Proceeding then to the farther shores of the Indian Ocean, the Viceroy was instructed to build a strong fortress upon the island of Anchediva (Anjediva). The two galleys, the timbers of which had been brought in the fleet, were to be put together here. Two caravels were appointed to patrol the coast around the station, which was regarded as of great importance. Hence they were to pass southwards along the coast to Cochin, looking for ships of the King of Calicut, "with whom the King for ever waged bitter war" and visiting Coulão, were by every means in their power to obtain leave to make a fortified settlement in that city. Finally, after the despatch of the annual homeward-bound fleet, an expedition was to be sent to the kingdom of Ormuz and the mouth of the Red Sea, to seek a site for a fortress that should act in some degree as a check upon the stream of Arab trade, which at that time bore not only the gold and silks of

Hindustan but also the spices of the Farther East to Mecca and the "Sultan of Babylonia".

Such were the orders under which Almeida sailed. If we reflect that less than six years previously India was a terra incognita, and the Cape only known by the fierceness of its storms, they appear marvellous in their comprehensiveness. We see, too, how wise was the policy that dictated them. Short as was Dom Manoel's acquaintance with the new world into which he adventured himself so boldly, it would seem that he had made himself master of the situation almost at a glance.

The traffic of the East was to pour into Europe through the gates of the Lisbon Alfandega. In order that this object might be attained, it was necessary that the first blow should be struck at Arab influence. Vasco da Gama, in the course of his memorable voyage, had found these "Mouros" in every city, and had not noted their riches and the extent of their influence in vain. The more important of the native kings, therefore, were to be conciliated with the special view of obtaining leave to build strong fortresses, which, connected by cruising bargantyms and caravels, should form a chain of nuclei of Portuguese influence. The "Mouros," when too strong, were to be temporised with; but, for the most part, the "ôte-toi, que je m'y mette" policy was that adopted. From the very beginning Dom Manoel recognised the enormous importance of mastering the entrance and the exits of the Indian Ocean. It was reserved for Albuquerque to conquer Malacca, but Almeida was charged to reduce Ormuz and gain possession of the strongholds round the Straits of Bab-el-Mandeb without loss of time. It was the outgoing streams of traffic that first demanded attention.

Upon the deeds of the Viceroy and his captains at this period we can only touch lightly. So rapid was the succession of events, and so packed with incident the history of his administration, that volumes, not pages, would be necessary to record them. It is not often that we hear of Magellan. Amid so large a company of distinguished men of "fidalgos e cavalleiros experimentados na guerra", of whom many had already served under Vasco da Gama, it could hardly be otherwise. His post could only have been a subordinate one, and we do not even know in which ship he sailed. However, that he made the best use of his opportunities is evident from the fact that he eventually became a most expert navigator. Later, when his name appears more frequently in the pages of the historians of that epoch, it is generally mentioned in connection with some distinguished act of bravery.

On the 22nd July the ships arrived off the bar of Quiloa. They were received badly, and the king declining to meet the Viceroy. The latter landed his forces and stormed the city, which was taken without the loss of a single Portuguese. No time was wasted, and the construction of the fort was begun upon the following day, the Viceroy himself personally aiding. On the 8th August (according to Correa the 13th August), a large garrison having been left to complete the work, and the rightful king, Mohammed Anconi, restored to his throne, the fleet started for Mombasa.

The city of Mombasa was one of the most important on the coast of Africa; it carried on a large trade with the interior, and was strongly fortified. Such a nut was no easy one to crack. The excuse for the attempt, however, was not long wanting, for the ships were fired upon as they arrived. Two days later, the city was stormed, and the Moors, although numbering ten thousand men, were overpowered by the superior skill and courage of their enemies. The fighting was severe, and the Portuguese had a very large number of wounded. Dom Lourenço, the only son of the Viceroy, first made himself famous at the assault. His great strength and extraordinary courage combined to make him almost worshipped by the men he led. Short as was his career, for he died in battle only two years later, his name became even more renowned throughout the East than did, later, that of Albuquerque. There is little doubt that the Portuguese owed their success in many cases to his personal influence and to their enemies' belief in his invincibility. After the fall of the city the king formally tendered his submission. He agreed to pay a yearly tribute of 10,000 serafins. A column of white marble was erected by the Viceroy to commemorate the event. Victors and vanquished became firm friends, and the king, "for the great love he bore Dom Lourenço" presented him with a valuable sword and a collar of pearls, worth 30,000 cruzados, upon his departure.

It was the Viceroy's wish to visit both Melinde (Malindi) and Magadoxo (Mogadishu). However, the season being now so far advanced, the custom of setting up a cross or a column in the countries, the pilots were strongly opposed to such a step. The plan was accordingly relinquished, and the fleet shaped its course across the Indian Ocean to the island of Anchediva (Anjediva), whither they arrived on the 13th September. The fame of their successes had preceded them. The Viceroy found letters from the King of Cananor informing him that there were 20,000 quintals of spice in his port ready for the homeward-bound ships, and that three rich Mecca galleons were daily expected in Calicut. Almeida began work, as usual, without the loss of a moment's time. The very next day after his arrival, the construction of the fortress was commenced. Ships were sent off to cruise in search of the Mecca squadron. The keels of a galleon and two bargantyms were laid down, and letters were sent to Cananor, Cochin, and Coulão to make known the Viceroy's advent. In twenty days the fortress was completed. The loot taken at Mombasa was sold by public auction, and the money handed to the treasurer of the fleet.

The King of Onor, a province lying about thirty miles to the south, had already made a treaty of peace with the Viceroy. Its duration was, however, of no great length, for being unwise enough to send an insolent message in reply to a request made to him by the Viceroy, the latter at once brought his fleet against him, and entering the river on the 16th October, burnt his ships and took the town with a readiness that soon brought the king to his senses. Dom Lourenço took his wonted place at the head of the storming party. However, he had little opportunity of displaying his prowess, for the enemy yielded almost without striking a blow, and the Portuguese lost only one man in the assault. The king, whose sin had been that of cupidity rather than an open defiance of the Viceroy, made a most ample submission. The latter behaved so generously to his adversary, that all former differences were forgotten in the friendship thus begun.

The rapidity of Almeida's movements, although characteristic of the man himself, owned at the same time another cause. The winter was fast approaching, and with it the north-east monsoon, whose favouring gales were to waft the home-returning fleet upon their voyage. The

Viceroy had not reached Cananor, still less Cochin, where he was to assume the reins of government. There was, therefore, no time for delay at Onor, and leaving this port as soon as possible, the fleet proceeded southwards to Cananor and came to anchor off the town on the 22nd October. The Portuguese had been upon the most friendly terms with the king of this country since the time of Vasco da Gama's first visit, and the Viceroy's arrival was welcomed with the greatest enthusiasm. The armada entered "gay with flags and standards, discharging salvos of artillery, the larger vessels remaining outside, but those of lesser draught anchoring in the bay, the galleys and the bargantym rowing. A sight that many people came to see, for in India they had not as yet seen galleys, the which are rowed with a great precision in the stroke."

The usual visits of ceremony having been paid, Almeida, who had hitherto called himself Governor, assumed the full rank and title of Viceroy. Next day he received an embassy from the powerful King of Narsinga, who was desirous of making a treaty with him. Learning from the resident Portuguese factor that nothing could be done in Cananor without a fortress - for the Arab merchants of the city had become greatly incensed with the growing influence of the newcomers, and had already plotted to kill the king - he sought leave to construct one. It was at once granted to him, and in five days, with the assistance of the natives, the erection of its walls, together with bastions to carry cannon, were completed. A day or two later it received its name - the Fort Saint Angelo - and Lourenço de Brito, with a garrison of 150 men, entered into possession. Correa gives a very different account stating that only a ditch and a palisade were made, and this almost surreptitiously.

Delaying a bare five days at Cananor, where two caravels were left to guard the coast, the fleet of Almeida, now much reduced in numbers, at length arrived at Cochin. Of the meeting between King Nambeadora and the Viceroy, Correa gives us a long account : the "king on his elephant with its trappings, and many people, the which the Viceroy left the fort to receive, accompanied by all his men, and before him his guard with trumpets and kettledrums, his captains dressed very gaily, the Viceroy himself clad in a coat of red satin, with a narrow black sash worked with gold, black buskins, a round cap, and an open black

damask cassock, which formed a train, as was then the custom."
Almeida next day publicly crowned the king with the greatest display
of ceremonial that lay within his power.

With the neighbouring states in a condition of hostility, overt or covert,
it was of the utmost importance to lose no chance of strengthening the
bonds of alliance with so powerful a prince. Almost at this moment,
indeed, news arrived of the rising of the Moors at Coulão port some
sixty miles farther south, and the murder of the Portuguese garrison, an
act that the Viceroy was not the man to leave long unpunished. The
duty devolved upon Dom Lourenço, and he performed it with his usual
quickness and success. In two or three days he returned to Cochin,
having burnt twenty-seven ships and killed numbers of the enemy
without the loss of a single man.

Meanwhile, the Viceroy was busy with the despatch of the
homeward-bound squadron under Fernão Soarez. Having loaded all the
pepper and spices in the Cochin factories, the ships proceeded to
Cananor, and took the remainder of their cargo from that port, which
they left on the 2nd January 1506, taking with them only sufficient men
for the navigation of the vessels; for, with the daily losses by fighting
and disease, and the scattered disposition of their forces, every sword
was of importance. The voyage was noteworthy from the fact that the
eastern coast of Madagascar was discovered for the first time. "They
arrived," says Goes, "off a land that not one of the pilots had ever seen
before.....and having sailed in sight of it for seventeen days, they
cleared it on the 18th February, the which, although at that time it was
not known, they found afterwards to be an island that the old
cosmographers call Madagascar, and the Moors the "Island of the
Moon." The ships arrived safely in Lisbon on the 23rd May 1506.

With the departure of the homeward-bound fleet, and the reduction of
Coulão, the Viceroy doubtless looked forward to a more peaceful
period in which to consider the many political questions that presented
themselves for solution. He was not destined to enjoy it either then or
indeed at any future time, for at the very moment when he least
expected it, a danger greater than any hitherto encountered menaced the
Portuguese power in India.

The advent of the Viceroy's fleet, the uniform success that had attended him in Africa, and the almost superhuman strength and courage with which Dom Lourenço was credited, had filled both the Moors and the Zamorim of Calicut with consternation. It was felt that if action was to be taken at all, it should be taken then. The homeward fleet had started, the Portuguese were considerably reduced in numbers, and no reinforcements were possible before the onset of the south-west monsoon. If a decisive blow could only be struck, if the fleet of the hated infidels could once be fairly annihilated, it might put an end for ever to their power in India. It was at all events worth trying. The Arabs saw ruin staring them in the face, and neither their creed nor their feelings inclined them to tame submission.

The Zamorim of Calicut accordingly summoned a meeting of all the leading Moors. Opinion was divided as to the course to be pursued. Some, recognising the formidable strength of the enemy, and mindful of the almost uninterrupted series of successes they had obtained, counselled alliance with the King of Portugal. They were overruled. It was felt that the time for this had passed, and that no alternative now lay before them but to cross swords. It was resolved, therefore, that a great armada should be equipped, which should attempt the conquest of Cochin itself, the very stronghold and seat of government of their enemies. Measures were accordingly taken to inform the Moors at every port of the plot and to request their aid. The vessels thus raised were to collect in Calicut.

Such a design could not long remain concealed. Dom Lourenço, being in Cananor, was visited by a man in the habit of a Moor, who, on being granted a private interview, revealed himself as an Italian, one Ludovico Vartema, a great traveller "qui studio orbis terrarum cognoscendi multas regiones peragravit," as Osorius tells us. This man had escaped from Calicut, and hastened to bring the news of the preparation of the armada. Unexpected and harassing as it was, Dom Lourenço did not lose heart. Despatching Vartema without loss of time to the Viceroy, who was then at Cochin, he set about the organisation of his own forces. The orders sent back by the Viceroy were not other than he had expected; that he was to fight "for the Catholic faith and for his honour, and bear himself as a Christian and his son."

The battle that ensued was one of the most celebrated of the many fought by the Portuguese in India. The armada, which was composed of 209 vessels - 84 being ships and the rest large praus - encountered Dom Lourenço's valiant little fleet on the 16th March 1506, a short distance to the north of Cananor. "It seemed," says Vartema, "like some huge forest, from the great masts of the ships." However, so little did Dom Lourenço fear the result, that he permitted his adversaries to pass until they were off Cananor - "per mostrarli quanto era l'animo de' Christiani." It was not until they were within a bombard-shot of the town that he commenced the engagement.

Against such an overwhelming force, the Portuguese could bring only eleven ships. Correa claims that there were 28 ships, but Vartema who was an eye witness states that there were eleven. They were manned, however, by men as brave as they were experienced, "all distinguished men, educated at the King's court - very noble men," Correa tells us. And very nobly indeed did they bear themselves. "For really, to say the truth, I have been in many a fight in my day, and seen many a fierce encounter," says Vartema, "but never have I seen braver men than these Portuguese." They had need of their courage, for they were but eight hundred fighting men against some thousands. The great ship of Rodrigo Rebello, in which sailed Dom Lourenço and the flower of his men, led the van, and turning neither to the right nor left, made straight for the enemy's flagship. Three times did she grapple with her, and three times were her grappling-irons cast off. At length their attempts were successful, and the Portuguese sprang on board, headed by their beloved chief, who "fought with his little halberd." The result was for the moment doubtful, for they found themselves engaged with six hundred of the enemy. It was not for long. Lourenço's valour bore everything before it, and before many minutes had elapsed, every man of the six hundred had been killed or driven into the sea.

Meanwhile the others had not been idle. João Serrão, brother to the Francisco Serrão who afterwards became the great friend of Magellan, was fighting as he never fought before, his ship attacked by more than fifty praus, from which he eventually shook himself free, though at the price of having almost all his men wounded. Simon Martins, the most daring of the Viceroy's captains, was in an even more desperate case, his low sloop being surrounded by four much larger vessels, who poured in a galling fire, until the Portuguese, their men all dead or wounded, and all their powder expended, were compelled to take refuge below deck. The Moors boarded, thinking she had struck, but they were quickly undeceived, for the captain, making a sally at the head of the survivors, cut down seven of them with his own hand, and the remainder were quickly driven overboard.

While these two desperate struggles were continuing, Dom Lourenço had laid his ship alongside a second antagonist. She proved to be a heavier craft than his first prize, and carried over fifteen hundred men. Their very number was probably against them, and Nuño Vaz Pereira boarding at the same time on the other side of the ship, the Moors found themselves between two fires, and were very soon overpowered. The enemy perceiving their two largest vessels taken, and many others either disabled or sunk, resolved on flight. The delight of the Portuguese was unbounded, for the victory, however much anticipated, was by no means safely within their grasp. "God be praised," exclaimed Dom Lourenço "let us follow up our victory over these dogs" and the order was at once given. A scene of the most frightful slaughter ensued. Quarter was neither given nor asked. The sea was dyed with blood, and the bodies washed ashore next day "formed as it were a hedge" upon the beach. More than 3,600 of them were counted.

Upon the Portuguese side between seventy and eighty fell, and over two hundred were wounded. Among the latter was Magellan, who, indeed, appears to have been habitually unfortunate in this respect, to judge from the expression used by Gaspar Correa "and at the affair with the Turks, and always in the armadas, and in Calicut, was he much wounded." He was cared for, no doubt, at the hospital at Cananor, whither, we are told, all the wounded were brought. The dead were buried at sea, in order that the Moors might not discover the extent of their antagonists' losses.

A victory so decisive was not without its effect, not only upon the Moors, but upon the native rulers, matters now appearing more settled, Dom Lourenço was despatched at the head of a small squadron to the Maldives. Owing to bad navigation, they missed their destination, but sighting Cape Comorin, eventually came to anchor off Point de Galle, and for the first time relations were established between Portugal and Ceylon. Magellan, meanwhile, was sent to Sofala under Nuño Vaz Pereira. As has already been stated, Dom Manoel's orders on the Viceroy's departure were that a fortress should be constructed in this city, but it will be remembered that the first port the latter entered in Eastern Africa was Quiloa. This was through no disobedience on the Viceroy's part, but the ship of Pero d'Anhaia, who accompanied Almeida as the future captain of Sofala, having gone ashore at the very moment of the sailing of the Viceroy's fleet, her officers and crew were forced to defer their voyage. Ultimately Sofala was reached and the fortress built, but Pero d'Anhaia's administration was a short one, for he was killed in the following year by the Moors.

Nuño Vaz sailed with instructions to take over the command. His orders, however, were that he should first visit Quiloa. In that port the greatest disorder prevailed, owing to a dispute as to the succession to the throne, and on his arrival he had to decide upon the merits of the two claimants. Sailing thence for Sofala, he established himself as captain of the settlement, but his term of office was even shorter than that of his predecessor. On the 8th September 1507, the fleet of Vasco Gomez d'Abreu arrived from Lisbon, and he had to resign his post. A few days later he left for Mozambique in the ship of Rui Gonçalves de Valadares. The pestilential climate of the coast had told terribly upon his men, and he landed with a great number of sick. So numerous were they, indeed, that his first care was to build a hospital. The captains themselves took turns in attendance upon the patients. Correa naively describes the treatment adopted: "Much did they occupy themselves," he tells us, "with the care and healing of the sick, to whom they gave many marmalades and conserves, in the eating of which they were greatly benefited."

The season being now far advanced, and the north-east monsoon established, Nuño Vaz Pereira and his comrades, unable to return to India, were forced to prolong their stay in Mozambique. They occupied themselves in building a church, and, it is needless to say, a fortress. Upon the change of the monsoon they sailed for Cochin, leaving a mere handful of men in charge under a feitor. From this fact it is evident that

Magellan could not have been present at the defeat of Dom Lourenço by Mir Hoseyn and Malik Jaz at Chaul in the spring of 1508. The expression already alluded to, that he was wounded "in the affair with the Turks," must therefore refer to the great battle off Diu, in which D. Francisco d'Almeida avenged the death of his beloved son.

Upon their arrival in India, Magellan and his comrades found the aspect of affairs much altered. They had left the country soon after a defeat of the most crushing kind had been inflicted upon their enemies. The power of Portugal seemed by it to have been fairly established in the East, and some of the lesser potentates, whose action appeared at one time doubtful, had formally acknowledged the Viceroy. Now all was changed. The fortress of Anchediva (Anjediva), which had cost them so much anxiety and so many lives, had been given up and razed to the ground. The King of Cananor, who had been most friendly, had been replaced by a successor whose sympathies were with the Zamorim of Calicut. The Portuguese had undergone a siege of many months in their fortress, and suffered unusual hardships. However, a far more serious danger confronted them. Hitherto the Moors had been the only foemen worthy of their steel. Now they were suddenly brought face to face with other enemies, who, at the very first rencontre, had put to flight their ships and slain their beloved leader, Dom Lourenço.

Their new foe was the Sultan of Egypt, or rather his admiral, Mir Hoseyn. The Moors, finding themselves powerless to cope unaided with their adversaries, sought help from Cairo. It was readily afforded them. Not only were the Sultan's revenues affected by the check in the stream of traffic that poured into the Mediterranean through his dominions, but the enemy was at his very gates, and action of some kind had become an imperative necessity. Unprovided, however, with a fleet in the Red Sea, and without wood wherewith to build it, he was forced to cut the latter in Asia Minor, and transport it on camels from Alexandria to Suez. Despite these difficulties, a fleet of ten ships was constructed at this port. It was placed under the command of the Emir Hoseyn. At the end of December 1507, it came to anchor off the great city of Diu, at the mouth of the Gulf of Cambay. Here the Emir joined forces with Malik Jaz, the governor of Diu. A few weeks later the armada sailed for Chaul, in which river the Portuguese fleet under Dom

Lourenço was at that time lying. The action that ensued, albeit a defeat for the Portuguese, was one of which they might justly be proud. Dom Lourenço, cut off from the rest of his fleet, and with his leg shattered by a cannonball, fought his sinking ship until her decks were nearly level with the water, and perished with the flower of his men, his end a fitting termination to a life brilliant in its untarnished honour, and conspicuous for deeds of the coolest daring.

Against these reverses, the Portuguese would have found it hard to make headway, had it not been that upon the northern shores of the Indian Ocean the name of Alfonso d'Albuquerque had already become a terror to the Muslims. Albuquerque had left Portugal with the understanding that he was eventually to supersede Almeida as Viceroy, and having finished his cruise upon the coasts of Arabia, turned southwards to India to deliver his papers. The two great captains met at Cananor on the 5th December 1508. Almeida refused to hand over his seal of office until he should have taken his revenge on Hoseyn and Malik Jaz - with which end in view he was then sailing for Diu. Albuquerque had no alternative but to give way.

Nuño Vaz Pereira, and with him, no doubt, Magellan had meanwhile returned safely from Mozambique to India in the summer, and had been almost immediately despatched to Ceylon. Whether Magellan went thither with him or not we do not learn from the records of contemporary historians, but it is more than probable that he accompanied his old commander, who got back from Ceylon just in time to join Almeida's avenging fleet. On the 12th December the armada sailed. It consisted of nineteen ships, which carried thirteen hundred Portuguese and four hundred Malabaris. On his way, the Viceroy, after touching at Baticala and Onor, made a descent upon Dabul, and so completely destroyed the city, that the action passed into a proverb, "May the vengeance of the Franks overtake you, as it overtook Dabul."

Arriving off Diu on the 2nd February 1509, the Viceroy found both Mir Hoseyn and Malik Jaz awaiting him. The former, thinking that the open sea offered the best chances of success, crossed the bar to meet the enemy. An engagement followed which advantaged neither party, and on the approach of night Mir Hoseyn retired to the harbour, resolving there to await the renewal of the Viceroy's attack. Next day the Portuguese boldly entered the river and the two fleets engaged. Almeida found opposed to him a force numbering over a hundred sail, which bore eight hundred Mamelukes, and many Christian soldiers, Venetian and Slav, all of whom were clad in chain-armour. A large number of Malabaris from Calicut and the formidable contingent of Malik Jaz crowded the smaller vessels. The Viceroy wished personally to engage the ship of Mir Hoseyn, but, at the earnest entreaty of his officers, allowed himself to be dissuaded, and deputied the task to his beloved captain Nuño Vaz Pereira.

With him, there is little doubt, went Magellan, in company with many of the most distinguished of the Viceroy's lieutenants. Thus manned, the Holy Ghost led the van, and fought her way to the great galleon of Mir Hoseyn. Desperate as was the struggle that ensued, the issue was not for long doubtful. The Egyptian admiral, boarded on both sides, was soon forced to yield, and the loss of the flagship so disheartened the captains of his other vessels, that the battle was from that moment practically decided. The ship of Malik Jaz, owing to her unusual strength, for a long time bade defiance to the Portuguese, but she was at length sunk by a broadside from the large bombards. The slaughter was even greater than on the occasion of the defeat of the Zamorim of Calicut. Between three and four thousand men were killed, and of the eight hundred Mamelukes but twenty-two survived.

The victory was decisive; Malik Jaz submitted, and Diu was entered in triumph by Almeida. However, it was not without its cost. Nuño Vaz Pereira fell, shot in the throat, and other brave souls with him. Great numbers, too, were wounded, and among them, Correa tells us, was Magellan. The engagement over, and a treaty of peace having been signed with Malik Jaz, the Viceroy returned with the fleet to Cochin. The power of the Portuguese in India was now fairly and indisputably established.

CHAPTER 3

SERVICE WITH ALBUQUERQUE

Almeida, who had not yet delivered the seal of office to Albuquerque, returned to Cochin on the 8th March 1509, and found his successor awaiting him. After his years of loyal service, after having at length brought security and success almost within measurable distance, he was called upon to resign his post. He had borne the burden and heat of the day, and now another was to reap the benefit of his toil. The trial was a most bitter one for him, and the differences in which he soon found himself involved with Albuquerque were not without excuse. Instead of resigning, he placed Albuquerque under arrest, and sent him to Cananor.

Whether Magellan joined with others in openly expressing disapproval of this action we do not know, but there is some reason to believe that he did so. On the 21st April there arrived at Cochin from Lisbon an armada destined for the reconnaissance of Malacca, under the command of Diogo Lopes de Sequeira. Almeida affected to think that this force was insufficient, and added another vessel, with a crew of seventy men, under the command of Garcia de Sousa, with whom he was not upon the best of terms. Some of the officers are mentioned by Barros and De Goes; among them Nuño Vaz de Castellobranco, who was sent "on account of the differences between him and the Viceroy". We learn that Magellan and Francisco Serrão, who later became his bosom friend, also sailed in the same vessel.

The little fleet, consisting of four ships of about 150 tons, and a "taforea", a sort of barge - sailed from Cochin on the 19th August, and sighting Ceylon upon the 21st, made for Sumatra. Sequeira was now in unknown seas - seas at least, which had never before been navigated by European vessels. His first port was Pedir, at the northern extremity of Sumatra. Having made a treaty of peace with the king both of this place and of the neighbouring city of Pacem, he proceeded without loss of time to Malacca, and anchored in the port on the 11th September 1509.

Malacca had been for years a familiar name to the Portuguese as the great mart for all the merchandise of the far East. Now that they had at last reached it, they found that it in no way fell short of their expectations. Hither, Barros tells us, had gathered Arabs, Persians, Gujaratis, Bengalis, Burmese, Liu-kiuans, Javanese, Chinese, and natives of the Philippines. The city, although not of any great depth, extended along the coast for a vast distance. The port was crowded with shipping, and the enormous trade carried on with all parts of the world was evinced by the busy scenes upon its quays. The advent of the Europeans, whose deeds in India were not unknown, was productive of a temporary panic. Confidence was soon restored, and on the third day the king formally received the envoys of Dom Manoel, and appeared desirous of showing them the greatest kindness and respect. His attitude was nevertheless intended to conceal his real designs, which were to seize Sequeira's fleet at the first opportunity, and inflict such a decisive blow upon the Portuguese as should effectually check their threatened move upon the gates of the Pacific.

Sequeira, it must be confessed, did his best to further them. No one ever adventured himself more confidingly into a nest of hornets. Warned that the Malays were not to be trusted by some friendly Chinese captains and again by a Persian woman, of whom one of the Portuguese was the lover, he persisted in ignoring the advice. His men visited the city and the natives Sequeira's ships "as though they had been at anchor off the city of Lisbon." The king's first plot was to invite the Captain-general and a large number of his people to a banquet. With their forces thus weakened, he simultaneously planned to attack his guests and the ships. Even Sequeira, however, declined to fall into so transparent a trap, and another ruse had to be adopted.

The Portuguese had expressed their desire of leaving as soon as they could get their cargo of spices, in order that they might not miss the monsoon for their homeward voyage. Taking advantage of this, the king informed Sequeira that he had gotten together a large quantity of pepper and other goods, which he would deliver to him if he would send all his boats ashore on the following day, together with plenty of men to load them. The Captain-general gladly acceded. Francisco Serrão in command of a large party, and with all the boats except that of the "taforea," proceeded ashore. With the strength of the fleet being thus reduced, the natives crowded to the ships with the ostensible purpose of trading. They awaited the signal for a general onslaught, which was to be given from the citadel.

Garcia de Sousa, more quick-witted than his commander, was not long in realising the impending danger. Without the loss of a moment's time, he drove the Malays out of his ship, and sent Ferdinand Magellan in the only remaining boat to the flaghip to put Sequeira on his guard. Magellan found the Captain-general playing at chess, surrounded by eight Malays, even then unwilling to believe that any treachery was contemplated. Hardly taking his eyes from the board, Sequeira merely ordered one of the sailors into the maintop to see if all were well with the shore party, and Magellan at the same moment left the ship. While aloft, the sailor chanced to look down, and saw a Malay standing behind Sequeira with his kris half drawn, while a comrade in front motioned to him not to strike, as the signal had not then been given. At the same moment Francisco Serrão and two or three others were seen running for their lives to the beach, and the puff of white smoke - the signal for the massacre - floated from the summit of the citadel. The sailor's warning cry of "Treachery ! treachery !" came not an instant too soon. Sequeira bounded from his seat, and escaping the blow from the kris of his would be murderer, ran to arms. The Malays, seeing themselves outnumbered, jumped overboard. Serrão meanwhile, in a small skiff and almost unarmed, was making desperate efforts to shake himself clear of a number of boats by which he was hard pressed. Already one of his men had been severely wounded, and the enemy had boarded their craft, when Magellan and Nuño Vaz de Castelbranco came to their rescue. Although a bare handful of men, they fought so desperately that the Malays were driven overboard, and the Portuguese reached their ship in safety. It is not too much to believe that the courage and presence of mind of

Magellan on this occasion greatly strengthened the bond of friendship between him and Serrão. To this friendship, as we shall see later, the great voyage of the greatest of navigators was more or less due.

The situation of the Portuguese at this moment was critical. Not only had the greater number of those on shore been captured or murdered, but a second party, who had landed upon a little island hard by, had also been cut off. Sequeira had hardly realised his position, when a large fleet of armed praus was seen rounding a corner and making for the vessels of the Portuguese. However great his folly, the Captain-general was no coward. Instant action was necessary, and he took it. Slipping his cables, he at once bore down upon the enemy, and so well were his guns served that the Malays were soon only too glad to retire, many of their ships being sunk and others hopelessly crippled.

Sequeira waited a day or two in the hope of ransoming some of his men. Sixty were missing, and although many were known to have been killed, he had reason to suspect that as many as thirty were prisoners. His efforts were fruitless, and accordingly, putting ashore two of his captives with an arrow through their brains and a message affixed to their bodies that "thus the King of Portugal avenged the treason of his enemies," he sailed for India. Correa's account of the Malacca difficulties differs in toto from the above, which, except for a few unimportant details, is that given by all the other old historians. In the Lendas da India, the Portuguese are attacked by night in a small fortress that they had previously obtained permission to erect.

The homeward voyage of the fleet was signalised by the capture of several junks. In one of these actions Magellan again distinguished himself in the same manner as at Malacca; for the Portuguese of Nuño Godin's ship being almost overpowered, Castelbranco and himself, with only four sailors, went to their assistance in the small boat of the "taforea," and brought the fight to a successful issue. In January 1510, the fleet arrived at Travancore, reduced to three vessels - one having gone ashore in the Straits, and one having been purposely burnt. In this port they learned the news of Almeida's departure from India, whereupon Sequeira, who had sided with him in his quarrel with Albuquerque, thought it better to sail direct for Portugal. Teixera's ship and the "taforea," bearing Magellan and his friend Serrão, proceeded on their course, and anchored a few days later in the harbour of Cochin.

Magellan and his comrades must have reached that capital almost simultaneously with Albuquerque. However great a failure Sequeira's expedition had been, that of the Viceroy to Calicut, whence he was now returning, had been even greater. Upon the 2nd January he had arrived off the city with a large armada. A few days later he left it, himself badly wounded. Seventy-eight of his best men killed, and over three hundred hors de combat, with no advantage, save the slaughter of a large number of Moors, accruing to his side. Neither his wounds nor his defeat, however, prevented Albuquerque from busying himself in the execution of his projects. He at once ordered an armada to be gotten ready to proceed against the cities at the entrance of the Red Sea, and despatched the rest of the homeward-bound fleet, the first part of which had already sailed to Portugal via Mozambique.

The three vessels of which this second division of the fleet was composed left Cochin about the middle of January. The chronology of this period of Magellan's history is a little obscure. After the fight at Calicut, Albuquerque is mentioned by Correa as sending Rebello thence to Cananor on the 10th January. It is probable, that he arrived at the latter city about the 14th. If Magellan was with the Viceroy in his first descent upon Goa, as Arana states, there is little enough of intervening time left for the preparation and despatch of the homeward fleet, the wreck upon the Padua Bank, the reaching of the mainland in the boats, the sending of the caravel to succour the shipwrecked party, and their return to Cananor. Most probably Magellan was not present at the first occupation of Goa.

One ship, commanded by Gomes Freire, sailing a little before her companions, had a prosperous voyage, reaching Mozambique in safety. The others, in one of which Magellan sailed, ran at night upon a shoal of the Great Padua Bank, and remained. The Padua Bank or Pedro Reef had more recently twenty-one fathoms as its minimum depth of water. It would naturally be concluded that the ships went ashore at some other place in the Lakadivhs. More especially from the fact that, according to one writer, the crew landed on an island or rock close at hand. However, it appears that the banks off this part of the coast were gradually sinking. On the Elicapeni Bank, there is more recently from 8-15 fathoms, while in 1835 Captain Byrom found 3-9 fathoms. Such a rapid alteration renders it quite possible for the wreck to have occurred on the "Bassas de Pedro."

The weather was good, and though the ships filled, they did not break up. The captains, Sebastian de Sousa and Francisco de Sa, were able to save not only sufficient provisions, but a good deal of the cargo also. The crews landed with their belongings upon a small island that was close at hand, and at daybreak a discussion took place as to the course to be pursued. It was resolved to make for the coast of India (distant about a hundred miles) in the boats. Owing to the want of room "there was much contention among them concerning which of them should go first. The captains, fidalgos, and persons of position desired so to do, but the sailors said that they should not unless they went also." In this state of affairs Magellan came to the rescue. Promising, with the ready coolness that, as we learn later, was so characteristic of him, that he would remain with the crews if they would swear to him that assistance should be sent immediately on the arrival of the boats in India. This was done, and the boats departed, reaching Cananor in eight days. Sebastian de Sousa kept his word, and sent Antonio Pacheco to their relief in a caravel without loss of time. Crew and cargo were safely got on board, and eventually the coast was reached with little more loss than that of the two vessels.

From Barros we learn one possible reason for Magellan's action on this occasion - that there was a friend whom, "since be was a person of no great importance," the captain was about to leave behind. We are not told his name, but there is little doubt that it was Francisco Serrão, and that it was his loyalty to him as a friend that prevented Magellan from considering his own safety. This incident is related by Herrera, Barros, Castanheda, and Damião de Goes, but the latter does not mention Magellan. Correa gives an account that differs in many particulars from that of the other historians. He states (a far from probable occurrence) that the crew remained in the vessels, which they shored up by means of the yards; that all this was arranged and ordered by Magellan; and that Gonzalo de Crasto - not Pacheco returned with the caravel. Whatever may have been the case, however, the deed was that of a cool, unselfish man, and it is recognised as such even by historians so adverse to him as Barros and Castanheda.

It is worthy of remark that, in Herrera's laudatory comments upon Magellan's action on this occasion, we learn one of the few facts concerning his personal aspect to which history has treated us: "Albeit his appearance was not greatly in his favour, since he was of small status".

At the moment of the rescue of Magellan and his comrades, Albuquerque was bound northwards with an armada of twenty-three ships for Ormuz, touching at Cananor and other neighbouring ports on his voyage. Whether the shipwrecked crews were incorporated with this fleet or not is uncertain, but it is by no means impossible that such was the case. Correa says that they returned to Cochin, while Castanheda implies that they went to Cananor. Barros, however, distinctly states that Pacheco returned with the rescued crew to Goa, and that they there found Alfonso d'Albuquerque. The Viceroy altered his plans en route, and leaving the siege of Ormuz for a future occasion. He made a descent upon Goa, which yielded to him on the 17th February 1510, almost without striking a blow. He was not at that time, however, in a position to hold the city against a large force, and three months later, May 30th, was compelled to evacuate it. It was only for a time. During his short tenure of the place Albuquerque had realised its importance. The next occasion on which Magellan appears upon the scene is at a council held by the

Viceroy on the 10th October 1510, upon questions connected with a second siege he had then resolved on.

The council was held at Cochin, and was composed of "all the captains of the King," to which rank it may be concluded that Magellan had by this time attained. The question for decision was whether the merchant ships then loading in Cochin should assist at the intended siege of Goa or not. Magellan, called upon to speak, gave a very decided opinion on the subject. He said that they "ought not to take the ships of burden to Goa, in as much as, if they went thither, they could not pass this year to Portugal.....and that there would not remain time for them to lay out their money, nor to do anything of what was necessary for the voyage." Albuquerque was of a different opinion. He said that "he would sail with as many ships and men as he could get together, and would go and take Goa, as he trusted in our Saviour's Passion that He would aid him". However, he added that he would not take any one away with him against his will. The captains, Correa tells us, paid little attention to this, being occupied with the profits resulting from the sale and embarkation of the goods that they had to convey to Portugal.

Magellan, we know, did not belong either actually or in spirit to such men as these. Although we do not find him mentioned by name in Correa's list of "valentes caualleiros" who accompanied Albuquerque in this expedition, he may well have come under the head of the "outros caualleiros honrados" who were present. The Viceroy arrived off Goa on the 24th November. The fleet consisted of thirty-four sail, which carried fifteen hundred Portuguese troops and three hundred Malabaris. On the following day the assault took place - a splendidly fought action, which resulted in the fall of the city and its occupation for the second time by Albuquerque. Under his administration, order and prosperity were rapidly restored. Money was coined. The ambassadors of the kings of Narsinga and Cambay arrived to establish relations with the Viceroy. The native women, embracing the Christian religion, became the wives of the conquerors, and trade was once more resumed.

Affairs once satisfactorily settled in Goa, Albuquerque, who in energy and ambition was no whit inferior to Almeida, determined on fitting out an armada "a buscar hos Rumes." Not only were the ships of the Caliph the bitter enemy of Lusitanian influence in the East, to be sought for and destroyed, but a fort was to be built at Aden, and another upon the Kamaran Islands in the Red Sea. The fleet left Goa at the end of March 1511. In doubling the Padua reefs they encountered such continued bad weather that they were forced to return. It was ultimately settled that they should proceed to Malacca instead.

In August, therefore, just two years subsequent to the sailing of Sequeira's expedition - an armada of nineteen vessels left Cochin for that city, bent on taking a full though tardy revenge for the treacherous slaughter of Serrão's comrades.

During their voyage they captured no less than five ships from Cambay. Having lost the galley of Simon Martins in a storm, they touched, as before, at Pedir in Atjeh, and confirmed their treaties with the king. At Paçem (Passir) they were again well received. Further south they encountered two junks and a caravel, all of which they captured. Unwittingly, they had begun their revenge, for upon the latter ship, after she had struck, they found the body of Nahodabeguea, the organiser of the plot against Sequeira.

De Goes relates a fable concerning this occurrence, embodying a belief that is not uncommon in many parts of the world. They find the body hacked to pieces, but no blood flows. On his wrist is a bracelet in which is set the bone of a species of large cattle found in Siam, called Cabis. On pulling this off, the blood gushes out and Nahodabeguea dies instantly.

On the 1st July 1511, the fleet arrived off Malacca, although Correa states that the fleet arrived in mid-June. It was not until six weeks later that the city fell. Although unprovided with fortifications, the number of cannon it mounted and of fighting men by whom it was garrisoned made its reduction no easy matter. In the history of Portuguese India the taking of Malacca by Albuquerque is perhaps the most striking event, not less from its political import than from the difficulty of the task and the richness of the booty. Upon the protracted struggle that ended so fortunately for the Viceroy's forces it is unnecessary to dwell.

Even at this period Magellan had not yet fought himself into the first half-dozen or so of distinguished captains whose names and individual deeds were thought worthy of mention by the chroniclers of that date. For the present, he remained for the most part hidden in the obscurity of the "outros caualleiros valentes" whose presence in the engagements is only rarely otherwise recorded. One writer (Herrera) however, speaks of him as "giving a very good account of himself" on this occasion. It is only what might have been expected from him, or indeed from any one of the courageous band who effected the downfall of the most important city of the East.

Against the twenty thousand fighting men, with three thousand pieces of artillery, whose workmanship, as we learn from the Commentaries of Albuquerque, could not be excelled even in Portugal, the Viceroy could bring a bare eight hundred Portuguese and six hundred Malabar archers. They had indeed need to give a good account of themselves, and for a protracted period the issue hung in the balance. "Assuredly," says Castanheda, "from the time we began the conquest of India until now was no affair undertaken so arduous as this battle.....nor one in which so much artillery was employed, or in which so many were engaged in the defence."

The fall of Malacca was of greater political importance than that of Goa. Not only was the city the key to the Eastern gate of the Indian Ocean, the gate through which the whole commerce of the Moluccas, the Philippines, Japan, and "far Cathay" passed on its road to the Mediterranean, but it was at the same time one of the largest marts in Asia. In its harbour rode the ships of countless nations and peoples, from "Cipangu" to Timor.

It is little surprising, therefore, that the news of Albuquerque's success spread far and wide throughout the Eastern world, and that the sovereigns of the neighbouring countries were anxious to solicit his protection. The alliances concluded with them tempted, if not to fresh conquests, at least to further explorations. The Spice Islands, an Eldorado even more glittering than the New World, had by this time passed from the cloud of uncertainty that hung around them, to become a reality almost within grasp. The Viceroy and his comrades had doubtless talked over their riches a hundred times, had met their ships and men, and had made themselves acquainted with such details as were possible of their navigation.

However, it must have been from Luigi Varthema, the Italian, the first European who had ever sailed into these waters, the traveller who had seen with his own eyes the hitherto unknown wonders of the Moluccas, that they derived their most trustworthy information. His accounts of "Maluch" and its cloves; of Banda the "isola molto brutta and trista", and its nutmegs, must have been fresh in their memories. Little wonder, then, that we find Albuquerque fitting out and despatching an expedition to these long sought for lands without a moment's delay. The streets of Malacca were hardly cleared of the debris of the assault, the conquerors hardly rested from their labours, ere Antonio d'Abreu weighed anchor with his three galleons, and sailed in quest of the unknown islands whose perfumed products were even more coveted than the gold of America.

The captains of the other ships were Francisco Serrão, and according to Argensola, Ferdinand Magellan. According to De Goes and Correa, the third vessel was commanded by Simão Afonso Bisagudo. The Portuguese forces had been so weakened by battle and disease that it was impossible further to reduce them to any considerable extent, and barely a hundred European soldiers sailed. The ships, however, bore numerous Malabaris and other mercenaries upon their roll, in addition to their ordinary complement of sea men. Leaving Malacca at the end of December 1511, the fleet followed a southern track, skirting the north coast of Java.

With regard to this first voyage of the Portuguese to the Moluccas the greatest discrepancies exist, in spite of the diffuseness of its narration by some of the contemporaneous historians, and the extreme importance of the enterprise. The question is whether Magellan really did sail with D'Abreu upon this occasion or not. Barros does not mention his presence, nor does the almost equally prolix Castanheda, and Correa, De Goes, and Galvão are also silent upon the subject. Again, from a document found in the Lisbon archives, it is known that Magellan was in that city in June 1512. If the expedition left Malacca for the Spice Islands in December 1511, or even in the middle of November, a very limited space of time is left for the completion of its work and the return of Magellan to Portugal. On the other hand, Argensola tells us very plainly that Magellan went as captain of the third ship. A still stronger argument perhaps exists in Magellan's own letter to Charles V in September 1519 in which he speaks authoritatively of the geographical position of the different islands of the Moluccas. These arguments in their turn are open to objection. Argensola is the least accurate of all the historians, and an obvious anachronism occurs in the same sentence with the passage quoted. Magellan's knowledge of the Moluccas, too, may very well have been obtained through his friend Francisco Serrão who at that time had been resident in Ternate for nearly eight years. The question, having regard to probabilities, must be answered in the negative, but it is of great interest. For, if Magellan did reach Banda, it may be justly claimed for him that at the period of his death in the Philippines he had in his own person completed the circumnavigation of the globe - an honour that is in general assigned to his successor, Sebastian del Cane.

They passed between that island and Madura, and holding an easterly course, left Celebes on their port-hand and entered the Banda Sea. The instructions given by Albuquerque were most explicit. No prizes were to be taken, no vessel was to be chased or boarded, and at every port the greatest respect was to be shown for the authorities and customs of the country. Further to secure their good reception, a junk preceded them, having on board a certain Nakoda Ismael, well versed in the navigation of these seas and in the commerce of their islands. Passing to the north of the volcanic islet of Gunong Api, they touched at Bouru, and finally reached Amboina in safety.

The distance between Amboina and Banda is such as, with a fair wind, might be easily accomplished in one day, even by the clumsily-built galleons of that period. Abreu chose, therefore, to visit this group, the home of the nutmeg, before proceeding northward to Ternate. Serrão's command - a Cambay ship taken at the siege of Goa had however become so unseaworthy that it was found necessary to abandon her. Officers and crew were taken on board the Santa Catalina to Banda, where a junk was purchased to take her place. So abundant was the supply of spice in that port, that they were able fully to laden their ships. Antonio d'Abreu resolved to return to Malacca without visiting Ternate, not only because he was unable to take more cargo, but also on account of the weather.

Perhaps the strongest argument against Magellan having sailed on this expedition with d'Abreu is afforded us by a consideration of the prevailing winds of those seas. Even had the fleet sailed in November, and reached Amboina in a fortnight, it is extremely unlikely that an attempt would have been made to beat back against the west monsoon. The east monsoon is fairly established in July. It may be said, with a confidence approaching certainty, that such of the fleet as returned to Malacca arranged their departure so that they might take advantage of it.

On the return voyage Serrão was destined again to meet with misfortune, or at least with what appeared at the time to be such. Getting separated from the rest of the fleet in heavy weather, his vessel struck on the reefs of the Schildpad Islands, and became a total wreck.

Of Serrão's future history, romantic and interesting as it is, it is impossible here to give a detailed account, though, from its connection with that of his friend Magellan, a glance at it is perhaps necessary. Thrown upon a deserted island, famous as the resort of pirates and wreckers who reaped the harvest of its formidable reefs, they feared that "if they met not their death from thirst and hunger, they might expect it from these corsairs." The very thing they most dreaded proved their salvation, and Serrão extricated himself from his dangerous position by a ruse as clever as it was laughable. Some pirates, having sighted the wreck, landed to hunt down the survivors. Serrão, meanwhile, had hidden his men close to the beach, and waiting until the newcomers had disembarked, quietly emerged from his place of concealment and took possession of their ship. His antagonists, with the prospect of being left without food or water, begged for mercy, which was granted upon condition that they should repair the wrecked junk. All reached Amboina in safety, and were well treated by the natives.

The kings of Ternate and Tidor were at that time engaged in a dispute about their boundaries, and not unwilling to obtain an aid of which both were wise enough to perceive the advantages, made overtures to the powerful foreigners, whose fame had by this time spread to the farthest boundaries of Malaysia. Serrão cast in his lot with that of the ruler of Ternate, and for the remainder of his life established himself in the Moluccas. From Ternate he wrote many letters to his friends, and especially to Magellan, "giving him to understand that he had discovered yet another new world, larger and richer than that found by Vasco da Gama." These letters, joined possibly with a personal knowledge of those regions, formed, it may safely be conjectured, no slight inducement to the undertaking of the voyage that ended Magellan's life and made his name immortal.

The letters written by Magellan to Serrão were found among the papers left at the latter's death. In them he promises "that be will be with him soon, if not by way of Portugal, by way of Spain, for to that issue his affairs seemed to be leading". A certain mystery enwraps the prolonged stay of Serrão in the Moluccas. It is almost certain, that it was contrary to orders, but that on the next visit of the Portuguese he was a person of such influence that they found it advisable to leave him alone. This is borne out by a document found by Munoz in the Seville archives.

Whether, then, Magellan did or did not see with his own eyes this promised land, one thing at least is certain, that the two friends never met again, In what ship or by what fleet he returned to Portugal we do not know, but that he did return about the period is conclusively proved, not only from the fact that the historians give the length of his Indian service as seven years, but from the evidence of certain documents of the Casa Real de Portugal, brought to light by the historian Munioz.

It was the custom in those days that all who belonged to the king's household should receive a stipend that, though merely nominal in value, corresponded to their rank. This stipend was known as the moradia. Magellan, borne on the books as "moco fidalgo," received a monthly pension of a milreis, and an alqueire of barley daily. On the 12th June 1512, we find him signing a receipt in Lisbon acknowledging the fact. It is probable that this receipt was signed not long after his arrival in Portugal. From a similar document, dated one month later (July 14th 1512), we learn of his promotion to the rank of "fidalgo escudeiro," which he presumably obtained for his services in the East. The increase in his pension was, comparatively speaking, considerable (850 reis). However, of far more importance was the improvement in his position at court; for, as we learn from Osorio, "each person was esteemed the more noble according to the amount of salary that he received."

Returned once more to his native land, Magellan remained there for nearly a year. Whether he retired to his estate at Sabrosa or breathed the more stirring air of the court at Lisbon, we are not informed. However, to one of his temperament - one who for seven long years had led a vivid life· of adventure by sea and land, a life of siege and shipwreck, of endless war and wandering, a country existence must have become impossible. To be with his fellows, with men who had tasted of the sweets and bitters of the wider life, to be within reach of news from India, to watch the preparations for further and perhaps greater expeditions - this must have been to him as the breath of his life, and we cannot doubt that he remained in Lisbon. It is wonderful that he should have remained so long. That he was not the man to sink into inaction either of mind or body we may be quite sure. We can picture him perfecting himself in the art of navigation or planning fresh explorations or conquests in the vast island-scattered seas through which well nigh spent with hunger and scurvy he was afterwards destined to wander for so many weary weeks.

Magellan's ability as a trained navigator is constantly referred to by writers of the period. It is not actually stated that he was a pupil of Martin Behaim, but he may quite well have been so. It was to India, doubtless, that Magellan looked as the scene of his future success - to the Farther India of which Serrão had written to him, and of which he himself later said that he would find his way thither, "if not by way of Portugal, then by way of Spain." It was not, however, in India that he was next to serve.

CHAPTER 4

SERVICE IN MOROCCO

In the summer of 1513 difficulties arose with the Moors of Azamor in Morocco. In the time of Dom João II a treaty had been concluded with them. Portuguese subjects resided in the city, their ships entered the harbour free of dues, and their goods passed the customs without charge. The peace remained unbroken until, tired of paying tribute, Muley Zeyam rebelled. Dom Manoel was not the monarch to leave an insult long unavenged. An armada was fitted out in Lisbon such as neither before nor since weighed anchor from the shores of Portugal.

Why so large a fleet was despatched is not clear. It consisted, all told, of more than four hundred ships, which bore no less than eighteen thousand men-at-arms in addition to the cavalry and sailors. The command was given by Dom Manoel to his nephew Jayme, Duke of Bragança. Leaving Belem on the 13th August 1513, the force arrived off Azamor on the 28th. A pretence of fighting was gone through, but the Moors were wise enough to realise that they had not sufficient strength to cope with so formidable an enemy, and so the city opened its gates without further bloodshed.

Among the many distinguished captains who entered them, we look in vain through the chronicler's list of names for that of Magellan, although we know, from his being mentioned in the pages of Barros very shortly after, that he must have been present. The Duke of Bragança returned in November to Portugal, and left Dom João de Meneses in command, a general noted for valour and energy, of whom it was said that "he ceased not for a moment from making cruel war against the Moors." The city was scarcely settled before a series of "entradas" or armed reconnaissances was instituted, which, making their descent where least expected, greatly harassed the Moors and kept the country in a perpetual state of terror. In one of these, under the leadership of João Soarez, Magellan was wounded in the leg by a lance, which appears to have injured some tendon behind the knee in such a manner that he remained slightly lame for the rest of his life.

Towards the end of March 1514, the Portuguese received information that the kings of Fez and Mequinez were preparing a large army for the recapture of Azamor. On the 12th April the patrols sent out from that city gave notice of the approach of the advance-guard, and Dom João de Meneses led his troops at once against them. Although the Moors were completely routed, leaving over two thousand of their men upon the field, the Portuguese also suffered considerable loss, and the advance of the enemy was unchecked. On Easter Eve they arrived at the river of Azamor. So great were their numbers, that seven days were occupied in the crossing, while behind them "everything was consumed, laid waste, and destroyed." The very size of the army was, however, the cause of its ruin. Already au bout de ses forces, it arrived in the neighbourhood of the city only to find the wells destroyed and the country devastated. The Portuguese had an easy task. With the aid of their native allies the invading host was soon put to flight. The booty was large. Over eight hundred horses alone were captured and a thousand Moors made prisoners.

Either on this occasion or very shortly after an incident occurred which, if we may believe the historians, was indirectly the cause of the differences between Magellan and his sovereign. Owing partly to his lameness and partly to his friendship with João Soarez, Magellan was selected, in company with another captain, Alvaro Monteiro, as quadrileiro mór in charge of the booty. Whether he had refused to wink at irregularities, and had hence become unpopular and open to unfounded accusations, or whether he was really guilty, it is impossible with certainty to discover. However, the fact remains, that, together with his comrade, he was accused by certain people of selling the cattle to the Moors, and permitting them to be carried off at night with his full knowledge and connivance. It is probable that under his old commander, Dom João de Meneses, he would have had little difficulty in clearing himself. However, the sudden death of the latter and the succession of Pedro de Sousa to the command of Azamor placed matters on a different footing. Magellan, desirous perhaps of personally explaining the affair, left Africa and returned to Lisbon.

Dom João de Meneses had died on the 15th May 1514. It must have been, therefore, at some date not far removed from this that Magellan presented himself before his sovereign. It is probable that he thought little or nothing of the charge that had been brought against him and that his conscience was clear. We are told that he took the opportunity of preferring his claims for promotion on account of his long service in the East, and petitioning for an increase of moradia. It was perhaps not the wisest of actions. Dom Manoel was by no means disposed lightly to regard the matter. The more so from the fact that he had received a letter from Pedro de Sousa informing him that Magellan had left Africa without his permission. It was in vain that the supposed culprit tried to justify himself. The King refused to listen to him, and ordered him at once to return to Azamor to answer the charges of which he stood accused.

Magellan had no alternative but to go, but on his arrival the authorities declined to proceed against him. No greater argument in favour of his innocence could be adduced. He returned without loss of time to Portugal, bearing the documents that, he confidently expected, would restore him to his sovereign's favour. Doubtless he looked forward with certainty to the coveted rise in the moradia - that minute increase that, paltry though it was in actual value, meant so much to those who were of the King's households. Foremost in his mind, however, must have been the hope of a command - of a return to India. He was doomed to disappointment. "The King always loathed him," Barros tells us. His reception was not more gracious than it had been on the occasion of their last meeting. Dom Manoel turned a deaf ear to his entreaties. Magellan, cruelly hurt at the ingratitude shown him after his years of honourable service, was left to realise that, so far as his king and country were concerned, his career was over.

The lapse of hundreds of years renders it difficult, perhaps, for us to judge between the two, but there is no doubt that such evidence as we have is in favour of subject rather than king. Mariz, in his Dialogos de varia Historia, has treated us to a eulogy of the stereotyped kind upon the latter - a florid tribute that has little genuineness in its tone.

If we turn to facts, however, the story reads differently. Vasco da Gama, to whom must at least be conceded the honour of discovering India, whatever may be said with regard to his cruelties, was left in obscurity by his royal master for eighteen years, and his services only properly acknowledged on the accession of the next monarch, Dom João III. Lord Stanley describes Dom Manoel as "of a most niggardly disposition, suspicious of his servants, and very jealous of directing personally all the details of government."

That the former attribute was true there can be no doubt. No better instance could be given than that on the occasion of the great defeat inflicted upon the Calicut armada, when the Viceroy doubled the pay of the men who had been wounded in the engagement, the King "did not approve of his action in this matter."

Osorius would have us believe that Magellan's application was refused on principle by the King. However, we gather from Barros and others that while he himself was denied, he was exposed to the double mortification of seeing others promoted whose success "was due to intrigue and patronage rather than to any merit of their own." The bitterness with which he felt the injustice of his treatment was in no way mitigated by the insinuation that his lameness was feigned in order to support his claims.

Of Magellan's movements subsequent to this affair we are unfortunately left for some time without any detailed account. Even without the general statement of the historian João de Barros that he "was always busied with pilots, charts, and the question of longitudes," we should have had little difficulty in guessing his occupation. He was unemployed, and was likely always to remain so, so long as Dom Manoel was on the throne. However, it is probable that this fact disturbed him very little, and that he had long decided what action he would take. It is not by any means certain, indeed, that he had not an alternative in his mind on the memorable occasion of his interview with the King - a question to which we shall have presently to return. Be that as it may, however, his future action was probably not a little influenced at this period by his becoming strongly united, if not by the bonds of friendship, at least by those of common interests, to a fellow-countryman, Ruy Faleiro.

Of Faleiro's antecedents we know little or nothing. Of what happened to him after the paths of the two lives diverged, we know almost less. However, for two years or more their histories were so closely linked together that it is impossible not to feel an interest in him. Like Magellan, though not a native of the wild Traz-os-Montes, he too was from the highlands of Portugal, and like him, he was in disfavour with his king. Both had as mistress the science of cosmography. However, while Magellan, the soldier who had served under Dom Lourenço, the sailor who was the first to navigate to Malacca was essentially the man of action, Faleiro was of a very different stamp. Student and dreamer, a lover of books and theories, he was little fitted for the practical life. His reputation as an astronomer and cosmographer was nevertheless undoubted, although his enemies declared it to be the work of a familiar spirit. His knowledge of the principles of navigation was probably as extensive as that possessed by anybody at that period. His treatise upon the means of calculating longitude was given to Magellan on his departure, to serve as guide and textbook throughout the voyage.

Each man doubtless found in the other much to be admired. While Magellan benefited greatly from his companion's acquaintance with the sciences, the fact that the latter did not accompany him upon his memorable voyage is not much to be regretted. Of uncertain temper, gloomy, and jealous of Magellan's influence and position, his presence would have served but to add one more difficulty to the many with which the indomitable navigator had to contend.

At what exact period this friendship or acquaintanceship originated does not appear. It is said by a contemporary historian that the two men had previously arranged to denaturalise themselves and offer their services to Spain. It is therefore more than probable that they were known to each other at the time when Magellan's humiliation at his sovereign's hands was still fresh in his memory. That that incident did not consist in the mere refusal of moradia there is every reason to believe, even had Barros not strongly implied the contrary. However, he tells us that it was shortly after his interview with the King that Magellan wrote to Serrão in the Moluccas, to tell him that he would be with him soon "if not by Portugal, then by way of Spain."

There can be little or no doubt that for a long time, perhaps for years, possibly ever since his Malaccan experiences had put him in relation with the farthest East, the project of reaching the Spice Islands by the western route had been the idée mère of the great navigator's restless brain. That it was this project that he laid before Dom Manoel is almost certain. Whether, like Columbus, he was laughed at as a visionary and a fool, we do not know. All we know is, that his plans met with a cold refusal.

At thirty seven, a born leader of men, of varied Eastern experience, a master of the art of navigation, his mind filled with an all-absorbing project, Magellan found himself condemned to a life of obscurity and inaction. The former might perhaps have been possible to him - inaction was not. Still more intolerable must have been the thought that, with his hands thus fettered, another might come and grasp the prize that he was now the only one to see. Already Christovão Jacques had led his ships far south along the coast of Patagonia, and Vasco Nunez de Balboa had seen the vast Pacific lying at his feet from the summit of the Darien sierra. To a man of Magellan's character and training but one course lay open, and that course he took. Bidding adieu for ever to Portugal, he publicly denaturalised himself, and passing into Spain, entered the service of the Emperor Charles V.

From Correa we learn something of the final severance of relations between Magellan and his sovereign. The former "demanded permission to go and live with some one who would reward his services.... The King said he might do what he pleased. Upon this Magellan desired to kiss his hand at parting, but the King would not offer it to him."

This action of Magellan drew down a perfect storm of abuse and invective, not only from Portuguese writers of that date, but from others to whom a more enlightened age and absence of the odium patrium should have taught broader views and a calmer judgment. With these violent outpourings whole pages might be filled. We have seen something of them in the will of Francisco da Silva Telles, and Osorius is perhaps even more unmeasured in his language. These are put into the shade by a later writer of Portuguese history. "The two monsters Magellan and Faleiro," he says, "traitors to the King whom it was their duty to serve, barbarians towards the country for which it was their duty to die, conspired to bring about a fatal war between two neighbouring and friendly powers." Manoel Faria y Sousa, and later Barbosa, are among the few who refused to join in this cuckoo cry of traitor. "The renderer of many a service to his country," says the latter, "the owner of a name whose glory he had made imperishable, he returned to Portugal, where he besought from the King some increase in his moradia..... The King, to the lasting injury of his country, refused this most just request, and Magellan, deeply hurt at his refusal, left a country so unworthy of such a well deserving son."

It is hardly necessary at the present day to offer an apology for Magellan's act of denaturalisation, although, were it so, the elaborate arguments of Lord Stanley of Alderley should prove more than sufficient. A great discoverer, whether in the realms of science or cosmography, belongs to no country, and, moreover, has no right to permit any false ideas of patriotism to check the advance of knowledge. That they were false ideas, and that Magellan in no way injured Portugal, is evident.

By the Tordesillas capitulation of 1494 the world had been divided into two halves, of which Spain was to have one, and Portugal the other. The western line of division had been agreed upon, but where the eastern fell geographical knowledge was not then sufficiently far advanced to discover. Upon which side of it the Moluccas were situated was unknown. However, his countrymen appear to have forgotten that no action of Magellan could affect the question. Either the islands belonged to Spain or they did not, and the great explorer, with all his geographical knowledge, was unable to shift their longitude one hair's breadth. Nor, even with the most critical eye, can we discover any ground for the anger of the historians save the extreme jealousy then existing between the two nations.

The custom of denaturalisation was fully recognised; it was not regarded as blameworthy, and it was at that period a common occurrence. Among navigators especially the taking service under a foreign power was almost as much a rule as an exception. Columbus, Cabot, and Vespucci are only three of many instances. However, even with this, Magellan was careful not to offend in the slightest degree against the country that, after his long services, had treated him so cavalierly. "Before consulting his own interests," says Faria, "he first did everything that honour demanded of him." By a clause in his agreement with the Emperor of Spain he pledged himself to make no discoveries within the boundaries of the King of Portugal, and to do nothing prejudicial to his interests. He did not sail upon his great voyage until two years after he had signed the act of denaturalisation.

Finally, it should be remembered that there was a sort of tacit understanding that the Spanish were to prosecute their discoveries to the west and the Portuguese to the east. Magellan's long planned expedition was to lead him into occidental waters, and it is probable that this fact was not without its effect upon his action. "Yet this," says Faria, "is the man whose honour has been so fiercely assailed by the great writers."

However, whether Magellan was justified in his action, or whether he was not, matters little as far as regards the result. The fact remains, that, for the second time, Portugal threw away the chance that fate had offered her. Hardly a quarter of a century before, King John II had ridiculed the ideas of Columbus, and regarded him as a boasting adventurer. Now Magellan learnt from his successor that "he might do as he pleased." The discovery of the New World and the circumnavigation of the globe are the two greatest deeds of geographical history, but Portugal, who had both within her grasp, cannot claim credit for either of them.

CHAPTER 5

GAINING THE SUPPORT OF CHARLES V

It was for Seville, the centre of the West Indian trade and the busiest city of Spain, that Magellan set out upon leaving Portugal, taking with him other navigators "suffering from a like disorder" - the neglect or enmity of their king. Faleiro, as we have seen, came under this head, but he was unable to travel with his friend. On the 20th October 1517, Magellan arrived at his destination. He found himself immediately among compatriots and men whose interests were of the same nature as his own. Foremost among them was one Diogo Barbosa, also a Portuguese, a commendador of the Order of Santiago, alcaide of the arsenal, and a person of considerable importance in Seville. At his hands Magellan received the greatest kindness and assistance. From his personal knowledge of the East this help was of double value. Nor did he limit it to advice and counsel. He persuaded Magellan to be his guest, and it appears that the latter resided at his house until his departure, three months later, for the Spanish court at Valladolid.

Diogo Barbosa, although he had held his post under the Spanish flag for nearly fourteen years, and had "served much and well in Granada and Navarre," had also drawn his sword for Dom Manoel and Portugal in the far East. In 1501 he captained a ship of the fleet of João da Nova, and sailed for India. Although this armada returned almost immediately, the voyage was conspicuous for the discovery of the two islands, Ascension and St. Helena. The former was discovered on the outward voyage, the latter on their return home in 1502. His son, Duarte Barbosa, was even more distinguished. At what exact period he had sailed from, and in what fleet he returned to his native land is unknown, but he had navigated the Indian seas for years, making notes of all he saw and heard. These notes - O Livro de Duarte Barbosa - a description of all the ports then visited in the Indian Ocean, and even beyond - he finished in the year 1516, a few months before Ferdinand Magellan came to live beneath his father's roof. Father and son were sailor-adventurers born and bred, and even if no family connection existed between them and Magellan, the bond uniting them must have been of no ordinary strength.

It was, moreover, of no disadvantage to the newcomers that the Alcaide
- mór or chief of the arsenal was also a Portuguese, and a person of
great distinction - Don Alvaro of Portugal. A brother of the celebrated
Duke of Bragança, who was executed by João II, he was only one of
many such refugees. All things considered Magellan could scarcely
have met with kinder or more influential protectors than those who
welcomed him on his arrival in the country of his adoption.

Close as was the friendship between host and guest, the two were
destined before very long to be still more nearly connected. The life of
Magellan had been, and was yet to be, one of the most vivid interest.
Full of vigour and incident, kaleidoscopic in its change of scene, never
resting, it ended in a grand success and a great disaster. Romantic in
many ways it doubtless was, but of romance in the present acceptation
of the word little or none has been handed down by the historians to
interest or amuse us. In the drama of life Magellan was not one to be
cast for the part of lover, although we feel that his character, from its
vigour and undaunted tenacity of purpose, must have strongly appealed
to women's admiration. Such a role, however, it fell to his lot at this
period to play. He made the part as short as possible.

Before the year 1517 had elapsed, within two months of his arrival in
Seville, Magellan married Beatriz Barbosa, the daughter of his friend
and host. Although the date of Magellan's marriage is given as 1518,
there is little doubt that it is incorrect. In his will of August 24th, 1519,
be speaks of his son being at that time six months old. This would fix
the date of the marriage at some time previous to May 1518. However,
we know that from January 20th until August of that year Magellan
was with the court at Valladolid and elsewhere. The probability is,
therefore, that Beatriz was married in order to accompany her husband
thither. This is made nearly certain by the evidence of her brother,
Jaime Barbosa, on the 3rd June 1520.

Magellan's courtship, it is to be presumed, had little or no effect upon
his plans. These had been carefully prearranged, and he lost no time in
furthering them to the best of his ability. His agreement with Faleiro
before leaving Portugal had been most explicit. Both were to be equal;
to stand on precisely the same footing. If anything should occur to

either touching the project they had in hand, he was bound to communicate with his comrade within six hours, and if either desired to renounce the arrangement and return to Portugal, be could do so on fulfilling the same conditions. Their project - the attempt to reach the Moluccas by way of America - was to be revealed to no third party until the arrival of Faleiro at Seville. However much its broad outline might be surmised, the details and the actual route were to remain a secret.

We have already considered the gradual development of the Hispano-Portuguese difficulty. The line of division fixed by the Bull of Pope Alexander VI on the 4th May 1493, fell it may be remembered, a hundred leagues west of the Azores and Cape Verde Islands. The protests of Dom João II of Portugal caused it, a year later, to be placed about 21 degrees further to the west, and Brazil - as yet undiscovered - fell to his country's share. As the knowledge of the South American coastline gradually progressed, the continent was found to trend westward until it was once more crossed by the dividing line, and again became Spanish. It was to this part, as yet dimly known from the explorations of Gonçalo Coelho and Christovão Jacques, and possibly from other sources, that Magellan and his friend Faleiro proposed to direct their course.

Columbus, as we know, considered his new world only as a portion of the old. Nor did his later discoveries undeceive him. It was only when, on the one hand, the work of Vasco da Gama and Albuquerque had begun to give a definite outline to the Indies, and, on the other, when each western sailing navigator found land at whatever latitude he might choose to cross the Atlantic, that the European world realised the existence of a new continent, and realised it as a vast, interminable barrier which stretched apparently from pole to pole.

Then came the search for some strait by which to pass it. The inward trend of the land at the Isthmus of Darien led later explorers to seek it there. Others, however, had tried before them. Columbus had attempted, upon leaving Cuba on his fourth voyage, to navigate westward with the idea of returning to Spain by sea. Far to the north, too, efforts had been made, and made in vain, although Sebastian Cabot wrote to Ramusio that he believed the whole of North America to be divided up into islands. However, the isthmus and the north alike proved impenetrable, and Magellan felt, even at that date, that it was not through the ice of a north-west passage that he was likely to reach the Moluccas. His route lay by the far south.

Whether he actually knew of the existence of the strait that bears his name is a question we shall have presently to consider. One thing we do know; that he went for the special purpose of seeking a passage from the Atlantic to the already known Mar del Sur, or South Sea, and that for the discovery of that passage be was prepared to push on to 70°S.

Magellan, we have seen, allowed nothing to delay the execution of his plans. Although bound not to reveal them in detail by his promise to Faleiro, he was equally engaged to bring them before the notice of those who had to do with Indian affairs. He offered, then, firstly to show Spain the shortest route to the Spice Islands, and, secondly, to prove that they lay within her legal boundaries. With his introductions he had no difficulty in gaining access to the authorities. It was to the Casa de Contratacion that he first applied.

On the history of this body - the India Office of Spain, and of all corporate bodies the most important at that time - it is unnecessary here to dwell. It had, among other rights and duties, the power of granting letters of marque, of giving instruction in navigation, of collecting information upon newly-discovered lands, and of settling all legal difficulties that might arise in connection with these and kindred matters. Whether the Casa was at that time too much taken up with other affairs - for it was just then the most eventful period of the history of the New World - whether it really considered Magellan's project as that of a visionary and a faddist, or whether it felt it unwise to adventure upon thin ice and court misunderstandings with the sister kingdom, we do not know. The result, however, was that the scheme, if not actually rejected, was shelved, and but for a chance circumstance might never have been carried out.

It happened that one of the three chief officials (who we learn from the

Ordinances, were a tesorero, a factor, and an escribano), a certain Juan de Aranda was very much more astute than his fellows. Possibly he saw his way to a share in the future glory of the expedition, and, as we shall see, in its pecuniary benefits, possibly he had no interest beyond the advancement of his country. It is not necessary, at this distance of time, to impute motives. The fact has merely to be recorded that he took the earliest opportunity of questioning Magellan more closely. Whether from his adroitness, or from the latter's feeling that he could be trusted, does not appear, but it was not long before he had persuaded the navigator to acquaint him with every detail. They were such as to commend the plan still more strongly to his favour. However, he was cautious. Before taking further steps he wrote privately to certain friends in Lisbon for information about the two men.

Our only source of information concerning this period of Magellan's life is "Habia escrito á Cobarrubias mercader é á Diego de Haro mercader que residian en Lisboa", in which Aranda was arraigned for having, while an official of the Casa de Contratacion, illegally contracted with Faleiro and Magellan to receive a certain percentage of the profits arising from the expedition. The evidence of the three parties in the case is given at length, followed by nine letters from Aranda to the King, bringing forward his services, how he had spent 1500 ducats over his two protégés, and had succeeded in preventing their return to Portugal, and finally how he had worked to get people to join the fleet. At a meeting of the Consejo de las Indias in Barcelona, June 25th 1519, under the presidency of the Bishop of Burgos, he was severely censured, and again on the 2nd July by the King's fiscal, but it seems that the affair was subsequently allowed to drop. The greater part of the very lengthy evidence tends to exonerate Aranda from blame. What he learnt was in their favour, and from that moment he threw himself heart and soul into the affair. He wrote instantly to the Chancellor of Castile, warmly counselling the despatch of an expedition, and recommending Magellan as "one who might do a great service to his Highness."

Meanwhile, at the beginning of December, Faleiro arrived in Seville. Aranda had as yet said nothing of the letters, but he now told the two friends of the steps he had taken. Magellan was merely vexed at his want of straightforwardness, but Faleiro was furious, and his anger was especially directed against Magellan, whom he upbraided for his "ligereza" and failure in the fulfilment of his promises. It was in vain that the latter pleaded that he had only acted, as he thought, for the best. Faleiro's temper, as ready to take offence as it was slow to forgive, caused a rupture between the two, which, though temporarily healed, was destined to break out afresh at no very distant date. Magellan's partnership with such a firebrand as Faleiro rendered his position most difficult, and such it remained almost up to the moment of the departure of the expedition.

It was perhaps not the best of times to choose for the initiation of plans such as these. Affairs in Spain were at this period in a condition that, at best, could not be regarded as other than uncertain. Charles V, who had at last made up his mind to visit his kingdom, had set out from Flanders, and landed in Villaviciosa, on the north coast of Spain, on the 13th September 1517. Proceeding with the army to Santander, he marched thence to San Vicente de la Barquera, and by Burgos and Palencia to Tordesillas, where his unhappy mother Joanna - for years hopelessly insane - still resided. On the 18th November he entered Valladolid. Ten days previously the Regent of Castile - Cardinal Ximenes de Cisneiros - wisest and most capable of rulers, had ended his long life while on his way to meet and welcome his sovereign. With his loss the affairs of the kingdom became yet more complicated. The King was surrounded by Flemings, anxious only to get what pecuniary benefit they could from their position. Himself hardly able to speak the language of his people, he looked upon the country merely as a means of affording supplies to aid him in his designs in Middle Europe. Mistrustful of their sovereign and bitterly jealous of his Flemish courtiers, the Cortes was summoned to Valladolid. It was into this mixture of nationalities and interests, this hotbed of brigue, that Magellan and Faleiro proposed to adventure themselves in order to expound their views upon an obscure point in geography, concerning which it was more than probable that no single one of their auditors would be interested.

On the 20th January 1518, the two men started together to ride from Seville to Valladolid. Aranda had arranged to go also. Francisco Faleiro, brother of Ruy Faleiro, went with them, and most probably

Beatriz, Magellan's wife. They joined the party of Doña Beatriz de Pacheco, Duchess de Arcos, and went by the Toledo road. Faleiro, still unforgiving, refused to travel in company with Aranda, and the latter, though he, left at the same time, took another route. He had begged them to await the arrival of the answer to the letter he had written to the Chancellor, but in vain. On his journey he met it, and finding that its tenor was in every way favourable to his protégès, he sent it on to them, together with a letter to say that he would wait for them at Medina del Campo, a town some thirty miles from Valladolid. The messenger met them as they were crossing the Sierra de Guadarrama, at Puerto de Herradon, and Faleiro's resentment had sufficiently cooled to permit of his acceding to Aranda's proposal. They met at the town indicated, and went to the same posada, and in a short time good relations were once more established between the trio.

They were now within easy distance of the court, but as yet Aranda had not found an opportunity of bringing forward a proposal he had doubtless long had in view. It was hardly to be supposed that such kindness as he had shown them - strangers, it must be remembered, who had no claim whatever upon him - should be entirely disinterested. Unaided and alone, it was in the highest degree unlikely that they would obtain the King's ear when business of much greater moment remained untouched; but to Aranda, the most important official of the India House, much was possible. To ensure the success of their scheme, he had undertaken a long and wearisome journey, had exposed himself to frequent rudeness at Faleiro's hands, and was now about to spend still more time and pains in introducing them at court. His kindness, however, did not end here. At Seville he had offered them his purse, and he again renewed his offer before arriving in Valladolid. Faleiro, Magellan tells us, had actually taken advantage of it. As the little party crossed the Duero, a few miles only from their destination, Aranda asked them if they would give him a share of the profits in the event of the King deciding to despatch an armada.

The request was not an unfair one, and Magellan's frank and generous character was ready to grant it at once. However, it was different with Faleiro. Suspicion held in his mind the place that gratitude should have occupied. A careless half-assent given by his comrade again aroused his anger. Precisely what occurred it is not easy to make out from the conflicting accounts of the three interested parties. It seems that Aranda suggested that he should receive one-fifth of the profits as his share, but only upon condition that the armada was commissioned at the expense of the King. If the cost of it had to be borne by the two navigators and their friends, he neither asked for nor expected any return. Faleiro at first would not hear of anything being promised, and his brother was of the same opinion. Magellan, wiser and less mean, proposed that Aranda should have one-tenth. The ill-temper of Faleiro, however, was such as quickly to cause a rupture. Aranda took it with his usual good-humour. "If they did not wish to give him anything, he did not want anything, and whether they gave it him or not, he would still advance their cause to the best of his ability, since by so doing he did a service to his sovereign." With this he rode on alone to Valladolid, while Magellan and his comrade stopped at Simancas to talk the matter over.

The result of their discussion was a resolve to offer Aranda an eighth share. Three days later they rode into Valladolid. Aranda came out to meet them, and took them to his inn, where they lay that night as his guests. Next day, anxious to be independent, they sought another posada. Aranda lost no time. He took them first to Sauvage, the Lord High Chancellor, who had succeeded to that post on the death of Ximenes. He then introduced them to the Cardinal Adrian of Utrecht and to the Bishop of Burgos. Finally, he procured them a personal interview with Charles V himself. All this, we gather, was done upon the day following their arrival, or if not, within a very short period after it. Aranda had gone a long way towards proving his title as a man of business. He went still further by having a document ready for the two navigators to sign, in which they legally bound themselves to fulfil the oral promises of the day before. This agreement was executed on the 23rd February 1518. The whole affair is instructive. Whatever their motives, interested or disinterested, those who aided the armadas in those days were apt to find their claims entirely ignored. The result of this venture of Aranda was a lengthy lawsuit, a loss of all the money he had advanced, and a public censure by the Consejo de las Indias. In it, it is worthy of note that Magellan has become Spanish even to his signature. Fernão de Magalhães has ceased to exist, and we make acquaintance for the first time with Fernando Magallanes.

Everything, so far, had gone well with the plans of the two friends, and Magellan might have been excused in feeling that success was within his grasp. Had he known more of those with whom he had to deal, he would not have been too sanguine. Three out of the four were Flemings, and the fourth - Fonseca, Bishop of Burgos - had made himself conspicuous for his bitter enmity to Columbus and other explorers of the New World. The Flemings were men of very unequal merit. Far superior to the others in ability and force of character was Charles's minister and guardian, Guillaume de Croy, Seigneur de Chièvres. A man of the court rather than of the schools, he nevertheless encouraged Charles in the study of history and the art of government, and, from his early appointment as his tutor, had contrived to gain extraordinary power over him. He exercised it in keeping his charge as much as possible away from Spanish influence, and, knowing and caring little for foreign affairs other than European, was not likely to interest himself much in projects of exploration. His avarice, which was boundless, was perhaps the only channel by which he might be approached. In this he was equalled, if not excelled, by Sauvage, the newly appointed successor to Ximenes, of whose character little more is known.

The third Cardinal Adrian of Utrecht, afterwards Pope Adrian VI, who was made Charles's preceptor under De Croy - was a person of no real ability. Of low extraction, a theologian of a conventional type, and a person of weak character, his advancement must always be regarded with wonder. Nominally he had acted in conjunction with Ximenes as Regent of Castile, but the latter, though on the best of terms with his coadjutor, had never even pretended to consult him. His opinion upon an affair of this kind was of little importance. That of Fonseca, Bishop of Burgos, on the other hand - the last of the four - was of very different weight. As President of the India House, he took an assured position as an authority upon colonial matters. Less a prelate than a man of business, Las Casas tells us he was well suited for such work as the fitting out of armadas. His character, nevertheless, was a despicable one. His hatred of Columbus has already been referred to. He thwarted Las Casas upon every point in his struggle to ameliorate the condition of the Indians. Cortez he declared a traitor and a rebel, and it is more than probable that he instigated a plot to assassinate him. To Balboa he was equally opposed. The most sanguine of project mongers would have gone to him with something more than diffidence.

These were the men, together with a boy-sovereign of eighteen, on whom Magellan's future depended. It might be imagined that support from the Flemings was an accidental possibility, but that none could be expected from Fonseca. Nothing is more certain, however, than the unforeseen. Whether the Bishop, venal and avaricious like his fellows, looked to the possibilities of future profit, or whether, having lost prestige from his opposition to the projects of Columbus, he was anxious to win it back over an expedition whose probable success he was wise enough to foresee, we do not know, but from the beginning be took up the cause of the two petitioners. From that moment its success was ensured.

Magellan came well prepared with arguments, animate and inanimate, to support his project. At the first formal meeting of the King's ministers he showed the letters from his friend Francisco Serrão, in which he told him that if he desired to get rich he should come to the Moluccas. He produced Vartema's account of his voyage to those islands; how they lay beneath the Equator, and far distant from Malacca. He showed a slave whom he had bought in the latter city, and who was a native of the Spice Islands, and a slave-girl from Sumatra, "who understood the tongues of many islands." "Other bids for credence did he make," we are told by Gomara, "conjecturing that the land (i.e., South America) turned westward, in the same manner as did that of Good Hope toward the east, since Juan de Solis had coasted it up to 40° S., with his course always more or less westerly. Since on the track thus taken no passage existed, he would coast the whole continent till he came to the cape that corresponds to the Cape of Good Hope, and would discover many new lands, and the way to the Spice Islands, as he promised."

Such an expedition, Gomara goes on to say, "would be long, difficult, and costly, and many did not understand it, and others did not believe in it. However, the generality of people had faith in Magellan as a man who had been seven years in India and in the spice trade, and because, being Portuguese, he declared that Sumatra, Malacca, and other Eastern lands where spices could be found belonged to Castile." The arguments and projects of the two navigators were illustrated by means of a globe that Magellan had brought with him from Portugal, which according to Argensola was a planisphere. Upon it were shown the continent, as he conceived it to exist, and his intended route. However, according to Herrera, the strait which it was his purpose to seek was intentionally omitted, in order that no one might anticipate him. Finally, when his companion had finished his demonstrations, Faleiro took up the argument and proved to his audience that the coveted islands lay within the line of demarcation arranged by the Tordesillas capitulation of 1494.

It was not to be expected that the project should meet with entire and instant approval. Some of the ministers rubbished it; others took no interest in it. However, upon further discussion the advice of Fonseca prevailed, and it was finally agreed to recommend the enterprise to the favourable consideration of the young King.

We can understand the delight with which the news of this resolution - tantamount to an actual order for the preparation of their armada - must have been received by Magellan and Faleiro. It only remained for them now to lay their proposals in due form before the King. Two ways - both commonly adopted at that time - were open to them. They could either fit out the expedition at their own cost, giving a certain percentage of the profits to the Crown, or, leaving the expenses to be borne by the King, sail as the captains of the ships, investing a certain fixed amount in articles of barter, and looking to their sovereign, upon their return, to confer upon them what benefits he thought fit.

Neither of the applicants was in the position to purchase and equip ships at his own expense. Faleiro was a poor student. Magellan, though a noble and a landowner, had profited no whit by his seven years' residence in the East. Most of those who survived the glorious uncertainties of that life made money. However, Magellan was not as other men, and whatever sin might be laid to his charge, that of greed was not one. In the East, we are told he lost the little that he had. However, there were plenty of rich and influential friends to assist him. His father-in-law, Diogo Barbosa, was a man of position, and Aranda was willing enough to place himself, purse and voice, at his disposal. Just at that moment, moreover, he had made an acquaintance that effectually banished all anxieties on the score of money. His acquaintance, who afterwards became his friend, was the great merchant Christopher de Haro.

The Haros were an Antwerp firm of traders - the Rothschilds of that day - who carried on an enormous and most profitable business with both the East and West Indies. In the various towns of these countries they had agents and clerks, who kept them informed upon every point of interest in trade, politics, and geography. Christopher de Haro resided in Lisbon, and had an agreement with Portugal concerning the Guinea trade. For some reason that does not appear, he had seven of his vessels sunk by the King's ships while on the coast. He sought indemnification, but his claim was ignored, and feeling that it would be wiser to quit a country where so little justice could be had, returned to Spain, his native land. He had but recently arrived. Magellan's project was the one above all others to commend itself to his favour. It gave him an opportunity of indirectly revenging himself upon Portugal, and at the same time of making a very profitable speculation. His ships had traded to the farthest East, had even reached China, and he knew what a monopoly of the spice trade would mean. He did not hesitate to offer all the aid that lay in his power.

Fortified with such strong support, the two Portuguese addressed their proposals formally to the King. They fell under two heads, those made with the understanding that the King should charge himself with the entire cost of the armada, and those suggested in the case of the expenses being borne by themselves.

In the first case they sought the concession of the following privileges :- That no other exploring expeditions should be sent out to the Spice Islands for a period of ten years, but that, if this could not be granted, they should have the right to a twentieth share of the resulting profits; that of all the lands and islands discovered by them a twentieth share of the annual profit should be theirs; that in this and every other succeeding expedition they should be permitted to send goods to the value of a thousand ducats for trading purposes; that in the event of the discovery of more than six islands, the Senorio of two should be conferred upon them; that of this first expedition, they should have one-fifth of the net profits; and finally, that the title of Almirante should be conferred upon them.

In the case of the armada being commissioned and despatched at their own expense, they besought the King to grant them the trade and ownership (scenario) of all the lands discovered by them, and the privilege of the sole right of exploration and discovery for ten years. In return, one-fifth of the profits were to be handed to the Crown.

The document was returned, with comments under each section, to Magellan, leaving the matter still undecided. A few days later, on the 22nd March 1518, a capitulation was granted by Charles V that definitely settled the terms under which the two explorers were to sail.

This document has been abridged here. It is taken from a copy in the Torre do Tombo, made from another copy, which is very illegible. The Spanish is rather antiquated, and much debased, apparently by Portuguese copyists, who have mixed up their own orthography. The Secretary's name was Francisco, not Fernan :

Contract and Agreement made by the King of Castile with Fernan Magellan for the discovery that he was to make, a copy of which he carried with him, signed by the Officers of the King of Castile, and made by his Secretary Fernan de los Cobos, and copied word for word.

Certificate given in Seville that the commendador Fernan de Magallanes, and the bachelor Ruy Faleiro, Portuguese, presented themselves at the Audiencia on the fourth of May, of 1518, before Dr. Sancho de Matienzo, the contador Juan Lopez de Ricalde, and the factor Juan de Aranda, judges and fiscals of their Highnesses, of the India House, residing in this city, in the presence of Juan Gutierrez Calderon, clerk of their H.H., and his Notary public, on behalf of Diego de Porras, chief clerk in civil and criminal causes of the said India House; and they presented to the judges two capitulations written on paper and signed by his Highness, and one sealed with a seal of coloured wax at the back and other necessary signatures, and two royal orders (cedulas) of H.H. signed with his royal name, all written by the secretary Fernan de los Cobos, the tenour of all which, one after another, is as follows.

The King : "Since you, Fernando de Magallanes, a knight, native of the Kingdom of Portugal, and the bachelor Ruy Faleiro, also a native of that kingdom, wish to render us a great service in the limits which belong to us in the ocean within the bounds of our demarcation, we order the following capitulation to be established with you for that purpose.

Firstly : That you are to go with good luck to discover the part of the ocean within our limits and demarcation, and because it would not be in reason that, while you go to do the above mentioned, that other persons should cross you to do the same, and taking into consideration that you undertake the labour of this enterprise, it is my favour and will, and I promise that for the first ten following years we will not give leave to any person to go and discover by the same road and course by which you shall go; and if anyone desire to undertake it and should ask our leave for it, before giving it, we will let you know of it in order that if you should be ready to make it in that time in which they offer, you should do so, providing an equal sufficiency and equipment, and as many ships as the other persons who may wish to make the said discovery : but, be it understood that, if we please to send to discover, or to give leave for it to such other persons as we please by way of the south-west in the parts of the islands and mainland, and all other parts which are discovered towards the part where they are to seek the strait of those seas, we may order it to be done, or give leave to other persons to do it, both of the mainland by the South Sea, which is discovered, or from the island of S. Miguel, if they wish to go and discover, they may do so. Also, if the governor and people who are now, by our orders, or may in future be in the said mainland, or other of our subjects may wish to discover in the South Sea, they may do so, notwithstanding the above, or any section or clause of this capitulation. Also, you may discover in any of those parts what has not yet been discovered, so that you do not discover nor do anything in the demarcation and limits of the most serene King of Portugal, my very dear and well-beloved uncle and brother, nor to his prejudice, but only within the limits of our demarcation."

In consideration of their goodwill and services, the next paragraph grants the right to levy upon any isles or countries settled by them after the expenses have been paid, a twentieth part, with the title of our Adelantados and Governors of the said countries and isles,

"you, and your sons and rightful heirs for ever, so that they remain for us and the kings that may come after us, and your sons and heirs being natives of our realms and married in them; and of this we will send you your formal letter of privileges."

The next paragraph grants the right to invest in goods each year the value of a thousand ducats, cost price, to sell in the islands and countries, and bring back the returns, paying only a twentieth in duty to the king without other payment. This only after the return from the voyage, not during it. Also to grant them greater favour, if more than six islands should be discovered; after six have been set apart for the king, they might mark out two from which they might take the fifteenth part of all the net profits and duties of the king after the expenses had been deducted. Also of all the net profit that there may be for the king on the return of the fleet, after this first voyage, deducting its expense, they may take a fifth part.

"In order that you may better carry this out, I will order the equipment of five ships, two of one hundred and thirty tons each, and two others of ninety, and another of sixty tons, provided with men, victuals, and artillery; that is to say, that the said ships shall be supplied for two years, and there shall go in them two hundred and thirty-four persons for their management : amongst masters, mariners, shipboys, and all other people that are of necessity, according to the memorial, and this we will order to be carried out by our officers in Seville.

Also if either of them died, this agreement was to be kept with, and by the other, as it would have been kept with both if they were alive."

The next paragraph says that a factor, a treasurer, an accountant, and clerks of the said ships, shall keep the accounts of all the expenses of the fleet.

"All which I promise and plight my faith and royal word that I will order it to be observed to you, in all and for all, according as is contained above, and upon it I have ordered this present to be given, signed with my name. Dated in Valladolid, the twenty-second day of March, of five hundred and eighteen years.

Yo el Rey.
By order of the King,
FRANCISCO DE LOS COBOS."

Another copy of the contract has the heading - Doña Juana and Don Carlos, her son, by the grace of God, Queen and King of Castile, Leon, Aragon, the two Sicilies, and Jerusalem, of Navarra, Granada, Toledo, Valencia, Galicia, the Mallorcas, Seville, Sardinia, Cordova, Corsica, Murcia, Jaen, the Algarves, of Aljazira, Gibraltar, of the Canary Isles, of the Indies, isles and mainland of the Ocean-sea, Counts of Barcelona, Lords of Biscay and Molina, Dukes of Athens and Neopatria, Counts of Roussillon and Cerdaña, Marquises of Euristan and Gociano, Archdukes of Austria, Dukes of Bergoña and Brabant, Counts of Flanders and Tirol, etc.

Accompanying the contract was another document, by which Magellan and his comrade were appointed Captains general of the armada, entitled from that moment to draw pay at the rate of 50,000 maravedis per annum from the Casa de Contratacion at Seville. By a cedula of 30th March of the following year (1519) Charles appointed Luis de Mendoza treasurer at a yearly salary of 60,000 maravedis, and Juan de Cartagena Veedor-general at 70,000 maravedis, and also captain of the third ship at 40,000 maravedis. On the 30th April, Antonio de Coca was made Contador of the armada at 50,000 maravedis.

A letter, also dated Valladolid, March 22nd 1518, and signed by the king, and the secretary Francisco de los Cobos, and signed at the back by Joanes Beijamanse, Fonseca Archiepiscopus, Episcopus, registered, Johan de Samana, Guillermo Chancellor, confers upon Magellan the power of deciding and executing short and summary justice by sea or land in case of suits or disputes arising in the fleet.

Another royal letter of the same date as the above orders the officers of the India House to provide Magellan with five ships, crews, provisions, etc., according to the memorial which is signed by our chancellor of Bargonha and by the Archbishop of Rosano and Bishop of Burgos; and bids them use all despatch.

Another royal letter, dated Aranda, 17th of April 1518, to Magellan and Ruy Faleiro, says that if, after they shall have sailed, either or both of them should die, and that they should have given to the people in the fleet instructions and orders that should be necessary for the discovery; and if they, profiting by them, should discover the isles and parts that they were going to discover, then their heirs and successors should enjoy the favours and privileges contained in the said capitulations. The document states that Magellan and Ruy Faleiro having presented the capitulations and letters and royal orders of his highness to the said judges, they summoned and required them to fulfil them according to their contents, and they requested this in the presence of the witnesses, Francisco de Santa Cruz, alguazil Lorenzo Pinelo, and Francisco de Collantes, porter of the Audiencia of the said House. Then the judges took the letters in their hands, and kissed them, and put them on their heads, as the orders of their king, and natural sovereign, whom may God suffer to live and reign many years; and they would answer more at length in complying with the orders. Witnesses the above-named.

On Monday, at the Audiencia de la Nona, on the thirty-first day of May of 1518 the judges, Dr. Sancho de Matienzo and the contador Juan Lopez de Ricalde, appeared before Juan Gutierrez Calderon, Clerk and Notary Public, and presented an answer signed with their names to the presentation made by the Portuguese captains of the royal orders and letters. And this reply is as follows : The said judges state that the king's letters order them to provide five ships, and men and provisions as may be necessary, in conformity with a memorial which the captains bring, signed by the great Chancellor of Burgundy and by the very Reverend Archbishop of Rosano and Bishop of Burgos, which said memorial up to this time has not been shown to us, and without it we cannot undertake anything so let his Highness send us orders according to that the said despatch signed, as has been said, by the chancellor and bishop; and we are ready to fulfil the orders which his Highness sends, having at the time moneys of his Highness in our power. This they said, and gave as their answers, and signed it with their names, Doctor Matienzo, Juan Lopez de Ricalde.

Magellan and Ray Faleiro asked from Juan Gutierres Calderon, Clerk and Notary Public, a certificate and legalised copy of what had passed for the conservation of their rights, which he accordingly gave him, dated on the said day and month (31st May) of 1518. The letter, the original of which appears to have fallen into the hands of the Portuguese at the Moluccas, is as follows :

The King : "Fernando de Magallams and Ruy Faleiro, Knights of the Order of St. James, our captains-general of the fleet, which we command to be equipped to go to discover, and the other separate captains of the said fleet, and pilots, masters, quarter-masters, and seamen of the said fleet : Inasmuch as I know for certain, according to the much information which I have obtained from persons who have seen it by experience, that there are spices in the islands of Maluco; and, chiefly, you are going to seek them with this said fleet, and my will is that you should straightway follow the voyage to the said islands in the form and guise which I have said and commanded to you, the said Ferdinand de Magallams; moreover, I command you all and each one of you that in the navigation of the said voyage you follow the opinion and determination of the said Ferdinand de Magallams, in order that first and foremost, before any other part, you should go to the said islands of Maluco, without there being any shortcoming in this, because thus it is fitting for our service, and after this done, the rest that may be convenient may be sought for according to what you have been commanded, and one and all neither do nor let them do anything else in anywise, under pain of losing their goods and their persons, at our discretion. Done in Barcelona, nineteenth day of April, year of one thousand five hundred and nineteen.

I, the King.
By order of the King,

FRCO DE LOS COVOS"

Charles, who in his bid for popularity had succeeded but ill with the Castilians, now resolved to visit Aragon. Summoning the Cortes of that country to meet him in Zaragoza, he marched thither in the beginning of April. Upon the way he stopped at Aranda de Duero, where his brother Ferdinand was then living, a prince so great a favourite with the Spaniards that the King's design, which was to send him out of the country was no ill advised step. However, in spite of the many intrigues and difficulties in which he found himself involved, and the barrier to external influences interposed by his Flemish courtiers, Charles found time to interest himself in the affairs of the future expedition. Magellan and Faleiro had followed the court, and being in constant communication with the King, were enabled to escape the delays which must otherwise inevitably have arisen. By certain cedulas issued by Charles at this time the pay of the two captains was raised to 146,000 maravedis, and they were granted a sum of 30,000 maravedis to defray initial expenses. The privilege of appointing a pilot was given to them, with the promise that, if approved by the Casa de Contratacion, he should have the title of "piloto real" conferred upon him. Not less welcome was a grant to the heirs of either navigator, in the event of his death, of all the privileges and profits to which the latter was entitled.

Although charged to proceed to Seville in order that they might place themselves en rapport with the officials of the India House and forward the preparation of the armada, Magellan and Faleiro were led to defer their journey. Leaving Aranda de Duero, Charles proceeded by Calatayud to Zaragoza, into which city he made a formal entry on the 15th May. The two friends followed in his train, for a check had lately come upon the progress of their scheme. Against want of money and interest, against the apathy or opposition of those in power, they had fought for months, and fought successfully; but now they were confronted by an obstacle not less serious, though long foreseen - the silent intrigues and loudly-expressed remonstrances of the Court of Portugal.

CHAPTER 6

PREPARING FOR THE VOYAGE

It could hardly be otherwise than that the news of Magellan's approaching voyage should reach Portugal. The defection of two such well known navigators, and the fact that they took others with them "sick with a like disorder," could not be passed unnoticed. The subsequent movements of the Consejo de las Indias at Seville were, no doubt, fully reported to Dom Manoel by the Portuguese "factor" resident in that city. However, it happened that a special circumstance brought the matter still more prominently forward. So prominently, in fact, that, advanced as were the preparations, the expedition was within an ace of being countermanded.

The question of the marriage of Dom Manoel to Doña Leonor, sister of Charles V, was at that time under consideration. Alvaro da Costa, the ambassador of Portugal at the court of Spain, was charged with the arrangement of the alliance. The treaty was concluded at Zaragoza on the 22nd May 1518, and ratified at the same place on the 16th July. It was the very period when Charles was most taken up with the project of Magellan, and Da Costa, naturally, was brought much in contact both with the affair and the principals concerned. They appear to have caused him far more anxiety than the marriage. From a letter to his sovereign, still existing in the Torre do Tombo, we get a glimpse of the means he employed to frustrate them. It was not the first time that the Portuguese, having been led by their ignorance and folly wilfully to reject one of the world's greatest chances, fought tooth and nail to counteract its outcome. When Columbus reached the shelter of the Tagus upon his first return from the New World, it was suggested by some of those at court that much future trouble with Spain would be obviated by his assassination. Not that these methods were confined to Portugal. The value of each discovery, owing perhaps to the rapidity with which it followed upon a previous one, was so little understood, that either of the two countries was ready at a moment's notice to take up an attitude of protestation, if not of something worse.

At first, Da Costa confined himself to simple dissuasion. In the course of various interviews with Magellan, he told the latter that, if he persisted in his enterprise, not only would he sin against God and his King, but would for ever stain the honour of his name, and, moreover, that he would be the cause of dissension between two kings who would otherwise, by the approaching marriage, still further strengthen the ties of friendship that already existed between them. Magellan's answer was that his first duty was to his King; that he had pledged his word to him, and that he too would sin against his honour and his conscience should he break it. To Da Costa's temptation of reward if he went back to Portugal he turned equally a deaf ear. Failing thus both in threats and persuasion, the Portuguese ambassador turned his attention to the King's ministers. The Cardinal, Adrian of Utrecht, weak and vacillating, half fearful of consequences and half mistrustful of the success of the expedition, played into his hands. "The Cardinal," writes Alvaro to his sovereign, "is the best thing here." Chièvres, too, was hardly against him; but Fonseca's convictions were so strong and his influence so great, that it was impossible to ignore them. Again foiled, Alvaro wrote to Dom Manoel. The news was received with renewed irritation, and discussed in various juntas and conselhos.

Some advised that Magellan should be bribed to return; others were against this, as affording a bad precedent. There were not wanting those who advised that he should be put out of the way. One of them was a bishop. Lafitau, in his Conquêtes des Portugais, hides, as a Jesuit, the name of this honourable counsellor. Faria and De Goes give it to us for eternal obloquy - it was Ferdinand Vasconcellos, Bishop of Lamego, who afterwards became Archbishop of Lisbon.

The news of his contemplated assassination reached Magellan while still in Zaragoza, but he paid but slight attention to it, and pursued his daily avocations, although exposing himself as little as possible, and "when night surprised them in the house of the Bishop of Burgos," Herrera tells us "the latter sent his servants to guard them home." Of Faleiro they made little account. His odd manner and uncertain temper led people to the conclusion that be was not quite of sound mind.

There were other reasons besides those of caution that called for the departure of the two navigators from Zaragoza. Their presence was needed in Seville. The Casa de Contratacion, as a body, had never been very favourable to their scheme. Some jealousy with Aranda possibly stood in the way; possibly the officials really did not believe in its chances of success. However, they opposed it, if not actively, at least with a dead wall of difficulties that rendered the future prospects of the expedition none of the brightest. Charles, with a quiet but firm hand, now put all these obstacles aside. In a letter written on the 20th July 1518, he informed the India House that it was his intention to carry out the proposed expedition; that certain moneys lately arrived from the West Indies were to be used for the purpose of defraying the expenses; and, finally, that he desired the armada should be fitted out in every way in conformity with the ideas and wishes of Magellan and Faleiro. However, at the same time that he wrote the letter, anxious to hasten these preparations, he intimated his wish that the two captains should depart for Seville without delay.

In order to mark still further his sense of the importance of the expedition and of his confidence in those to whom he had intrusted its command, Charles signified his intention of conferring upon Magellan and his comrade the honour of the Order of Santiago. They were decorated with the cross of Comendador in the presence of the Council, and at the same time the conditions of the agreement concluded at Valladolid on the 22nd March were formally confirmed. A few days later, at the end of July, the two Comendadores left the court for Seville.

In answer to the remonstrances expressed by Alvaro da Costa, Charles had written to Dom Manoel to explain the object of Magellan's voyage. In his letter he assured his future brother-in-law that nothing should be done in any way to the detriment of Portugal, and that if he had not complied with his wish, it was because the explorations proposed would not be carried beyond the limits of Spanish waters. His reasoning was in vain. Alvaro renewed his complaints and remonstrances, and Chievres being ill, succeeded in obtaining a private interview with the King. The sum and substance of it he gives in the letter addressed to Dom Manoel, and dated from Zaragoza, September 28th 1518, to which allusion has already been made :

"Sire - Concerning Ferdinand Magellan's affair, how much I have done and how I have laboured, God knows, as I have written you at length; and now, Chievres being ill, I have spoken upon the subject very strongly to the King, putting before him all the inconveniences that in this case may arise, and also representing to him what an ugly matter it was, and how unusual, for one king to receive the subjects of another king, his friend, contrary to his wish, a thing unheard of among cavaliers, and accounted both ill-judged and ill-seeming. Yet I had just put your Highness and your Highness's possessions at his service in Valladolid at the moment that he was harbouring these persons against your will. I begged him to consider that this was not the time to offend your Highness, the more so in an affair which was of such little importance and so uncertain; and that he would have plenty of subjects of his own and men to make discoveries when the time came, without availing himself of those malcontents of your Highness, whom your Highness could not fail to believe likely to labour more for your disservice than for anything else; also that his Highness had had until now so much to do in discovering his own kingdoms and dominions, and in settling them, that he ought not to turn his attention to these new affairs, from which dissensions and other matters, which may well be dispensed with, may result. I also represented to him the bad appearance that this would have on the year and at the very moment of the marriage, - the ratification of friendship and affection. And also that it seemed to me that your Highness would much regret to learn that these men asked leave of him to return, and that he did not grant it, the which are two faults - the receiving them contrary to your desire, and the retaining them contrary to their own. And I begged of him, both for his own and for your Highness's sake, that he would do one of two things - either permit them to go, or put off the affair for this year, by which he would not lose much; and means might be taken whereby he might be obliged, and your Highness might not be offended, as you would be were this scheme carried out. He was so surprised, sire, at what I told him, that I also was surprised; but he replied to me with the best words in the world, saying that on no account did he wish to offend your Highness, and many other good words; and he suggested that I should speak to the Cardinal, and confide the whole matter to him. I, sire, had already talked the matter over with the Cardinal, who is the best thing here, and who does not approve of the business, and he promised me to do what he could to get off the affair. He spoke to the King, and thereupon they summoned the Bishop of Burgos, who is the chief supporter of the scheme. And with that certain two men of the Council succeeded in making the King believe that he did your Highness no wrong, since he only ordered exploration to be made within his own limits, and far from your Highness's possessions; and that your Highness should not take it ill that he should make use of two of your subjects - men of no great importance - while your Highness himself employed many Spaniards. They adduced many other arguments, and at last the Cardinal told me that the Bishop and the others insisted so much upon the subject, that the King could not now alter his determination. While Chievres was well, I kept representing this business to him, as I have just said, and much more. He lays the blame upon those Spaniards who have pushed the King on. Withal he will speak to the King, but on former occasions I besought him much on this subject, and he never came to any determination, and thus, I think, he will act now. It seems to me, sire, that your Highness might get back Fernão de Magalhães, which would be a great blow to these people. As for the bachelor (Ruy Faleiro), I do not count him for much, for he is half crazy. Do not let your Highness think that I went too far in what I said to the King, for beside the fact that all I said was true, these people do not perceive anything, nor has the King liberty up to now to do anything of himself, and on that account his actions may be less regarded (por iso se deue de syntyr menos sues cousas). May the Lord increase the life and dominions of your Highness to His holy service. From Saragoga, Tuesday night, the 28th day of September.

I kiss the hands of your Highness. ALUARO DA COSTA."

This letter was not the last of its kind, for though the protestations of the Portuguese ceased for the time being, they were again renewed upon the removal of the court to Barcelona. Nor did they end until Magellan finally weighed anchor at San Lucar de Barrameda, and started on his voyage.

We must return to Seville, whither the two newly made knights had meanwhile arrived. Their presence was regarded by Fonseca as likely to smooth the difficulties made by the Casa de Contratacion. This body, although definitely instructed by the King's cedula in March, as we have seen, demurred somewhat to the arrangement therein contained, and wrote again asking for a confirmation of a despatch signed by the Chancellor of Burgundy, expressing themselves, however, as ready to fulfil the King's orders "if we have at the time money of his Highness at our disposal." The reply was Charles's letter of July 20th already mentioned, charging them to fit out the fleet according to the ideas and wishes of its commanders. It is probable that they themselves carried this document and presented it in person. However, whatever may have been the way it reached its destination, its effect was magical. "We are greatly pleased," write the officials, "at the arrangement concluded .....it is a very honourable and advantageous undertaking, as we inform the Bishop of Burgos." They add that a certain sum of money had arrived from India, and ask whether it should be used for the expenses. Everything seemed to be couleur de rose. However, even at the hands of the Casa de Contratacion Magellan and his friend had yet to experience difficulties and unpleasantnesses, and to learn that the King of Spain, despite the lengthy titles heading his cedulas, was not all powerful.

The altered attitude of the India House, together with the energy of Magellan, gave an impulse to the work of preparation that must have gone far towards compensating the great navigator for the months of disappointment and heart-burnings through which he had passed. Now his way seemed clear before him, and he worked with double vigour, writing letters to the King and the Bishop of Burgos to inform them of the progress of affairs. At the outset, good-natured and a hater of quarrels, he had ceded to the fitful temper and morose disposition of his comrade, and permitted him to take the lead; but when it came to practical work - to the fitting out of a fleet and to the choice of his men, then the experience gained by years of service in the East necessarily placed Magellan in a position of authority that was beyond the power of Faleiro to question. So long as they had to bow the knee in kings' houses, petitioners and place-seekers, they were equals; but upon the ship's deck in Seville, away from the flattery laden air of the court and almost within sound of the sea, there was little doubt as to which meant to command. So, little by little, it came about that Faleiro, albeit nominally on the same footing - the "conjunta persona" with Magellan - fell insensibly into the second place.

The preparations, then, were pushed on with all speed. The King, in his letter of July 20th 1518, had informed the officials of the Casa de Contratacion that since so many articles were to be obtained both better and cheaper in Biscay, he had sent thither to purchase them. Other materials were apparently brought from Flanders. The ships, as we learn from documents in the Seville archives, were all bought at Cadiz. The duty of purchasing them devolved upon Aranda, who was probably totally lacking in the technical knowledge necessary for such a responsible task, for we learn from the Portuguese factor Alvarez, then residing in Seville, that they were not in the best condition. "They are very old and patched," he says, "..... and I would be sorry to sail even for the Canaries in them, for their ribs are as soft as butter." In Charles's original capitulation to the two captains he had promised that two should be of 130 tons, two of 90, and the fifth of 60. Those obtained for the expedition were tolerably close to the promised tonnage, being in the aggregate only twenty tons short.

The names and burden of the five vessels were as follows :- Santo Antonio, 120 tons; Trinidad, 110 tons; Concepcion, 90 tons; Victoria, 85 tons; Santiago, 75 tons. It is difficult to assign an exact value to these "toneles de porte." They may perhaps be taken as roughly representing the ordinary tons of the present day. What they were, how rigged and masted, we do not know. From a few chance words of Herrera we learn that the poop and forecastle of each was provided with high obras muertas - with castles, in short, as was not unusual at that period. Such vessels are seen in the illustrations of De Bry, and indeed in Columbus's own sketch of the Oceanica Classis. It is, however, nearly certain that all the ships in Magellan's fleet were decked, while but one of the three that the discoverer of America took on his memorable voyage was thus advantaged.

The ships once obtained, Magellan occupied himself unremittingly in overhauling them and putting them in a seaworthy condition before starting upon his long and dangerous voyage. It was when engaged in this work, on the 22nd October, that an incident occurred which once more brought forcibly before him the fact that the emissaries of Portugal were still at work to thwart his plans. He had no longer Alvaro da Costa at hand to tell him that he was a renegade to his face, and to connive at his assassination in secret, but his place was taken by an individual even more unscrupulous - Sebastian Alvarez, the factor of the King of Portugal at Seville, and it was probably at his instigation that the incident arose.

On the day in question, Magellan had taken advantage of the tide to careen the Trinidad at an early hour. At daybreak he ordered four flags bearing his own arms to be placed upon the four capstans. In this position it was the custom always to carry the captain's flag, while the royal ensign and that of the vessel itself were flown at the mast-head. On this occasion these latter were not hoisted, having been sent to be painted, and Magellan, engaged with his work, had not noticed their absence.

As the work proceeded, a gradually increasing crowd of idlers watched its progress. It was maliciously suggested by some one that the capstan flags bore the arms of the King of Portugal, and, in the midst of considerable disturbance and murmuring, an alcalde arrived upon the scene. Without consulting Magellan, he incited the bystanders to tear them down. The crew now summoned their captain, till then engaged below, who explained to the official that "the arms were not those of the King of Portugal; that they were his arms, and that he was a vassal of the King of Spain." Sailor and aristocrat, Magellan was not one to bandy words with an alcalde, and he returned to his work without further discussion. The alcalde was not so easily satisfied, and insisted upon the removal of the obnoxious flags. Sancho Matienzo, the chief official of the India House, who arrived at this juncture, advised Magellan to yield for the sake of calming the mob. Sancho Matienzo, a well known person at that period, was a Canon of Seville and a personal friend of Magellan. Magellan agreed, but the moment was a bitter one for him, for among the crowd he recognised an agent of the King of Portugal, whom he felt to have been the instigator of the riot. There is little doubt that the caballero in question was Sebastian Alvarez. Meanwhile, the alcalde had gone in search of the port-captain (teniente del almirante), whose appearance was the signal for a renewal of the tumult. Arriving on the scene, he called upon his men to "arrest the Portuguese captain who flew the ensign of the King of Portugal," at the same time roughly demanding of the Comendador "where were the flags, and why were they hoisted upon the capstans ?" Magellan's answer was that he was not responsible to him for his actions. The port-captain instantly called upon the alguaciles to arrest him, but Matienzo cautioned the irate official that if he laid hands upon the King's captain he would have to answer for it to the King. His interference so enraged the alguaciles and companions of the teniente, that they rushed upon him with their drawn swords, threatening to kill him. Seeing the highest official of the India House thus treated, Magellan's people - or such of them, he naively remarks, as had been paid in advance - thought it best to decamp.

The ship was at the moment in a somewhat dangerous position. Magellan, ever ready of resource, saw in this fact a means of strengthening his hand. He threatened to leave it, and to make the officials responsible for any damage that might occur. Already conscious, perhaps, of having gone too far with Matienzo, the port-captain thought it best to alter his tactics. He eventually left the ship, contenting himself with arresting some of the crew and disarming others. The teniente del asistente, to whom Magellan had appealed for support, refused to interfere.

Two days later Magellan wrote a full account of the affair to Charles V, begging him to order a searching inquiry to be made. The fearlessness and independence of the letter is characteristic of Magellan. He asks for full satisfaction, reminding Charles that "the insult was offered not to Ferdinand Magellan, but to one of your Highness's captains." He requests that the principal actors in the émeute may be punished, and that for the future he may be secured against the recurrence of such acts of violence. We have not Charles's answer, but we have Herrera's account of it. The King expressed his regret at the incident, and his approval of Matienzo's action. He censured the teniente del asistente and the Sevillians for refusing to aid Magellan, and ordered the officials who had taken the chief part in the disturbance to be severely punished. His prompt action and readiness to support the two

Portuguese on this occasion went far towards smoothing their difficulties for some time to come.

In January 1519, Charles V left Zaragoza. He arrived at Lerida in the beginning of February, and entered Barcelona on the 15th of that month. Fonseca, the staunch friend and supporter of the explorers, accompanied him, and kept their undertaking and its many needs constantly before his notice. Fearing anticipation by Portugal, he counselled the prompt despatch of the fleet at all costs. At Seville the two treasurers of the armada, Alonso Gutierres and Cristobal de Haro - the great East India merchant already mentioned - were doing their best to forward the preparations. Money was greatly needed. The coffers of the India House were well-nigh exhausted, and Charles, who regarded Spain as the milch-cow of the Netherlands, was not likely, even if it lay within his power, to replenish them from his own pocket. At this juncture Haro offered his purse. We learn from the letter of Alvarez, by which private information was given to the King of Portugal of the affairs of the armada, that he advanced four thousand ducats, the fifth part of the whole cost. Haro himself claims to have given 1,616,781 maravedis. His coadjutor, Gutierres, also aided and with permission of the Bishop of Burgos, other Seville merchants joined in the venture. In this manner the entire cost of the armada, 8,751,125 maravedis, was finally defrayed.

From the court in Barcelona, the King's cedulas were now despatched in quick succession. Writing on the 10th March 1519, he grants to the merchants who have advanced money the right of investing an equal sum in the three expeditions next succeeding. On the 30th of the same month Luis de Mendoza was appointed treasurer to the fleet, with a salary of 60,000 maravedis per annum during the voyage. At the same time Juan de Cartagena was gazetted captain of the third ship and Veedor-general, for which he was to receive pay at the rate of 110,000 maravedis. Gaspar de Quesada was nominated captain of the fourth or fifth ship on the 6th April, and a few days later Antonio de Coca was made Contador of the armada at 50,000 maravedis.

On the 18th April Charles orders that, ready or not ready, the fleet must sail before the end of May. On the following day issues a species of sailing orders, charging the officers and crew "to defer to the opinion and orders of Magellan, and to proceed straight to the spicery." The despatch of a second armada by the same route appears to have been early contemplated, for in a cedula of the 30th April, Francisco, brother of Ruy Faleiro, is assigned a salary of 35,000 maravedis to reside in Seville and take in hand the affairs of the fleet "which was to be sent after that of which Magellan and his brother were in command." A week later, May 5th, the King desires that the number of the crew of the squadron should be limited to two hundred and thirty-five men, and directs that, if possible, it may further be reduced. It was left to Magellan, "por cuanto tiene mas experiencia," to choose his men. The captains were directed to declare in writing the course they meant to take, and the rules to be followed in making observations. At the same date Charles granted certain entretenimientos to Magellan's wife, ordering that during the voyage her husband's pay should be received by her. He also offered to reward the pilots and masters according to their services upon their return to Spain; but whether he yielded to the petition of the former to raise their pay to three thousand maravedis per mensem does not appear.

Such is the gist of some of the many cedulas that the labour of Munioz disinterred from the mass of papers in the Seville archives. The last, and most lengthy of all, was despatched from Barcelona on the 8th May, and contains the most minute instructions for the voyage. So minute and diffuse are they indeed, that a bare reference to the subjects touched upon can only be given here. The document is divided into seventy-four heads, and might with advantage have been furnished with an index. The captains are cautioned not to overload their ships, and to keep the orifice of their pumps well out of the water. They are to communicate every day if the weather permit, and to follow certain rules with regard to lights at night, while in the case of a ship getting lost, full details are given as to the course to be pursued. There are instructions about landing in unknown countries, about making friends with the chiefs, about dealing with "Moros," about prizes, and about the distribution of prize-money. The last article is specially interesting as showing the comparative value of each rank in the service at that time. The captains are specially enjoined to treat their men amorosamente, to personally visit the wounded and the sick, and to prevent the surgeon from taking any fees. Stringent regulations are given with regard to the rations, which are to be issued every other day, and from time to time to be carefully inspected. A dozen or more of the seventy-four heads relate to trade and barter; others guide the morals of the crew, who are not to swear, and not to play games of chance, such as dice and cards, "for from such often arise evil, and scandal, and strife." Insult and violence offered to women were to be severely punished, but a tolerable amount of liberty appears to have been allowed to the crew, and every one was permitted to write home as he thought fit. There are wise regulations about guarding against fire, and still wiser anent building houses in the tropics, counselling their erection in good air, on the slopes of the mountains, and not on marshy ground or shut-in valleys. The document ends with a long list of the "quintaladas" permitted to the different members of the ship's company. The quintalada was the free freight allowed to officers and crew. It was permitted to every one, from captain to cabin-boy, and varied from 8000 to 75 pounds according to rank. It paid a duty of one twenty-fourth to the Crown. Finally, while the King orders that "under no condition whatsoever shall they touch at or explore land, or do anything within the boundaries of the most Serene King of Portugal," he nevertheless takes care to direct that, in the case of a Portuguese ship being found in Spanish waters, she should be called upon to quit the neighbourhood and to surrender her cargo.

Charles's strong support with regard to the émeute about the flags on the 22nd October had rendered inadvisable, for the time being, at all events, any interference on the part of the agents of the King of Portugal. It is possible that another reason existed. Gomara tells us that at one time Dom Manoel was not greatly disturbed about Magellan's projected voyage, being persuaded in his own mind that there was no other route to the Spice Islands save and excepting that taken by his own ships. However, as the months passed, and the armada approached completion, this faith became less secure, and before long another attempt was made to persuade Magellan to relinquish the expedition. The author was Sebastian Alvarez, the Portuguese factor at Seville, and the instigator of the disturbance just mentioned. A letter written by him to Dom Manoel on the 18th July 1519, is still existing. It throws a flood of light upon the various plots surrounding the explorers.

After acknowledging two letters from his royal master, from which it may be concluded that he had not failed to keep him well informed with regard to Seville affairs, he goes on to acquaint him of the arrival of Cristobal de Haro and Juan de Cartagena, bringing instructions more or less at variance with those of Magellan. Upon this, he says, the officials of the Casa de Contratacion summoned the latter, and demanded to know, amongst other things, why he took so many Portuguese with him. Magellan answered that, as captain of the fleet, he should do as he chose, without rendering an account to them. High words passed. The factors of the India House ordered pay to be given to all except the Portuguese, and, charged with the complaints of both parties, a messenger was despatched at once to Charles V to obtain his decision. Having put Dom Manoel in possession of these details, Alvarez thus proceeds :

"And seeing the affair begun, and that it was a convenient season for me to say what your Highness commanded, I went to Magellan's house, where I found him filling baskets and chests with preserved victuals and other things. I pressed him, pretending that, as I found him thus engaged, it seemed to me that his evil design was settled, and since this would be the last word I should have with him, I desired to bring back to his memory how many times, as a good Portuguese and his friend, I had spoken to him, dissuading him from the great mistake he was committing. And after asking pardon of him, lest he should be offended at what I was about to say, I reminded him how many times I had spoken to him, and how well he had always replied to me, and that from his replies I always hoped that in the end he would not go, to the so great injury of your Highness. And what I always told him was, that the path he had chosen was beset with as many dangers as the wheel of Saint Catherine, and that he ought to leave it and take that which led to Coimbra, and return to his native land and to the favour of your Highness, at whose hands he would always receive benefits. In our conversation I brought before him all the dangers I could think of, and the mistakes he was making. He said to me that now, as an honourable man, he could only follow the path he had chosen. I replied that unduly to gain honour, and to gain it with infamy, was neither wisdom nor honour, but rather lack of wisdom and honour, for he might be sure that the chief Castilians of this city in speaking of him held him for a low person and of no breeding, since, to the disservice of his true king and lord, he embarked in such an undertaking, and so much the more since it was set going, arranged, and petitioned for by him. And he might be certain that be was considered as a traitor, engaging himself thus in opposition to your Highness's country. Here he replied to me that he saw the mistake he made, but that he hoped to observe your Highness's service, and by his voyage to be of assistance to you. I told him that whoever should praise him for such an expression of opinion did not understand it; for unless he touched your Highness's possessions how was he to discover what he said ? Besides, it was a great injury to the revenues of your Highness, which would affect the whole kingdom and every class of people, and it was a far more virtuous thought that inspired him when he told me that if your Highness ordered him to return to Portugal that he would do it without further guarantee of reward, and that when you granted none to him, there was Serradossa, and seven yards of grey cloth, and some gall-nut beads open to him. So then it seemed to me that his heart was true as far as his honour and conscience were concerned. Our conversation was so long of duration that I cannot write it. At this juncture, sire, he began to give me a sign, saying that I should tell him more ; that this did not come from me, and that, if your Highness commanded me, that I should tell him so, and also the reward that you would grant him. I told him that I was not a person of such weight that your Highness would employ me for such a purpose, but that I said it to him as I had on many other occasions. Here he wished to pay me a compliment, saying that if what I had begun with him was carried on without the interference of others, your Highness would be served, but that Nuño Ribeiro had told him one thing, which meant nothing (q nio fora nada), and João Mendez another, which bound him to nothing, and he told me the favours they offered him on the part of your Highness. He then bewailed himself greatly, and said he was much concerned about it all, but that he knew nothing which could justify his leaving a king who had shown him such favour. I told him that it would be a more certain matter, and attended with a truer honour, to do what he ought to do, and not to lose his reputation and the favours your Highness would grant him. And if he weighed his coming from Portugal (which was for a hundred reals more or less of moradia that your Highness did not grant him, in order not to break your laws), and that there had arrived two sets of orders at variance with his own, which he had at the hands of the King, Don Carlos, he would see whether this insult (desprezo) did not out balance it - to go and do what it was his duty to do, rather than to remain here for that for which he came. He was greatly astonished at my knowing so much, and then he told me the truth, and how the messenger had left - all of which I already knew. And he told me that certainly there was no reason why he should abandon the undertaking, unless they failed to fulfil anything in the terms of the agreement; but that first he must see what your Highness would do. I said to him, what more did he desire to see than the orders ? and Ruy Faleiro, who said openly that he was not going to follow his lantern, and that he would navigate to the south, or he would not sail with the fleet; and that he Magellan thought he was going as admiral, whereas I knew that others were being sent in opposition to him, of whom he would know nothing, except at a time when it would be too late to save his honour. And I told him that he should pay no heed to the honey that the Bishop of Burgos put to his lips, and that now was the time for him to choose his path, and that he should give me a letter to your Highness, and that I, out of affection for him, would go to your Highness and plead his cause, because I had no instruction from your Highness concerning such business, and only said what I thought I had often said before. He told me that he would say nothing to me until he had seen the answer that the messenger brought, and with this our conversation finished. I will watch the interests of your Highness to the utmost of my power. I spoke to Ruy Faleiro twice, but he replied nothing to me, save how could he do such a thing against the King, his lord, who conferred such benefits upon him; and to all that I said to him he gave me no other answer. It seems to me that he is like a man affected in his reason, and that this his familiar has taken away whatever wisdom he possessed. I think that if Fernão de Magalhães were removed that Ruy Faleiro would follow what Magalhães did."

The rest of the letter of Alvarez, which is one of great length, need not be quoted. He gives the King of Portugal information about the ships and their armament, together with a list of the Portuguese who had at that time taken service in the fleet. A passage concerning the proposed route and the charts and instruments provided is, however, of interest :

"The route which it is reported they are to take is direct to Cape Frio, leaving Brazil on the right, until they pass the boundary-line, and thence to sail W. and W.N.W. direct to Maluco, which land of Maluco I have seen laid down on the globe and chart which Fernando de Reynell made here, the which was not finished when his father came here for him, and his father finished the whole and marked these lands of Maluco, and on this pattern are constructed all the charts which Diego Ribeiro makes. And he makes all the compasses, quadrants, and globes, but does not sail with the fleet; nor does he desire anything more than to gain his living by his skill.

From this Cape Frio to the islands of Maluco by this route there are no lands laid down in the charts they take. May God the Almighty grant that they make a voyage like that of the Cortereals, and that your Highness may remain at rest, and ever be envied, as your Highness is, by all princes."

Such a letter as this gives us some idea of the difficulties with which Magellan had to contend. They were augmented by the relations existing between his colleague and himself. Always of uncertain temper, Faleiro had of late become still more difficult to deal with. What was his real condition it is impossible to say. Although the suggestion has been stoutly combated by some historians, the balance of evidence is in favour of the fact that he became insane. Both Acosta and Sebastian Alvarez in their letters to Dom Manoel already quoted, speak of him as being half-crazy. From what we know of his previous history, the supposition is not an impossible one, and is even probable, perhaps. The contemporary writers for the most part support it. Argensola tells us that having gone out of his mind, he was sent to the madhouse in Seville. Gomara says that he went mad from the fear that he would be unable to fulfil his promise, and Oviedo speaks of him as muy loco, having lost both his health and his reason. By others it is hinted that the madness may have been feigned with the idea of commanding the squadron which was to follow that of Magellan. Barros gives a still more ingenious story that Ruy Faleiro, being an astrologer, cast his own horoscope, and finding that the voyage would be disastrous and end in his death, he feigned madness at the last moment to avoid sailing. Herrera tells us that differences arose between the two commanders, and it seems that Alvarez was instrumental in fomenting them. However, whatever may have been the difficulty, the King had ultimately to dismiss Faleiro. By a cedula dated from Barcelona on the 26 July 1519, he ordered that he should remain in Seville to superintend the preparations of the second fleet, and Magellan from this date remained practically in sole command, in spite of Juan de Cartagena, to whom Faleiro's ship was given, being spoken of in some documents of the India House as his "conjunta persona." His position was further strengthened by an order from the King that Luis de Mendoza, the captain of the Victoria, and treasurer of the fleet, who had been insolent and inclined to question his authority, should render unhesitating obedience. We may be sure that with this Mendoza's hatred of Magellan was in no way mitigated. It culminated before long, as we shall see, in the mutiny of Port St. Julian, where a swift and terrible punishment was the reward of his treason. It would have been better for him had he been dismissed his ship, as were two mutinous Portuguese at this period. The plots of Alvarez had already begun to work, and disaffection was rife long ere the ships left the Guadalquivir.

One of the points upon which Charles V had most strongly insisted was that the number of Portuguese borne upon the ship's books should be reduced to the smallest possible limits. In a letter written from Barcelona on the 17th June 1519, Charles V sent a special order to Magellan and Ruy Faleiro that no one of that nationality should accompany the expedition except four or five for the service of each of them. Later, hearing several of the grumetes are Portuguese, he writes that they must be dismissed. Writing again on the 5th July to Ruy Faleiro, who had sought permission for his brother to accompany him, the permission is given, but only on condition that he should form one of these five. On the 26th July the same order is reiterated. Nevertheless, circumstances brought it about that many more ultimately sailed. It may well be imagined that there were not wanting people who ascribed the worst of motives to Magellan with regard to the matter. To clear himself he presented an informacion to the India House on the 9th August, drawn up in the then customary form of question and answer, and giving the evidence of five men of known position and character, among whom we find the name of Sebastian del Cano.

From it we learn several facts of interest. It tells us how in the streets and squares and quays of Seville the public crier announced the departure of the fleet, and called for volunteers; how the people said the pay was too small, and would not go; how the officers were sent to Cadiz and Malaga and other ports, and still could not get their complement; and how, finally, a number of foreigners, and among them several Portuguese, were enrolled, with whom the captains were, nevertheless, quite satisfied. Of the varied nationalities and tongues thus brought together one reads with astonishment. Several of Magellan's officers were accordingly sent to other ports to endeavour to get the necessary complement, and Charles's regulations as to the admission of Portuguese had ultimately to be relaxed. In a later Cedula permission is given for the enrolment of twenty-four, twelve to be nominated by the Emperor, and twelve by Magellan. We find, however, that thirty-seven at least sailed on the voyage, and as some of these entered themselves as of Seville or some other Spanish port, it is probable that even this number is not inclusive and final.

Of Portuguese there ultimately sailed no less than thirty-seven, probably even more, for our sources of information, though wonderfully full, are not absolutely complete. Besides the Spaniards, Portuguese, and Basques, the thirty or more Italians, who were largely Genoese, Neapolitans, or Sicilians, were the greatest in number. There were nineteen French. There were also Flemings, Germans, Greeks, Corfiotes, Africans, Malays, Moors, Madeirans, and natives of the Azores and Canary Islands. There was one Englishman, a certain Master Andrew of Bristol. Despite the fleet sailing from Seville, only seventeen men are entered as of that city. The Biscayans, as was always the case on such expeditions, were largely represented.

From various causes - the haste in the despatch of the ships, combined with the difficulty in obtaining hands; the shipping of some of the crew in the Canaries; and, perhaps, the purposed omission of certain names owing to the ships having become more largely manned by Portuguese than would have seemed desirable to the authorities - it is impossible to arrive at the exact number of persons who sailed with Magellan upon the voyage. From the official lists, and from the casual occurrence of names in the numerous and lengthy autos fiscales connected with the expedition, we gather that at least 268 individuals embarked. The actual names of such a number are given. It is more than probable that there were others who were neither entered in the ships' books nor the subject of casual mention. It may be affirmed with tolerable certainty that between 270 and 280 persons manned the five ships that formed the squadron.

The flagship, the Trinidad carried a crew of at least 62 men, the San Antonio 57, the Concepcion 44, the Victoria 45, the Santiago 31. Of the other 29 who are mentioned by name, we do not know the ships. An examination of the ships' books shows that each vessel carried a captain and one or more pilots - who were without exception Portuguese - a maestre and contramaestre who would correspond to the mates of a merchant vessel - a purser, steward, carpenter, barber, caulker, and cooper. Two classes of sailors were borne - the marineros, or A.B.'s, and the grumetes, or ordinary seamen. Of the former the flagship carried 14, and 10 grumetes; the other vessels a few less. Upon each ship were three gunners or lombarderos. All these men were foreigners, generally French, but sometimes Germans or Flemings. The master-gunner of the flagship was Maestre Andrew, of Bristol, the only Englishman in the expedition. Three or four chaplains seem to have accompanied the fleet, but only one surgeon, the Bachelor Morales, whose duties must indeed have been arduous. Various pages and body-servants of the officers completed the lists of the ships' crews. The young men of good family, who took part in the expedition from love of adventure or desire for advancement in military service, shipped as sobresa'ientes or supernumeraries. In this class came Duarte Barbosa, Magellan's brother-in-law, and Alvaro de Mesquita, his cousin.

Despite the difficulty in obtaining men, the preparations were by this time nearly finished. From a letter of Magellan to the India House we learn that his chief anxiety was to obtain possession of Ruy Faleiro's book of the various methods of taking observations. He desires to take

Francisco Faleiro as captain in place of his brother, but fears that even then the latter may not see fit to put him in possession of the coveted book. His fears, however, were groundless, for though Francisco Faleiro decided not to sail with him, but to await the following expedition, the book upon which Magellan so greatly depended for his observations was presented to him by his former friend and comrade before sailing.

Before starting upon an expedition of such magnitude as this, it was the custom, as we have already seen, to attend a solemn church service en masse. Upon this occasion the ceremony was one of more than usual interest. It must have been felt by all that the voyage before them was of no ordinary character. They were not bound for the now well-known West Indies, nor about to sail the trite waters of the Indian Ocean. Their very first experiences would be in almost unknown lands and seas. So, when the Corregidor of Seville, Sancho Martinez de Leyva, solemnly entrusted Magellan with the royal standard in the church of Santa Maria de la Victoria, and received from him the oath that, as a good subject of the King, he would carry out his enterprise, there must have been few of the onlookers to whose minds the difficulties and dangers of their future path did not present themselves. To Magellan the captains and officials of the armada swore a like oath of allegiance, promising to follow the course ordered by him and to obey him in everything: Alas for man's sincerity and honour ! Many of those who knelt before the altar were at that moment pledged to join in open mutiny against their leader directly the fitting opportunity should arrive.

The preparations were now sufficiently far advanced to permit the fleet to leave the quays of Seville. On Wednesday the 10th August 1519, the vessels weighed and dropped down the river to the port of San Lucar de Barrameda, at its mouth. Here they remained for more than a month. It was now evident that, so far as the actual start of the expedition was concerned, the efforts of the Portuguese had failed, and their predictions proved incorrect. To within a few months of his sailing, Magellan had been represented to Dom Manoel as "a boaster and a man of little worth, who would not carry out his promises." Now they formed a different opinion. The plots and intrigues to let and hinder the expedition did not therefore cease even with its departure. Dom Manoel sent ships to the Cape, and also to Santa Maria in the Rio de la Plata, with orders to intercept their passage. These having failed in their object, Diego Lopez de Sequeira was instructed to send six ships from Cochin to the Moluccas for the same purpose - an order he was unable to fulfil on account of there being no vessels available at the time.

Unconscious of these added dangers, Magellan worked hard at the innumerable matters of business connected with his immediate departure. Together with his captains, he went backwards and forwards between Seville and the ships, supplying the various omissions which at the last moment so frequently declare themselves. One of his last acts was to address a memorial to Charles V, assigning the geographical position of various places more or less connected with the line of demarcation among them the Moluccas - giving as his reason "that the King of Portugal may assert that they lie within his limit, and that no one understands the matter as he (Magellan) understands it."

CHAPTER 7

MAGELLAN'S FINAL WILL

On the 24th August 1519 Magellan made his final will. The document is still in existence in the Seville archives. It bears evidence of strong religious influence, if not religious feeling. In it he desired that one-tenth part of his share of the profits of the expedition (which share was to be one-fifth of the whole) should be taken and divided into three equal shares, one of which was bequeathed to the Convento de los Minimos of Victoria de Triana, where he was to be buried if he died in Seville. The other two shares were to be equally distributed between the monastery of Monserrat in Barcelona, the convent of San Francisco in Aranda de Duero, and San Domingo de las Duenas in Oporto. Of the effects he might die possessed of in the fleet and of his real and personal property in Seville, he desired that a fifth share should be expended in saying masses for his soul.

The rule and seignorial rights of the lands he might discover he desired should pass in regular succession, first to his son Rodrigo, or, to the child that might be born to him - his wife being then pregnant - or, failing direct descent, to his brother Diogo de Sousa, or to his sister Isabel. If the property should pass to the side branch, the holder of the mayorazgo should, in the event of the survival of Doña Beatriz, his wife, pay to her annually a fourth part of the revenue and a sum of two hundred ducats. Magellan's son Rodrigo died in 1521; his second child was stillborn; his wife died in 1522; Duarte Barbosa was killed in the surprise of May 1st 1521, the father, Diogo Barbosa, dying in 1525, the Crown took possession of the estate, which was claimed by Jaime Barbosa and other sons of Diogo. The case, after having remained seven years unheard, was again brought forward on the 6th June 1540. The claimants had spent all their money and were reduced to want, and though Magellan had given his life in the service of Spain nineteen years before, they had not received a maravedi. What was the ultimate result we do not learn, but knowing what we do of Spanish justice at that period, we can guess.

Of the 50,000 maravedis of pension conferred by the Casa de

Contratacion upon his life and that of his wife, the latter was to pay annually to the said sister Isabel the sum of 5,000 maravedis. His son or sons were left residuary legatees. His heirs were to take the name and arms of Magallanes, and to reside and marry in Spain.

Magellan appointed as executors his father-in-law, Diogo Barbosa, and Don Sancho de Matienzo, the canónigo of Seville who had supported him on the occasion of the riot instigated by Alvarez. At the same time that he made his will he addressed a letter to the King, asking that the 12,500 maravedis presented to him on the occasion of his decoration with the Order of Santiago might be paid to the convent of Victoria de la Triana, he having already promised it to them.

The following is Magellan's final will :

"In the name of the Most High and Mighty God our Lord, who is without beginning and reigns without end, and of the most favoured Glorious Virgin, Our Lady, Holy Mary, His blessed Mother, whom all we Christians own as Queen and Advocate in all our actions; to their honour and service, and that of all the Saints of the courts of Heaven. Amen.

Know all ye by these presents, that I, Hernando de Magallanes, Comendador, His Majesty's Captain-general of the Armada bound for the Spice Islands, husband of Doña Beatriz Barbosa, and inhabitant of this most noble and most loyal city of Seville, in the precinct of Santa Maria, being well and in good health, and possessed of such my ordinary senses and judgment as God our Lord has, of His mercy and will, thought fit and right to endow me; believing firmly and truly in the Holy Trinity, the Father, Son, and Holy Ghost - three persons and one only true God, as every faithful Christian holds and believes, and ought to hold and believe, and being in fear of death, which is a natural thing from which no man can escape; being willing and desirous of placing my soul in the surest and most certain path that I can discern for its salvation, to commit and bring it unto the mercy and forgiveness of God our Lord, that He, who made and created it, may have compassion and pity upon it, and redeem and save it, and bring it to His glory and His heavenly kingdom.

Whereas I am about to proceed in the King's service in the said Armada, by these presents I make known and declare that I make and ordain this my Will, and these my bequests, as well of my goods as of my body and soul, for the salvation of my soul and the satisfaction of my heirs, Firstly, the debts owed by me and to me owing : they are such as will be found written in my book of accounts, the which I confirm and approve and acknowledge as correct. The following are the legacies bequeathed by me :-

Firstly, I commend my soul to God our Lord, who made and created it, and redeemed me with His precious blood, and I ask and beseech of the ever-glorious Virgin Mary, Our Lady, His blessed Mother, that, with all the Saints of the heavenly kingdom, she may be my intercessor and supplicant before her precious Son for my soul, that He may pardon my sins and shortcomings, and receive me to share His glory in the kingdom of heaven. And when this my present life shall end for the life eternal, I desire that if I die in this city of Seville my body may be buried in the Monastery of Santa Maria de la Vitoria in Triana - ward and precinct of this city of Seville - in the grave set apart for me; And if I die in this said voyage, I desire that my body may be buried in a church dedicated to Our Lady, in the nearest spot to that at which death seize me and I die; And I bequeath to the expenses of the chapel of the Sagrario of the Holy Church of Seville, in grateful remembrance of the Holy Sacraments which from the said church I have received, and hope to receive, if it be the will of God our Lord, one thousand maravedis; And I bequeath to the Holy Crusade a real of silver; And I bequeath to the Orders of the Holy Trinity and Santa Maria de la Merced of this city of Seville, in aid of the redemption of such faithful Christians as may be captives in the country of the Moors, the enemies of our holy Catholic faith, to each Order a real of silver; And I bequeath to the Infirmary of San Lazaro without the city, as alms, that they may pray to God our Lord for my soul, another real of silver; And I bequeath to the hospital de Las Bubas of this city of Seville, to gain its intercession, another real of silver; And I bequeath to the Casa de San Sebastian in Tablada, to gain its intercession, another real of silver; And I bequeath to the Holy Church of Faith in Seville another real of silver, to gain its intercession; And I desire that upon the said day of my burial thirty masses may be said over my body - two cantadas and twenty-eight rezadas, and that they shall offer for me the offering of bread and wine and candles that my executors desire; And I desire that in the said monastery of Santa Maria de la Vitoria a thirty day mass may be said for my soul, and that the accustomed alms may be given therefor; And I desire that upon the said day of my burial three poor men may be clothed - such as I have indicated to my executors and that to each may be given a cloak of grey stuff, a cap, a shirt, and a pair of shoes, that they may pray to God for my soul; And I also desire that upon the said day of my burial food may be given to the said three paupers, and to twelve others, that they may pray to God for my soul; And I desire that upon the said day of my burial a gold ducat may be given as alms for the souls in purgatory. And I confess - to speak the truth before God and the world and to possess my soul in safety - that I received and obtained in dowry and marriage with the said Doña Beatriz Barbosa, my wife, six hundred thousand maravedis, of the which I made acknowledgment before Bernal Gonzalez de Vallecillo, notary -public of Seville; and I desire that before everything the said Doña Beatriz Barbosa, my wife, may be paid and put in possession of the said six hundred thousand maravedis, her dowry, together with the arras that I gave her.

And forasmuch as I am proceeding in the King's service in the said Armada, and since of all the gain and profit that with the help of God our Lord may result therefrom (save and excepting the first charges of the King), the share allotted to me is one-fifth of the whole, in addition to that which I may acquire from the merchandise which I take with me in the said Armada of all this which I may acquire from the said Armada I desire to set aside one-tenth part, touching which, by this my will and testament, I desire and order, and it is my wish, that the said tenth may be expended and distributed in the manner following :

Firstly, I desire and order, and it is my wish, that one-third of the said tenth part may be given to the said monastery of N. S. Santa Maria de la Vitoria in Triana, for the construction of the chapel of the said monastery, and that the monks of the said monastery may henceforth for ever engage to pray to God for my soul.

Furthermore, I desire, and it is my wish, that the remaining two-thirds of the said tenth part shall be divided into three equal parts, of which one part shall be given to the monastery of N. S. Santa Maria de Monserrat, in the city of Barcelona; another to the monastery of San Francisco in the town of Aranda de Duero, for the benefit of the said monastery; and the third to the monastery of San Domingo de las Dueñas, in the city of Oporto, in Portugal, for such things as may be most necessary for the said monastery; and this bequest I make that they may pray God for my soul.

Furthermore, I will and desire, and it is my wish, that of the half of the rest of my estate of the said Armada belonging unto me, together with that of the other estate of which I am possessed in this said city of Seville, one-fifth part may be set aside to fulfil the necessities of my soul, and that my executors out of this said fifth part may fulfil these necessities of this my will and testament, and whatever more may seem fitting unto them for the repose of my soul and conscience.

I desire, moreover, that there may be paid to Cristobal Robelo, my page, the sum of thirty thousand maravedis from my estate, the which I bequeath unto him for the services he has rendered unto me, and that he may pray God for my soul.

And by this my present will and testament, I declare and ordain as free and quit of every obligation of captivity, subjection, and slavery, my captured slave Enrique, mulatto, native of the city of Malacca, of the age of twenty-six years more or less, that from the day of my death thenceforward for ever the said Enrique may be free and manumitted, and quit, exempt, and relieved of every obligation of slavery and subjection, that he may act as he desires and thinks fit; and I desire that of my estate there may be given to the said Enrique the sum of ten thousand maravedis in money for his support; and this manumission I grant because he is a Christian, and that he may pray to God for my soul.

And whereas His Majesty the King has granted unto me, my sons, and my heirs in tail male the governorship of certain lands and islands that I may discover with the said Armada, according to the terms contained in the Capitulacion made with His Majesty, together with the title of Adelantado of the said lands and islands discovered, and also the twentieth part of their produce, and other benefits contained in the said Capitulacion; by these presents, and by this my will and testament, I declare and name for this mayorazgo - in order that, upon my decease, he may succeed to the above - Rodrigo de Magallanes, my legitimate son, and the legitimate son of the said Doña Beatriz Barbosa, my wife, and thereafter unto any legitimate son that God may grant him; and should he have no legitimate sons born in wedlock to have and inherit the above mayorazgo, I desire and command that the other legitimate son or daughter whom God may give me may inherit, and so successively from father to son; And if by chance a daughter should hold the mayorazgo, in such a case I desire that the son whom God may give her to inherit the said mayorazgo, shall take the name of Magallaes [sic], and bear my arms without quartering them with any others; And, should he fail to take the name of Magallaes and to bear my arms, in such case I desire and order, and it is my wish, that a son or nephew or nearer relation of my lineage may inherit the said mayorazgo, and that he may live in Castile, and bear my name and arms; And if - which may God forbid - the said Rodrigo de Magallaes my son should die without leaving sons or daughters born in wedlock, and that I should beget no other sons nor daughters to succeed to the mayorazgo, I desire and order, and it is my wish, that Diego de Sosa, my brother, who is now living with His Serene Majesty the King of Portugal, may inherit the above, and come and live in this kingdom of Castile, and marry in it, and that he adopt the name of Magallaes, and bear the arms of Magallaes, as I bear them - the arms of Magallaes and Sosa; And if the said Diego de Sosa, my brother, have neither sons nor daughters born in holy wedlock to inherit the aforesaid mayorazgo, I desire and order, and it is my wish, that Isabel de Magallaes, my sister, may inherit the said mayorazgo, provided that she call herself Magallaes, and bear my arms, and come to reside and marry in this kingdom of Castile.

And furthermore, I desire and order, and it is my will, that if the said Diego de Sosa, my brother, or the said Isabel de Magallaes, my sister, succeed to the aforesaid mayorazgo, they shall be obliged to assist the said Doña Beatriz Barbosa, my wife, with the fourth part of all that the said my mayorazgo produces, fairly and justly, and without let or hindrance soever; And I desire that the Comendador Diego de Barbosa, my father-in-law, may undertake the charge of the person, goods, and mayorazgo of the said Rodrigo de Magallaes, my son, and of the child or children with whom the said Doña Beatriz Barbosa, my wife, is now pregnant, until they reach the age of eighteen years, and that during this period the said Comendador Diego Barbosa may receive and collect all the produce and rents which the said estate and mayorazgo may produce, and give and deliver to the said Doña Beatriz Barbosa, my wife, his daughter, the fourth part of all that may therefrom result, until such time as my sons aforesaid be of the age stated; the said my wife, Doña Beatriz Barbosa living widowed and chastely; And if she should marry, I desire that there may be given and paid to her the sum of two thousand Spanish doubloons, over and above her dowry and arras, and the half of the accumulations thereon.

Furthermore, I desire, and it is my will, that the said Comendador Diego Barbosa may take and receive, as his own property, one fourth part; and that he may expend the remainder in the maintenance and education of my sons; And likewise, I desire and order, and it is my wish, that if the said Diego de Sosa, my brother, or the said Isabel de Magallaes, my sister, inherit the aforesaid my mayorazgo, that above and beyond that which I have desired may be given each year to the said Doña Beatriz Barbosa, my wife, they shall be obliged to give each year to the said Comendador Diego Barbosa, for the remainder of his life, two hundred ducats of gold, to be paid from the estate of the said mayorazgo.

Furthermore, I desire that, if the said Comendador Diego Barbosa collect the aforesaid my estate, he may give of it to the said Isabel de Magallaes, my sister, for her marriage, such as seems fitting to the said Comendador Diego Barbosa.

Furthermore I desire that of the fifty thousand maravedis that I have for my life and that of the said Doña Beatriz Barbosa, my wife, from the Casa de Contratacion of the Indies in this city of Seville, the said Doña Beatriz, my wife, may give to the said Isabel de Magallaes, my sister, the sum of five thousand maravedis per annum until the arrival of my estate resulting from this my present voyage, when the said Comendador Diego Barbosa can give her that which I have arranged and desired in this my will that he should give her for her marriage.

And this my will and testament having been fulfilled and discharged, together with the bequests and clauses therein contained, relating to the aforesaid my possessions, whether fixtures, movables, or livestock, in compliance with that herewith prescribed and expressed, I desire that all and everything of the said possessions which may remain over and above may be had and inherited by the said Rodrigo de Magallaes, my legitimate son by the said Doña Beatriz, my wife, and by the child or children of which the said Doña Beatriz is now pregnant, being born and living the period that the law requires, whom - the said Rodrigo de Magallaes, my son, and the child or children of which the said my wife is pregnant - I appoint and establish as my legal residuary legatees, equally the one with the other; And if, which may God forbid, the said my son, or child borne by my wife, die before attaining the proper age for the succession, I desire that the said Doña Beatriz Barbosa, my wife, may inherit the said my estate, save and excepting that of the mayorazgo, and I appoint and establish her as my residuary legatee.

And for the discharge and quitment of this my will and testament, and of the bequests and clauses concerning the said my estate therein contained, in compliance with that herewith prescribed and expressed, I hereby appoint as my executors for the payment and distribution of the said my estate, without hurt to them or theirs, Doctor Sancho de Matienzo, Canon of Seville, and the said Comendador Diego Barbosa, my father-in-law; And I bequeath to the said Doctor Sancho de Matienzo for the burden thus laid upon him in the fulfilment and discharge of this my will the sum of thirty gold ducats and two pesos.

Done in Seville, in the King's Customs of this city of Seville, Wednesday, the twenty-fourth day of the month of August, in the year of the birth of our Saviour Jesus Christ one thousand five hundred and nineteen. And I, the said Comendador Hernando de Magallaes, sign and confirm it with my name in the register, in the presence of the witnesses Diego Martinez de Medina, Juan Rodriguez de Medina, and Alfonso Fernandez, notaries of Seville."

CHAPTER 8

THE SHIPS AND THEIR CREWS

Before entering upon the narrative of Magellan's final expedition, the issue of which was to stamp him as the greatest of the world's discoverers, we must turn for a moment to consider the materials with which he was provided. To the ships themselves allusion has already been made. They were for the most part old, small, and in anything but good condition. The Trinidad, though not the largest, was the most seaworthy and most suitable for capitana, and at her mast-head Magellan accordingly flew his pennant. Juan de Cartagena captained the San Antonio, the largest vessel of the fleet. The Concepcion was commanded by Gaspar Quesada, and the Victoria by the traitor Luis de Mendoza, treasurer of the armada, who had already been reprimanded by the King for insolence to the Captain-general. The little Santiago was given to João Serrão, whose long experience in the East and great knowledge of navigation rendered him one of the most important members of the expedition.

The command of the Santiago by Serrão was, as it happened, an affair of no little moment to Magellan. However, for his old friend and comrade it is more than possible that the mutiny of Port St. Julian might have proved too much for him, and the great discovery of Magellan's Straits might have been postponed to deck another brow with laurels. Upon the Portuguese in the fleet, despite his altered nationality, Magellan relied even more as friends than as navigators. By the time the squadron had crossed the bar, the originally permitted number of five had greatly increased. Among the 280 men, more or less, who sailed, thirty-seven, as we have seen, were Portuguese, and of these many held most important posts. On the Trinidad were Estevão Gomez the pilot, Magellan's brother-in-law-Duarte Barbosa, Alvaro de la Mezquita, and eight others. The San Antonio bore the cosmographer Andres de San Martin and João Rodriguez de Mafra. All the pilots of the fleet, indeed, were Portuguese, just as the gunners were foreigners; and João Lopez Carvalho and Vasco Gallego navigated respectively the Concepcion and the Victoria.

The armament of the fleet was on an extensive scale. The artillery comprised sixty-two culverins, ten falconets, and ten large bombards. Small firearms were not then greatly used, and only fifty arquebuses were carried. There were, however, a thousand lances, two hundred pikes, ten dozen javelins, ninety-five dozen darts, sixty crossbows, with 360 dozen arrows, and "sundry swords that the captain took." One hundred corselets, with gauntlets, shoulder-pieces, and casques, appear in the list, together with an equal number of cuirasses. Finally, we learn that as much as 5,600 pounds of powder were put on board.

The "instrumentos" with which the navigators were provided were of the simplest nature. Twenty-three parchment charts by Nuño Garcia, six pairs of compasses, twenty-one wooden quadrants, seven astrolabes, thirty-five compass-needles, and eighteen hour-glasses formed the entire list; and not all of these, we are told, were ultimately taken. The number of articles for barter was, however, very large. In the "Priuie Notes given by a Gentleman to the Marchants of the Muscouie Company," with which Hakluyt has made us acquainted, the importance of such expeditions being provided with "looking-glasses for women, great and fayre," is dwelt upon, and Magellan's squadron was amply supplied with these, together with 500 pounds of "crystals, which are diamonds of all colours." Knives, fish-hooks, stuffs, and velvets, ivory, quicksilver (2240 pounds), and brass bracelets all figure largely in the list; but it appears that bells were considered to be the most useful objects of barter. Of these, no less than 20,000 were taken.

The cost of the fleet, with its stores and armament, was for those days considerable. From papers existing in the Seville archives, we know the exact amount to a maravedi. The entire expenditure was 8,751,125 maravedis. However, some of the stores having been left behind, the sum was reduced by 416,790 maravedis. Of the whole sum, about one quarter was supplied by Cristobal de Haro and his friends. The rest was at the King's expense.

From various documents existing in the Seville archives we gather extraordinarily precise details, not only as regards the articles supplied to the Armada, but also as to their price and their exact distribution among the different ships. This information is of much interest, showing as it does what stores were at that period considered necessary. It also throws light upon various events connected with the preparation of the fleet of which we should otherwise have remained in ignorance. The following were the costs in Maravedis :

Ships and their fittings : 228,750 for the Concepcion; 300,000 for the Victoria; 330,000 for the San Antonio; 270,000 for the Trinidad; and 187,000 for the Santiago; bringing ships from Cadiz to Seville, and expenses of Juan de Aranda in going to Cadiz 24,188; Workmen careening ships, etc. 13,482; Carpenters for repairing ships 104,244; Caulkers for caulking ships 129,539; Sawyers for sawing planks, etc. for ships 6,790; Wood for beams and planking, etc. 175,098; Nails used in repair of ships, together with the supply for the voyage 142,532½; Oakum used in repair of ships, together with the supply for the voyage 31,670; Pitch, tar, and resin used in repair of ships, together with the supply for the voyage 72,267½; Grease used in repair of ships, together with the supply for the voyage 53,852; 173 pieces of canvas for sails, etc. 149,076; Twine for sewing the above, with needles and awls, and money paid for making 32,825; Masts, yards, and spare spars 37,437; Skiff purchased for the Trinidad 3,937½; Pumps, bolts, and nails 15,475; Oars and sweeps 6,563; Leather bags. hose, and leathers for the pumps 9,364; Pulleys and blocks 1,285½; 3 timbers for knees 3,687½; 8 large blocks 4,204; Standing and other rigging, and rigging 34,672½; 3 large pitch ladles 511; 13 lighters of ballast for the ships 1,962; 32 yards of coarse canvas for making sacks for the ballasting 807; Pay of workmen and sailors during the preparations for the voyage 438,335½; Thirteen anchors 42,042; 8 saws, large and small 1,008; Bits and braces, large and small 1,762; 6 pickaxes to dig the ditch to careen the ships 663; 76 hides to make pitch-brushes to pay the ships 2,495; Fuel used in pitching the ships 4,277; Pilots for bringing ships from San Lucar to Seville 1,054½; 221 quintals of cables and hawsers and 1000 arrobas of hemp to make the rigging and cordage, which, together with cost of manufacture (38,972ms.) and money paid for sedge and esparto -grass rope (14,066 ms.), make 324,170½; 80 flags, and the painting of them, with a royal standard made of taffety 25,029; Cost of the "bergantym" 49,504; Expenses of Duarte Barbosa in Bilbao when he went to buy the articles for the ships, together with those of Anton Semeño 84,144.

Artillery, Munitions, Arms : 58 culverins, 7 falconets, 3 large bombards, and 3 "pasamuros," all from Bilbao 160,135; 50 quintals of gunpowder from Fuenterrabia and freight 109,028; 165 pounds of powder for proving the artillery in Bilbao 5,477; Shot and cannonballs of iron and stone 6,633; 6 molds for making cannonballs 3,850; 221 arrobas 7 pounds of lead for bullets, save 84 arrobas used as plates for leading the seams of the ships 39,890; Paid for mounting the artillery 3,276; Wages of the lombarderos 8,790; 100 corselets with armlets, shoulder-plates, and helmets, and 100 breastplates with throat-pieces and helmets from Bilbao 110,910; 60 crossbows with 360 dozen arrows from Bilbao 33,495; 50 arquebuses from Biscay 10,500; Coat of mail and two complete suits of armour for the Captain-General from Bilbao 6,375; 200 shields from Bilbao 6,800; 6 sword-blades for the Captain from Bilbao 680; 95 dozen of darts, 10 dozen javelins, 1000 lances, 200 pikes, 6 boarding-pikes, etc., from Bilbao 44,185; 120 skeins of wire for the crossbows, etc. 2,499; Cleaning the arms, 6 pounds of emery, leathers, tacks, buckles, etc. 3,553; 50 flasks and prickers for the arquebuses, and 150 yards of fuses 5,611.

Stores : The costs of Stores in Maravedis (ms.) were : biscuit, 363,480 Maravedis (i.e., 2138 quintals 3 pounds, at 170 maravedis per quintal), plus hire of sacks, portage, etc., total 372,510 maravedis; wine, 508 butts from Jerez, 511,317, and costs thereon, total 590,000; 50 cwts. beans, 90 cwts. chick-peas, 2 cwts. lentils 23,037; 47 quintals 3 arrobas of olive-oil 58,425; 200 barrels anchovies, 238 dozen large dried fish 62,879; 57 quintals 12 pounds dried pork 43,908; 7 cows for the voyage (14,000 ms.), 3 pigs (1180 ms.), and meat for workmen, total 17,740; 984 cheeses, weighing 112 arrobas, 26,434; 417 pipes, 253 butts, 45 barrels for the wine and water (230,170 ms.), staves, oil-vessels, barrels for the cheeses, jars for vinegar, etc., total 393,623; 21 arrobas 9 pounds of sugar, at 720 ms. per arroba 15,451; 200 arrobas vinegar 3,655; 250 strings of garlic and 100 strings of onions 2,198; 18 quintals of raisins, & etc. 5,997; 16 quarter casks of figs 1,130; 12 cwts. of almonds in their shells 2,922; 54 arrobas 2 pounds of honey 8,980; 2 quintals of currants 750; 3 jars of capers 1,554; Salt 1,768; 3 quintals 22 pounds of rice 1,575; 1 cwt. of mustard 380; Preserved quince 5,779; Medicines, unguents, salves, and distilled waters 13,027; 5 pipes of flour 5,927.

Hardware and Storeroom Articles : Copper kitchen utensils : 6 large cauldrons, weighing 280 pounds (6165 ms.), 5 large pots, weighing 132 pounds (3700 ms.), 2 baking ovens, weighing 171 pounds (7695 ms.), 1 pot weighing 27 pounds (1215 ms.), and large vessel for pitch, weighing 55 pounds (2200 ms.) etc., total 21,515; 10 large knives 884; 42 wooden pint measures for the rations 516; 8 arrobas of candles, and grease for 42 arrobas more, etc. 3,440; 89 lanterns 1,430; 9½ pounds ornamented wax candles for the consecration of the ships 495; 40 cart loads of wood 8,860; 40 yards of coarse canvas for tablecloths 1,280; 14 large wooden trenchers 476; Chain for large cauldron 158; 12 bellows 256; 22½ pounds beeswax for waxing thread and for the crossbows 1,530; 12 large knives (calabozos) for the steward's room 768; 5 large iron ladles 204; 100 mess-bowls, 200 porringers, 100 choppers, 66 wooden platters, 12 mortars, 62 trenchers, all from Bilbao 5,834; 20 lights for the lamps 240; 12 funnels 330; 5 hammers 125; 18 extra trenchers 995; Brass pestle and mortar for the dispensary 653; 35 padlocks, given to the stewards 3,622; Irons, handcuffs, and chains, etc. 3,091; 20 pounds of steel for the pikes, etc. 240; An arroba of stamped iron weights 297; 50 spades and pickaxes 2,400; 20 bars of iron 1,600; 56 iron pikes and hammers and 2 large iron mallets 2,531; 2 great ship's lanterns 1200; 8 pair of pincers 360; Boat hooks, awls, etc. 1,224; 50 quintals 20 pounds of iron in small bars 24,938; Mats and baskets for the entire fleet 10,639; Fishing gear - 2 seines (chinchorros), (costing 8500 ms.), 6 chain hooks (125 ms.), floats for the seines (425 ms.), fishing-lines and cords (8663 ms.), harpoons and fish-spears from Biscay (8715 ms.), 10,500 fish-hooks (3826 ms.); total 30,254; Forge, bellows, anvil, and fittings from Biscay 9,147; 15 blank account-books, 5 wherein to keep the accounts of the fleet, and 10 for the officials to keep current accounts 1,211; Stevedores' wages for lading the ships 2,635; 2 grindstones, and a hone for the two barbers 2,125; 5 drums and 20 tambourines, given to the people of the fleet to serve for their pastime 2,895; The furniture (el ornamento) and all the necessary appliances for the chaplain to say Mass 16,513; 3700 paid the pilots for bringing the ships from Seville to San Lucar, and 1,985 from San Lucar over the bar to the sea totalling 5,685; Paid Rodrigo de Garay for his work 11,250; Paid Juan de la Cueva for his work 7,500; Carriage of quicksilver, vermilion, and other articles 12,014; Paid courier who came from Portugal and returned to the Court .5,625; Paid for posts and couriers to and from the Court 45,000; Paid to the Caravel, and for rations for the messenger sent wish letters to the Canary Islands 6,750; Paid to Luis de Mendoza to purchase various necessaries in the Canary Islands 15,000.

Charts and Nautical Instruments : Paid Nuño Garcia to buy parchments for the charts 1,125; 1 dozen skins of parchment given to Nuño Garcia 900; Another dozen skins of parchment given to Nuño Garcia 864; 7 charts constructed by the orders of Ruy Falero 13,125; 11 charts made by Nuño Garcia by the orders of Fernando Magallanes 11,250; 6 charts caused to be made by Ruy Falero, and one sent to the King 13, 500; 6 wooden quadrants made by Ruy Falero 1,121; 1 wooden astrolabe made by the said Ruy Falero 750; 1 planisphere ordered to be made by the Captain Magallanes for the King 4,500; Paid to the said Magallanes for 6 metal astrolabes with rulers 4,500; Paid to the same for 15 compass needles 4,080; Paid to same for 15 wooden quadrants, bronze-fitted 1,875; Gilt compass in a box, sent to the King with chart mentioned above 476; Leather case for the planisphere 340; 12 hourglasses bought by the Captain 612; 2 compass needles that the Captain has 750; 6 pairs of compasses 600; Paid to Nuño Garcia for 2 compass needles 750; Paid for the correction of an injured compass needle 136; 4 large boxes for four compasses, which Ruy Falero had made 884; 16 compass needles and six hourglasses, sent by Bernaldino del Castillo from Cadiz 6,094.

Articles of Trade and Barter : 20 quintals of quicksilver; 30 quintals of vermilion; 100 quintals alum; 30 pieces valuable coloured cloth at 4000 ms. per piece; 20 pounds of saffron; 3 pieces "veintenes," (pieces of cloth containing 2000 threads to the warp) silver, red, and yellow; 1 piece Valencia stuff; 10 quintals of ivory; 2 pieces of coloured velvets; 200 common red caps; 200 coloured kerchiefs; 10,000 fish-hooks; 1000 maravedis-worth of combs; 200 quintals of lump copper; 2000 brass bracelets; 2000 copper bracelets; 10,000 bundles of yellow matamundo; 200 small brass basins of two sorts; 2 dozen large basins; 20,000 small bells of three kinds; 400 dozens of German knives of the commonest kind; 40 pieces of coloured buckram; 50 dozen scissors; 900 small looking-glasses, and 100 larger size; 100 quintals of lead;

500 pounds of crystals, which are diamonds of all colours; totalling 1,679,769 maravedis.

We learn from the same document that four months' pay was given in advance, and that the number of persons receiving it was 237. Either some of those who accompanied the expedition did not receive pay - as, for example, the sobresalientes, many of whom were doubtless young men of good family - or some forty or more persons must have joined the fleet on the eve of its departure, which we have reason to believe was the case.

Another document informs us how the various stores and provisions were distributed among the five vessels of the squadron. A proportionate division of the latter was made according to the ship's burthen. The flagship took two cows, the other vessels one each. One surgeon alone being carried, all the medicines went with him on the Trinidad. The two ornamentos with robes and all necessaries for Mass were carried on the flagship and the San Antonio.

Our knowledge of the events of Magellan's great yet disastrous expedition is drawn from limited sources. Of those persons who actually took part in it, only four have left any description of its incidents. In Ramusio's Navigationi et Viaggi occurs an exceedingly brief account by an unknown Portuguese, so brief, indeed, as to be almost valueless. In the Seville archives there exists a derrotero or log-book, supposed to be written by Francisco Albo, the contramaestre of the Trinidad, but it is little more than a collection of nautical observations, which, though of the greatest interest in furnishing data for the actual course sailed by the vessels of the fleet, tell us little or nothing of the ordinary incidents of the voyage. A third account is that of the so-called Genoese pilot. From the fact that the manuscript is in the Portuguese language, and, moreover, in remarkably pure Portuguese, it has been conjectured that the author was not a Genoese. The narrative is tolerably full, but it bears no evidence of having been written by a pilot, and it is further worthy of remark that no Genoese sailed as pilot in the fleet.

The chief source of information we have, however, is neither of the foregoing. When the despatch of the fleet was finally decided upon, a certain Italian gentleman - Antonio Pigafetta by name - a native of Vicenza, being in Barcelona, and "desirous of seeing the wonderful things of the ocean," obtained permission to accompany Magellan on his voyage. Through the many adventurous months of wandering that fell to his lot, he kept his journal, finally publishing it upon his return. In it hearsay evidence is largely mixed with personal experience, but upon the whole it gives by far the best and fullest account of the expedition. There are reasons for supposing that it was originally published in French - reasons too lengthy to discuss here. It was dedicated to the celebrated Grand Master of Rhodes, Villiers de l'Isle Adam - Pigafetta himself being a Knight of Rhodes - and a copy was presented by him to the Regent, Louise of Savoy, mother of Francis I.

The most careful account written by mere historians of the event, who had taken no part in the voyage, is that of Maximilian Transylvanus, an under-secretary at the court of Charles V. This person, who had married Cristobal de Haro's niece, was a natural son of the Archbishop of Salzburg, and a pupil of the celebrated Peter Martyr. Upon the arrival of the survivors of the expedition at Valladolid (whither they had gone to present themselves to the Emperor), they were carefully interrogated by both Peter Martyr and Maximilian. The former, we are told, wrote a long account of the affair. "This viage," says Eden in his translation of the Decades, "was written particularly by Don Peter Martyr of Angleria, being one of the counsayle of Themperours Indies, to whom also was commytted the wrytynge of the hystorie and examination of al suche as returned from thense into Spayne to the citie of Siuile in the yeare MDXXII. However, sendynge it to Rome to bee prynted in that miserable tyme when the citie was sacked, it was lost, and not founde to this day, or any memory remaynynge thereof, sauynge suche as sum that redde the same haue borne in mynde."

Maximilian's account, however, remains. It was written on the 24th October 1522, to his father, and reached him in Nuremberg in the following month. The description of such a voyage naturally attracted much attention. The manuscript, which was in Latin, was printed in Cologne in January of the following year, thus probably preceding the Navigation et Descouurement of Pigafetta.

In addition to these sources, both Correa and Herrera give descriptions of the voyage that bear evidence in a greater or less degree of first-hand information. Among the mass of documents in the Seville archives are sundry informaciones and other papers throwing considerable light upon the mutiny and other salient incidents of the expedition.

CHAPTER 9

FROM SPAIN TO SOUTH AMERICA

All was now ready, and the Captain-general rejoined his ship and hoisted his pennant. Every day, Pigafetta tells us, officers and men had gone ashore to hear mass at the church of Nossa Senora de Barrameda, and now, on the eve of sailing, Magellan gave orders that all should confess, "in the which he himself showed the way to the others." Next day, Tuesday the 20th September 1519, a favourable breeze having sprung up, he gave the order to weigh, and a little later the ships cleared the river and commenced the memorable voyage that, through almost unparalleled suffering and disaster, was to win an immortal name for its survivors as the first circumnavigators of the globe.

The squadron's course on leaving Spain was shaped southward for the Canaries. Immediately on getting to sea, Magellan instituted a strict system of signalling at night by means of lights, and appointed the watches, as was even at that time customary. The admiral's ship led the van, bearing on the poop the farol or lantern, which it was the duty of his fleet to keep in sight. The night was divided into three watches - the first at the beginning of night; the second, called the medora, at midnight; and the third towards daybreak. The last was known as la diane, or the watch of the morning star. Each night they were changed; those who had kept the first watch kept the second on the following day, the second the third, and so on. In accordance, too, with the customary rules laid down by the India House, the crew of each vessel was divided into three companies - the first belonging to the captain or contramaestre, who took it in turns to command; the second to the pilot; and the third to the maestre. "The Captain-general, a discreet and virtuous man, careful of his honour," says Pigafetta, "would not commence his voyage without first making good and wholesome ordinances."

On the 26th September the fleet arrived at Tenerife. The log-book of the "Genoese pilot" gives the 29th as the date. Remaining three or four days to take in wood and water, they then sailed for a port called Monte Rosso on the same island, where they again delayed two days to supply themselves with pitch, or, according to Herrera, to await a caravel which was to bring them fish. It was while they were in Tenerife that an incident occurred which early brought home to Magellan the difficulties that lay in his path.

Of the existence of disaffection among his crew Magellan must have been well aware. Before starting, two of his men had been dismissed for insubordination. We have seen how, in Sebastian Alvarez' letter to Dom Manoel, he hints at a prearranged conspiracy. Pigafetta tells us that the captains of the other ships hated their leader, and the fact must have been patent enough. However, though he may have been fully conscious of the danger that threatened him, this danger had not as yet assumed definite shape. Now, at the very beginning of his voyage, at the moment of adventuring himself into unknown seas, it was to do so. A caravel arrived bearing a secret message from his father-in-law, Diogo Barbosa, warning him to "keep a good watch, since it had come to his knowledge that his captains had told their friends and relations that if they had any trouble with him they would kill him." Argensola gives us the same story that "his captains had resolved not to obey him, particularly Juan de Cartagena." The news, which probably was no news to Magellan, did not dishearten him one whit. He sent back answer to Barbosa that, were they good men or evil, he would do his work as a servant of the Emperor, and "to this end," he added, "he had offered his life." His letter, Correa tells us, was shown by Barbosa to the Corregidores, "who greatly lauded the stout heart of Magellan."

Pigafetta, ere leaving the Canaries, duly chronicles the semi-fabulous story of the island of Hierro - old even in those days, for Pliny records it - how its single tree is perpetually enveloped in a cloud from which it distils an unfailing supply of water. A story founded upon fact, as we know now, for both in Madeira and the Canaries the laurel and other heavy foliaged evergreens condense abundant water from the daily mists. The fleet left Tenerife at midnight on the 3rd October (on the 2nd according to Herrera's account) running under foresails only until they cleared the land, when they closed and held a south-west course until noon on the following day, when the observations taken placed them in 27° N. latitude, having made a run of twelve leagues.

From here they followed in the wake of the admiral's ship, steering sometimes south, sometimes south by west, and early on the following morning the San Antonio, running under the stern of the Trinidad, demanded the course. The pilot replied that it was south by west. It having been previously settled, Herrera tells us, that, until they reached the latitude of 24° N., the course was to be south-west, Juan de Cartagena demanded to know why it was changed. Magellan replied that "he was to follow him and not ask questions." The captain of the San Antonio retorted that he ought to have consulted the captains and pilots, and not to have acted thus arbitrarily. He added that it was an error of judgment to keep so near the African coast. Magellan's reply was to the same effect as his first answer - that the squadron must follow his flag by day and his lantern by night.

For fifteen days the fleet held good weather, passing between Cape Verde and its islands without sighting either, and running along the African coast. Between the cape and Sierra Leone they encountered calms and baffling winds for twenty days or more, during which time they advanced only three leagues upon their way. Provided with few or no data in physical geography, they had chosen what we now know to be a disadvantageous course. Following on the calms they had an entire month of head winds and very heavy storms. So heavy indeed were some of these squalls, that the vessels dipped their yardarms, and the captains were more than once on the point of ordering the masts to be cut away. Striking all sail, they ran under bare poles at the mercy of the wind. Pigafetta, to whom the sea and its natural phenomena were novelties, gives us a vivid account of the terrors of this period. "In these tempests," he says, "the Corpo Santo or St. Elmo's fire often appeared, and in one that we experienced on a certain very dark night, it showed itself at the summit of the mainmast with such brightness that it seemed like a burning torch, remaining there for a space of more than two hours; the which was of such comfort to us that we wept for joy. And when it left us, it cast such a vivid light in our eyes that for near a quarter of an hour we remained as blind men, crying out for mercy, for we gave ourselves up for lost."

For nearly sixty days they encountered rain while in the neighbourhood of the Line, "a thing very strange and unaccustomed to be seen," according to the ideas prevalent at that time. Sharks often came round their ships "large fishes with terrible teeth, and were caught by hooks; but the sailors do not seem to have appreciated the flesh, which they pronounced, in the case of the large ones, to be hardly fit to eat, while the smaller fish were little better. Notes of a like naive nature follow upon birds. The men had fitted the well-known legend of the bird of Paradise - heard doubtless by the old hands in some far Eastern port - to some petrel or diver. "They make no nest," it ran, "because they have no feet, and the hen lays her eggs on the back of the cock, and there hatches them."

The slowness of their progress during this early part of the voyage caused some anxiety as to the sufficiency of provisions, and the crew were accordingly placed on diminished rations. Four pints of water only were allowed daily, a smaller measure of wine was given, and the weight of bread reduced to a pound and a half. The voyage was destined to be attended by unusual difficulties and disasters, even for those perilous times - disasters only equalled by the world-famed success of its issue - and foreshadowings of the miseries awaiting the navigators in the Pacific early darkened their path.

Their troubles with regard to the insufficiency of stores were, however, at that time of no very great moment. They were forgotten before a more serious difficulty than any that had hitherto arisen. The dissensions that had already commenced between Juan de Cartagena and his chief had shown no sign of abatement as the voyage progressed. Before the Line was reached they culminated in open rupture. It was the custom, ordained by the King and embodied in his letter of instructions to Magellan, that every evening, whenever the weather rendered it possible, the captains should communicate with the flagship, to salute the admiral and to take his orders. One day the quartermaster of the San Antonio, hailing the Trinidad, gave as greeting, "Dios vos salve, señor capitan y maestre, é buena compañia." Magellan, resenting the studied omission of his proper title of Captain -general, informed Juan de Cartagena that he expected to be rightly addressed in future. The latter replied that "he had sent the best man in the ship to salute him, and that another day, if he wished, he would salute him through one of the pages." For three days, however, he failed altogether to comply with the rule.

The route from Spain towards South America

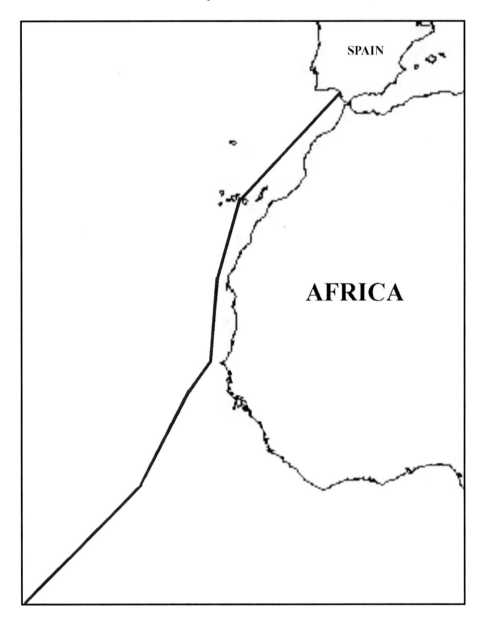

Magellan, though not the man tamely to submit to insults from his subordinates, took no immediate action, but a day or two later, a court-martial being held upon a sailor of the Victoria, Cartagena was summoned with the other captains to the flag-ship. The trial over, a discussion of the course to be steered followed. Cartagena, emboldened by Magellan's quiescence and the success of his former insults, renewed them without more ado. However, he had mistaken his man. Magellan, seizing him by the breast, and exclaimed, "You are my prisoner." Cartagena called in vain upon those present to aid him and to seize Magellan. No one stirred, and he was led off in custody to the stocks, and entrusted to the keeping of Luis de Mendoza, captain of the Victoria. The command of the San Antonio was given to the contador, Antonio de Coca. It was a pity for the offender that the prompt and resolute action of the admiral upon this occasion did not serve as a warning to deter him from future insubordination.

Steering a more westerly course, the fleet approached the New World, and arrived off Cape St. Augustin, near Pernambuco, on the 29th November. They continued to hug the coast, and on December 8th were close to land, and in only ten fathoms. Next day they found themselves in latitude 21° 31' S., in sight of a very high mountain near Cape St. Thomas. Rounding Cape Frio, they anchored in Rio harbour, which, since they entered it on the day of that saint, the 13th December, they called the Bay of Santa Lucia. Here they remained a fortnight, taking in wood and water and trading with the natives, "a good people and numerous," as Albo records. Pigafetta has left a lengthy record of their stay here, and of the customs and peculiarities of the country and its people, partly from his own observation, partly from that of former voyagers, notably Vespucci. The pineapples "a very sweet fruit, more tasteful than any other" - sweet potatoes, fowls, and tapir were much appreciated by the sailors after their reduced rations. They were to be had in abundance and upon the easiest terms. For a knife or a fishhook five or six fowls might be obtained; for a comb or mirror enough fish for ten men, and for a little bell a large basket full of sweet potatoes. A still better bargain was made by Pigafetta himself, who exchanged the king from a pack of cards for six fowls. Besides articles of food, parrots and other birds were brought for sale by the natives, who were ready enough to barter away their children for an axe or a large knife. The admiral, however, forbade the purchase of any slaves, hot only on account of the difficulty of feeding them, but in order that the Portuguese, within whose country the territory lay, should have no ground of complaint.

It is unnecessary to dwell on Pigafetta's evidently hearsay or borrowed account of the Indians and their customs. He speaks of their sleeping in "nets of cotton that they call amache," and of their boats called canoe. On the authority of João Carvalho, the pilot of the Concepcion, who had resided with them for four years, he describes their cannibal customs, and dilates upon the wonders of the country. His account of his personal experiences is more interesting. Brazil, it must be remembered, had been discovered twenty years at the time of Magellan's voyage. It is worthy of record that Carvalho took with him upon this voyage a son whom he had by a native wife during his former residence in Rio. It had not rained for two months before the visit of the fleet, and the arrival of the strangers coinciding with the termination of the long drought. The people thought they had brought the rain with them, and were easily converted to Christianity. Mass was said twice on shore while the ships lay in the bay, and the natives assisted with the utmost devotion at it, "remaining on their knees with their hands joined in great reverence, so that it was a pleasure and a pity to see them." It is remarkable that none of the historians of the voyage mention the presence of Portuguese in Rio de Janeiro, although there is every probability that some may have been there at the time, since a trading station had been established in the bay some years before.

The fleet, well furnished with fresh provisions, resumed its voyage on the 26th December. Before doing so, however, an attempt had been made by the cosmographer Andres de San Martin to fix the longitude of the bay. On the 17th December the altitude of the moon and Jupiter were observed, and from their position it was computed that the latter was in conjunction with the moon at the place of observation at 7h. 15m. after noon of the previous day. The tables of Regiomontanus were supposed to give the time of the conjunction at Seville. Herrera describes the observation at some length : it led to no definite conclusion, for the result obtained was evidently erroneous, and Andres ascribed the error to the almanac.

Sailing along the coast on a W.S.W. course, the vessels arrived off the Bahia de los Reyes (probably the Bay of Paranagua, in latitude 25° 28' S. upon the last day of the year). No landing was effected, and they continued their route to the southward, still hugging the coast and constantly taking soundings. They were well acquainted, even in those days, with the art of arming the lead, and Herrera tells us on more than one occasion what bottom was found. On the 8th January, being in shoal water, they anchored for the night. On the 10th January (11th January according to Herrera) they were passing very low land, with no landmarks save three hummocks, which appeared to be islands. These the pilot Carvalho declared to be Cape Santa Maria, saying that he recognised it from the account of João de Lisboa, who had been there. Losing the land here on their then course, they ran back northwards in search of shelter, having met with a terrific storm of thunder and lightning, and anchored. On the following day they weighed and proceeded W. ¼N., but the water becoming very shallow, the Santiago was sent ahead. They were at the mouth of the great river where Juan de Solis lost his life at the hands of the cannibals - the Rio de la Plata of today.

Their exploration of the river was a careful one. The account given of it by Herrera differs somewhat from that of Albo the pilot, but in general outline it is the same. For two days they followed up the stream. The pilots grumbled at the risk, for the greatest depth they found was three fathoms, and Magellan gave the order to anchor. They remained here six days, taking in water, and catching great quantities of fish. Many natives gathered in canoes, and, mindful of the fate of Juan de Solis, Magellan ordered three boats to be manned and armed, upon which the people fled ashore. The Spaniards landed and tried to catch them, but in vain. "They made such enormous strides," says Pigafetta, "that with all our running and jumping we could not overtake them." The country was found to be beautiful, but without sign of habitation. At night, an Indian dressed in goatskins came alone in a canoe and visited the flag-ship without a sign of fear. The admiral presented him with a cotton shirt and a jersey of coloured cloth, at the same time showing him a silver plate, to ascertain if he knew the metal. The native gave him to understand that there was much of it among his tribe, but

Magellan's hopes of barter were doomed to disappointment, for the man went away next day and did not return.

By Albo's log-book we learn that the vessel or vessels sent on in advance were absent fifteen days, and that two other ships were also sent southwards. Of these, the San Antonio was one, and in her Magellan himself went, anxious to examine the coast with his own eyes. Albo's description of this incident, especially when read side by side with Pigafetta's account, is of great interest. Both the reconnaissances were made with the object of seeing if there might not by chance exist a strait leading into the Pacific. The mere fact that Magellan sought for a strait here (or perhaps sought to disprove its existence) proves nothing with regard to the great question of what he knew concerning the straits that now bear his name. Such a strait, according to the Italian, had been rumoured, or its possibility surmised. However, twenty leagues to the south, Magellan reached the opposite bank of the river, and fresh water still washed the sides of his ships. He had to do, then, with the mouth of a great river only, and with nothing more; and the fine della terra, which Cape Santa Maria had been supposed to form, was not yet.

Rejoining the other ships, and beating back against strong head-winds to "Monte Vidi," Magellan anchored with his squadron off the site of the present city. On the morning of February 3rd he weighed and resumed his voyage to the south. Next day a leak was discovered in the San Antonio, but it was got under after a delay of two days, and on the 6th February the course was once more resumed. Keeping close to the coast off Cabo San Antonio, they rounded what is now known as Cape Corrientes, which, owing to its sand hills and shoals, they called Punta de las Arenas. On the 12th February they encountered a very severe storm of thunder and lightning and rain, the worst of which being over, the "glorioso cuerpo" of St. Elmo appeared to them, "the which some call that of San Pedro Gonzalez, others of Santa Clara, and others again of San Nicholas." Whichever it may have been, it afforded them much spiritual consolation, and "many who held the matter in derision," says Herrera, "not only saw it, but believed in it, and affirmed its truth."

13th February they found themselves among shoals (the "Bajos anegados" of Ribero's map), and the Victoria bumped several times, but fortunately did not remain. They thought it best, however, to keep off shore, and a course was steered that took them out of sight of land for two or three days. It does not appear whether Magellan thought that during this time he may have missed the possibility of a strait, or whether some other reason came into play. Either on the 22nd or the 23rd February he decided partially to retrace his steps, and a W.N.W. course was set. It brought them, February 24th, to the mouth of the Gulf of San Matias, which they entered "to see if there were not an outlet for the Moluccas." None appeared, and at the approach of night, finding no proper anchorage, they again stood out to sea. The bay received its name from its discovery upon San Matthias' Day. It was here that they appear to have first felt the effects of the oncoming winter. Herrera speaks of the great cold they experienced, and chronicles a succession of storms that separated the ships for three or four days.

Three days later, February 27th, they arrived at an inlet to which they gave the name of Bahia le los Patos, or Duck Bay, from the number of penguins frequenting it. A boat with six men was sent to get wood and water, but, fearful of the natives, they went to a small island instead of visiting the mainland. Upon it they found so many "sea wolves" (probably some species of the Otariidae or fur-seals), and penguins that they were astounded. The whole fleet could have been laden with them. Unable to discover either wood or water, the sailors filled their boat with these creatures. However, with a storm springing up, they found themselves unable to return. They were forced to spend the night upon the rock, fearing that they would either be devoured by the "wolves" or die from the cold.

Page 117

The route along the coast of South America

Next morning a number of men were sent to their rescue, who found their boat upon the rocks, and concluded that they had perished. On shouting out for their comrades, an enormous number of seals sprang out, of which they killed many; and searching farther, they came upon the missing men buried beneath the seals they had killed, and half dead from cold and exposure. On their return to the fleet another storm came on, so heavy that the cables of the Trinidad parted, and only one held. Close to the rocks, and horribly afraid, they promised a pilgrimage to N.S. de la Victoria, and commended their souls to God. With morning the storm ceased, and there was not sufficient wind for them to get under way. However, their troubles were not over, and they had yet to learn the meaning of autumn and winter on the shores of Patagonia. At midnight another storm burst upon them, lasting three days, and carrying away their forecastles and poops. Again they vowed pilgrimages in their distress, and again their prayers were heard. The three holy bodies, San Anselmo, San Nicholas, and Santa Clara appeared at the mastheads, and the storm ceased.

CHAPTER 10

MUTINY IN PORT ST. JULIAN

Great as their anxiety and hardships had been, it seemed that they were destined to grow worse as the fleet advanced. A few days later they arrived at a bay with a narrow entrance, which appeared, since it was roomy inside, to be suitable for them to winter in. They entered it, and in six days encountered severer storms and ran greater danger than had yet fallen to their lot. A boat that went ashore to water upon their arrival was unable to return, and the crew subsisted as best they could upon shellfish. "At last," Herrera tells us, "at last it pleased God that they should leave that bay, and they named it the Bay of Toil," ("Bahia do los trabajos"- possibly Bahia de los Desvelos, in latitude 48° 15' S.). How long a time had been passed in it does not appear, but considerable delay must have occurred either in the bay itself or its immediate neighbourhood, for it was not until the 31st March 1520, that the fleet anchored for the winter in Port St. Julian in latitude 49° 20' S. The weather had become too severe for a farther advance. Well sheltered and abounding in fish, the harbour seemed in every way a suitable one. However, it was destined to be no haven of rest to Magellan, for it was here that the mutiny, so long planned and so long foreseen, at length broke out.

Upon their arrival, one of the first steps taken by the Captain - general was to place officers and crew once more upon diminished rations. Bearing in mind the long winter they had before them, no wiser action could have been taken. However, such actions, however wise or even necessary they may be, are rarely popular, and this was no exception to the rule. The sailors grumbled, as sailors will grumble, and, hating Magellan, and anxious only for the failure of his expedition, it is little probable that the Spanish captains showed much energy in checking them. Matters grew daily worse. The extreme cold they were beginning to experience, the frequent storms they encountered, their disbelief in the existence of a strait, combined to render them oblivious alike of potential honours and of duty.

They openly demanded either that they should be put on full rations, or that the homeward voyage should be at once commenced. It was evident, they said, that the land stretched without a break to the Antarctic Pole, and that there was no hope of finding any strait. Also the winter, from whose rigour some had already died, was upon them. Therefore, to remain meant the loss of ships and men, which were of more importance than all the cloves and spices of the Moluccas. They alleged that it was not the intention of the King that they should continue to seek the impossible. It was sufficient that they had arrived at a point whither no one hitherto had been bold enough to penetrate. They added that if they went farther south they would in all probability be wrecked upon some inhospitable coast, where every soul would perish.

Magellan's answer was such as we might expect from him. Although so many were against him, nothing was further from his intention than to yield. The voyage, he said, was undertaken at the King's orders, and come what might. He added that it was imperative to push on to the termination of the continent and to the strait, which they could not fail to find. The winter, indeed, made their task impossible for the moment, but upon the advent of spring they could continue, if they pleased, to latitudes where the days were three months long. He marvelled that Castilians should be guilty of such weakness. As for the want of provisions, there was little cause for complaint. In the bay in which they lay at anchor there was plenty of wood, good water, and an abundance of fish and birds. Neither the bread nor wine had as yet run short, nor would they.

Since Magellan himself was determined to die rather than shamefully to turn back, he felt sure that among such comrades as embarked on such an expedition there could be no lack of that spirit of valour that always animated the Spanish nation. He asked them, therefore, to endure patiently until the winter should pass. The greater their labour and privation, the greater would be their sovereign's reward. They were to reveal to him, he concluded, an unknown world abounding in gold and spices, which would bring wealth to each and all concerned in its discovery. The demands of the crew, and Magellan's speech in reply, are almost identical in Oviedo and Herrera. Both perhaps are borrowed from the letter of Maximilian Transylvanus, that they also resemble almost word for word.

For a time, we learn, the crews were content, satisfied with the arguments he had advanced, but it was not for long. The treachery of his captains was at work, and the murmurings broke out afresh. The men began to talk to one another of the long-standing hatred between the Portuguese and Spaniards, and of Magellan being a Portuguese. They said that he could do no greater service to his country than to lose this fleet and all its sailors. They added that it was incredible that he should wish to find the Moluccas even if he could. It would be enough if he could delude the Emperor for a year or two with false hopes. Even their course, they said, was not towards the Moluccas, but towards snow and ice and perpetual storms.

This time Magellan took other measures to repress the discontent. As a man of spirit and honour, Gomara tells us, he showed his teeth, and seized and punished the offenders. His action was, however, too late to ward off the blow that was about to fall. An early warning of the coming storm was afforded not long after the arrival of the fleet in Port St. Julian. Magellan had given orders that upon Easter Day all should go ashore and attend mass, and that afterwards the captains of the ships should dine at his table.

Some changes had been effected in the command. It will be remembered that, upon the degradation of Cartagena, Antonio de Coca had been appointed captain of the San Antonio. We do not learn what action of his deprived him in his turn of his post, but deprived he was. Arana tells us that Magellan mistrusted him. Whatever may have been the cause, his command was conferred upon Alvaro de Mesquita - a first cousin of Magellan. It is not improbable that the appointment of a Portuguese was obnoxious to the Spaniards. At any rate, both Gaspar Quesada and Luis de Mendoza refused to attend mass, and Mesquita alone dined with his kinsman on board the Trinidad. Magellan, we are told, looked upon the affair as of ill augury, and his suspicions proved only too well founded.

The blow fell the very same night. In the middle watch Gaspar

Quesada, captain of the Concepcion, accompanied by Juan de Cartagena, Juan Sebastian del Cano, and some thirty armed men, boarded the San Antonio. They entered the cabin of Alvaro do Mesquita with drawn swords. Resistance was useless. He was immediately put in irons, secured in the cabin of Geronimo Guerra, and a guard placed over him. The disturbance at once brought the maestre, Juan de Lorriaga, upon the scene, a faithful Basque, who had no thought of joining the rebels, even in face of such serious odds. He called upon Quesada instantly to leave the ship, and upon his refusal, ordered the contramaestre, Diego Hernandes, to summon the crew to arms. Quesada, exclaiming, "We cannot be foiled in our work by this fool," sprang at him and stabbed him repeatedly with a dagger, leaving him for dead. Lorriaga died from the effects of his wounds on 15th July. The contramaestre had meanwhile been overpowered and made prisoner. So rapidly and unexpectedly had the affair taken place, that the crew, deprived of their officers, had no alternative but to submit. They were at once disarmed, and the arms placed in the cabin of Antonio de Coca, who had cast in his lot with the mutineers.

Measures were next taken to secure the ship against recapture. The command was given to Juan Sebastian del Cano, to whose name the stain of mutiny must ever attach, despite the honour so justly won by him at a later period. The artillery was mounted, and the decks cleared for action under his orders. Antonio Fernandes and Gonçalo Rodrigues, two Portuguese who had resisted Quesada's authority, were put in irons, together with a certain Diego Diaz, who had helped them. The stores were broken open, and the wine, bread, and other provisions freely distributed. In this and other matters Antonio de Coca, the former captain of the San Antonio, was active in assisting Quesada, as was also Luis del Molino, the latter's body-servant. The chaplain of the ship, Pedro de Valderrama, though occupied in confessing the apparently dying maestre, observed them, and mentioned the fact in his evidence before Magellan. It obtained for Molino a sentence of death, but for lack of an executioner his life was spared, upon the condition that he himself should execute his master.

The ship Victoria, whose captain, Luis de Mendoza, treasurer of the armada, had always been a bitter enemy of Magellan, had from the beginning given in its adherence to the mutineers, although a marked element of loyalty existed among the crew. The sublevados were therefore in a very strong position. They held the Concepcion, the San Antonio, and the Victoria, and were headed by Quesada, Juan de Cartagena, Antonio de Coca, and Mendoza. Of the little Santiago we hear nothing. Her captain, Serrão, was the brother of Magellan's staunchest friend, and of her crew of thirty-two, one-half only were Spanish. It is unlikely that any attempt was made to interfere with her, either by force or persuasion. Quesada and his party felt strong enough to carry out their plans without her assistance.

Such was the state of affairs to which Magellan woke upon the morning of the 2nd April. The San Antonio had been carried so rapidly and quietly that no suspicion of the truth had occurred to the officers of the flagship. It first dawned upon them, the chronicler Herrara tells us, on Magellan sending a boat to the San Antonio to pick up some men for a watering-party. They were hailed and told to keep off, and informed that the ship was under the orders of Gaspar Quesada, and not Magellan.

Hearing the news, and at once suspecting the serious nature of the affair with which he had to deal, Magellan ordered the boat to go round to the ships and ask for whom they declared. Quesada's reply was, "For the King and for myself," and like answers were given from all except the Santiago. Shortly afterwards a boat arrived with a letter from Quesada. He had seized the ships, he said, in order henceforward to do away with the possibility of a repetition of the bad treatment which officers and crew alike had received at the hands of Magellan. However, if Magellan would agree to their demands, they were ready once more to acknowledge his authority. Magellan, in reply, said that he would meet them on his ship, and would hear what they had to say. However, the mutineers, fearing that they would be seized if they ventured on board the Trinidad, declined to see him, excepting on the San Antonio.

Magellan had before him a task of which the difficulty would have appeared to most men almost invincible. Unless he won the day, the theories and hopes of his lifetime were doomed to complete and final failure. With the Santiago only, the continuation of the voyage was impossible. To return once more to the Seville quays, having achieved nothing after so great a flourish of trumpets at his departure was of course to return to disgrace and oblivion. At any risk and cost, therefore, the mutiny must be suppressed, but how it should be suppressed was another matter. We have seen enough of Magellan's life and actions under Almeida to know that in cool daring few men were his superiors. However, openly to attack the three revolted ships with no assistance other than the little Santiago would have been madness, and no one knew it better than he. If he was to succeed at all, it must be by finesse - by the exercise of that faculty that, Herrera tells us, supplied him with a way out of every new difficulty as it arose.

Magellan did succeed. His first action was to seize the boat of the San Antonio that brought him Quesada's message. Bearing in mind the large proportion of foreigners upon the Victoria, and the fact that he knew many of them to be loyal to him, he decided to address himself first to the capture of that vessel. He hoped, if he was successful, to be more than a match for the others. The skiff, accordingly, carrying the alguacil Gonzalo Gomez de Espinosa and five men bearing concealed arms, was despatched with a letter to Mendoza, summoning him at once to the flagship. Mendoza smiled at its contents - as though he would say, "I am not to be caught thus." He did not calculate upon the instructions given by Magellan. As he shook his head in refusal Espinosa drew his dagger and stabbed him in the throat, and at the same instant he was cut down by another of Magellan's men. He fell dead upon the deck. The dangerous position of the alguacil and his handful of men had, of course, been foreseen. A boat with fifteen picked men of the Trinidad, captained by the trusty Duarte Barbosa, brother-in-law of Magellan, had been kept in readiness. Almost at the moment that Mendoza fell, the Victoria was boarded with a rush. Hardly an effort at resistance was made. Either overawed at the death of their captain or loyal in reality to the leader of the armada, the crew surrendered at once. Barbosa hoisted Magellan's ensign, and, weighing anchor, placed the captured ship in close proximity to the capitana at the entrance of the port. The Santiago took up a similar position upon the other hand. The three ships together effectually guarded the harbour's mouth, preventing the escape of the others, and Magellan held the game in his own hands.

The mutineers were summoned to surrender, but refused, and it was conjectured that the two ships would attempt to escape under cover of darkness. Early in the day the Trinidad had been cleared for action. An order had been issued to "make a plentiful provision of much darts, lances, stones, and other weapons, both on deck and in the tops." The watch was now doubled; the men were allowed a good meal, and the strictest injunctions were given to guard against the escape of the vessels.

A little after midnight the San Antonio hove in sight. She was supposed to be bearing down upon the flagship, but was in reality dragging her anchors. Upon the quarter-deck was Gaspar Quesada, who, armed with lance and shield, called upon his men. No one stirred, and the Trinidad, opening fire with her large bombards, grappled her and poured her boarders over her side. At the same moment she was boarded on the starboard hand by the sailors of the Victoria. Their cry "Por quien estais?" met with the answer, "For the King and Magellan." Quesada and his fellow-mutineers were quickly seized, and the captain and pilot, Alvaro de Mesquita and Mafra, set at liberty. Not a man was killed; hardly a blow struck. Mafra alone had any narrow escape of death, a ball from the flagship passing between his legs as he sat imprisoned below deck.

The mutiny was now over. Juan de Cartagena, perceiving the loss of the San Antonio and the surrender of Quesada, realised that nothing was to be gained by further resistance. When the boat from the Trinidad came alongside and called upon him to surrender, he obeyed the order at once. He was placed in irons and brought back to the flagship, there to await his sentence.

Next day the body of Mendoza was brought ashore. He was publicly cried as a traitor, the body was drawn and quartered, and the quarters spitted on poles. An inquiry was then held upon the circumstances of the mutiny, of which no details are given us. Forty men were found guilty of treason and condemned to death. However, partly because they were necessary for the service of the fleet, partly because he did not wish to make himself unpopular by too severe measures, Magellan pardoned them. Such a clemency, however, could not be extended to Quesada nor Cartagena, whose insubordination had been an affair of old date. Quesada, doubly guilty by the brutal manner in which he had stabbed the maestre of the San Antonio, was sentenced to be executed. On Saturday, the 7th April, he was taken on shore and the sentence carried out. His head being struck off by his servant, Luis del Molino, and his body quartered, as in the case of Mendoza.

A different fate was reserved for Juan de Cartagena. Whether, since he had been directly appointed by Charles V, Magellan did not wish to take his life, or whether he considered that there were extenuating circumstances connected with his case, we cannot tell. A violent death at least was spared him, and he was sentenced to be marooned upon the departure of the fleet. With him the priest Pero Sanchez de Reina suffered a like punishment. Herrera speaks of a clerigo frances as being the culprit, leaving it to be inferred that it was Bernardo Calmeta, the chaplain of the San Antonio. In the "List of Deaths in the Fleet of Hernando de Magallanes" it is, however, distinctly mentioned that the offender was Pero Sanchez de Reina. It is nevertheless worthy of remark that Calmeta's name is not to be found among those who returned to Spain, nor among those who perished in the expedition. His offence was a grave one, for he was found guilty of trying to incite the crew to mutiny for a second time, even after the failure of the plot and the justice executed upon its authors. No one would listen to him, and he was soon denounced and made prisoner.

Of Antonio de Coca's punishment we hear nothing. We know only that he reached the Mariana Islands with the fleet and died there. Others, among them Andres de San Martin, the cosmographer, are said to have been punished by Magellan. However, as we learn this from the evidence of the crew of the San Antonio, which ship deserted the fleet a few months later, and as we know much of the evidence to be untrue, no reliance can be placed upon the assertion.

Magellan's action in the mutiny of Port St. Julian has been made the subject of the severest strictures, more especially by those of the school of fireside criticism. His stratagem of capturing the Victoria has been stigmatised as assassination. By one author he is described as "a man of cruel and savage disposition," who "ruthlessly slaughtered his own comrades." However, such expressions are as incorrect as they are violent. In times of mutiny, when right is no longer might, and the loyal crew are confronted by overpowering odds, legal measures are occasionally impossible, and fairness worse than a mistake. Mendoza, a mutineer and ipso facto worthy of death, only met his punishment - and met it, it should be remembered, at the hands of an alguacil - a few hours before it would otherwise have been inflicted. As a mutineer, moreover, he was well aware of the risks he ran - well aware that, if Magellan could, he would kill him. Finally, we cannot judge sixteenth-century matters by today's standards. The taking of a man's life was in those days a small matter. However, in expeditions such as these, the preservation of discipline was an affair of vital importance. In this case, had the attempt on the Victoria failed, the complete collapse of the work of the armada must inevitably have followed.

Magellan has also been accused of having acted illegally in the punishment of the mutineers. In the letter of Maximilian Transylvanus this charge is brought against him. However, though there may be a difference of opinion as to the justifiability of Mendoza's death, there can be none whatever upon this question. The "Titulo de Capitanes," granted by Charles to Magellan upon the 22nd March 1518, gives the latter full power over the persons and property of those sailing with him. Correa, too, is definite upon the point. "The Emperor gave him power of rope and knife over every person who went in the armada." It is satisfactory to find that the punishments of Quesada and Cartagena were as strictly legal as they were well deserved.

The mutiny was the turning-point of Magellan's career. Thenceforward, whatever desire to question his authority may have existed it remained unexpressed. The inflexible determination of the man, his strength of will, his readiness of resource, showed officers and crews alike that obedience was the best policy. Had they known what suffering and what peril lay in their path, it is doubtful whether the resolution and energy of any single individual would have availed to stop their defection. However, Ruy Faleiro had only cast his own horoscope; and so it happened that Magellan sailed southward to the discovery of the strait that bears his name.

It is a singular fact that of the four persons who accompanied the expedition and wrote an account of it, two should have remained absolutely silent upon the subject of the mutiny. The other two - the "Genoese pilot" and Pigafetta - have thought it worthy of only the barest mention. The account of the latter is remarkable for its extraordinary inaccuracy. "The Captains of the other four ships," he writes, "plotted to kill the Captain-general," and he then goes on to say that it was Cartagena who was executed and quartered, while Gaspar Quesada was marooned. It seems incredible that an eyewitness - which he undoubtedly was - should have failed to remember circumstances such as these. The fact somewhat lessens the value of his book as a credible narrative. However, we know that such parts of the diary as were written on the spot, detailing his own experiences, are almost always accurate. Our real knowledge of the affair is due to three documents existing in the Seville archives - an information drawn up by Magellan at the time, giving the examination of witnesses; a letter of the Contador Recalde to the Bishop of Burgos, containing the evidence of the deserters of the San Antonio; and, lastly, an account of the evidence taken in Valladolid, October 18th, 1522, concerning certain events of the voyage. The historian Herrera has a tolerably full and correct account of the tragedy, but that of Correa, though nearly as full, is inaccurate in many points, as indeed it is often wont to be.

CHAPTER 11

DISCOVERY OF THE STRAIT OF MAGELLAN

Order having once more been established, Magellan kept all hands busily at work during the remainder of his sojourn in Port St. Julian. The vessels were careened and caulked, and such repairs as were found necessary were carried out. The San Antonio especially stood in need of them. The mutineers, in chains, were kept working at the pumps until the carpenters had rendered such work no longer needful. It was not until the day of departure from the bay that they were set at liberty.

Towards the end of April Magellan determined to undertake a reconnaissance of the coast in the vicinity. The fear of a more or less prolonged inaction and its effect upon the men most probably led him to this step. The Santiago, from her handiness and small draught, was chosen for the work, and her choice was the more indicated from the fact of Serrão being her commander. Few men were so well versed in the art of seamanship and navigation; fewer still were endowed with his experience. He had long used the Eastern seas both as subaltern and captain. From the time of his first command under Rodrigo Rabello in 1506 until his departure on the expedition, he had been constantly in active service. As brother, moreover, of Magellan's great friend, Francisco Serrão, the Captain-general knew that every trust could be reposed in him. He received instructions therefore to sail along the coast to the southward, examining each bay and inlet. He was not to carry his explorations too far. If after a certain time nothing worthy of note was met with, he was to retrace his steps and once more rejoin his comrades in Port St. Julian.

It is to Herrera that we are indebted for an account of the voyage. The Santiago, working slowly along the coast, arrived on the 3rd May at the mouth of a river of considerable size, nearly sixty miles from the harbour whence she had set out. Serrão named it the Rio de Santa Cruz. The fish were so abundant that he was induced to prolong his stay for six days to lay in a supply. The seals, or sea-wolves, as the sailors termed them, were equally numerous, and of such large size that the

Spaniards were astounded. One of them, deprived of the skin, head, and entrails, weighed nearly five hundredweight.

Having replenished their stock of provisions, the explorers continued their voyage. However, they had barely gone three leagues, when, on the 22nd May, they encountered one of the short but violent storms which at this season render the coast of Patagonia so dangerous. The ship was put under storm canvas, but the rudder having become injured by the heavy seas, she refused to obey her helm, and a sudden squall from the east drove her ashore. Fortunately, she took the ground in such a manner that the crew were able to save themselves by dropping from the end of the jib-boom, but they had barely time to escape with their lives. In a few minutes the ill-fated Santiago was in pieces. Her crew, to the number of thirty-seven men, found themselves without provisions of any kind, exposed to the hardships of a most inclement climate. They were separated by seventy miles of pathless wilderness from the succour of their comrades. The only good fortune attending them was of a negative kind. However, one life was lost - that of the African slave of the captain.

For eight days the castaways remained in the neighbourhood of the wreck, hoping possibly to secure some articles of food or otherwise, which might prove of service in the desperate journey that lay before them. Their hopes were vain. Among the jetsam, however, were numerous planks. Mindful of the fact that between them and safety lay the river they had just discovered (the great Rio de Santa Cruz, a barrier three miles in width), they started on their march laden with sufficient of these to enable them to construct a raft wherewith to cross it. However, short as was the distance they had to traverse, they became so exhausted by exposure and want of nourishment that they were forced to abandon the greater part of their load. They did not arrive at the river until the fourth day. It may be wondered why such toil and hardship were undertaken when a raft might have been built at the riverside. It is probable, however, that the shipwrecked men were unprovided with axes, and that there was also insufficient wood for the purpose. Here at least they were safe from starvation, for, as they had previously discovered, its waters abounded in fish. It was resolved that the main body of the crew should encamp upon the banks, while two of the strongest of their number should cross in the little raft they had constructed, and endeavour to make their way to Port St. Julian.

For eleven days they struggled on, living at one time upon roots and leaves, at another upon such shellfish as they were able to collect upon the shore. At first they attempted to follow the coastline, as affording them better means of subsistence. However, they were soon obliged to relinquish this plan, owing to the marshes that barred their passage and forced them to strike inland. At length the welcome harbour was reached. So altered were they from the hardships they had undergone, that they were recognised with difficulty by their old comrades.

The weather continued so unsettled, that Magellan considered it better to try to reach the shipwrecked party by land, rather than expose another of his vessels to the risk of loss. He accordingly at once despatched a relief party of twenty-four men, laden with wine and biscuit. Like their two comrades, they experienced great hardships from the rigours of the climate and the roughness of the country. No water was to be found on the road, and they were forced to melt the little snow they could discover to supply themselves with drink. On arriving at the river, they found their companions safe, although exhausted by exposure and privation. In parties of two or three - for the little raft could hold no more - the castaways were brought across the river, and the homeward march began. It speaks well for the courage and endurance of the Spaniards that they eventually reached the fleet without the loss of a single man. Good fortune afterwards attended them with regard to the ship's stores and artillery, the greater part of which were saved and picked up by Magellan on resuming his voyage to the south.

Upon their return, the crew of the Santiago were distributed among the four remaining ships. Serrão, who had displayed both courage and ability in his conduct of the shipwrecked crew, was rewarded by the command of the Concepcion. The ultimate result of the two disasters that had befallen Magellan was greatly to strengthen his hand. In lieu of three disaffected and traitorous captains - Quesada, Cartagena, and Mendoza - the commands were held by Portuguese, in whom he could place complete and absolute reliance. Serrão, as we have seen, took the

Concepcion, while the San Antonio and Victoria were captained by Alvaro de Mesquita and Duarte Barbosa, the former of whom was Magellan's first cousin, the latter his brother-in-law.

The winter was now fairly established, and the cold became more severe. Nor was the weather they experienced such as to tempt a renewal of their explorations along the coast. However, the Captain-general, anxious to learn something of the interior of the country, thought it advisable to despatch a small expedition with that object. Four men only were sent. They were well armed, and were furnished with instructions to penetrate, if possible, to a distance of thirty leagues, to plant a cross, and to put themselves upon a footing of friendship with any natives they might, happen to meet. The nature of the country was, unfortunately, such as to render the expedition a failure. Neither food nor water was to be found. The men were forced to be content with the ascent of a high mountain at some little distance from the coast. Planting a cross upon its summit, and giving to it the name of the Mount of Christ, they retraced their steps. They arrived at the ships, informing Magellan that the country was intraversable and without resources, and appeared to be entirely unpeopled.

It was not long before the latter piece of information at least was proved to be incorrect. The fleet had remained at anchor for weeks in Port St. Julian, and no trace of natives had been seen. One morning, however, the sailors were astonished by the appearance of a man of gigantic stature upon the beach, who sang and danced, pouring sand upon his head in token of amity. Magellan sent a man ashore with instructions to imitate the action of the savage, and, if possible, to make friends with him. This he succeeded in doing, and the newcomer was brought before the admiral. Spaniards and native were equally surprised. The latter marvelled, Gomara tells us, to see such large ships and such little men; and pointing to the sky, seemed to inquire whether they were not gods who had descended from heaven. The Spaniards, wondering at the great stature of their visitor, concluded that they had come upon a race of giants. "So, tall was this man," writes Pigafetta, "that we came, up to the level of his waist belt. He was well enough made, and had a broad face, painted red, with yellow circles round his eyes, and two heart-shaped spots on his cheeks. His hair was short and coloured white, and be was dressed in the skins of an animal cleverly sewn together." The description given of this animal leaves no doubt that it was the guanaco. The skin of the same creature served to make boots for these people. It was the unwieldy appearance thus given to the feet that led Magellan to apply to the race the name of Patagão.

The man seemed most peaceably disposed, though he did not lay aside his arms - a short, thick bow, and a bundle of cane arrows tipped with black and white stones. Magellan treated him kindly, and ordered that he should be given food. He was shown some of their objects for barter, among others a large steel mirror. So overcome was he on catching sight of himself, says Pigafetta, that he jumped backwards with an unexpectedness and impetuosity which overset four of the men who were standing around him. He was, neverthetheless, not unwilling to accept a small mirror as a present, and some beads and bells having been added. He was put ashore under the care of four armed men.

A companion met him upon landing, and confidential relations having been thus established, the Spaniards had no difficulty in persuading the natives to visit their ships. Others, accompanied by their wives, were not long in showing themselves, and eventually several came on board. "The women," we are told, "were loaded by them with all their belongings, as if they were so many beasts of burden. We could not behold them without wonder." They were not so tall as the men, but much fatter, and had breasts half as long as a man's arm. With them "they brought four of those little beasts of which they make their clothing, leading them with a cord like dogs coupled together." The use of these, they said, was to tie up and entice others within range of the arrows of the hunter, who was hidden near. The Spaniards were anxious to secure some of these guanacos. They got together eighteen of the natives and set half of them to hunt on either side of the entrance of the harbour. However, we are not told the result of their endeavours.

Many visits were thus paid by the natives to the fleet, and Pigafetta was enabled to obtain a small vocabulary of their language. One of them, who seemed especially tractable and pleasing, remained with the ships some days. He was taught the Paternoster and Ave Maria, which he pronounced well, but in an exceedingly loud voice, and the priest eventually baptized him with the name of Juan Gigante. Magellan gave him a number of presents, with which he was much pleased, and on the following day he returned bringing a guanaco. Magellan, hoping to obtain some more of these animals, directed that further presents should be made him. The man was never seen again, however, and it was suspected that he had been murdered by his companions.

The manners and customs of the Patagonians are described at some length by the supposed Genoese pilot as well as by Pigafetta. The fact that they devoured with great relish the rats that were caught on the ships filled the sailors with astonishment, which was not lessened by perceiving that they did not stop to skin them. Still more astonishing was their power of thrusting arrows down their throats without injury. It was apparently done more as a tour de force than for any definite purpose, although Pigafetta regarded it as a species of medical treatment, "in luogho di purgarsi," as he describes it.

In spite of Magellan's fixed rule that the fleet should, not be burdened with useless mouths, especially now that the rations had been reduced, he was so much struck with the gigantes, as they termed them, that he resolved to bring some of them back with him to Spain as a present to the Emperor. It was some little time before he was able to put his project into execution, for fifteen days elapsed before another native was seen. At length, upon the 28th July, four appeared upon the beach, and were brought on board the Trinidad. Magellan was anxious to keep the two youngest, but having an idea that their capture might not be an easy matter, he decided to use strategy rather than force. Loading them with presents, so that their hands were full, he then offered them a pair of irons, and, as they were unable to take them, showed them how they fitted upon the legs. A couple of strokes of the hammer riveted the bolts, and the two unlucky natives were prisoners before they realised their position. When they did so, they became furious, invoking Setebos, their Great Spirit, to their aid. Their two companions were conducted ashore with their arms bound by a party of men who were instructed to bring the wife of one of the captives, "who greatly regretted her, as we saw by signs." The huts of the natives were reached the same day, but as it was late, the pilot Carvalho, who was in charge of the party, decided on waiting till the following day. It happened that on the road, one of their charges had attempted to escape, and in the struggle that ensued he was wounded in the head. His companions said nothing at the time, but next morning they spoke a few words to the women, and immediately all took to flight. At a little distance they halted to exchange shots with the Spaniards, and in the encounter Diego de Barrasa, man-at-arms of the Trinidad, was struck in the thigh by an arrow and died immediately.

Magellan attempted to follow the Patagonians, either with the idea of punishing them, or more probably with the hope of capturing a woman of the tribe. However, he was unsuccessful, and it seems that - by nature a wandering people - they disappeared for a time from the neighbourhood.

The action of the Spaniards upon this occasion was, of course, totally unjustifiable according to our ideas. However, it must be remembered that the humanitarianism of the present day was at that time not even in its infancy. A selvaje was looked upon as hardly other than an animal, and giants, such as these were supposed to be, must have approximated them still more closely.

The actual height and size of the Patagonians remained for a long time a matter of dispute. An assemblage of very tall people always causes an over estimation of their height. There is no doubt that Pigafetta's diary gives a bona fide record of the impression produced upon the mind of himself and his comrades. Lieutenant Musters, who was the greatest authority upon the country, gave the average height of the men as six feet, while some reached six feet four inches or more. Their muscular development was very great. According to Darwin, their height appeared greater than it really was due to large guanaco mantles, their long flowing hair, and general figure.

No doubt Magellan regarded it as his duty to bring such curiosities to his Emperor, and did not consider his breach of faith as other than a perfectly justifiable proceeding. The two captives were placed in different vessels. We learn from the account of the Genoese pilot that one arrived in Spain, brought thither in the San Antonio, when she deserted the rest of the squadron in the Straits. According to other accounts, however, he died before reaching that country.

Herrera's account of the intercourse of the Spaniards and Patagonians differs widely from the above in certain points. He relates their first meeting differently. He describes the death of Diego de Barrasa as occurring in a chance rencontre with the natives. He records the despatch of a punitive expedition of twenty men as a sequel, adding that not one of the enemy was encountered.

In the letter of Maximilian Transylvanus there occurs a lengthy description of a visit of seven men of the fleet to a Patagonian but some distance inland, followed by an attempt to capture three of the natives. One only was caught and brought on board, but his death occurred within a few days. Neither of these accounts, it should be remembered, are first hand.

Weary, no doubt, of the continued inaction, and anxious to leave a place that must each day have brought the remembrance of the mutiny to his mind, Magellan resolved to pass the remainder of the winter in the Rio de Santa Cruz, which had been discovered by Serrão in the ill-fated Santiago.

The ships were now repaired and refitted, and in good order, and the admiral hoped to make the passage without encountering one of the frequent storms that render this coast so dangerous in winter. He accordingly gave orders to prepare for sea.

Before their departure, however, a sentence had to be carried into effect - that of the marooning of Juan de Cartagena and his fellow-culprit, Pedro Sanchez de Reina. In the pay list of the voyage, published by Medina, this name appears as Pedro Sanchez de Viena. For some reason that we do not learn, they were put on shore nearly a fortnight before the sailing of the fleet on Saturday, August 11th. They were provided with "an abundance of bread and wine," Herrera says. However, it must have been a bitter punishment for them to watch the departure of their comrades and to reflect how small was their chance of life - a chance still further diminished by the altered relations of the Spaniards with the natives. They were "judged to be worse off, considering the country in which they were left, than the others who were drawn and quartered."

On the 24th August, every member of the expedition having confessed and received the sacrament, the fleet left the bay. Before their departure Andres de San Martin took observations to determine the latitude. The result he obtained was 49° 18' S., which is wonderfully correct. They shaped their course S.W.¼W., and two days later arrived off the mouth of the Santa Cruz river. Their passage was not accomplished without danger, for the ships were nearly lost in a heavy squall. "God and the Corpi Santi, however," writes Pigafetta, "came to our aid," and they reached the shelter of the river and anchored in safety. The latitude was, fixed; with very tolerable accuracy, at 50°. In this port, of desolate character, two months were passed. The time was spent in provisioning the ships with such wood as could be obtained, and with fish, of which there was abundance. On the drying and preserving of a sufficient supply of these their future comfort - perhaps even their future plans - depended, for the stores of the fleet had already begun to reach an alarming stage of diminution. Visits were paid to the coast to the southward, where the wreck of the Santiago had taken place, and such articles as had since been washed ashore were recovered.

No occurrence worthy of note befell the navigators during their delay in the river, if we except a supposed eclipse of the sun, recorded by the historian Herrera, but by no single one of those actually present who have left us an account of the voyage. In an age of writing that erred even more in ellipsis than garrulity, this latter circumstance could not, however, be advanced, as a conclusive proof of its non-occurrence. "On the 11th October," we are told, "while in this river, an eclipse of the sun was awaited, which in this meridian should have occurred at eight minutes past ten in the morning. When the sun reached an altitude of 42½ degrees it appeared to alter in brilliancy, and to change to a sombre colour, as if inflamed of a dull crimson, and this without any cloud intervening between ourselves and the solar body. Not that the body of the sun, either wholly or in part, was obscured, but its clearness appeared as it might in Castile in the months of July and August when they are burning the straw in the surrounding country. This lasted till it reached an altitude of 44½ degrees when it regained its original brilliancy."

What conclusion to draw from the above passage it is difficult to decide. The haziness of the sun could only have been due to some atmospheric cause. An annular eclipse of the sun certainly did take place October 11th, 1520. However, it was not visible upon the coast of Patagonia, the central line crossing the meridian of the Santa Cruz river, more than 30° north of the Equator.

With the advent of October the weather improved, and on the 18th Magellan judged the spring to be sufficiently far advanced for the continuation of his voyage. The fleet was got under way. Feeling sure that lie must ere long come upon the object of his search, the admiral ordered the ships to keep along the coast as before. For two days they were baffled by head-winds and bad weather, fighting their way southward inch by inch. At length the wind shifted to the north, and they ran before it on a S.S.W. course for two days more. On the 21st October 1520, they found themselves in sight of land; "and there," says the pilot Albo, "we saw an opening like unto a bay." They were off Cabo de las Virgenes, and Magellan had found his long hoped for strait at last !

We must pause here for a moment to consider a question of the greatest interest - a question that has never yet been satisfactorily answered. Did Magellan know, as a certain fact, of the existence of the strait ? Or was his discovery of it due to a carefully reasoned out argument based upon the presumed homology of the Cape of Good Hope ? Or was it from the blindest of chances, from the sort of fortune that guides a caged bird, panting for liberty, to the broken bar of its prison ?

In Pigafetta's account of the voyage there occurs a very remarkable passage, so clearly and definitely expressed, that, did it only emanate from a more accurate author, the matter would seem at once and for ever set at rest. "We all believed," it runs, speaking of the strait, "that it was a cul-de-sac; but the captain knew that he had to navigate through a very well concealed strait, having seen it in a chart preserved in the treasury of the King of Portugal, and made by Martin of Bohemia, "a man of great parts." The matter is also alluded to by Gomara, but he throws doubt upon it, and says that "the chart showed no strait whatever, as far as I could learn". His evidence, as that of a contemporary historian, is not without weight. Herrera, speaking of the offer made by Magellan and Faleiro at the Spanish court, tells us that they proposed to conduct their ships to the Moluccas "by means of a certain strait, at that time not known of by any one". A few lines farther on, he gives the story of Martin Behaim's chart, and adds that "from him they obtained much information concerning this strait." M. Ferdinand Denis, in his Portugal, gives us some information as to the provenance of this chart but he offers no opinion as to the truth of the statement. We have yet another of the great historians who discusses the possibilities of Magellan's foreknowledge of his strait - Oviedo, who wrote in 1546, a period that is within measurable distance of the great navigator's voyage. In one passage he speaks with no uncertain voice "of which strait and voyage none had knowledge or remembrance until the renowned Captain Ferdinand Magellan discovered and showed it to us." However, elsewhere the claims of Martin Behaim are discussed. He decides that, whether the discovery was due to his suggestion or to the pluck of Magellan, the latter is worthy of all praise, and "more is owing to his capacity than to the science of the Bohemian."

All the foregoing, it will be observed, are the opinions of people writing after the event. For the journal of Pigafetta we know to be in many places no journal at all, but to have been written up some time after the occurrence of the various incidents, possibly even not till his arrival in Spain. The question will be asked, Is there any passage of a date anterior to the voyage that would lead us to conclude that the great navigator suspected the existence of an opening from the Atlantic into the Pacific ? It may be answered in the affirmative. Whether that suspicion amounted to actual knowledge it is difficult to say. However, not only have we the record of Herrera as to the examination of Magellan before Charles V's ministers, and the exhibition of Pedro Reynel's globe, but a document is still existing which places the matter beyond a doubt. In the capitulation granted by the King to Magellan and Faleiro on the 22nd March 1518, the phrase "para buscar el estrecho de aquellas mares" - to go in search of the strait is used. It would seem from the use of the definite article as if some actual known or rumoured strait was intended.

We may now turn to the evidence of various maps and globes. There occurs in the Tratado of Antonio Galvão, which was afterwards Englished by Richard Hakluyt in 1601, an account of "a most rare and excellent map of the world, which was a great helpe to Don Henry (the Navigator) in his discoueries". It may have been the starting-point of Magellan's theory of the existence of a Pacifico-Atlantic passage. "In the yeere 1428 it is written that Don Peter, the King of Portugal's eldest sonne, was a great traueller. He went into England, France, Almaine, and from thence into the Holy Land, and to other places. He came home by Italie, taking Rome and Venice in his way : from whence he brought a map of the world that had all the parts of the world and earth described. The Streight of Magelan was called in it the Dragon's taile." Galvão, par parenthese, mentions another map, which his friend Francisco de Sousa Tavarez, had himself seen, made in 1408, which marked the navigation of the Indies and the Cape of Good Hope. These two are doubtless those alluded to by Ferdinand Denis, and the clear account of them renders them at any rate worthy of mention as a piece of evidence. However, they are, after all, but of slight weight in the scale. Of quite another value are two still extant globes, which demand a careful and detailed consideration.

These globes were constructed by Johann Schöner, Professor of Mathematics in Nuremberg, in the years 1515 and 1520. Both are so alike in their outline of South America, that as far as concerns the question under consideration they may be regarded as one.

A Pacifico-Atlantic passage is in them boldly drawn. It is represented in or about latitude 45° S., and in the earlier, or Frankfort globe a line is traced embracing the coast beyond the strait and enclosing the legend "Terra ult. incognita," thus implying - almost without a shadow of doubt - that this strait had been at that date already visited and recognised as a waterway between the two oceans. South of this an indefinite mass of land is figured, to which the name of "Brasilie regio" or "Brasilia Inferior" is given. Some distance off the eastern mouth of the strait is placed a small group of islands.

What had Schöner in his mind when he gave this strait a place upon his globes ? What were his sources of information ? Was it fact or conjecture that guided his pencil ? These are the questions we have to answer.

Some light is thrown upon them by a work of the cosmographer that was published at the same time as his early globe, and intended to be in great measure illustrative of it. In it he speaks of his "Brasiliae regio" - that the country was not far from the Cape of Good Hope; that the Portuguese had explored it, and had discovered a strait going from east to west; that this strait resembled the strait of Gibraltar; and that "Mallaqua" was not far distant there from.

All this information was, nevertheless, not gathered at first hand by Schöner. Shortly before he wrote, but how long we do not know, for the title page bears no date, was published a certain pamphlet in bad German, anonymously, and was apparently a confused translation of a Portuguese original - the "Copia der Newen Zeytung aus Presillg Landt." From this he apparently took his description almost word for word, and the question thus shifts itself a point further back into the examination of the provenance and authorities of the "Copia."

We do not get very much information from the work itself, but what we do get is very interesting. The captain of the ship, whose voyage it describes, was a "fast güt frewndt" of the writer. The expedition is stated to have been fitted out under the auspices of the Portuguese government by various private gentlemen, among whom was "Christoffel de Haro." It is exceedingly probable then that it was either that of Gonzalo Coelho or of Christovão Jacques, and the probability is in favour of the latter. That it was little known about, and only chronicled en passant by the historians, was no doubt owing to the fact that it was a purely commercial venture, in which the obtaining of a good cargo of Brazil-wood and slaves was of greater importance than cosmography.

Dr. Wieser, although admitting that there is strong reason to believe the "Copia" to be the outcome of the voyage of Christovão Jacques, and consequently allowing the strait depicted on Schöner's globes to have been discovered by that explorer, does not admit that it was the strait of Magellan. He dismisses all possibility of such being the case upon the one argument that the "Copia" speaks of it as being in 40° S.. The Nuremberg globes and this "Zeytung" can no longer, he says, be adduced in proof of the strait having been discovered before the voyage of Magellan.

A careful consideration of the facts will not necessarily lead every one to the same conclusion as that arrived at by Dr. Wieser. The "Zeytung" is no learned geographical disquisition published by some king's pilot or great cosmographer. It is a very sketchy and mediocre work, written by one who was merely a "fast güt frewndt" of the captain. We cannot therefore place too great dependence upon the accuracy of his "viertzig grad hoch." It is easy to see that the exact position of the strait did not interest the author as much as the animals and products of the "Presillg Landt" he describes. Schöner, too, although adopting his text almost word for word, does not accept his latitudes, and the strait is figured in 45° S. Why he should not have placed it yet further to the south it is difficult to say. If we turn to Ruysch's mappamundi, made in 1507, we find, written across the lower part of the "Terra Sancte Crucis," a statement to the effect that the Portuguese ships had at that time penetrated as far south as latitude 50°.

The fact that certain islands are figured in Schöner's globes in the neighbourhood of the strait is of some interest. Whether they are or are not the Falklands it is difficult to say. In the 1520 globe they bear the text "Ins. delle Pulzelle." That Davis, for whom the honour of the discovery of the Falkland Islands is claimed, should have called them the Virgin's Land, if a coincidence, is at least a curious one.

Perhaps the most important fact in connection with the question of Magellan's foreknowledge of his strait, is that of Christopher de Haro having been the chief person concerned in the fitting out and despatch of the ship whose voyage was the cause of the publication of the "Zeytung." We must not forget the friendship existing between him and Magellan, nor that he contributed more than a fifth part of the cost of his armada, nor that the great house of which he was one of the leading members, had probably more sources of information at command than any monarch. Look at the matter how we may, certain broad facts remain :- that both Coelho and Christovão Jacques pushed far south along the shores of South America before Magellan sailed on his great voyage, though how far is unknown; that a pamphlet, likewise indisputably of an anterior date, describes a Pacifico-Atlantic strait at some length; and finally, that Schöner considered the information he was possessed of to be sufficiently trustworthy to figure this strait upon his two globes of 1515 and 1520.

Shortly, then, we have three reasons, or groups of reasons, for supposing that the existence of Magellan's Strait was known prior to the visit of that navigator. Firstly, the passage in Pigafetta deliberately stating that such was the case, and the mention of the fact by various historians; secondly, the use of the phrase "to go in search of the strait" in Charles V's capitulacion of 1518; and lastly, the evidence of various maps and globes and the "Zeytung aus Presillg Landt." Let us now consider the arguments that can be adduced on the other side of the question.

According to Pigafetta, Magellan derived his information from a chart existing in the King's treasury. We are not told when he saw it. Towards the end of his service with Portugal he was out of favour with the King. He was, indeed, never regarded by him with anything but dislike, and it is therefore improbable that he would be the only person permitted to see it. Gomara, too, says that when Magellan passed into the service of Spain, and his intention of visiting the Moluccas became known, Dom Manoel remained content when he learned that he had promised not to take the route by the Cape, "thinking that he could find no other way nor navigation for the Spices other than that which he (the King) had." Dom Manoel would hardly have felt so reassured had he a chart depicting the straits in his possession, and knew that Magellan had consulted it.

The uncertain, slow, and groping route followed by the fleet is also apparently in favour of a want of definite knowledge on the subject. However, it is quite possible that Magellan wished either to assure himself that no more northerly passage had escaped notice, or to make a tolerably complete survey of the coast. Finally, the assertion made by the admiral that he would push on even to latitude 75° S. to find the object of his search shows considerable indefiniteness. We must not forget that the historians are - save Galvão - one and all silent as to its former discovery.

On the whole, then, the balance of evidence is in favour of a more or less inexact knowledge of the existence of some Antarctic break in the vast barrier which America opposed to a western passage. No less indefinite statement can be made with any certainty. It is indeed possible that the wish was father to the thought. The explorers of those days, having tried Central and Northern America in vain, and feeling that the land to the south of the Terra Sancta Crucis alone offered them a chance, eventually persuaded themselves into a belief in the real existence of the object of their desire. There were reasonable arguments in favour of it also. The fact that the southern part of the continent ever trended to the west, that the vast mass of Africa terminated in a cape, appeared of no little import to navigators at the beginning of the sixteenth century. An idée mère does not take long in growing into a conviction. The shortest route to the enchanted East was the problem that filled the mind of every one. So they were ready to push their explorations to the farthest limits, that their ships might float on the waters of the Pacific. No weightier evidence of the all absorbing nature of the work of discovery in those days could be adduced. Whether Magellan had a previous knowledge of his strait or not, we can understand how strong was his determination to do his best to find one.

CHAPTER 12

PASSAGE OF THE STRAIT OF MAGELLAN

The explorers, we have seen, reached the entrance of the Straits on October 21st, 1520. According to Thevet, it was Magellan himself who first described it. It is not improbable that the great desire of his life should lend the leader of the expedition a preternatural keenness of vision, and reward him as it rewarded Columbus. In the narrative of the anonymous Portuguese published by Ramusio, the strait is called after the Victoria, "because the ship Victoria was the first that saw it."

Be that as it may, however, the order was given for the fleet to enter. On their starboard hand they passed a cape, which since it was St. Ursula's day, they called the Cape of the Eleven Thousand Virgins. The pilot Albo took the latitude, and found it to be 52° S. (although Cape Virgins is in latitude 52° 20' S.). The bay within was spacious; and seemed to afford good shelter.

The admiral gave orders that Serrão and Mesquita should continue the reconnaissance in the Concepcion and San Antonio. Meanwhile, the flagship anchored in company with the Victoria to await their return, which was not to be deferred for more than five days. It is probable, assuming Pigafetta's account to be correct, that the vessels anchored in Lomas Bay, upon the south side of the strait. For he distinctly tells us that the mouth of the "First Narrows" remained unknown to them until discovered by the San Antonio and her consort. This could not have been the case had they anchored in Possession Bay, and they could not well have chosen any other spot. Lomas Bay is also the most natural shelter for a ship.

During the night one of the characteristic storms of these regions broke upon them, lasting until noon on the following day. It blew, most probably, from the north-east, for they were forced to weigh anchor and make an offing, standing on and off until the weather moderated. The San Antonio and Concepcion were in equally bad case. Endeavouring to rejoin the others, they found themselves unable to weather the cape that separated them from the anchorage. It was probably the eastern horn of the Great Orange Bank. They were obliged to put about, seeing nothing but certain destruction before them, for the bay, as they thought it, appeared as such - no opening being visible at its head. As they gave themselves up for lost, they rounded Anegada Point, and the entrance of the "First Narrows" revealed itself. Up these they ran, thankful for their escape, and emerged from them to find themselves in the great bay beyond (St. Philip or Boucant Bay - the Lago de los Estrechos of Oviedo). They prosecuted their explorations to the entrance of Broad Reach. They then returned, having rapidly surveyed the neighbouring waters, and assured themselves that the strait led onwards for an immense distance to the south.

Magellan had meanwhile awaited them with more than ordinary anxiety. It was feared that they had been lost in the storm, more especially from the fact that certain "smokes" had been noticed on shore. These they afterwards learnt were caused by fires lit by two men from the missing ships, with the object of revealing their presence. However, at the time they were considered to point rather to the conclusion that a shipwreck had occurred. While the crews of the two vessels were speculating upon the fate of their comrades, the San Antonio and Concepcion suddenly hove in sight, crowding all sail and colourful with flags. As they approached, they discharged their large bombards and shouted for joy, "upon which," says Pigafetta, "we united our shouts to theirs, and thanking God and the Blessed Virgin Mary, resumed our journey."

The accounts given by the two crews were so different that it is probable that the vessels separated during their reconnaissance, and that one pushed on much in advance of the other. They gave it as their opinion that the inlet led onward to the Pacific. Not only had they ascended it for three days without finding any sign of its termination, but the soundings in the channel were of very great depth, and in many cases they could get no bottom. The flood, moreover, appeared stronger than the ebb. It was impossible, they said, that the Strait should not be found to continue.

After penetrating three or four miles within the "First Narrows," the admiral signalled the fleet again to anchor, and despatched a boat ashore to survey the country. Most likely the appearance of habitations had attracted his eye, for Herrera tells us that at the distance of a mile inland the men came upon a building containing more than two hundred native graves. On the coast they found a dead whale of gigantic size, together with a great quantity of the bones of these animals, from which they concluded that the storms of that region were both frequent and severe. Passing the Second Narrows, the squadron entered Broad Reach, and anchored on the 28th October off an island at its head. According to Albo's diary there is every probability that the anchorage at the north of Elizabeth island, subsequently known as Royal Road, was that chosen by Magellan. Cape San Severin of Herrera is either Cape St. Vincent or the headland of Gente Grande Bay.

From the sketchy and confused accounts that have come down to us, it is impossible to reconstruct an exact itinerary of the passage of the Strait, or to present events in any certain chronological order. We are in possession of a few facts that are practically incontestable. We know that the fleet emerged from the straits upon the 28th November; that on 21st November Magellan issued a general order demanding the opinion of his captains and pilots upon the question of continuing the voyage; that the San Antonio deserted, and that she deserted almost without doubt in the beginning of November. Herrera gives an account of a council held by Magellan with regard to the advisability of the prosecution of the voyage in which Estevão Gomes, pilot of the San Antonio, spoke. However, Barros gives Magellan's "Order of the Day" in extenso, which bears the date 21st November. It seems hardly probable that there were two councils upon this subject, or that, if there were, some reference to the fact should not have been made, but it is of course possible. It is also singular that in Magellan's "Order" of 21st November, and Andres de San Martin's reply to it, there should be no allusion to the desertion of the San Antonio.

Order of the day of Magellan, 21st November 1520 : "I Fernan De Magalhaes, Knight of the Order of St. James, and captain-general of this fleet, which his majesty sent for the discovery of the spices, etc. I make known to you, Duarte Barbosa, captain of the ship Victoria, and to the pilots, masters, and quarter-masters of that ship, as I have understood that it seems to you all a serious matter, that I am determined to go forward, because it seems to you that the weather is little fitted for this voyage on which we are going; and in as much as I am a man who never rejected the opinion or counsel of any one, but rather all my affairs are discussed and communicated generally to all, without any person being affronted by me; and since, because of that which happened in the port of S. Julian with respect to the death of Luis de Mendoça, Gaspar de Quexada, and the banishment of Juan de Cartagena and Pero Sanches de Reina, the priest, you, from fear, desist from telling me, and counselling all that may appear to you to be for the service of his majesty, and the safe conduct of this fleet, and you have not told it me nor counselled it : you err in the service of the emperor and king our sovereign, and go against the oath and plighted homage which you have made to me; for which I command you on the part of the said sovereign, and on my part beseech you and charge you, that with respect to all that you think is fitting for our voyage, both as to going forward, and as to turning back, that you give me your opinions in writing each one for himself : declaring the circumstances and reasons why we ought to go forward or turn back, not having respect to anything for which you should omit to tell the truth. With which reasons and opinions, I will say mine, and my decision for coming to a conclusion as to what we have to do. Done in the Channel of All Saints, opposite the river of the islet, on Wednesday, twenty-first of November, in fifty-three degrees, of the year one thousand five hundred and twenty."

Andres de San Martin replied, giving his opinion that, though he doubted there being any opening in the channel by which to go to the Moluccas, yet he thought they should go forward till the middle of January, as long as the summer and long days lasted.

Magellan received this and the other opinions, which he had asked for only to please and content his people. He gave a full answer, with long reasons for going forward. He swore by the habit of St. James, which he wore, that so it seemed to him to be for the good of the fleet. This opinion was notified to the fleet, and next day he set sail.

With regard to the chronology of minor events we have to confine ourselves to probabilities. According to Herrera, Magellan took the opinion of his officers at an early period of his passage through the straits. All with one exception were for pushing on. They had provisions for three months still remaining. Fired by the spirit of their chief, it seemed to them a disgrace to return to Spain at this juncture. What had they to show for all the bitter months of hardship through which they had pawed ? Where were the riches of which they were in search, the islands over which they, had been granted seignorial rights ? So utterly unknown was the Pacific, so vague the ideas at that time prevalent as to the actual size of the globe they were then circumnavigating for the first time, that there seemed to them no impossibility in the idea that the Spice Islands were already almost within their reach. It was folly at least not to carry on their explorations a little farther now that the summer was before them.

The only voice raised in opposition was that of Estevão Gomes, pilot of the San Antonio. Although a countryman of the admiral, and indeed a kinsman also, he had been for some time upon bad terms with his relative. Pigafetta tells us the hatred he bore him arose from the fact that the despatch of Magellan's expedition did away with hopes he had formed of himself leading a voyage of exploration. Whatever ill-will may have pre-existed was probably increased by the command of the San Antonio having been conferred upon Alvaro de Mesquita instead of himself, the king's pilot. The slight was none the less galling from the fact that his rival was a mere supernumerary borne upon the books of the Trinidad, and probably owed his fortune rather to his near relationship to the admiral than to any skill as a navigator or seaman.

The arguments brought forward by Gomes were plausible enough. Now that they had apparently found the strait, he said it would be better to go back to Spain and return with another armada. For the way that lay before them was no small matter, and, if they encountered any lengthened period either of calms or storms, it was probable that all would perish. Magellan replied as those who knew him probably expected him to reply, albeit unmoved in manner "con semblante muy compuesto" - "that if they had to eat the leather on the ships' yards he would still go on, and discover what he had promised to the Emperor, and that he trusted that God would aid them and give them good fortune." However, the opposition of Gomes, whose skill as a pilot was beyond question, must have rendered his position a difficult one. Foreseeing the possibilities of further grumbling, if not mutiny, he issued an order that no one, under pain of death, should discuss the difficulties of the task that lay before them, or the scarcity of provisions with which they were threatened. It is doubtful how far this would have availed had his crews known what misery was in store for them. For the admiral's words came literally true; and, broken down with scurvy, and privation in their long passage across the Pacific, the men did eat the leather on the yards, and the ships still pressed onward for the Moluccas.

Next day the fleet made sail on a S.S.E. course down Broad Reach, approaching a point on their port hand, which was some point between Gente Grande and Useless Bays, possibly Cape Monmouth. Beyond they came to three channels, of which, according to Herrera, intelligence had been already brought by the Concepcion and San Antonio - which two ships had been despatched on a second reconnaissance from Elizabeth Island. Of these three fjords, "one led in the direction of the Scirocco (S.E.), one to the Libeccio (S.W.) and the third towards the Moluccas," (Admiralty and Magdalen Sounds, and Froward Reach of the main channel). The fleet anchored at some place in the neighbourhood of their mouths, and Magellan ordered the two pilot ships to explore the south-eastern arm. Meanwhile, in company with the Victoria, the flagship followed up the main channel, having left instructions for the future course to be pursued by Mesquita and Serrão.

Rounding Cape Froward, the admiral continued onward for fifteen leagues, when he anchored in a river to which he gave the name of the River of Sardines, from the abundance of those fish they obtained there. The ships watered and cut wood, which they found so fragrant in burning, that "it afforded them much consolation." Shortly after their arrival in this port they sent on a boat well manned and provisioned to explore the channel further. In three days it returned with the joyful intelligence that they had sighted the cape that terminated the strait, and had seen the open sea beyond. So delighted were the explorers with this happy termination to their anxieties, that salvoes of artillery were discharged, and Magellan and those with him wept for joy.

Four days or more (six according to Herrera) had now elapsed, without sign of the two other vessels. The admiral accordingly decided to leave the River of Sardines and retrace his steps in search of them. It is difficult to identify the River of Sardines with any degree of accuracy. From Pigafetta's evidence it would be such a distance from the exit of the straits that the boat journey there and back would take three days. It would not be necessary to proceed beyond Tamar Island to sight Cape Deseado and the open sea. It is possible to reach Tamar Island from any point in the neighbourhood of Carlos III Island and return within the time given. Herrera tells us that after leaving the San Antonio at Cape Valentyn, the admiral, went forward for one day, and then anchored in a river that is evidently the River of Sardines.

Albo says that after rounding Cape Froward they went on about fifteen leagues and anchored. His journal renders it probable that it lay east of the entrance to Otway Water. A passage farther on in Pigafetta tells us that the River of Sardines was close to the River of Isles. That the latter had an island opposite to it, upon which Magellan planted a cross as a signal. This island must almost certainly have been one of the Charles Islands, which are full in the fairway of the channel, and admirably suited for the construction of a cairn or signal to attract the notice of any passing ship. Port Gallant and Port San Miguel, therefore, most probably correspond to the River of Sardines and the River of Isles. In the Anuario Hidrographico de Chile, Andrews Bay is suggested as the River of Sardines.

On their way they had leisure to examine the striking scenery by which they were surrounded. On entering the straits, they had found the country desolate and poor, more or less devoid of vegetation, and consisting of nearly level plains. Here they were, as Herrera tells us, "in the most beautiful country in the world - the strait a gunshot across," separating high sierras covered with perpetual snow, whose lower slopes were clothed with magnificent trees. The extraordinary suddenness of the change in the scenery of the straits is dwelt upon by Darwin in his Voyage of the Beagle. The distance between Port Famine and Cape Gregory in the "Second Narrows" is about sixty miles. "At the former place we have rounded mountains concealed by impervious forests, which are drenched with the rain brought by an endless succession of gales; while at Cape Gregory there is a clear and bright blue sky over the dry and sterile plains." It was not long before they met with Serrão's ship, the Concepcion, but she was alone. Magellan, suspecting perhaps that some accident had happened to the San Antonio, at once hailed and demanded news of her. Serrão had none to give. She had outsailed them almost from the moment of their departure from Cape Valentyn, and they had not seen her since.

Upon receiving the news, Magellan at once instituted a search. Admiralty Sound, for the exploration of which the San Antonio had been detailed, was examined to its inmost recesses without result. The Victoria was then despatched northwards with the idea that the missing ship, having misunderstood orders, might return upon her track under the belief that she would meet her consorts at Elizabeth Island. However, Broad Reach was found to be deserted, and though the Victoria sailed back to the very entrance of the straits, no trace of the vessel was to be seen.

It was scarcely possible that any misunderstanding could have occurred. In the "Instruccion" given by the Emperor to Magellan and Faleiro on the 8th May 1519, the fullest rules were laid down with regard to the course to be pursued upon the accidental separation of a ship from the squadron. One of two things had happened - the San Antonio had either been lost, and lost with all hands, for otherwise their search must have revealed some traces of her, or she had deserted. The men of the Victoria, having placed ensigns in two conspicuous positions with letters of instruction buried at their feet, returned to the admiral with the news. He was awaiting them with the other ship in the River of Isles, in close proximity to his former anchorage, the River of Sardines.

The intelligence was a great blow to Magellan, the greater because it occurred at the very moment of his success, and at a time when every ounce of food was of importance in the further prosecution of his journey. The San Antonio was the largest vessel of the armada, and carried a proportionately large quantity of stores. Unwilling to realise it, he was anxious to delay some time longer, in the hope that some unforeseen circumstance might have happened, and that at any moment the missing ship might return. However, reflection convinced him of the uselessness of so doing, and he resolved to continue his journey. Barros tells us that, wishing to know what had occurred, Magellan requested the astrologer, Andres de San Martin, to cast the horoscope. He was informed that the ship had returned to Spain, and that her captain was a prisoner. Correa also has this story.

There were now but three vessels of the fleet remaining - the capitana or flagship, the Victoria, and the Concepcion. The desertion of the San Antonio had doubtless caused a new fear in the heart of the leader of the expedition - the fear that her example might be not without its effect, and that even now that he held success in his grasp, it might at any moment be wrested from him. He was no man of inactivity, masterly or otherwise. His custom was ever to meet his dangers and difficulties halfway, and disarm them. And so, rather than permit the thoughts of officers and men to dwell upon the weakened condition of the fleet, and the still more serious loss of provisions, without discussion, he sent an order to each ship that the various authorities should express their opinion upon the advisability of continuing the voyage.

This order, to which allusion has been already made, came into the hands of the historian Barros among various papers of Andres de San Martin. It was promulgated on the 21st November in the River of Isles. The astrologer's reply was subjoined, and is the only one remaining to us. He was of opinion that they should go forward, "so long as they had the full bloom of summer with them," and continue their discoveries until mid-January, albeit he did not consider that the straits offered a proper route to the Moluccas. He strongly counselled that the ships should always anchor at night, not only for security's sake, but in order that the crew, toil-worn and weak as they were, should obtain sufficient rest. It is almost incredible that the ships - and sailing ships, it must be remembered - should have attempted such difficult navigation in unknown waters by night. Yet from this we can only conclude that such was the case.

Whether the suggestion was adopted or not, Barros does not inform us, but he gives us the general tenor of Magellan's reply, which was of the usual character. The admiral, it is suggested, only requested the opinions of his officers as a mere matter of courtesy, his intention being to turn back for no one. He gave many reasons for pushing on, adding that God, who had brought them thus far to the discovery of their long-looked-for strait, would in due and fitting time bring them to the ultimate realisation of their desires. Next day, having given a general notification of his opinion, he weighed anchor amid salvoes of artillery, and made his way towards the Pacific. From passages in the diary of Albo and the so-called Genoese pilot, Magellan is supposed to have passed on the south side of Carlos III Island but there are not sufficient grounds for this supposition. Presuming the fleet to have sailed from Port San Miguel, it is unlikely that they would have crossed the straits to navigate a much less evident passage. Had they passed on the north side, it is argued, they would have been led off the track in to Otway Water. However, the entrance to Otway Water is so obviously not the main channel, that it would never have led them to an exploration of its recesses. Moreover, they knew the way from the crew of the boat who had already sighted the Pacific.

The constant fires seen upon the southern side of the straits had led Magellan to give to the land the name that it bears to this day, the "Tierra del Fuego." It remained for Schouten and Le Maire, nearly a hundred years later, to prove the truth of his surmise concerning it - that it was no continent, but merely an island or group of islands. "To the left," says the letter of Maximilian, "they thought the land to consist of islands, for on that side they sometimes heard the beating and roaring of the sea, as though upon some farther shore." They must have been nearing the exit.

They passed Cape Deseado - "the longed-for cape," as they termed it - on the evening of the 28th November 1520, (according to Albo and Pigafetta, the 27th according to the anonymous Portuguese, and the 26th according to the Genoese pilot). The little armada then sailed out upon the hitherto unknown waters of the South Pacific. The account given by Herrera of the passage of the straits differs in certain particulars from that here given. The concurring statements of Pigafetta and either of the two pilots have, however, been taken as preferable whenever such concurrence exists. Elsewhere, what is evidently supplemental in Herrera's narrative has been introduced with as strict a regard for chronology as rare occurring dates render possible.

Before we leave the strait we must pause for a moment to glance at its nomenclature. Magellan, it has been often said, conferred upon it his own name, but that this was the case we do not learn from any contemporary narrative. Pigafetta figures it as the "Streto Patagonico". According to the diary of the anonymous Portuguese, it was called "Victoria Strait", since that ship first sighted it, "though some called it the· Strait of Magalhães, since our captain was named Fernão de Magalhães." On the arrival of the vessels at the narrow channel beyond Clarence Land the name of Todos os Santos, or Todolos Sanctos, was conferred upon it - it being All Saints' Day, the 1st November. In 1580, Sarmiento re-christened it the Strait of the Mother of God. However, as may be imagined, the name of its discoverer was too closely associated with it to be put aside, and it has remained, and perhaps will always remain, the Strait of Magellan.

We must turn now to the San Antonio, whose base desertion had thrown still further difficulties in the path of the explorers. It appears that, from the moment of separating at Cape Valentyn, the pilot Gomes had determined to put into execution his project of returning to Spain. On the third day, having proved Admiralty Channel to be merely an inlet, the vessel turned northward once more. They did not sight Serrão's ship, the Concepcion, which was probably already bound westward up the straits. One author, indeed, tells us that the San Antonio slipped past the entrance of the inlet at night, with the express purpose of avoiding her. Whatever may have been the case, when the time came to shape their course for the rendezvous prescribed by the flagship, Estevão Gomes and Geronimo Guerra, who was a relation of Cristobal de Hare, and had been brought up by him, and who had been made tesorero of the ship by Magellan himself, resisted Mesquita's authority, and proposed an immediate return to Spain. What followed is not clear. The mutineers, who had laid their plans well, and won over a large proportion of the crew to their side, declared on their arrival in Seville that the captain stabbed Gomes, and that he in turn retaliated by stabbing the captain. The last at least was true. Mesquita was seized and placed in irons and, according to Oviedo, put to the torture in order that they might obtain from him a statement to exculpate the mutineers. The date of this occurrence is given in Recalde's letter as the 8th October - a manifest error, as the fleet did not enter the straits until the 21st October. The incident must have occurred fully a month later.

Geronimo Guerra was made captain, and with Gomes as pilot the ship made sail to clear the straits as quickly as possible. It was proposed at first to return to Port St. Julian, in order to pick up their two comrades, Cartagena and the priest, who, it will be remembered, had been left there as a punishment for their share in the mutiny. However, whether it was thought better to proceed at once to Spain, or whether a visit was actually paid to the spot without finding their companions, the fact remains that the San Antonio never brought them back to their native land. Argensola says distinctly that these men did return in the San Antonio. However, had they done so, we should have had some mention of the fact in the official letter of Recalde to the Bishop of Burgos. Moreover, the result of this letter, as we learn from Herrera was an order from the Casa de Contratacion to send a ship to rescue them. We hear nothing further of this rescue. It is more than probable that the ship was never despatched, and that the two mutineers expiated their sins with their lives. The San Antonio shaped her course for the coast of Guinea, where they took water and provisions, the former having already failed from the protracted length of the voyage. From this or other causes the Patagonian they were bringing home fell sick and died. On Wednesday, 6th May 1521, the vessel arrived at the port of Seville.

Gomes and his comrades had, of course, a well concocted story to hide their treachery. They complained that the flagship had failed at the rendezvous, and having searched for her in vain they had no alternative but to return to Spain. However, they did not confine themselves to excuses. The gravest accusations were brought against Magellan - that he was guilty of great harshness and cruelty, that he sailed at random, and that he lost time and wasted the provisions by endless delays, and that all this was to no good end or profit whatsoever. Magellan, unable to make a defence, was held for a culprit. Mesquita whose loyalty had procured him some stabs from a poignard, the rack, and six months in irons - was thrown into prison as his accomplice. It was in vain that Magellan's father-in-law, Diogo Barbosa, came to his aid, for he remained there until the return of the Victoria. The result of the inquiry instituted by the India House, however, was such that Gomes and Guerra, together with two others more especially implicated in the mutiny, were also incarcerated. Beatriz, Magellan's wife, though not actually placed under lock and key, was strictly watched, "in order that she should not escape to Portugal until the facts of the case are better understood."

It is from the letter of the Contador Lopez de Recalde, already alluded to, that we gather most of the details of the San Antonio incident. Two years later, in a memorial presented to Charles V, Diogo Barbosa alludes to the treatment allotted to the various persons concerned in it with a blunt frankness that is unusual even for those days. He complains that the mutineers "were very well received and treated at the expense of Your Highness, while the captain and others who were desirous of serving Your Highness were imprisoned and deprived of all justice." "It is from this," he adds, "that so many bad examples arise - heartbreaking to those who try to do their duty." It must be allowed that his remarks, if not those of a courtier, have at least the merit of being true, and that had Spain treated better those who were at that time only too ready to shed their blood in her service, it would have been not without material effect upon the history of her colonies.

Passage of the Magellan Strait

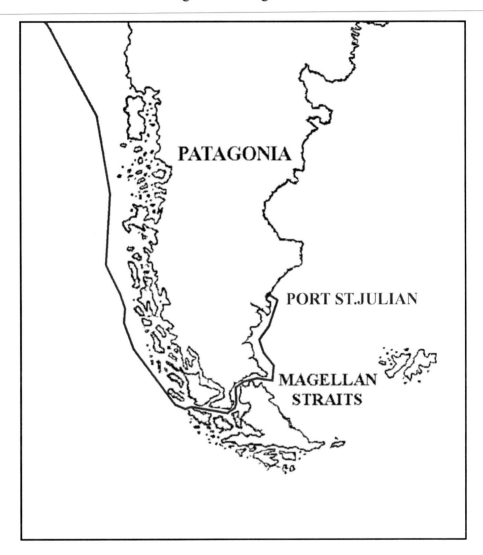

CHAPTER 13

VOYAGE ACROSS THE PACIFIC

The three remaining ships of the squadron, the Trinidad, Concepcion and Victoria, passing Cape Deseado, directed their course to less inhospitable shores and a warmer climate. Their passage of the strait had cost them thirty-eight days. Herrera, Oviedo and Maximilian give the period as twenty-two days. This may possibly mean the actual time occupied in sailing, or perhaps the number of days passed in traversing the narrow part to which the name "Canal do Todos Santos" was more particularly applied. Although its length was in reality not more than 320 miles, the many incidents that had arisen and the protracted time that they had spent within its limits led them to exaggerate its size. The distance from mouth to mouth was variously estimated at from 350 to 400 miles.

On reaching the Pacific, the other Patagonian captured in Port St. Julian died. He had been kept on board the flagship, and had apparently reconciled himself in part to his position. To Pigafetta he had become an object of curiosity and interest. "I conversed by signs or as best I could with the Patagonian giant we had on board, making him tell me the names of things in his language, whence I was able to form a vocabulary. When he saw me take the pen in my hand he used to tell me the names of the objects around us, or of some action he might imitate.....When he felt himself gravely ill of the malady from which he afterwards died, he embraced the Cross and kissed it, and desired to become a Christian. We baptized him, and gave him the name of Paul."

Faring northward to escape the cold, the explorers encountered such favourable weather that the difficulties and privations they had passed through were well-nigh forgotten. The sudden, violent tempests had given place to steady winds that wafted them on their course over the surface of a placid sea. Thankful for their deliverance from their troubles they gave the name of the Pacific to the vast ocean that had afforded them so friendly a reception. "Well was it named the Pacific" Pigafetta writes, "for during this time (three months and twenty days) we met with no storm." At first their course led them along the wild seaboard of western Patagonia. On the 1st December they were some fifty or sixty miles distant from the coast in latitude 48° S., and from that time to the 16th followed a direction that kept them within measurable distance of the land.

From South America across the Pacific

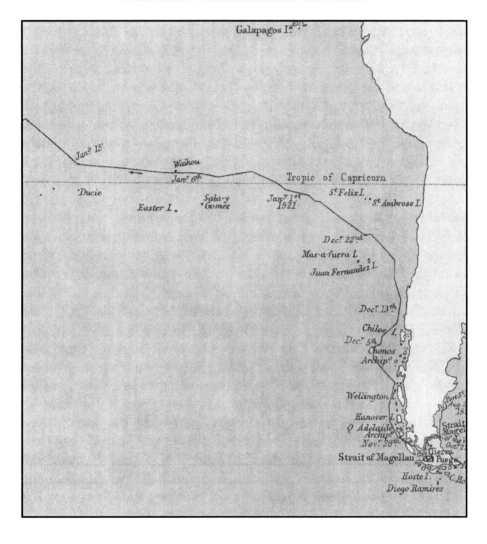

The abundance of fish astonished the sailors. Pigafetta describes the albacores and bonitos, "which pursue other fish called colondrini (swallows). On being followed, these spring from the water and fly about a bowshot - so long as their wings are wet - and then regain the sea. Meanwhile, their enemies follow their shadow, and arriving at the spot where they fall, seize upon them and devour them - a thing marvellous and agreeable to see."

On the 16th December the general direction of the course of the armada was altered for the first time. Magellan, thinking he had pushed sufficiently far northward, bore away upon a more or less north-westerly track for the lands and islands of which he was in search. Day after day passed, but no land was met with to break the monotony of the apparently endless waste of waters that surrounded them. On the 24th January 1521, after nearly two months' sailing, an islet covered with trees was sighted. On approaching, it was discovered to be uninhabited, and, as they could find no bottom with the lead, the course was once more resumed. Its latitude was fixed by the pilot Albo at 16° 15' S., and the name of St. Paul's Island was given to it.

Eleven more days of sailing upon a course varying from N.W. to W.N.W., brought them again in sight of land. Antonio de Brito, in his resume of the voyage sent to the King of Portugal, mentions this island as being 200 leagues from St. Paul's. According to the anonymous Portuguese, the distance separating the two is 800 miles. Small and uninhabited like the first, it afforded them neither water nor fruit. "We found only birds and trees," says Pigafetta, "but we saw there many of the fish called Tiburoni." The island was accordingly called the Isla de los Tiburones, or Shark Island, and "since we found there neither people, nor consolation, nor sustenance of any kind, the name of Desaventuradas - the Unfortunate Islands - was given. to this and St. Paul's Island." Maximilian and Herrera record that the fleet delayed here two days, but we know from Albo's diary that this could not have been the case. Meinicke identifies San Pablo, or St. Paul's Island, with Puka-puka in the Tuamotu Archipelago (latitude 14° 45' S., longitude 138° 48' W.), and Shark Island, or the Tiburones, with Flint Island in the Manihiki group (latitude 11° 20' S., longitude 151° 48' W.).

Across the Central Pacific

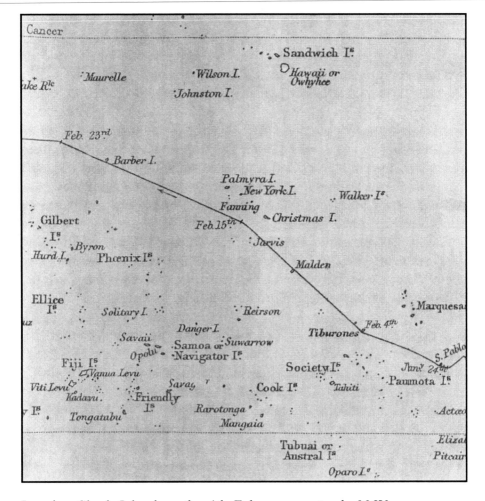

Leaving Shark Island on the 4th February, a steady N.W. course was held. The disappointment felt at not being able to obtain provisions was great, for the condition of the majority of those in the fleet was now most pitiable. The rations were reduced to the smallest limits. "Such a dearth of bread and water was there," writes Gomara, "that they ate by ounces, and held their noses as they drank the water for the stench of it." The Italian historian gives a still more vivid account of their sufferings. "We ate biscuit, but in truth it was biscuit no longer, but a powder full of worms, for the worms had devoured its whole substance, and in addition it was stinking with the urine of rats. So great was the want of food that we were forced to eat the hides with which the main yard was covered to prevent the chafing against the rigging. These hides, exposed to the sun and rain and wind, had become so hard, that we were obliged first to soften them by putting them overboard for four or five days, after which we put them on the embers and ate them thus. We had also to make use of sawdust for food, and rats became such a delicacy that we paid half a ducat apiece for them."

The result of such privations may be easily imagined. Scurvy broke out, and broke out in its worst form. The sufferings of the invalids were aggravated by the lack of any reserve of suitable food for them, and many died. According to Herrera twenty men perished. However, consultation of the official "List of deaths" reveals the fact that only seven were recorded between the departure from the straits and the arrival of the fleet at the Mariana Islands. Others suffered greatly from pains in the arms and legs. Few were altogether well, but Pigafetta was one of them. "I ought to thank God," he says, "for not having had the slightest illness during the whole of the period."

Day after day the ships sailed onward until they reached the Line. Aware from the accounts of his friend Francisco Serrão that the Moluccas did not offer such opportunities for victualling and refitting as he now desired, Magellan thought it best to shape his course further to the north, in the hope, perhaps, of attaining some part of China, with whose wealth and extent he was well acquainted from the accounts of the Chinese traders with whom he had mixed at Malacca. As they progressed upon their voyage, great attention was paid to the navigation. Exact means of estimating their position, it is true, they were without. They were capable of calculating their latitude with tolerable accuracy, although their errors in the estimation of longitude were astounding. So inaccurate were their methods that Albo, on arriving at the Philippines, was no less than fifty-two degrees and fifty-five minutes in error. We know from Pigafetta that the log was in use in those days, as well as the existence both of deviation and variation of the compass. He writes that "According to the measure we made of the voyage by means of the chain at the poop, we ran sixty or seventy leagues a day." Magellan, having ordered a certain course, inquired of the pilots how they had laid it off on the charts. They replied, "as he had ordered it." Upon which he said that "they had laid it off wrong, and that they must apply corrections for the error of the compass, which in this part of the world was not attracted with such force as it is in its own quarter - that is, the northern hemisphere." Columbus upon his first voyage also noted the phenomenon, and endeavoured to explain it.

With its load of human suffering and anxiety, the armada pressed on for yet another month with a steady and favourable wind. Their position resembled that of Columbus before sighting the new world, as day after day their despairing glances were bent westward in hopes of land. Then came their reward, and an end, or at all events a temporary end, of all their miseries. On the 6th March land was sighted. A number of praus came out to meet them, and all anxiety as to the existence of a population was at once set at rest. For ninety-eight days they had sailed over an utterly unknown sea, "a sea so vast that the human mind can scarcely grasp it," Maximilian writes in his letter.

The group of islands thus discovered by the fleet subsequently became known as the Mariana Islands (also the Marianas), which up until the early 20th century were sometimes called Islas de los Ladrones (the Ladrones). It is not absolutely certain which island or islands Magellan first sighted and visited, but there is not much doubt about the matter. Maximilian is the only author of any authority who gives individual names to these islands. Oviedo and Gomara copy from him. He calls them Inuagana and Acaca. The former is probably Agana in Guam, and Acaca or Açaça may perhaps be Sosan in Rota Island. In all probability the high peak of Rota was the first land to show itself above the horizon. Steering for this, Guam must have come into view on their port bow, and discovering it to be the larger of the two, Magellan altered course to S. W., in order to approach its shores.

Their visit to the islands was a short one. "The inhabitants were a people of little truth," as the Genoese pilot describes them. Hardly had the ships come to an anchor when the natives stole the skiff from under the stern of the admiral's ship, cutting the rope by which she was made fast, and carrying her off with great speed and adroitness. They boarded the vessels and robbed the newcomers of everything that they could lay hands on. It was impossible to keep them off. Before long the order had to be given to eject them from the ships. They found themselves involved in a mêlée, which, according to Herrera, became so serious that the Spaniards had to use their artillery, killing numbers of the natives. Magellan, much annoyed at the loss of his skiff, weighed anchor and stood on and off during the night lest he should be surprised. In the morning he returned, and landing in person with a force of fifty or sixty men, burnt the village and a number of boats, regained the skiff, and took a quantity of provisions. The natives, who seemed at one time disposed to offer a stout resistance, fled at the first discharge of the arquebuses. No casualties occurred on the side of the Spaniards, but the islanders lost seven or eight men killed. They appear, from Pigafetta's account, to have been quite unacquainted with the use of bows and arrows, for when wounded by one of the latter they would draw it out of their bodies and look at it with great surprise, an incident which aroused the compassion of their antagonists. Their only arms were spears tipped with fish-bone.

Their praus - stem and stern alike, and fitted with an outrigger - struck with astonishment those who saw this species of boat for the first time. Their speed especially filled them with wonder. As the vessels left the port they were pursued by these craft. So dexterously were they handled that they passed between the ships going at full sail and the boats they towed astern. "They did this so quickly and skilfully," says Pigafetta, "that it was a marvel." It seems still more curious that, considering the relations existing between their visitors and themselves, the people should be quite willing to engage in barter, and that immediately after Magellan had burnt their village, boats should put off laden with provisions for that purpose. Possibly their love of gain overcame every other consideration. "They are poor, but ingenious, and, above all, thieves," says Ramusio, "and for that reason we called these islands the Robber Islands." We learn from the diary of the Genoese pilot that Magellan gave them the name of Islas de las Velas Latinas, or the Lateen-sail Islands, from the number of craft thus rigged with which they abounded.

Reaching the Philippines

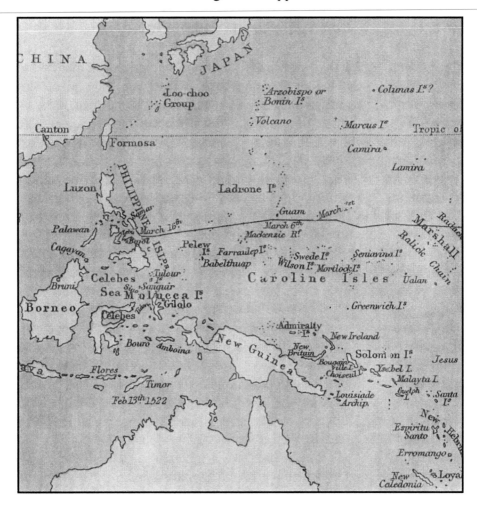

Greatly improved in health from the fresh fruit and vegetables they had procured, the explorers left the Marianas on the morning of the 9th March. On this day the sole Englishman in the fleet - "Master Andrew of Bristol" - died, the succour having come too late to save his life. The course was set W. ¼S., and held for seven days.

CHAPTER 14

ARRIVAL IN THE PHILIPPINES

On the 16th March they saw land - the southern point of Samar Island of the Philippines. Finding the coast beset with shoals, they bore away to the southward and fell in with the conspicuous island then, as now, known by the name of Suluan. From thence they reached the neighbouring island of Malhou, and anchored for the night. It appeared to be uninhabited. Next day, being anxious to rest his sick, Magellan ordered tents to be set up on shore and a pig to be killed for them - which animal, no doubt, was obtained during their stay at the Marianas. The sight of the fleet attracted the notice of a passing prau, and on Monday, March 18th, the Europeans made acquaintance for the first time with the inhabitants of the Philippine Islands. They were of a very different nature to those of the Marianas. The boat contained some notables from the little island of Suluan, who welcomed the newcomers without fear. Magellan ordered some caps, looking glasses, bells, and other trifles to be given to them, and in return was presented with fish and palm-wine. Pigafetta's "figs a foot long, and two cocchi," which he also mentions among the gifts, we have little difficulty in recognising as bananas and coconuts. Friendship with the natives was still further cemented by their visiting the ships. The hopes of the Spaniards were roused by being shown various spices, which must have enabled them for the first time to realise the proximity of the Moluccas.

To the archipelago thus discovered the Captain general gave the name of St. Lazarus, for he had first sighted the group upon the day sacred to that saint. It was not till long after, that the later appellation of the Islas Philippinas was conferred upon them in 1542 after Philip II, the son of Charles V. Meanwhile, curiously enough, they became known to the Portuguese as the Eastern Islands while the Spaniards called them the Islas del Poniente, for, as we have seen, the latter power sailed westward round the world, and the Lusitanians eastward. This circumstance was the cause of yet another oddity. To the first circumnavigators the necessity of altering their day on passing the meridian of 180° was unknown, and so the error persisted until later centuries of Hong Kong and Manila calling the same day Monday and

Sunday. It was not until the 31st December 1844, that the matter was ~~rectified by the omission of that day from the Manilan calendar.~~

The natives returned to the fleet on the 22nd March as they had promised. They brought an abundance of fruit, coconuts, oranges and bananas, and a cock, "to give us to understand that they possessed fowls in their country." It is probable that this bird was the jungle-fowl (Gallus bankiva), which was caught and tamed in large numbers by the natives of the Philippines, and was subsequently used for crossing with the domestic fowl. Their chief, who accompanied them, had gold rings in his ears, and bracelets of the same metal, worn by most of them, attracted the covetous eyes of the Spaniards. With the free supply of vegetable diet the sick improved rapidly. Each day the admiral went ashore to visit them, and every morning gave them coconut milk to drink with his own hands. The personal visits of their leader no doubt contributed not a little to their recovery. After a rest of nine days it was considered that the voyage might be safely resumed, and the order to weigh anchor was accordingly given on the evening of Monday, 25th March.

While it was being carried out, an accident happened to Pigafetta that came near to bringing the chevalier and his diary to an abrupt conclusion." I was going," he says, "upon the bulwarks to fish, when I put my foot upon a spar wet with rain, and slipping, fell overboard without being perceived by any one. When half drowned, it chanced that my hand touched the sheet of the mainsail, which was in the water, and to this I clung and began to shout out until they heard me and came to my aid with the boat, the which help," he reverently adds, "was not due to any merits of my own, but to the protection of that fount of pity, the Virgin Mary." It was the day of the Annunciation of the Blessed Virgin Mary.

Leaving Malhou, the fleet struck across to the eastern shores of Leyte, or Seilani, as it was then called, and coasting them arrived on the morning of March 28th at Mazzava or Mazaba, a small island that subsequently appeared on the charts as Limassaua. Here for the first time they exchanged sign language for a more satisfactory means of communication, for Magellan's slave, Enrique of Malacca, found that his Malay was understood. The natives were nevertheless so shy that they would not approach the ship, and the presents that Magellan desired to give them had to be put upon a plank and floated towards them. Two hours afterwards the king came in a large canoe and had a long conversation with the interpreter. Although declining to go on board the Trinidad, he permitted some of his men to do so. They received good entertainment at the admiral's hands. In return the king was desirous of presenting him with a large bar of gold, but Magellan refused, although at the same time thanking him much for his offer.

The next day, which was Good Friday, Enrique was sent on shore to obtain provisions. He returned with the king, who brought dishes of fish and rice to Magellan with his own hand. Magellan gave him a Turkish robe of red and yellow and a red cap, and the ceremony of accepting each other upon terms of brotherhood, or casi-casi, was gone through. Pigafetta does not give us more details. The ceremony was probably that of "blood brotherhood," consisting in each of the parties tasting the blood of the other, a widespread custom in the Malay Archipelago. The day was spent in making a prodigal display of the wonders of western civilisation; exhibiting the objects of trade, discharging the artillery, showing the charts and compasses, and describing the events of the voyage. At the admiral's account of the immense size of the Pacific the king was greatly astonished. Equal astonishment was caused by the men in suits of complete armour, who received the cuts and thrusts of their comrades unharmed. At the end of these performances Magellan asked if two of his officers might go ashore with the king to see the things of his country. Permission was given, and the Chevalier Anthony Pigafetta was chosen to be one of them. He has left us a very clear and detailed account of their experiences.

"When we landed," he says, "the king raised his hands to heaven, and then turned towards us. We did the same, and so, indeed, did all the others. The king then took me by the hand, while one of his chiefs took my comrade's, and we were led in this manner under a canopy of canes where there was a balangai or canoe, like a galley, on the poop of which we sat, conversing by signs, for we had no interpreter. The king's followers remained standing, armed with swords, daggers, spears, and shields. A dish of pork with a large vessel full of wine was brought, and at each mouthful we drank a cup of wine. If, as rarely happened, any was left in our cups, it was put into another vessel. The king's cup remained always covered, and no one drank from it but he and I. Before drinking he raised his hands to heaven, and then turned to us, and at the moment that he took the cup in his right hand he extended towards me the closed fist of his left, so that at first I thought he was about to strike me. Thus he drank, while I went through the same gestures towards him, seeing that every one did the same towards his companion when drinking. With these ceremonies or signs of friendship we took our dinner, and I was unable to avoid eating meat on Good Friday.

Before the hour of supper I presented to the king the many presents I had brought with me. I enquired the names of numerous objects, and wrote them down. They were struck with astonishment on seeing me write, and on hearing me repeat, in reading, the names they had given me. Then came supper time. They brought two large china dishes, the one filled with rice, the other with pork in its gravy. We ate our supper with the same ceremonies and gestures as before. We then repaired to the palace of the king, in shape like a sort of hay-loft or rick, covered with banana leaves, and supported on four large beams which raised it from the ground, so that we had to ascend to it by means of ladders. On our arrival the king made us sit upon a cane mat with our legs crossed like tailors on a bench, and after half an hour a dish of fish was brought, cut in pieces and roasted, another of freshly-gathered ginger, and some wine. The king's eldest son having entered, he was made to sit next me, and two more dishes were then brought, one of fish with its sauce and the other of rice, to eat with the prince. My companion, having eaten and drunk too much, became intoxicated.

For candles they used the gum of a certain tree called anime, wrapped up in leaves of the palm or banana. The king now made a sign to us that he desired to retire to rest, and departed, leaving the prince with us, in whose company we slept on cane mats with cushions stuffed with leaves.

Next morning the king came to seek me, and taking me by the hand led me to the place where we had supped to have breakfast; but the boat which had been sent to take us off having found us, we took our departure at once. The king was in the best of humours, and kissed our hands on parting, while we kissed his. There came with us a brother of his, the king of another country, accompanied by three other men. Magellan kept them to dinner with him, and made them presents of various objects."

The petty king last mentioned, Pigafetta learnt, ruled over the district of Caraca in Mindanao, his jurisdiction extending to the island of Suluan, the land first sighted by the fleet. He was known as the Rajah Calambu, and his brother as the Rajah Siani. Gomara calls the Rajah Calambu, the Rajah Calavar, and says that they made friends with him". He is described by the chevalier as having a silk cloth on his head, a dagger with a long handle that was all of gold, and chewing of betel.

The following Sunday, the 31st March, was Easter day. It was the anniversary, too, of the mutiny in Port St. Julian. If Magellan reflected, as he doubtless did, upon the events of that day, it must have been to thank God and his patron saint for the changed aspect of affairs. Then the outlook for him was well-nigh as dark and hopeless as it could be, and he was about to stake his all upon one desperate chance. Now, though disease and desertion had thinned his ranks, he had practically won the game. His great aim had been accomplished, and he had found his straits. The barrier believed to extend from pole to pole to separate the Atlantic from the Pacific had been proved not to exist. He had left behind him the perils of that vast ocean that his ships had been the first to penetrate, and had crossed the meridian of the Spice Islands. He had discovered an unknown and extensive archipelago, as rich in gold, apparently, as it was fertile, and had made friends with some of its kings. Everything pointed to a happy issue of the voyage and a continuation of the successes that he had so deservedly won. No shadow had as yet crossed his path; no warning of the blow that was so soon to fall.

Good Christian and devout Catholic as he was, therefore, Magellan gave orders that the Easter services should be celebrated with the utmost ceremonial. The two kings attended, kissing the cross, and

kneeling with joined hands like their visitors. At the elevation all the
ships fired their broadsides. After mass had been said, a cross and
crown of thorns was brought and presented to the kings, with
instructions that it should be set up on the summit of the highest
mountain in the neighbourhood, that all might see and adore it. This
they expressed themselves most willing to receive. Magellan then
asked if they were at war with any one, for if such were the case, he
would go and defeat their enemies with his men and ships, and render
them obedient to their authority. "The king answered that there were,
indeed, two islands with which he was at war, but that it was not then a
fitting season to proceed against them, albeit they thanked him for his
offer. The captain replied that, if it pleased God that he should return,
he would bring enough men to conquer all those countries. It was
arranged that after dinner the cross should be planted on the summit of
the mountain, and the festa having been concluded by a volley from our
musketeers who were drawn up in battalions, the kings and the captain
embraced each other, and we returned to the ship. After dinner, it being
mid-day, we all went ashore in our doublets, and in company with the
two kings ascended to the summit of the highest mountain in the
neighbourhood, and there planted the cross. The captain then explained
the advantages it would bring them. Each one of us adored it, reciting a
Paternoster and an Ave, whereupon we descended, crossing the
cultivated grounds and going to the balangai, where the king caused
refreshment to be brought."

Magellan was now anxious to resume his voyage, and inquired which
were the best ports for provisions and trade, wishing to turn some of his
many articles of barter into gold and spices. He was told that there were
three - Ceylon, Zzubu, and Calagan, but that Zzubu was the largest and
had the most traffic. Ceylon was another name for the island of Leyte;
Zzubu is Cebu, and Calagan the district of Caraca in Mindanão. "He
thanked them and deliberated to go there," says Pigafetta, "for thus his
unlucky fate willed that it should be." Upon inquiring for pilots, the
king offered to conduct them himself if they would wait for a day or
two while he got in his rice harvest, at the same time begging for
assistance in the fields. This was readily granted by the Spaniards, "but
the kings had eaten and drunk so much the day before that, either
because they were intoxicated or because they were ill, they slept the

whole day and we could do nothing." By dint of hard work upon the two following days, however, the harvest was got in. On Thursday, April 4th, the fleet weighed anchor and continued the voyage, after a stay of a week at the island.

From Limassaua their course led them north-westward along the shores of Leyte, which they hugged closely to avoid the reefs barring the passage between that island and Bohol. Passing the little island of Canigan (Camigão), they touched at another to which Pigafetta gives the name of Gatigan, a name that it is impossible with any certainty to identify. Presumably this island lies somewhere between Camigão and the Camotes Islands. It is perhaps Jimuquitan or Apit Island. Here the voyagers were much struck by the Pteropi or "flying foxes" - the huge fruit-eating bats of which so many species inhabit the Malay Archipelago. Pigafetta declares that they were as large as eagles, and describes the capture of one, saying its flesh resembled that of a fowl in taste. The mound-building Megapodesgallinaceous birds peculiar to the Austro-Malayan subregion, were also met with and their habits well described. "As large as fowls are certain black birds with a long tail, which lay eggs like (i.e. as big as) those of a goose and cover them with sand, and leaving them thus exposed to the sun's heat the chicks are hatched." From Gatigan a westerly course was steered, but, having outsailed the prau of the King of Limassaua, who was piloting them according to his promise, they bore away for the Camotes group, where they awaited him. The good navigation of the Spaniards much astonished him on his rejoining them. At the Captain-general's invitation he went on board the Trinidad, and on Sunday the 7th April the fleet entered the port of Cebu.

Before arriving at the town many villages were passed; evidence that the district was one of the richest in the Archipelago. On reaching the anchorage, Magellan commanded that the ships should be dressed, and that simultaneous broadsides should be fired, "at which," as may be imagined, "the people were greatly frightened." A messenger was at once sent ashore with the interpreter, who reassured the natives by telling them that the artillery had been fired in honour of the king, and as a sign of peace and friendship. The king in answer asked the business of the newcomers, whereupon the interpreter informed him that his master was an officer of the greatest king in the world, and that be was on his way to the Moluccas, but upon hearing of his courtesy and good fame from the King of Limassaua, he desired to visit him. The King of Cebu, emboldened by the pacific attitude of the Spaniards, replied that it was well, but that he required that every one entering the port should pay tribute. The interpreter was in no way intimidated. His king, he said, paid tribute to no one, and if he wished for peace he could have peace, and if he wished for war he could have war.

It happened that at that moment a Siamese trader was in the port, a Moro versed from boyhood in the affairs of the East. The conquests of the Portuguese in India and their widespread and increasing influence were well known to him, and, desirous of saving the king from the results of a rupture with the Spaniards, he informed him of the successes of the Europeans in greater India, and counselled him to make peace. The King of Limassaua added his influence to the same end, and eventually the most cordial relations were established between Magellan and the king. A formal treaty of peace was concluded, the ceremony of blood brotherhood performed, and an agreement entered into whereby the Spaniards were to have the exclusive privilege of trading in the king's dominions.

Magellan, from the very earliest accounts we have of him, appears to have been a man in whom the religious spirit was very largely developed. On the occasion of the conclusion of the treaty - which was arranged on board the flagship by the nephew of the King of Cebu he alluded at some length to matters of the Christian faith. The statement that when their parents were old they paid no more attention to them, and the command passed to the children, drew from him the rebuke that the Creator expressly imposed upon sons the duty of honouring their father and mother, threatening with eternal punishment those who transgressed this precept. His impassioned address caused many of his auditors to express their desire of becoming Christians, and they begged that he would leave them two of his people to teach them the principles of that religion. Magellan's answer was that of a man singularly free from bigotry. He warned them against adopting Christianity either from fear or from the hope of deriving any temporal advantage from it. He said that he would never harm any one who desired to continue in the belief and observances of his own faith and laws, although he would not conceal the fact that those who became Christians would be more beloved and better treated by his people.

In whatever form his sentences reached the ears of his audience through the medium of the interpreter, the effect produced was all that Magellan could desire. The natives at once declared that they desired to become Christians, not from fear, nor from the wish to please their visitors, but of their own free will. They put themselves, they said, in his hands and desired him to treat them as his servants. The captain, with tears in his eyes, embraced the chiefs, and swore by the faith that he had in God, by the fealty that he vowed to his king, and by the habit of Santiago that he wore, that perpetual peace should thenceforward reign between the kings of Spain and Cebu.

Later in the day Pigafetta was despatched with one of the officers to the king, bearing the presents usual on such occasions. These were a robe of yellow and purple violet silk, a red cap of fine material, and some strings of crystal beads, borne upon a silver dish; together with two gilded glass beakers, which the envoys carried in their hands. They were well received by the king, and his people, standing round, told him of Magellan's speech, and how he exhorted them to embrace the Christian religion. The king asked them to remain to sup with him, but Pigafetta and his comrade made their excuses and returned to the ship. Next day, the 10th April, they again went ashore early. Martin Barreta, who had sailed as a supernumerary of the Santiago, had succumbed to the privations endured when crossing the Pacific. A few hours later his comrade, Juan de Aroche, also died. Permission was sought to bury them, and was readily granted. The grave was dug in the open space in the middle of the town, and the funeral conducted with all possible pomp, in order to impress the people. Later the place was consecrated as the Christian cemetery. The Spaniards little guessed how many of their number were destined to leave their bones in Cebu, still less would they have dreamt, had they known it, that none of them should lie at rest within the consecrated area.

Magellan's next object was to commence barter. In those days this was carried out with some ceremony. A store or large building of some kind was obtained on shore, filled with merchandise, and placed under a strong guard. When all was prepared the shop, for such it really was, was opened, and bartering began. On this occasion the objects were ready for display in two days. The people regarded them with the greatest wonder. For bronze and iron they were ready to exchange gold, giving value to the amount of fifteen ducats for fourteen pounds weight of iron. For small objects they gave pigs, goats, and rice. Magellan gave strict orders that no great desire to obtain gold should be shown, "otherwise," writes the Italian historian, "every sailor would have sold his all for gold, which would for ever have ruined our future trade." It is interesting to note that many appurtenances of civilisation were found existing among the natives. They were possessed of measures of capacity, and knew the use of weights. Formed by a spear-shaft suspended in the middle by a cord, they had on the one arm a basin attached by three strings, and at the other a leaden weight to obtain the equilibrium. "The people live with justice, and good weight and measure," we are told.

The king having expressed his wish to become a Christian, preparations were made for the celebration of his baptism with a becoming amount of ceremonial. In the open space already alluded to in the centre of the town a scaffolding was erected, and decorated with hangings and palm fronds. On Sunday, the 14th April, the rite was performed. Forty men in armour preceded Magellan and his officers, before whom the royal standard was borne. On arriving at the place prepared, Magellan and the king sat in two chairs one covered with red and the other with violet velvet, while the notables sat around on cushions. Before the king was baptized, Magellan instructed him in the meaning of the ceremony, and told him that if he wished to be a good Christian he must burn all his idols and worship the Cross. The idols are described by Pigafetta as being made of wood, hollowed out behind, with the arms and legs apart, and the feet turned upwards. They had a rather large face with four very large teeth, like those of a wild boar, and all of them were painted. A large cross was raised in the marketplace, and the people were told that they must adore it at morning and at mid-day upon their knees. The priest then baptized him, together with the prince, his nephew, the King of Limassaua, and others to the number of fifty or more. All were clad in white. The king, or rather rajah's, name, for he was of the latter rank, was Humabon or Hamabar, according to Gemara. The name of Carlos was given to him, in honour of the emperor; to his nephew that of Hernando, either out of compliment to Magellan, or to the emperor's brother; while the King of Limassaua became Juan, and the Moorish trader, who also appears to have embraced the new faith, Christopher.

The Spaniards returned to the ships for dinner, after which the chaplain and many others again went ashore to baptize the queen. She was led to the place with forty of her ladies, and while waiting was shown a figure of the Virgin and Child carved in wood, which she expressed a desire to have presented to her by Pigafetta. She took the name of Joanna, after the unhappy mother of Charles V, while the wife of the Rajah of Limassaua was baptized as Isabella. The example thus set by their rulers was followed immediately by the lower classes, and on that day no fewer than 800 persons were received into the Church. The news soon spread, and the people arrived in hundreds, until in eight days all the inhabitants of Cebu were baptized, and some belonging to other neighbouring islands. Maximilian Transylvanus records that the number was 2200, but it very possibly exceeded this considerably.

It seems probable, from Pigafetta's account, that the authority of this King or Rajah of Cebu was not so fully recognised by the surrounding chiefs and kinglets as it should have been. Magellan, now that he had concluded an alliance with him, was, of course, anxious to strengthen his position as much as possible. With this object in view he summoned a meeting of his two brothers and various chiefs who had exhibited a tendency to disobedience. He informed them that if they did not render a proper homage to their sovereign he should order them to be put to death, and their property to be confiscated. Such a notice his auditors were not in a position to gainsay, and they promised to obey. One of them, however, seems to have repented afterwards, and having again refused to submit to his authority, a punitive expedition was sent against him that plundered and burnt his village, and erected a cross over the smoking ashes. "Had they been Moors," writes Pigafetta, "we should have set up a column as a sign of their hardness of heart, for the Moors are more difficult of conversion than are the Gentiles." It seems probable that this village was one of the King of Mactan, although we are not actually told so.

For these services and in token of affection, the king presented Magellan with a pair of large gold earrings, two bracelets and two anklets set with precious stones. Spaniards and natives were now upon the best of terms, but Magellan, finding that the idols were not burnt, as he had ordered, and that offerings of meat were still made to them, reproved his converts severely for their breach of faith. They excused themselves by saying that they were preserved to restore to health a sick man, brother of the prince, (who Maximilian describes as a grandson of the king) "the most valiant and wisest man on the island," who lay so ill that for four days he had not spoken. Filled with zeal for his religion, Magellan said that if the king had true faith in our Lord, and burnt all the idols, and caused the sick man to be baptized, he would at once recover, and so sure was he of this, he added, that if it were not so he would cheerfully consent to forfeit his head. The king agreed. A procession was accordingly arranged with the greatest pomp and show that lay in the Spaniards' power. Formed in the great square by the cross, it proceeded to the house of the sick man, who was found unable either to speak or move. He was baptized, and Magellan asked him how he felt. The "faith cure" was not long in taking effect, for the patient answered immediately that by God's grace he was tolerably well.

"This great miracle was done under our very eyes," says the pious old historian. On the fifth day the man rose from his bed, burnt an idol that he had in his house, and proceeding to the seashore, where were several temples in which it was the custom to eat the meat offered to the idols, caused them to be destroyed. The natives tore them down, shouting "Castille, Castille," and declared that if God gave them life they would burn as many idols as they could find, even if they were in the house of the king himself. The influence and prestige of the Spaniards had now reached such a point that it seemed impossible that anything should ever occasion its downfall. Yet, as we shall see, it was to last for a few days only, and to be annihilated with a rapidity and completeness even more astonishing than that of its establishment.

CHAPTER 15

THE BATTLE OF MACTAN

It is probable that Bulaya - the village burnt by order of Magellan, on the occasion of the chastisement inflicted on the rebel chiefs - was situated on the little island of Mactan or Matan, whose rajah, Silapulapu, had rendered an unwilling obedience to the authority of the Cebu potentate. He could not understand, he said, why he should do homage to one whom he had been accustomed for so long to command. The action taken by the Spaniards had not rendered his attitude in any way more submissive. While he was meditating upon some method of revenge, one of his chiefs, by name Zula, sent a small present to the admiral, together with a secret message to the effect that if he did not give a more suitable offering it was through no fault of his own but rather from fear of the rajah. Zula added that if Magellan would help him with a boat and a few of his men, he would undertake to subdue his chief and hand over the island to the Spaniards.

Upon receipt of the message, Magellan at once resolved to take the affair in hand. Although at first opposed to the enterprise, the King of Cebu was anxious to assist him when he saw that he was determined upon going. João Serrão, the captain's staunch adherent and right-hand man, the old and tried warrior of a hundred fights, was altogether against it. Not only was nothing to be gained by it, he argued, but they had already lost a number of men. It would be unwise to leave the vessels as unprotected as they would be obliged to leave them, for the expedition needed a considerable force. However, it was in vain that he protested. Filled with religious enthusiasm at his successes in Cebu, Magellan desired to push them still farther, until the whole archipelago should recognise the authority of Spain and be received into the bosom of the Catholic Church. He was one, moreover, to brook no opposition from an individual whom he regarded as a rebel rather than an enemy. Action with him followed close upon resolve. Nothing, apparently, could ever make him reconsider a determination, and if he took counsel it was for form's sake only. So Serrão's wiser words of caution were put aside, and the expedition was prepared. At the last moment his officers besought him not to go in person. However, he would not have been Magellan had he listened to them. Good shepherd as he was, writes Pigafetta, he refused to desert his flock.

At midnight on Friday, 26th April, all was ready, and the expedition left Cebu. The Spaniards numbered sixty men all told. The Rajah of Cebu, the prince, a number of the chiefs, and a force of about a thousand men accompanied them in a fleet of twenty or thirty war canoes. The Europeans had three boats only. The little island of Mactan is close to Cebu, forming in fact its harbour, and the spot chosen for landing was probably not more than four or five miles distant from the fleet. It was reached three hours before daylight. No attempt was made to surprise and carry the town. The captain desired to try persuasion before force. Few men, probably, loved the din of battle more dearly than did he, or joined with more readiness in a desperate undertaking. However, here the affair seemed mere child's-play, and he probably did not think it possible that any number of naked natives could be a match for the sixty armour clad Europeans he brought against them. So, with characteristic straightforwardness, he sent the Moorish trader to Silapulapu, informing him that if he would submit and pay the tribute, no harm should be done to him, but if not, "he would learn how our lances wounded."

The answer returned was defiant enough, that "if the Spaniards had lances so also had they, albeit only reeds and stakes hardened by fire; that they were ready for them, but they besought them that they would not attack before morning, as they expected reinforcements at daylight."

This message, the most transparent of ruses, was of course recognised by Magellan as such. Warned, no doubt, by their previous encounter, the natives had ditched and staked the town and had dug pitfalls. A night attack would have been all in their favour, but they did not succeed in deceiving their enemies. The King of Cebu also counselled waiting for daylight. When it arrived, he begged Magellan to be allowed to lead the assault. With his thousand men and a few Spaniards to aid and inspire them he declared the victory to be certain. Magellan, it is needless to say, would not hear of it. He ordered his friend and ally to remain in the canoes with his men. He begged that they would look on, and note how his men could fight.

Owing to the coral reef surrounding Mactan, the boats from the fleet were unable to approach the shore. So far off, indeed, had they to remain that it was necessary to wade for a "distance of two good crossbow shots" before the attacking party set foot upon the beach. Of the sixty men, Magellan and forty-eight landed, the other eleven remained with the boats to guard them, and to serve the bombards. Gomara and Maximilian state that Magellan took forty men only. Herrera says that fifty-five landed. However, Pigafetta's account, here given, must be preferred. It is that of a participator in the engagement, and is evidently written with care and accuracy.

As they stepped ashore, the dawn of the 27th April 1521 broke over the island. It was Saturday, a day specially chosen by the admiral, as he had a great veneration for it. Alas ! for his choice ! Alas ! for the spectacle of prowess that he had charged his Cebu allies to watch ! Of valour, indeed, there was enough and to spare, but it availed nothing against the blunder he had made of under estimating the strength of his opponents. From the moment of landing it became evident that a determined resistance would be made. Numbers of natives - varying, according to different accounts, from fifteen hundred to six thousand - surrounded them. Pigafetta, who was himself of the attacking party, records that they were divided roughly into three bodies, of which one opposed their advance, while the others assailed them in flank. The captain accordingly marshalled his men in two companies, as affording a better means of defence. It is probable that the ground greatly favoured the natives. It probably was not then, the custom in the Philippines to build the houses of a village in very close proximity to each other. The trees and gardens by which they are generally surrounded, together with the thick bush that covers the uncultivated ground, afforded the best of cover to the islanders. Close fighting was impossible. Therefore, while the Spaniards were hardly able to fire a shot with any certainty, they were exposed to a continuous and galling fire of spears and arrows. Showers of stones were also thrown, and though the men were well protected about the body by their corslets, it was not long before some of the missiles began to tell upon their limbs.

It seems that but few arquebusiers were of the party, such as there were kept up a desultory fire with the crossbow men for some time, but to little effect. The natives, seeing the comparative harmlessness of the European weapons, grew emboldened. Magellan, realising that the ammunition was being wasted, shouted to his men to reserve their fire, but his orders were disregarded in the confusion of the mêlée.

The attacking party were now getting so hard pressed that Magellan directed a small detachment to advance and set fire to a group of houses not far distant. The plan was not attended with the success that he had desired. So infuriated were the islanders at the destruction of their property - for the wind having aided the Spaniards, twenty or thirty of the houses were soon in flames - that they returned to the attack with redoubled energy, and, cutting off some of the incendiary party, succeeded in killing two of them. From this moment the issue of the day was practically decided. Magellan, whose right leg had been pierced by an arrow, saw that a further advance was impossible, and gave orders to retreat. In vain, however, did he command that the movement should be executed slowly and in order. Had his orders been carried out, the result of the battle might have been different. However, to the Spaniards, spoilt by facile victories, a reverse was attended with unknown terrors, and the greater part of them fled immediately in wild disorder. Six or eight only were left to support their gallant commander in a steady retreat to the beach, surrounded by swarms of natives who poured in a heavy fire of arrows and spears upon the courageous little band. So heavy was it, says Pigafetta, who stayed by his beloved captain to the last, that we could hardly offer any resistance. Then the water's edge was gained, but no aid could be obtained from the boats. Their distance from the fight was so great that it was useless to bring the bombards into action, and friend so mixed with foe that even had they been within range it would have been impossible. So, fighting hand to hand, and step by step retreating, the coral reef was traversed, until they were distant a bowshot from the shore, and the water reached their knees.

Then the end came. The natives, confident in their numbers, and caring little for the weapons of the Europeans, pressed them still harder. Twice the captain lost his helmet, and a little later he received a spear wound in the right arm. The islanders recognised his rank, and directed their attacks especially against him; and finding the bodies of their antagonists invulnerable, they endeavoured to wound them in the legs or face. The length of their spears being greater than that of the Spanish lances, gave them still further advantages. However, in spite of this, the resistance of Magellan and his men was determined and obstinate to a degree. The King of Cebu, recognising the gravity of their situation, had landed some of his men to draw off the attack, but it was too late. The rest must be told in Pigafetta's own words.

"Thus we fought for an hour or more, until at length an Indian succeeded in wounding the captain in the face with a bamboo spear. He, being desperate, plunged his lance into the Indian's breast, leaving it there. However, wishing to use his sword he could only draw it half way from the sheath, on account of a spear wound he had received in the right arm. Seeing this, the enemy all rushed at him, and one of them with a long terzado, like a large scimitar, gave him a heavy blow upon the left leg which caused him to fall forward on his face. Then the Indians threw themselves upon him with iron-pointed bamboo spears and scimitars, and every weapon they had, and ran him through - our mirror, our light, our comforter, our true guide - until they killed him. While the Indians were closely pressing him he several times turned around towards us to see if we were all in safety, as if his obstinate resistance had no other object than to give time for the retreat of his men. We who fought with him to the last, and were covered with wounds, when we saw him fall, made for the boats, which were then on the point of pushing off..... There perished with him eight of our men [seven according to the official list of deaths, but one succumbed later to his wounds], and four of the Christian Indians. We had, besides, many wounded, among whom I must count myself. The enemy lost only fifteen men. He died, but I trust that your Illustrious Highness [Pigafetta's book was dedicated to Villiers de l'Isle Adam, Grand Master of Rhodes] will not permit his memory to be lost, the more so since I see born again in you the good qualities of so great a captain, one of his leading virtues being his constancy in the worst misfortune. At sea he endured hunger better than we. Greatly learned in nautical charts, he knew more of the true art of navigation than any other person, in sure proof whereof is the wisdom and intrepidity with which no example having been afforded him he attempted, and almost completed, the circumnavigation of the globe."

So died Magellan, his life wasted in a miserable skirmish with natives. The manner of his death has been related by various historians, the most trustworthy of whom differ in no essential point. The account of Pigafetta, who fought by his side, is doubtless correct. However, in a desperate struggle such as that in which the great navigator perished, it is not astonishing that the minor details of the onlookers' stories should vary. Thevet states that he was killed by an arrow, which is partly borne out by Nicholas of Naples, a sailor of the Victoria, in his examination as a witness in support of Jaime Barbosa's claim to Magellan's estate in the year 1540. "I was by his side and saw him killed by arrows and a lance-wound which pierced his throat." Whether Magellan met his death by spear or arrow, however, matters little. He fell as we should expect him to fall, fighting bravely, and up to the last moment of his life thinking of others rather than himself.

When the King of Cebu heard the news he burst into tears. With the victory in their power they had deliberately thrown away every chance, and had suffered a most disastrous defeat. Silently, and with bitter sorrow at their hearts, the Spaniards decided to return, and the little flotilla recrossed the bay to Cebu. Their anguish was the more poignant since the body of their commander remained in the enemies hands. The same evening a special messenger was sent to Silapulapu demanding it, and offering to give whatever merchandise he desired upon its return. It was in vain that he pleaded. The rajah's reply was that for nothing in the world would they give back the captain's body, for they desired to preserve it always as a monument of their triumph. It was in vain, too, that Barbosa, the brother-in-law of Magellan, made renewed offers. The victors were inflexible, and the bones of the brave old warrior and explorer rest to this day in Mactan.

We do not know with any certainty where he fell. However, the Spanish have attempted to identify the village upon which the attack was made, and a monument was erected to his memory on the spot. Magellan needs no monument. His name is written for ever, not only on his straits, but upon the heavens, whose face, as astronomer and navigator, he had scanned so often, in fair weather and foul, in every quarter of the globe.

From the history of the last voyage of Magellan alone a fair idea might be gathered of the great commander's character, even had we known nothing previously about him. Its leading features do not alter. As he was in his youth in India - cool in danger, unselfish, and possessed of a determination almost without parallel - so he remained to the end, until he fell in the little island of Mactan, before the cane spears of a horde of naked natives. On the very occasion of his death he exhibited these qualities in a most striking manner. The details of the engagement that we are possessed of show that his actions were distinguished as much by coolness as by bravery. To his unselfishness, without a shadow of doubt, he owed his death. "His obstinate resistance had no other aim than to give time for the retreat of his men," Pigafetta tells us. Yet the expedition was undertaken in defiance of the advice of his officers and the entreaty of his friends. His fate was the outcome of an excess of self-reliance, of too blind a confidence in his own unaided judgment. Magellan was a born leader of men from sheer force of character and strength of will. However, there was more than mere energy in him. That he was a man of considerable intelligence there is no doubt from the evidence of other writers besides Pigafetta, and entirely apart from the question of whether he was or was not previously aware of the existence of the straits of which he went in search. However, the most charming trait in his character is the carelessness of self that reveals itself so often in the history of his life, the readiness to sacrifice himself on all occasions for others. How he died we have just seen. However, we must not forget his action on the occasion of the wreck on the Padua bank, when he volunteered to remain with the sailors; or the aid that, at imminent risk of his life, he afforded Serrão at the attempted massacre of the Portuguese at Malacca. With his own hands he tended his sick crew in the Philippines, after having shared on equal terms with them the privations of their voyage across the Pacific. With mutineers and traitors, in fact with all who rebelled against authority, even if only mere shirkers or grumblers, he was no doubt a hard master. However, to those who served him faithfully and did their duty he ever remained a staunch friend. Moreover, he bears a name of untarnished honour.

A question of no little interest yet remains for consideration - the question of what rank ought to be assigned to Magellan as a navigator and explorer. In the history of geographical discovery there are two great successes, and two only, so much do they surpass all others - the discovery of America, and the first circumnavigation of the globe. Columbus and Magellan are the only possible competitors for the supremacy. Were the vote of the majority taken, it would without a shadow of doubt be recorded in favour of the former. We can see easily enough that it could not well be otherwise. Fortified by the dangerous possession of a little knowledge, the mass would grant the palm to him who first brought the vast continent of America to the ken of Europeans. However, without detracting in any way from the ample, honour that is his just due, an unbiassed comparison of his great voyage with that of Magellan leaves the latter navigator with the verdict in his favour on almost every point. If it be claimed for Columbus that he crossed an ocean of vast size whose western half was unknown to the inhabitants of the old world, it is equally incontrovertible that Magellan traversed a far vaster sea, upon whose waters no European ship had ever floated. When Columbus started on his voyage, his work lay immediately before him. Magellan did not arrive at the Pacific until more than a year after he weighed anchor from San Lucar de Barrameda, for months of which he had undergone great and continued hardships. While the great Genoese made land on the thirty-sixth day after leaving the Canaries, the little armada of Magellan struggled for no less than three months and eighteen days across the unknown waste of the Pacific. Little wonder that they said it was more vast than the imagination of man could conceive ! As an explorer then, the merits of Magellan must be ranked as superior to those of the discoverer of the New World. The long-foreseen mutiny, the ceaseless tempests and cold of Patagonia, the famine that stared him in the face, failed to daunt him. He carried out an expedition infinitely more lengthy and difficult in the face of incomparably greater hardships.

It is more difficult to adjudicate upon the respective merits of the two great discoverers as navigators. Columbus was an acute observer, and though his deductions were by no means always correct, they evince considerable ingenuity and reasoning power. We know that be was a maker of charts and maps before he started upon his great voyage, and that he was in communication with the leading cosmographers of the day. Nevertheless, he can hardly be called one of them. Girava indeed, writing in 1556, speaks of him as "a great sailor, but a poor cosmographer." Whether his judgment is correct or not we cannot well decide at this our present date. Columbus's discovery of America is surrounded with such a halo of glory that we are blinded by its brilliance, and forget that it was, after all, but an accident. For he died, as we know, in the belief that he had reached Asia; ignorant of the fact that a yet vaster ocean than that he had already traversed lay between him and the object of his desire. It was a magnificent mistake, a mistake which in its results was worth a hundred accurate reasonings, but it was a mistake nevertheless.

Magellan we know to have been a cosmographer and navigator of exceptional skill. He is mentioned constantly as such during the period of his service in the East. Returning to Portugal, he applied himself heart and soul to his favourite science, his chief study being to establish some trustworthy method for obtaining longitude. His long acquaintance with Ruy Faleiro, who appears to have been one of the ablest astronomers of the day, perfected him in his science so far as it then went. He left Seville with a reputation hardly inferior to that of his instructor. It is probable that Pigafetta's Treatise of Navigation was the outcome of Magellan's teaching. The successful way in which the latter conducted his ships upon his last great voyage speaks highly of his skill. It is asserted by one of Magellan's detractors that he reached the Philippines by mistake, intending to proceed to the Moluccas, but being ignorant of their position. Not only was he perfectly well acquainted with their situation, as is evidenced by the letter written by him to Charles V immediately before starting on his voyage, but we are especially told by the Genoese pilot that Magellan kept to the north on purpose, knowing that it was impossible to refit and obtain proper provisions in the Moluccas. Neither as geographer nor astronomer can Magellan be ranked beneath Columbus. Lord Stanley's dictum that he is "undoubtedly the greatest of ancient and modern navigators," is an opinion that a careful investigation obliges us to accept.

Few details have been handed down to us concerning the personal appearance of Magellan. We know, as has already been stated, that he was rather below than above the ordinary height, and that the wounds he received in Africa had made him slightly lame. However, our knowledge is practically limited to these facts. M. Ferdinand Denis, in his Portugal, gives an engraving of a portrait of the navigator. Sr. Vargas y Ponce, in his Relation del Ultimo Viage al Estrecho de Magallanes, gives a beautifully engraved portrait, executed by Selma, from a painting then (1788) in the possession of Don Felipe Vallejo of Toledo. This painting was a copy of another existing in the gallery of the Duke of Florence, and ascribed, probably erroneously, to Titian.

CHAPTER 16

TREACHERY IN CEBU

Upon the arrival in Cebu of the survivors of the Mactan disaster, one of the first duties performed was the election of a successor to the post of captain-general. A dual command, a not unusual custom in those days, was resolved upon, and the choice of the electors fell upon Duarte Barbosa, and João Serrão. Both were navigators of no ordinary merit, who had seen long service under Almeida and Albuquerque in India, and both were Portuguese by birth.

At the time of the conversion of the Cebu people, it will be remembered, a large store had been opened in the town, and much bartering had been carried on. We do not know whether the Spaniards had any definite reason to suspect treachery. However, if such was the case they took the best measures to induce it, for one of their first acts was to transport this merchandise again to the ships. A more ill-advised step could hardly have been conceived. Their defeat at Mactan had seriously damaged their prestige in the eyes of the islanders, and it behoved them to make as light of it as possible. The withdrawal of the goods from their store was tantamount to a confession of weakness. In short, it was courting attack.

The disaster came soon enough, whether the distrust exhibited by the Spaniards was or was not a factor in it. What actually tempted the King of Cebu to the base act of treachery of which he was guilty seems uncertain. By some historians it is said that the chiefs who had made difficulties in submitting to his authority, united to form a common cause. They informed him that if he did not assist them in exterminating the Spaniards and seizing their ships, they would kill him and lay waste his country. Others declare the treachery to have originated in the fleet itself - a story related so circumstantially that it is impossible not to give some credence to it. Magellan's slave, Enrique of Malacca, the interpreter to the expedition, had been wounded slightly in the Mactan affair, and remained obstinately in his bunk, and declining to move. As his injury was very trivial and his services were greatly needed, Barbosa rated him soundly, telling him that though

Magellan was dead he was still a slave and the property of Doña Beatriz, that disobedience was not for dogs such as he, and that he would get a sound beating if he did not do what he was told with readiness and alacrity. The man obeyed and showed no resentment at the time, but he nursed his revenge and resolved to betray the Spaniards at the first opportunity. Going in secret to the King of Cebu, he told him that his masters had decided to attack the town and carry him away captive on their ships, but that if he would follow his advice he might turn the tables upon them, and soon become owner of all their belongings. Maximilian and Gomara, give the same story, as does Pigafetta, and Sebastian del Cano in the evidence given by him before the Alcalde Leguizamo in October 1522, with the exception that they make Serrão, not Barbosa, rate Enrique. Improbable as the story was, its acceptation no doubt fell in with the king's desires. He resolved at once upon a plan for the massacre of his former friends and the seizure of their vessels.

It had been previously settled that an offering of jewels should be made by the native king to the King of Spain in recognition of his authority and protection. All having been arranged, a message was sent to the commanders to intimate that the present was ready, and that they were desirous of offering it in due form. They therefore begged their presence, and that of every one who could be spared from the fleet, at a feast. Barbosa accepted without hesitation, but Serrão had misgivings. However, the arguments or banter of his friend gained the day, and he agreed to go.

On the morning of Wednesday, May 1st, the two captains rowed ashore in company with twenty-seven others. According to Pigafetta, only twenty-four were with them, but the above number must be correct, for two turned back, and twenty-seven appear in the list of killed. Fortunately for Pigafetta, a wound that he had received in the face on the occasion of the Mactan affair prevented his joining the party, which included many people of importance. The cosmographer, Andres de San Martin, the escribanos Sancho de Heredia and Leon de Espeleta, and the priest, Pedro de Valderrama, were of it. With them, too, was one Luiz Affonso de Goes, a Portuguese, supernumerary of the Trinidad, João Carvalho, the pilot, and Espinosa, the alguacil. In the official death-roll, under the date of April 27th, the day of the Mactan tragedy, we find the name of Cristóbal Rabello, who is described as captain of the Victoria. Under the date of May 1st occurs the entry of Luis Alfonso de Lois, (sic) who is given a like description. Yet we know that Duarte Barbosa had been appointed captain of that ship after the mutiny. How can these apparently conflicting statements be reconciled ? A possible explanation is afforded by a few stray words in the bulky pay-list of the armada, under the name of Duarte Barbosa. They state that the Captain-general placed Barbosa under arrest in Sta. Lucia Bay because he went away with the natives. He was guilty of a like offence in Cebu, being away three days from his ship, although the admiral sent a message to him to bid him return. He may, perhaps, have been deprived of his command in consequence and succeeded by Rabello, while after the engagement at Mactan he would take command of Magellan's ship, while de Goes captained the Victoria. It is far more probable that the entries are wrong, and that Barbosa never lost his command. He at least drew pay as captain all this time, and the promotion neither of Rabello nor de Goes is mentioned in the pay-list.

The king awaited them upon the beach, surrounded by numbers of his people, to escort them to the place where the feast had been prepared. However, treachery was in the air, and others beside Serrão had an instinctive feeling of some approaching disaster. Espinosa and Carvalho, seeing Valderrama led away alone in a suspicious manner, resolved instantly to turn back. Their caution saved them, but they alone of all the party escaped with their lives. Hardly had they got back to the ships and related their story when a great disturbance was heard on shore. The natives had gradually surrounded their guests, and on a given signal had fallen upon them with spear and kris. Hopelessly outnumbered, the Spaniards fought to the end, selling their lives as dearly as they could. Carvalho, who was now in command, and had apparently hove short his cables in anticipation of the disaster, weighed immediately, and approaching the shore poured broadsides into the village. At the same moment a group of natives came down to the water's edge dragging with them João Serrão, bound and bleeding from many wounds. They were desirous of bartering his life for cannon and merchandise. Serrão shouted to his friends the terrible story of his comrades' death. He implored Carvalho to cease firing, or he too would be murdered, and then, turning to his captors, said that if they took him to the ships they would receive whatever they demanded. This they refused to do, fearful of retaliation on the part of the Spaniards. Serrão was a fellow countryman of Carvalho, and was, moreover, his compadre, his boon companion. It seemed hardly necessary to appeal to him for succour in such an hour. However, seeing that no steps were being taken to despatch a boat to his assistance, Serrão implored that this might be done before it was too late. No boat, however, was sent. He did not know, and he could not believe, that his friend intended, in cold blood, with a depth of cowardice and treachery beyond parallel, to leave him to be murdered. However, so it was. As the ships slowly made sail and stood out to sea, his friend's baseness dawned upon him. In the name of their friendship he again and again begged and implored his help. Then, seeing that it was in vain, he solemnly cursed him, praying God that at the last great day he would require Carvalho to render an account of his actions in this affair. It appears from the account of Pigafetta that it was a far viler sin than cowardice of which Carvalho was guilty - that he refused to rescue Serrão in order to get the command.

As the vessels left, their crews, watching, saw the natives turn upon their captive. A little later and loud cries came from the midst of the crowd, portending his death. At the same time another party was seen tearing down the cross that had been erected near the church. Rapid and complete as had been the conversion of the natives, their recantation was no less so.

CHAPTER 17

THE SPICE ISLANDS

With grief and despair in their hearts the members of the now much-weakened expedition resumed their voyage. Not only were they greatly reduced in numbers, but the comrades they had lost were the strongest of the party. Many also were men of importance in the command or navigation of the ships. On mustering all hands it was found that only 115 remained of the original 270 or more who left Seville. The account of the Genoese pilot states the number to have been 108 men, that of Barros 180. The latter number is evidently incorrect. The San Antonio left Seville with nearly seventy men on board, and since she received her share of the Santiago's crew, it is probable that she did not desert with much fewer than eighty men. The list of deaths up to this time numbered seventy-two. This would leave about 120 men. The Concepcion, too, was leaky and unserviceable. So, rather than run the risk of being undermanned and of losing her cargo, they resolved to burn her, after transshipping the best of her stores into the other vessels. This was accordingly done off the island of Bohol, and, while Espinosa was made captain of the Victoria, Carvalho was confirmed in his command as Captain-general, a post that he did not very long retain.

The course was now shaped to the southward for the Moluccas. Coasting the western promontory of the great island of Mindanão, where they touched and made friends with the natives, they bore away for Borneo, having on their way undoubtedly received intelligence of the city now known as Brunei. Their track took them to the island of Cagayan Sulu. Pigafetta speaks of the very large trees in it, and records that its few inhabitants were Moors banished from Borneo, who regarded the newcomers as gods. Provisions were now running very short, and their first object being to obtain them, they enquired for Palawan, where they heard that rice was procurable. They were directed northward again, and after running twenty-five leagues hit off its southern end, and coasted it for a considerable distance to the north-east. So reduced were they that but eight days provisions remained. They had for some time under consideration the project of establishing themselves in some island and supporting life as best they could upon the fish and vegetables it might chance to afford them. Such a rash step was fortunately unnecessary. Palawan was found to be a promised land, abounding in pigs, goats, poultry, and fruits, and more important still, in rice. They placed themselves upon a footing of blood-brotherhood with the chief in whose district they had landed, and after a few days' stay left on the 21st June for Borneo. The MS. of Sao Bento da Saude has "21st day of July." They had been astonished to find in the port an African named Bastião, who spoke Portuguese tolerably well, having acquired it in the Moluccas, where he had become a Christian. With some difficulty they prevailed upon him to act as pilot, but when the time came for their departure he was nowhere to be found. The Spaniards did not permit themselves to be discouraged. Finding a ship about to enter the harbour they took her, and compelled three Moors whom they found aboard, and who said that they were pilots, to conduct them to Brunei.

Passing between the islands of Balábac and Banguey, the Trinidad and Victoria hugged the Bornean coast, and sighting "an exceedingly great mountain, to which they gave the name of St. Paul" (subsequently called Kina Balu), anchored at some islands near the mainland (the Mantanani Islands). The Bornean coast is beset with shoals and sand banks, necessitating the utmost care in navigation, and the ships crept cautiously along, anchoring at night near the mouth of the Brunei river. Here they landed their pilots, together with a representative from the fleet, leaving them to make their way by land to the city to prepare the Sultan for their arrival, while the ships, having watched the course taken by some junks, were enabled to pick up the very difficult channel by which it is approached, and navigate it successfully for some distance. Next day praus arrived with presents from the Sultan, and piloted them to the usual berth, which appears to have been three or four leagues from the city.

Pigafetta describes Brunei as a vast collection of houses built entirely on piles in the water. Its situation, in a lake-like expansion of the river, was singularly picturesque and quite unique in character. It must, however, have been of a large size, for the Italian narrator speaks of the "25,000 fires or families" of which it was composed. The palace of the

Sultan was built on shore. Its great halls hung with silk brocades, its rooms full of courtiers, and the elaborate ceremonial observed. Elephants with their magnificent trappings, bore the Spanish officers to the Sultan's residence.

Although the people of Brunei had treated those of the fleet with apparent goodwill, it seems that the latter, after trading for three or four weeks, were not without suspicions of treachery. Their experience at Cebu had made them thoroughly mistrustful. They had definite cause for alarm, for five of their number, having been sent on shore to obtain wax with which to caulk the vessels, were detained by the Sultan. At the same time some large junks came to anchor in close proximity to the Trinidad and Victoria, and between them and the bar. Next morning the watch were alarmed at seeing two hundred praus or more advancing upon them from the city, divided into three squadrons. The two ships at once got under weigh, and making straight for the junks, opened fire upon them without further ceremony, capturing one and driving others ashore. The result of the action intimidated their smaller antagonists, and the praus returned. Next morning, the 30th July, the Spaniards sighted a large junk, which they attacked and captured without difficulty. Their prize was commanded by a son of the King of Luzon himself, Captain-general of the Sultan of Borneo. He was returning from a punitive expedition to the south part of the island, of which some districts appear at that time to have been desirous of Javanese rather than Bornean rule.

With these hostages Carvalho doubtless hoped to get back the men who had been detained by the Sultan, Sripada. One of them was his own son by a Brazilian woman. The other two, for two had already got back to the ships, were ordinary seamen - two Greeks of Corfu and of Naples. It is probable that they were deserters, or had perished in some street quarrel, for they were not returned. The death-roll of the expedition makes two others to have been left behind in Borneo, one of whom was the escribano of the Trinidad. Carvalho, who was apparently a man of bad character, had meanwhile permitted the Luzon prince to escape, having secretly received from him a very large ransom, which he appropriated to his own use. The others, to the number of fourteen or sixteen, were kept prisoners on board, and with them three women of great beauty who had been found in the junk. They were destined as a present to the Queen, writes Pigafetta, but Carvalho kept them for himself.

Retracing their course, the Trinidad and her consort sailed north-east along the Bornean coast in search of a port in which to careen and repair before continuing the voyage to the Moluccas. Passing Cape Sampanmangio, the flagship took the ground and remained for some hours, but was eventually got off without injury. Shortly after, a harbour was found which seemed suitable for their purposes. It was in an islet off Banguey or Balambangan islands, so far as can be made out from the indefinite records left us. According to Herrera, this port was on the Bornean coast, while Pigafetta speaks of it as being in Palawan. A stay of no less than six weeks was made here. The ships were beached, thoroughly overhauled and caulked. Each man worked according to the best of his knowledge and ability, but in the face of many difficulties. The greatest labour had to be gone through in obtaining wood for their work, the ground being covered with briars and thorns, and the men without shoes to protect their feet.

On the 27th September the explorers once more resumed their voyage. During their stay in Port St. Mary - as they named the harbour - they lost the bombardier of the Victoria, who died from the wounds he had received in the engagement at Mactan. Either on leaving the port, or at an earlier period - as we prefer to follow Herrera or the Genoese pilot - Carvalho was deprived of his command. His conduct had for a long time proved his incapacity for the position. Gonzalo Gomez de Espinosa, the alguacil, was appointed commander-in-chief, and Juan Sebastian del Cano took the post of captain of the Victoria. His conduct on the occasion of the mutiny in Port St. Julian had been deserving of great blame, but the ranks had been greatly thinned by the desertion of the San Antonio and the disasters in the Philippines, and with his known ability as a navigator, the choice could not well have fallen upon any other. Making an easterly course for the island of Cagayan Sulu, the vessels fell in with a junk, which they engaged and captured. It had on board the Governor or Rajah of Palawan, with whom they had previously been on terms of friendship. Under Magellan such acts of semi-piracy would not have been encouraged, but it was characteristic of the new command that every strange ship should be looked upon as fair game. As a ransom they demanded four hundred measures of rice, twenty pigs, as many goats, and a hundred and fifty fowls, to be paid within eight days. This figured as a tribute to the King of Spain. On receiving it, on the 7th October, they returned the rajah some of his krisses and arquebuses, and, having added a few presents, permitted him his freedom.

Rounding Cagayan Sulu, the vessels sighted the island of Sulu, and would have visited it but for a headwind that compelled them to bear away for the southwest point of Mindanão. This they coasted, and, passing between it and Basilan, sailed for some distance up the Gulf of Mindanão. Here they fell in with a large prau, which, following their usual custom, they captured, after a desperate resistance in which seven of her crew were killed. For the first time the nearness of their goal was revealed to them, for they found that the captain had actually been in the house of Francisco Serrão in Ternate. The end of their troubles was approaching, and the riches of the Spice Islands, the long-sought Eldorado of the old world, were about to become a reality.

Upon the details of the course of the two ships after leaving Mindanão it is not necessary to dwell. They steered southward, passing the Sanghir and Talaut islands, and, sighting the northern extremity of Celebes, altered course to the south-east. On Wednesday, the 6th November, they passed between Mean and Zoar - subsequently known as Tifore and Mayo islands, and a little later the high peaks of Ternate and Tidor appeared to their delighted gaze. How overjoyed the half-starved and toil-worn mariners must have been we can imagine. "The pilot who had remained with us," says Pigafetta, "told us that they were the Moluccas, for the which we thanked God, and to comfort us we discharged all our artillery. Nor ought it to cause astonishment that we were so rejoiced, since we had passed twenty-seven months, less two days, always in search of these Moluccas, wandering hither and thither for that purpose among innumerable islands."

On the afternoon of Friday, November 8th, 1521, the Trinidad and Victoria rounded the southern point of Tidor, and anchored in twenty fathoms, close to the shore of that island, discharging their broadsides as a salute to the king. Next day he came on board in state. An astrologer and prophet, Almanzor, as he was named, declared that he had divined the arrival of the strangers. He met them with the warmest welcome. "After such long tossing upon the seas, and so many dangers," he said, "come and enjoy the pleasures of the land, and refresh your bodies, and do not think but that you have arrived at the kingdom of your own sovereign." Whether he regarded the Spaniards in the light of future allies who would help him against his enemies does not appear, but this explanation of the warmth of his reception seems the most probable. He doubtless dreaded the aid that the Portuguese were able to afford the people of Ternate if they so desired. The Spaniards, anxious to make treaties with him and without delay to load their ships with the coveted spices, encouraged his friendship to the utmost of their power. They loaded him and those of his suite with presents. So much did they give him, indeed, that they were requested after a time to cease their gifts, for "he had nothing worthy to send to our king as a present, unless, now that he recognised him as his sovereign, he should send himself." In spite of his humility of speech Almanzor was of kingly presence and bearing. Servants carrying golden vessels for water, betel, and other necessaries stood always in attendance, and his son bore a sceptre before him. Under no conditions would he bow or even incline his head, so that in entering the cabin of the flagship he was obliged to do so by the opening from the upper deck, so as not to stoop, which he would have been obliged to do had he entered by the door from the waist of the ship.

On the 10th November, Carvalho and others went ashore, and after a long conversation with the king a treaty appears to have been signed, by which he acknowledged the sovereignty of Spain. He asked for the royal standard and the emperor's signature, and seeing the eagerness of the Spaniards to commence the lading of their ships, informed them that though he had not in Tidor a sufficiency of cloves ready, he would himself go to the island of Batchian, where he trusted he should find enough.

Although Magellan was no longer with them, it may be imagined that the Spaniards lost no time in making inquiries for Francisco Serrão, his great friend and relation, of whom they must have heard so much. He was dead. The manner of his death was more or less shrouded in mystery, but they learnt that it had taken place seven or eight months previously, almost indeed at the same time as Magellan. He had been Captain-general of the King of Ternate when that king was at war with the Sultan of Tidor. Having succeeded in beating the latter in various engagements, he compelled him to give his daughter in marriage to the King of Ternate, and to send him many sons of the chiefs of Tidor as hostages. The King of Tidor never forgave him. Serrão, having visited that island some years later to trade in cloves, was caused to be poisoned by the king. According to others, he was poisoned by a Malay woman who acted under Portuguese orders. Argensola states that Don Tristão de Meneses despatched him back to India, being afraid of his acquiring too much power, and that he died on board ship on his way to Goa.

On Monday, November 11th, one of the sons of the King of Ternate came to visit the ships, having with him the Javanese widow of Serrão and her two little children. Aware of his hostility to their host, Espinosa and his officers were uncertain how to act. However, Almanzor sent them a message to do as they thought fit. They accordingly had their interview with him in their boat, and presented him with various gifts. In his prau was a certain Indian named Manoel, servant of one Pedro Affonso de Lorosa, a Portuguese who had formerly resided in Banda, but after Serrão's death had settled in Ternate. From this man the Spaniards learnt that although enemies of the Sultan of Tidor, the Ternate chiefs were at heart in favour of Spain. On hearing this they wrote to Lorosa, telling him to visit the fleet without fear.

The prices for barter were agreed upon, and a house arranged for the accommodation of the merchandise on the following day. It is interesting to note the estimate of the respective values of articles in those days. The standard measure of cloves was the bahar of 406 pounds. This could be obtained for ten ells of red cloth, fifteen of yellow, fifteen hatchets, thirty-five glass goblets, seventeen catties of cinnabar or quicksilver, twenty-six ells of common linen, a hundred and fifty knives, fifty scissors, forty caps, ten Guzerat cloths, or a hundredweight of bronze. The Brunei gongs were as much esteemed then, and for every three of them - doubtless the spoil of some of their prizes - they were able to purchase two bahars. All these prices nevertheless were prospective for as yet no cloves or spices of any kind were to be obtained. The Sultan sent one of his sons to the island of Motir, and announced his intention of visiting Batchian in person in order to see what could be done. The Spaniards, anxious to please him in every way, gave him the three women and the men they had captured in the Prince of Luzon's junk. They killed all the pigs they had on board, which had always been a source of great annoyance to him as a Mohammedan.

On the evening of the 14th November the Portuguese Lorosa arrived in a prau, and they were enabled for the first time to obtain news from civilised lips of what had passed in the Moluccas. He had come with Serrão in the first expedition of 1511, and was well acquainted with native politics. Lorosa told them that Don Tristão de Meneses, whose large ship had left for Banda only a few months before, had brought news of the departure of Magellan's armada from Seville. Lorosa informed them that the King of Portugal had sent ships both to the Cape of Good Hope and to the Rio de la Plata to intercept it, and that, learning later that Magellan had passed westward, he wrote to the Viceroy of India, Diogo Lopez de Sequeira, to despatch a fleet of six vessels to the Moluccas against him. This, Sequeira was unable to do, owing to renewed difficulties with the Arabs in the Red Sea. A galleon that he had sent later under the command of Francisco Faria had been unable to reach its destination. The trade of Portugal in the islands must have been considerably developed, even at this date. Lorosa informed his hearers that a great number of junks went yearly from Malacca to Banda to purchase nutmegs, returning by way of Ternate to complete their cargo with cloves.

Two days later the Moorish king of Gilolo, an ally of Almanzor, visited them, and was given a quantity of presents. Great numbers of the natives of Ternate also came, their boats laden with cloves, desirous of commencing trade. However, Espinosa, who did not wish to offend the Sultan, thought it best not to begin to sell the merchandise until his return from Batchian. This took place on the night of November 24th, amid great rejoicings. The Sultan's prau passed between the Trinidad and Victoria with drums beating, while the Spanish ships fired their broadsides in his honour. The Captain-general was informed that for four days there would be a continuous supply of cloves. The Sultan was punctual to his promise, and next day they began the lading of the ships. "As they were the first cloves we took aboard, and as they were also the chief object of our voyage, we discharged many bombards for joy."

On the following day the Sultan informed them that it was the custom, when the first loads of cloves were embarked on a vessel, that he should give a feast to the crews and merchants. He begged them, therefore, to attend an entertainment be proposed to give at which the King of Batchian would also be present. Espinosa and his men, however, who had not forgotten the Cebu incident, instantly suspected treachery, and refused. Their suspicions were, nevertheless, unfounded, for, though they learnt afterwards, on trustworthy authority, that certain of the chiefs had counselled their assassination, they also learnt that the Sultan had indignantly rejected so base a suggestion. His loyalty to Spain and admiration of the Spaniards were doubtless sincere enough. Nor was he the only person to express a desire to become a vassal of the emperor. Many of those in authority in the neighbouring islands were also ready to place themselves under Charles's protection. On 16th November a treaty was signed with the King of Gilolo, on the 19th of the same month with the Rajah of Makian, and on the 16th or 17th December with the King of Batchian and various notables of the island of Ternate. The King of Batchian sent a slave and two bahars of cloves as a present to the emperor. He was desirous of presenting ten bahars, but so heavily laden were the ships, Pigafetta tells us, that Espinosa was afraid of taking more.

Among his presents was one that greatly pleased and astonished the Europeans - some skins of the bird of Paradise. The mention made of them by Maximilian Transylvanus in his letter to the Cardinal of Salzburg is perhaps the first record that we have of the existence of these birds. However, it is hard to believe that the Portuguese, who had at this time been for ten years upon the islands, were not perfectly well acquainted with them. The natives of New Guinea seem, from Pigafetta's account, to have prepared the skins in precisely the same manner as that in use at the present day. To the Malay traders, judging from Maximilian's letter, they were apparently common objects. "The Mohammedans, who travelled to those parts for commercial purposes, told them (the Kings of Marmin) that this bird was born in Paradise, and that Paradise was the abode of the souls of those who had died, wherefore these princes embraced the religion of Mohammed, because it promised wonderful things about this abode of souls." The fact that the skins were prepared with the feet cut off doubtless caused the fable given us by Maximilian and copied by a hundred authors - that they passed an entirely aerial existence, never alighting upon the ground nor upon any tree that grew upon it. Sometimes, reports ran, they were seen to fall dead from the sky. For these reasons, and from their beauty, the skins were much valued, and they were supposed to render their wearers safe and invincible in battle.

If there had been an insufficient supply of cloves at the time of the arrival of the fleet, there was certainly no lack of them as the weeks wore on, and the time for sailing approached. The Sultan issued a proclamation that all who had them might sell, after which, says Pigafetta, "we bought them like mad." The prices in consequence went down very much. For four yards of ribbon a bahar was obtainable, and at length, each man wishing to have his share in the cargo, and having no more merchandise to barter, gave one his mantle, and another his coat, and another his shirt or other garments to obtain them.

On Monday, 16th December, they bent new sails to the ships, each adorned with the Cross of St. James of Galicia, and with the motto, "This is the Device of our Good Fortune." Eighty barrels of water were put on board each vessel, and the preparations for departure pushed forward. Their wood they had arranged to obtain at the little island of Mareb, whither the king had sent a hundred men to cut it. Anxious to be provided with the best sources of information concerning the Moluccas and their trade, they offered Lorosa, the Portuguese, a high salary, and succeeded in persuading him to accompany them to Europe. He embarked at the risk of his life, for a Ternate chieftain - a friend of the Portuguese - attempted to seize him, with the intention of delivering him to the commandant of Malacca. Lorosa escaped upon this occasion. However, an unlucky fate having thrown him a few months later into the power of his countrymen, he paid for his desertion with his head.

The time had now arrived for the departure of the Trinidad and her consort. The Sultan of Tidor was inconsolable. He was as an unweaned child, he said, whom its mother was about to leave. He was the more disconsolate since he had got to like not only the Spaniards but so many of the products of their country. He besought of them that they would not fail to return as quickly as possible. Meanwhile, the Sultan begged that he might be left some artillery in order that he should be the better able to defend his country. He was accordingly presented with some arquebuses that had been taken in the prizes captured off the Bornean coast, besides some swivel guns and four barrels of powder.

On Wednesday, December 18th, all was ready. Much as the weary and wave-tossed explorers longed for rest and the pleasant land of Castile, they were heartily sorry to leave the Moluccas, where they had obtained so warm a welcome and so valuable a cargo. No one could bid adieu to so beautiful a country without regret. The charm of existence there, once tasted, can never be forgotten. "What need is there of many words ?" says Maximilian. "Everything there is humble and of no value, save peace, ease, and spices. The best and noblest of these, and the greatest possible good, namely, peace, seemed to have been driven by men's wickedness from our world to theirs." Alas ! it did not long remain there. For half a century or more from the time of which he spoke, the most atrocious acts of cruelty and treachery daily wrote the annals of the islands in blood.

Passage through the Spice Islands

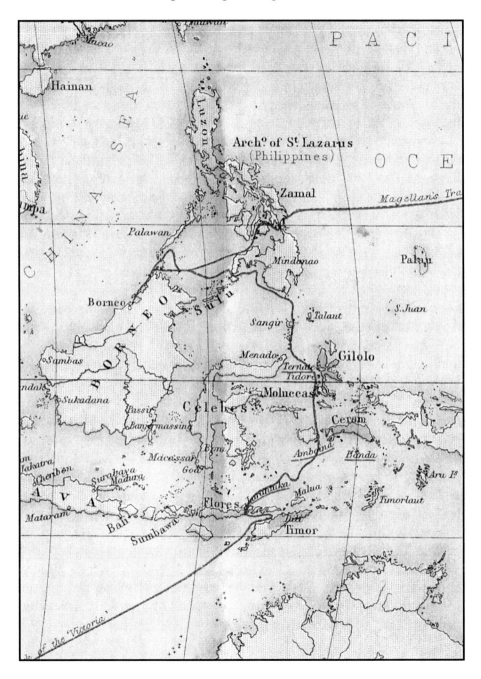

The Sultans and Rajahs of Tidor, Gilolo, and Batchian, together with a son of the King of Ternate, came to bid farewell to their visitors, and to accompany them as far as the island of Mareh. The Victoria was first aweigh, and standing out a little waited for the flagship, which was in difficulties with her anchor. While engaged in this, a leak of the most alarming kind was suddenly discovered; "the water rushed in with as much force as if it came through a pipe". However, nowhere could they discover its exact situation. Learning what had occurred, del Cano returned and took up his former anchorage. The men were kept day and night at the pumps, but in vain, and the leak gained on them. Such divers as were available were employed, but to no purpose, and the Sultan sent to a distant part of the island for three other men who were possessed of special skill. These dived with their long hair loose, so that the inrush of the water should act upon it, and thus indicate the leak. However, although they remained more than an hour in the water, they were unable to find it.

The condition of the Trinidad was evidently serious, and a meeting was held to decide upon their course of action. Eventually it was settled that the Victoria should take advantage of the east monsoon, and sail for Spain without delay. Meanwhile, the flagship should discharge cargo, undergo a thorough refit, and start at the change of the monsoon for Panama. This decision arrived at, the captain of the Victoria, fearing that she also might spring a leak on account of the heavy cargo and the long voyage before them, thought it better to lighten her of some of her cloves. This was done, and some of the crew were put ashore, preferring to remain in the Moluccas, since they feared the ship could not last out the voyage. Those that were to remain behind busied themselves in writing letters to their friends and relations in Spain, and on Saturday the 21st December, at midday, del Cano started on his voyage. The ships took leave of one another by a mutual discharge of bombards. Amid tears and embraces, the friends of many months mutual hardships bade adieu. The greater number were destined never to see each other again. Gonzalo Gomez de Espinosa, with fifty-three men, remained with the flagship.

CHAPTER 18

THE FATE OF THE TRINIDAD

Before completing the history of Magellan's voyage, we must detail the fate of the Trinidad. Her condition was such as to necessitate the discharge of all her cargo, and a thorough examination of her timbers. She was accordingly dismantled. Her artillery, cargo, spars, and fittings were sent ashore, and placed under guard in the store that the Sultan of Tidor had allowed them to erect, and the vessel having been careened, the work of her repair was at once commenced. While engaged upon it, Espinosa received a visit from the King of Gilolo, who begged for cannon or firearms to aid him in subduing some rebels with whom he was fighting. A small number of Spaniards were sent to his assistance, and before they returned, the Indians had worked so well under the direction of the captain that the ship was ready for sea.

It was decided to leave certain goods and articles of barter upon the island, as much that a centre of Spanish influence might be established, as that trade should continue until the arrival of the next armada. Luis del Molino was therefore selected as officer in charge. Juan de Campos acted as clerk and treasurer, and Alonso de Cota, Diego Arias, and Master Pedro - one of the Flemish bombardiers - formed the remainder of the garrison. Carvalho, the deposed Captain-general, had died on the 14th February.

On the 6th April 1522, the Trinidad sailed upon her long voyage to Panama - a destination she was fated never to attain. She was manned by a crew of fifty four men all told, and took a cargo of a thousand quintals, or nearly fifty tons of cloves. The course resolved on led them northwards, coasting the west shores of Gilolo until its terminal cape was reached. Rounding it they came in sight of Chão or Porquenampello and Pyliom - two islands subsequently known as Morti and Rau - and passed between them and the mainland of Gilolo on a southerly course. Their object was to make "Quimar," a district under the authority of the Sultan of Tidor, where fresh provisions were awaiting them. Quimar and its port Zanufo, Camafo, or Camarfya (which are doubtless synonymous), have been variously identified with

Morotai or Morti, and the N.E. arm of Gilolo. The port at which they called is more probably Komo, on the northern peninsula of that island, a conjecture further borne out by the Paris MS., which says that on leaving it they "steered seventeen leagues eastward, and came out of the channel of the island of Batechina (Gilolo) and the island Chão."

After a stay of eight or nine days they again made sail on the 20th April (the 25th April, according to the Paris MS). Steering eastward, they ran out into the open sea, when they set an E. ¼N. course. Head winds, however, compelled them to alter it, and they ran to the N.E. and N.N.E. until, on the 3rd May (May 6th according to the Paris MS.), two small islands were sighted. To these which were in all probability Warwick and Warren Hastings Islands - they gave the name of the islands of St. Anthony. The ship was now navigated for the Ladrones, one of the northern islands of which - conjecturally Agrigan - was visited, and a native taken on board. It is difficult to explain why, on leaving this group, a persistent north-easterly course should have been held, but so it was. They met, as might well be imagined, with constant head winds. Espinosa was probably more fitted for an alguazil than a captain. We are not informed who undertook the navigation of the ship. It was probably Juan Bautista Punzero, to whom de Brito declares the arrival of the fleet at the Moluccas to have been due, or possibly the Genoese Leon Pancaldo or Pancado - certainly not Espinosa, who was a person of no education and could not even write his own name. The latitude of 43° N. was finally reached, but long before this they had begun to run short of provisions. Eventually they were reduced to rice, and rice only. Ill provided with clothes and accustomed for so long to a tropical climate, they were unable to endure the cold. Disease found them a facile prey. To crown their misfortunes, they encountered a severe storm that lasted for five days and caused them the loss of their mainmast, besides considerable injury to their poop and forecastle. Under these circumstances it was found impossible to proceed, and Espinosa resolved to return by way of the Marianas to Tidor. His effort to regain the island he first visited was unsuccessful, and he brought up off Saipan, or Pamo (otherwise Mao), as it was then called. Here the native he had picked up on his outward voyage ran away, together with three of the sailors, who were fearful of the epidemic that was at that time so rapidly reducing the crew in numbers. Oviedo tells us how, more than three years later, the ships of Loyasa came across one of these men, Gonzalo de Vigo, in Tinian. His two companions had been killed by the natives. This deserter was of much use to them, and he was taken on to the Moluccas. The return from the Marianas to Gilolo was effected in six weeks, and they anchored off Dui, an island near its northern point. Further than that it was impossible for them to proceed. Three-fifths of their number were dead, and the rest were so disabled by scurvy and other disorders that they could no longer navigate the ship.

Meanwhile, a considerable change had taken place in the aspect of affairs at Tidor. On the 13th May, little more than a month after their departure, a fleet of seven Portuguese vessels, manned by over three hundred men, and under the command of Antonio de Brito, sailed into Ternate roads. His visit had, perhaps, been partly induced by finding in Banda - the port whence he came - one of the five Spaniards left behind in Tidor by Espinosa, who had doubtless gone thither for the sake of trade. De Brito's first step, as appears by his own letter to the King of Portugal, was to demand the surrender of the storehouse and its contents, together with the men in charge. They had no course open to them other than to yield to such a force. Possession was at once taken of the building, and the stores appropriated. The Captain-general demanded of the Sultan what right he had to admit the Castilians when the Portuguese had been so long established in the islands.

Espinosa had not been long at his anchorage before the news of the arrival and doings of the Portuguese was brought to him. He resolved, nevertheless, to give himself up to de Brito, so deplorable was his condition. Spain was, moreover, upon good terms with Portugal, and he hoped for fair treatment. He therefore sent a letter by Bartholomew Sanchez, clerk of the Trinidad, to the Portuguese Captain-general, begging succour. No answer arriving, Espinosa weighed anchor. He struggled on for a few miles to the port of Benaconora where he was at length met by a caravel and other small craft with Simon d'Abreu, Duarte de Resende, Don Garcia Enriques, and twenty armed Portuguese. They gave the captain a letter from de Brito (dated 21st October 1522). They at once took possession of the ship, seizing all the papers and log-books that could be found, as well as her astrolabes and quadrants. She was then brought in and anchored off Ternate, and her cargo discharged. It was the last voyage she was destined to make. During her unloading a heavy squall caught her, and she went ashore and broke up. Forty bahars of cloves were lost in her. However, her timbers and fittings were saved, and served in the construction of the fortress the Portuguese were then erecting in Ternate, and in the repair of their ships.

It was in vain that Espinosa protested against the action taken by the Portuguese. They replied that he had done his duty to his sovereign, and that they should do the same to theirs. He asked that they would at least give him a certificate of the items of the ship's cargo, in order that he might render an account of it to the emperor. However, he was told that if he wished an account rendered, he should render it himself from the yardarm of his vessel. He was called upon to deliver the royal standard, but this he declined to do. He said that since he was in their power they could of course seize it, but that he was unable, as an officer of the emperor, to surrender it.

When the Trinidad was brought to her last anchorage she had on board but nineteen survivors of the fifty-four men who had sailed in her but six months previously. Pedro Affonso de Lorosa - the Portuguese who had deserted from Don Tristão de Meneses - was also with them. His fate did not remain long in doubt, for he was executed shortly after his arrival. Of the five men left in Tidor in charge of the stores one had died, three were prisoners of the Portuguese, and Luis del Molino was at large among the islanders. On receiving a message from Espinosa he came in and gave himself up. From these men the others learnt what had taken place in their absence. The Portuguese had levelled the factory and storehouse to the ground, seizing all the rigging and fitting of the ships, together with the cloves and other spices that had been collected. Espinosa and his men were able to realise what was before them. Could they have seen the letter written by Antonio de Brito upon the subject to his royal master, their fears would scarcely have been alleviated. "So far as concerns the master, clerk, and pilot" - it runs - "I am writing to the Captain-general that it would be more to your Highness' service to order their heads to be struck off than to send them there (i.e., to India). I kept them in the Moluccas, because it is a most unhealthy country, in order that they might die there, not liking to order their heads to be cut off, since I did not know whether your Highness would be pleased or not. I am writing to Jorge de Albuquerque to detain them in Malacca, which, however, is a very healthy climate."

With this laudable desire for their speedy decease in the heart of their captor, it may be imagined that the outlook of the Spaniards was not of a very promising nature. The sick were, however, sent to a temporary hospital. Great mortality prevailed at first in the Moluccas, as we learn from de Brito's letter. Within two months of his arrival he had lost fifty of his men, and only fifty remained in health. The remainder went to the fortress upon Ternate, which the Portuguese were at that time engaged in building. There they were set to work upon it - Espinosa himself being ordered to labour with the others, an order that he declined to obey. It is negatively to the credit of de Brito that he thought it best not to press the matter. However, they were subjected to many indignities, being openly and grossly abused before the natives in order that the authority and repute of the emperor might be as far as possible belittled.

In this manner the twenty-three prisoners were detained in Ternate. At the end of February 1523, with the exception of two carpenters whom de Brito needed, they started on their homeward voyage. The voyage destined to be protracted from months into years, and to end at last with the safe return of but four of their number. Terrible as had been the mortality on board the Victoria, it was as nothing compared with that of the Trinidad.

The men were first taken to Banda. Four of them who left Ternate together never reached the island, and of the junk in which they sailed no tidings were ever heard. The others were detained in Banda for four months and then despatched by way of Java, at whose ports they touched, to Malacca, where they came into the hands of Jorge d'Albuquerque, who was at that time Governor. More delays took place here. We have seen how de Brito gave actual instructions for their detention, lamenting, nevertheless, the healthiness of the climate. It was, however, sufficiently malarious or insanitary to bring four of the unhappy wanderers to the grave. Anton Moreno, an African slave of Espinosa, was appropriated by Albuquerque's sister, and it was not until five months had passed away that the voyage of the survivors was resumed.

From Malacca the prisoners, for such they still were, were sent to Cochin. They appear to have embarked in two or more ships. The junk in which Bartholomew Sanchez, Luis del Molino, and Alonso de Cota sailed was never more heard of, and when the others reached their destination the annual homeward-bound fleet had sailed. Despairing of ever getting back to their native land, two of their number, Leon Pancaldo and Juan Bautista Poncero (who originally sailing as maestre of the Trinidad, was described in various lists as Punzerol and Ponce de Leon) ran away and concealed themselves on board the Santa Catalina, each ignorant of the other's presence. This ship was bound for Portugal, but on arriving at Mozambique the two stowaways were put ashore, with the intention of returning them to Cochin. Both men, however, succeeded in disappointing their captors. Juan Bautista died. Leon Pancaldo hiding himself just as Diogo de Mello's ship started for Cochin, managed to ship on board a homeward-bound vessel commanded by Francisco Pereira. Upon his arrival at Lisbon he was thrown into prison, but was eventually set free by order of the king.

Meanwhile, the others remained behind at Cochin. Vasco da Gama, then viceroy, had remained deaf to their entreaties for release. On Christmas Eve, 1524, he died, and was succeeded by Don Enrique de Meneses, who, more compassionate than his predecessor, consented at length to their departure. However, their numbers had sadly decreased. Four, as we have seen, had died during their detention in Malacca, and three more had fallen victims to their hardships in Cochin. Juan Rodriguez of Seville had escaped in the ship of Andres de Sousa, which was bound for Lisbon. There remained but three men, Gonzalo Gomez de Espinosa, the captain; Gines de Mafra, seaman of the Trinidad; and Master Hans or Aires, bombardier of the Victoria. There is a discrepancy in the various documents concerning this third individual. According to some, it was Morales the surgeon who returned with Espinosa and died in the Lisbon prison, while the bombardier Aires came back in the Victoria, and was one of those who went to court to be presented to Charles V. Their troubles were not over upon landing in the Peninsula, for they were thrown into the common prison, where, overcome by his previous sufferings and the treatment to which he was subjected, Master Hans died. Espinosa and Gines de Mafra remained incarcerated for seven long months, when the former was released. Mafra, having in his box some log-books and nautical works or notes written by Andres de San Martin, was supposed to be a pilot, and was detained longer. On proving his rank and condition he was permitted his liberty a month later. However, the books were seized, and afterwards, as far as can be learnt, came into the hands of João de Barros the historian. Barros writes of having got papers and books from Duarte de Resende, who "took them from the astrologer Andres de San Martin," besides those he obtained from Espinosa.

Four men, and four men only, thus remained alive out of the fifty-four who sailed in the Trinidad from Ternate - Gonzalo Gomez de Espinosa, alguacil of the fleet; Gines de Mafra, of Jerez, marinero; Leon Pancado (or Pancaldo), of Saona near Genoa, marinero; Juan Rodriguez (el Sordo), of Seville, marinero, formerly of the Concepcion. Hans Vargue ("Maestre Ance") - a German - was master-gunner of the Concepcion, and was afterwards borne on the Trinidad. He reached Lisbon with Espinosa and Gines de Mafra, and being thrown into prison with them immediately on his arrival, perished there. Espinosa was well received by his sovereign, who rewarded him, and - if we may credit a passage in Oviedo - granted him a patent of nobility and a life pension of 300 ducats. However, so mean were the officials of the India House that they actually docked him of his pay during the time that he was a captive in the hands of the Portuguese, alleging as a reason that it was incontestable that while in that condition he was no longer in the service of Spain ! On the 14th January 1528, Espinosa instituted a plaint to recover this money. A long procés was the result, but whether he gained his cause or not is not recorded.

CHAPTER 19

THE RETURN OF THE VICTORIA

The crew of the Victoria consisted of sixty men all told, of which forty-seven were Europeans and the rest natives. Touching at Mare, and taking on board the wood that had been cut for them, the Victoria shaped a S.W. Course that took her to the west of the Batchian group. Anchoring at one of the Xulla Islands on their way, they reached Buru on Friday, the 27th December, and obtained fresh provisions. On New Year's eve they were off the Lucopin or Schildpad Islands, and sighting the great island barrier that stretches from Timor to Sumatra on the 8th January 1522, passed through it in a storm so severe that all vowed a pilgrimage to N.S. de la Guia. What passage was chosen by the Victoria is uncertain, but there is no doubt that it was either Flores Strait or Boleng Strait, from details in Pigafetta and Albo's log-book. The ship was allowed to run before the gale on an easterly course, coasting the southern side of the chain, and eventually the island of Mallua - subsequently Ombay (now Alor) - was reached in safety.

Here they spent fifteen days. The ship stood in need of caulking, and the crew were kept at work at it. The people of Ombay seemed to have been of Papuan origin, judging from Pigafetta's account of their "hair raised high up by means of cane combs with long teeth," and also by the beard being encased in reed tubes, "a thing," he adds, "which seemed to us most ridiculous."

On Saturday, January 25th, del Cano sailed, from Ombay, and having run some twenty miles to the S.S.E., arrived at the large island of Timor. The Portuguese at that time had no settlements upon it, and indeed had never even visited it. However, it was renowned throughout the archipelago for its trade in sandalwood and wax. At the time of the Spaniards' visit a Luzon junk was trading in the port at which they touched. Having some difficulty in getting provisions, the captain ordered one of the chiefs who had visited the vessel to be detained until he ransomed himself with live stock. However, on receiving this, del Cano gave him an equivalent value in articles of barter and sent him away satisfied. The Victoria then continued her voyage, coasting the north-western side of the island until its terminal cape was reached. On the 13th of February she was put on a S.S.W. course across the Indian Ocean for the Cape of Good Hope. Gomera records the visit of the Victoria to Ende or Flores island, which would tend to prove that she passed through Flores Strait. His account also speaks of a mutiny at Timor. Oviedo also has a passage that seems to bear this out. Both probably, borrowed from Pigafetta's words. However, the official death-list does not make any mention of such executions, while, on the other hand, it records the deaths of fifteen men on the high seas and the desertion of two others. Pigafetta tells us that the ship left Tidor with a complement of forty-seven. We know that she reached the Cape Verdes with thirty-one - a number that exactly tallies, presuming that Pigafetta did not count himself. We are therefore forced to reject the story of the mutiny.

Day after day that course was held, except indeed when necessity compelled them, as it too often did, to strike all sail for purposes of repair. On the 14th March they kept a point or two more to the west, and four days later, while taking their mid-day observations, land was sighted ahead. An attempt was made to fetch it and anchor, but they were unable to do so, and they accordingly lay to until the following day. No landing, however, was effected, and the ship bore away to the north. The island was that subsequently known as Amsterdam Island.

Their long voyage had already begun to tell both on ship and men. On the 3rd April they were again compelled to strike all sail and busy themselves with the repairing of the ship. What these repairs were we are not told, but they were probably connected with the state of her hull, for she was then leaking considerably. The crew, after such long service within the tropics, felt the cold greatly. The meat had all become unfit for food. Their lack of salt had not permitted them properly to cure it, and hence all hands were reduced to a diet of rice, and rice only. Upon such rations there is little wonder that sickness broke out. So enfeebled were the crew that it was debated whether they should not make for Mozambique, where the Portuguese had been long established. "However, the greater number of us valued honour more than life itself," says Pigafetta, "and so we resolved at all hazards to attempt the return to Spain."

Across the Indian Ocean

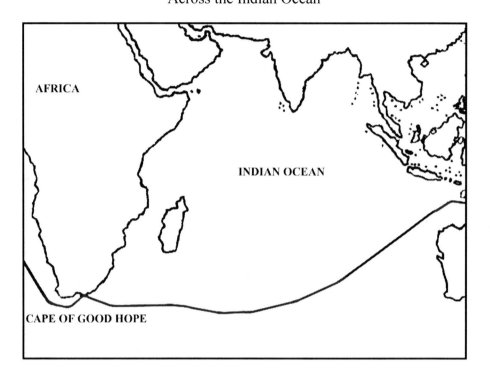

From the 7th April to the 16th April the Victoria held her course between the fortieth and forty-first parallels of latitude. South of this she did not sail, and with a strong wind and heavy sea she bore to the north on the following day. For nearly a month they pressed on, until on the 8th May they sighted the high land of South Africa, and anchored on the following day. They were at fault both in latitude and longitude, for they had imagined themselves to have passed the meridian of the Cape. Running along the south coast they arrived off the mouth of the Rio del Infante, or Keiskamma river, on the 11th. They were not destined to pass the dreaded Cape without accident, for in heavy weather on the 16th May they carried away their foretopmast and sprung their fore-yard. Two days later they passed Cape Agulhas. Correa writes that the Victoria met and spoke with the ship of Pero Coresma, then on her way to India, off the Cape. The incident is mentioned by him alone, and is probably one of his many inaccuracies. Again they had to stop for repairs, and again they struggled on. Scurvy and starvation had reduced them to the greatest misery and distress.

Nearly one third of their own number had died, and nine of the thirteen natives. Pigafetta was almost the sole person in health. "We noticed a curious thing in throwing the bodies overboard," he wrote; "the Christians remained with the face turned up to heaven - the Indians with the face downwards."

The Line was crossed on June 8th, and on the 1st July a meeting was held to decide whether they should or should not touch at the Cape Verdes. The conclusion was foregone, for dire necessity had rendered it impossible for them to proceed further. They arrived on Wednesday, July 9th, at Santiago, and anchored in the port. Knowing that they ran great risk of being seized, instructions were given to those who went ashore to conceal who they were, and to pretend that they came from America, giving out that the other two ships of their squadron had preceded them to Spain, but that they had been delayed by the loss of their foretopmast on the Line. We learn from Albo's diary that they were well received and supplied with provisions by the Portuguese. On the night of Sunday 13th July, they put to sea, the weather being threatening and the port unsafe. In the morning they returned and lay on and off while they sent a boat for rice. One trip was made, but she did not again return. They waited until next day in vain, and then stood in towards the port, when a boat came alongside and ordered them to surrender. The secret had leaked out, either by the bragging of one of the crew at a wine shop, or as Maximilian tells us, by an attempt made by a sailor to sell some of his cloves. This latter statement is borne out by the evidence of Albo and Bustamante. In his answer, del Cano temporised, and asked for the return of his boat and men. However, seeing some caravels preparing to get under weigh, they crowded all sail and escaped, leaving their comrades in the hands of the Portuguese. They had now but eighteen Europeans and four natives left on board - scarce enough to work the ship; for although improved in health and strength by the fresh provisions, and cheered by the prospect of their rapidly approaching return, the greater number of them were upon the sick-list. Their sufferings were not to endure much longer.

From the Cape of Good Hope back to Spain

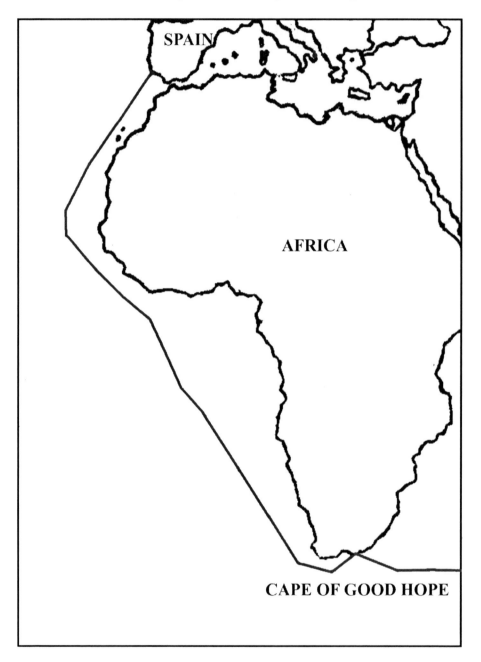

Soon the welcome shore of Spain hove in sight. It proved to be Cape San Vincent, and keeping away to the east and south the Victoria arrived off San Lucar de Barrameda on Saturday the 6th September 1522. On Monday the 8th September - three years all but twelve days from the date of their final departure from Spain - they anchored near the mole of Seville. The First Circumnavigation of the Globe was accomplished, and a voyage brought to a conclusion that was, and is, without parallel in its history of determination and suffering, disaster and success. With what delight must they not have discharged their salvoes of artillery, and recounted their adventures to the crowds who flocked to welcome them. Yet, amid their joy, the vows that they had promised so often in the hour of danger were not forgotten. On the day following their arrival all who were able to walk went in procession, barefoot and carrying tapers, to the shrines of Santa Maria de la Victoria and Santa Maria de Antigua. They offered their heartfelt thanks for their safe return.

From Pigafetta's journal we learn that thirty-one men of the Victoria eventually returned home. Herrera also gives the names of thirty-one as going to Court to relate their adventures to the Emperor. Thirteen of these had been seized by the Portuguese in the Cape Verde Islands, but they were released shortly afterwards and sent at once to Seville.

Herrera's list has been copied by numerous writers, even by those of a later date, such as Lord Stanley of Alderley and De Barros Arana, without any attempt, apparently, to verify it. It is nevertheless very erroneous, as a careful consideration of the documents relating to the expedition shows. The following lists have been corrected as far as is possible to give the names of the eighteen men who returned to Seville on the Victoria :

Miguel de Rodas, contramaestre of the Victoria

Miguel Sanchez, of Rodas, marinero of the Victoria

Martin de Isaurraga, of Bermeo, grumete of the Concepcion

Nicholas the Greek, of Naples, marinero of the Victoria

Juan Rodriguez, of Seville, marinero of the Trinidad - Three men of this name sailed on the voyage. The other two were borne as marineros on the Concepcion. One died on the voyage; the other, nicknamed "el Sordo," was one of the four survivors of the Trinidad.

Vasco Gomez Gallego, Portuguese, grumete of the Trinidad - Not Vasco Gallego, pilot of the Victoria, who died February 28th, 1521.

Martin de Judicibus, of Genoa, superintendent of the Concepcion

Juan de Santandres, of Cueto, grumete of the Trinidad

Hernando de Bustamante, of Merida or Alcantara, barber of the Concepcion

Antonio Pigafetta, of Vicenza

Francisco Rodriguez, of Seville, a Portuguese - marinero of the Concepcion

Antonio Ros or Rodriguez, of Huelva, marinero of the Trinidad

Diego Gallego, of Bayonne - marinero of the Victoria

Juan de Arratia (or de Sahelices), of Bilbao, grumete of the Victoria

Juan de Acurio, of Bermeo, contramaestre of the Concepcion

Juan de Gubileta (or Zuvileta or Zubieta), of Baracaldo, page of the Victoria

Francisco Albo (Or Alvaro or Calvo, the pilot who has left us the log-book record of the voyage) of Axio, contramaestre of the Trinidad.

Juan Sebastian del Cano (Juan Sebastián Elcano), of Guetaria, master of the Concepcion

Herrera gives the following names in his list as also being among the survivors : Lorenzo de Iruna, Juan de Ortega, Diego Garcia, Pedro de Valpuesta, and Martin de Magallanes. All these men, however, died on the voyage, and their deaths are recorded in the official list. It is a curious circumstance that they should all without exception have died near the termination of the voyage. Lorenzo de Iruna succumbed as the Victoria was rounding the Cape. Martin Magellan, the last of the five, died on the 26th June 1522, almost within sight of the Cape Verde Islands.

Before the advent of the Victoria it was not realised that circumnavigation of the globe implied the loss or gain of a day, according to the east or west direction of the voyage. The Spaniards were accordingly much astonished, on reaching civilisation, to find themselves out in their calculations. The fact is given to us by Ramusio in his introduction to Maximilian's letter, and Eden, in the quaint language of his day, also comments upon it.

The papers in the Seville archives give us full details of the spices brought back in the Victoria. The bulk of the cargo consisted of cloves, and of these, exclusive of the quintalades or free freight permitted alike to officers and men, there were 520 quintals, or about twenty-six tons of our weight. The value of this was estimated at 7,888,684 maravedis, and in addition there was a certain quantity of cinnamon, mace, nutmeg, and sandalwood that raised the value. On the whole, despite the frightful losses both of ships and cargo during the voyage of the armada, the venture had been successful. Deducting the value of the Victoria and her fittings, and of the articles of barter aboard her, from the original cost of the entire expedition, the value of the spices was found to exceed the latter.

The thirteen men left at the Cape Verde Islands were released and sent on to Lisbon very shortly afterwards in a homeward-bound ship from Calicut. The united crew were received by the emperor at court. These were :

Maestre Pedro, from Tenerife, of the Santiago - Maestre Pedro, who is probably identical with Herrera's Pedro de Indarchi, was shipped in Tenerife on 1st October 1519.

Richard, from Normandy, carpenter of the Santiago - Variously called Ricarte, Rigarte, Ripart, Ruxar, or Ruger Carpintete. His birthplace is given as Bruz (?) or Ebras (?).

Pedro Gasco, of Bordeaux, marinero of the Santiago

Alfonso Domingo, marinero of the Santiago

Simon de Burgos, Portuguese, servant of the Captain, Luis de Mendoza, Victoria

Juan Martin, of Aguilar de Campo, servant of the Captain, Luis de Mendoza, Victoria

Roldan de Argote, of Bruges, bombardier of the Concepcion

Martin Mendez, of Seville, accountant of the Victoria

Gomez Hernandez, of Huelva, marinero of the Concepcion

Ocacio Alonso, of Bollullos, marinero of the Santiago

Pedro de Tolosa, of Tolosa in Guipuzcoa, grumete of the Victoria

Felipe de Rodas, of Rodas, marinero of the Victoria

Juan de Apega - This man, mentioned by Herrera, is probably identical with Juan Ortiz de Gopega of Bilbao, steward of the San Antonio

Of the Indians, all except one were sent back to the Moluccas in Loyasa's expedition in 1525. That one unwittingly owed his detention to his over-shrewdness. "On arriving in Spain," says Oviedo, "the first thing he did was to inquire how many reals went to a ducat, and how many maravedis to a real. And going to the vendas and grocers' shops, he was wont to buy a maravedi's worth of pepper, informing himself on all points concerning the value of spices in our country; and so sharp was he about it that the authorities feared his knowledge, and hence he himself brought it about that he never returned to his native land." The after history of that intrepid and amusing traveller, the Chevalier Antonio Pigafetta, shall be related in his own words : "Then, leaving Seville, I repaired to Valladolid, where I presented to His Sacred Majesty Don Carlos neither gold nor silver, but other things far more precious in the eyes of so great a sovereign. For I brought to him among other things a book written with my own hands, giving an account of all the events which had happened from day to day in our voyage. Thence I set out as best I could, and went to Portugal, where I related to King John the things which I had seen. Returning by way of Spain, I came to France, where I presented some things from the other hemisphere to the Regent - mother of the most Christian King Don Francis. Then I turned my face towards Italy, where I gave myself, and what slight services I could render to the renowned and most illustrious Signor, Philip de Villers Lisleadam, the most worthy Grand Master of Rhodes."

The ultimate fate of the Victoria we learn from Oviedo. After making one voyage in safety to the West Indies, she was again despatched to Cuba. However, though she reached her destination she never returned, caught in some Atlantic gale, her timbers, rotten from age and tropic seas, must have proved unequal to the strain. Such at least we may conjecture, for neither of her, nor of those that sailed in her, were any tidings ever heard.

The fame of Magellan's voyage resounded through the length and breadth of the Peninsula, and reached all parts of Europe. Charles V, who had just arrived from Germany, on learning of the arrival of the Victoria wrote at once from Valladolid to Sebastian del Cano, instructing him to appear at court with two of the best instructed of his crew. The whole number, as we have seen, were ultimately presented. Charles was generous to del Cano beyond his deserts. He was granted an annual pension of 500 ducats, and a coat-of-arms commemorating the services he had rendered to Spain. Fortune befriended him indeed. The little we know of him in Magellan's voyage - for until his appointment after the wholesale massacre at Cebu he was comparatively an obscure personage - is far from being in his favour. He took an active part in the mutiny at Port St. Julian, and gave evidence at Valladolid upon certain events of the voyage that was so biased, and in some cases so untrue, that he forfeits much of his claim to our admiration. Neither can he be given any very great credit for his navigation, for it must not be forgotten that when he took the command the hitherto unknown Pacific had been crossed, and the ship was far beyond the longitude of the Moluccas, and distant from them only six hundred miles. Antonio de Brito, moreover, in his letter to the King of Portugal, tells us that after the death of Magellan, Juan Bautista Poncero was the chief navigator. However, to del Cano fell the good fortune of bringing home the Victoria, and, as her captain, the honours accorded upon the occasion of such a great event naturally fell to his share.

It may be imagined that the arrival of the Victoria was a matter of no little joy to Alvaro de Mesquita, the unhappy captain of the San Antonio. It will be remembered how the mutineers of that vessel, deserting their captain - general in his hour of need, overpowered their commander and brought him, wounded and in irons, to Seville. Although their story was but half-believed, Mesquita was still kept incarcerated, as was the manner of those times. Now, set at liberty, he was rewarded in common with his former friends and comrades, upon whom pensions and various distinctions were conferred. For some reason, perhaps the length of time that had elapsed since the occurrence, a corresponding punishment does not seem to have overtaken the mutineers.

We have done now with the great expedition of Magellan, and with the return of "that unique, that most famous ship, the Victoria," as Oviedo calls her. "The track she followed," he exclaims, "is the most wonderful thing and the greatest novelty that has ever been seen from the time God created the first man and ordered the world unto our own day. Neither has anything more notable in navigation ever been heard or described since the voyage of the patriarch Noah." The extravagant terms of admiration, the flowery periods, the elaborate metaphors characteristic of the period in which they lived, were lavishly used by the historians who chronicled the voyage. The keynote was struck by

Maximilian Transylvanus in his Salzburg letter, and the theme has been introduced by every one who has written upon the subject, from Argensola and Gomara to Camoens. The latter, indeed, seems to have borrowed the idea of a famous verse in the Lusiad from Oviedo, and turns Magellan's praise into Gama's. However, all this praise and glory came too late for Magellan's family, as they did for the immortal commander. Whilst he himself lay at rest in a little islet in the far Pacific, neither his wife nor child were fated to live much longer. In September 1521, five months after Magellan's death in the Philippines, his son Rodrigo died. In March of the following year, 1522, "having lived in great sorrow from the news which she had received of the death of her husband," Magellan's wife Beatriz also died, before the voyage for which her husband became so famous had even been completed.

CHAPTER 20

PIGAFETTA'S JOURNAL OF THE VOYAGE

Antonio Pigafetta was an Italian navigator. He was one of the few people that completed the entire journey around the world. He kept a journal in which hearsay evidence is largely mixed with personal experience, but which gives by far the best and fullest account of the expedition.

****

Since there are several curious persons (very illustrious and very reverend lord) who not only are pleased to listen to and learn the great and wonderful things that God has permitted me to see and suffer in the long and, perilous navigation, that I have performed (and which is written hereafter), but also they desire to learn the methods and fashions of the road that I have taken in order to go thither, (and who do) not grant firm belief to the end unless they are first well advised and assured of the commencement. Therefore, my lord, it will please you to hear that finding myself in Spain in the year of the Nativity of our Lord, one thousand five hundred and nineteen, at the court of the most serene king of the Romans, with the reverend lord, Mons. Francis Cheregato, then apostolic proto-notary, and ambassador of the Pope Leon the Tenth, who, through his virtue, afterwards arrived at the bishopric of Aprutino and the principality of Theramo, and knowing both by the reading of many books and by the report of many lettered and well-informed persons who conversed with the said proto-notary, the very great and awful things of the ocean, I deliberated, with the favour of the Emperor and the above-named lord, to experiment and go and see with my eyes a part of those things. By which means I could satisfy the desire of the said lords, and mine own also. So that it might be said that I had performed the said voyage, and seen well with my eyes the things hereafter written.

Now in order to decypher the commencement of my voyage (very illustrious lord); having heard that there was in the city of Seville, a small armade to the number of five ships, ready to perform this long voyage, that is to say, to find the islands of Maluco, from whence the spices come : of which armade the captain-general was Fernand de Magaglianes, a Portuguese gentleman, commander of St. James of the Sword, who had performed several voyages in the ocean sea (in which he had behaved very honourably as a good man), I set out with many others in my favour from Barcelona, where at the time the Emperor was, and came by sea as far as Malaga, and thence I went away by land until I arrived at the said city of Seville. There I remained for the space of three months, waiting till the said armade was in order and readiness to perform its voyage. And because (very illustrious lord) that on the return from the said voyage, on going to Rome towards the holiness of our Holy Father, I found your lordship at Monterosa, where of your favour you gave me a good reception, and afterwards gave me to understand that you desired to have in writing the things which God of His grace had permitted me to see in my said voyage; therefore to satisfy and accede to your desire, I have reduced into this small book the principal things, in the best manner that I have been able.

Finally (very illustrious lord), after all provisions had been made, and the vessels were in order, the captain-general, a discreet and virtuous man, careful of his honour, would not commence his voyage without first making some good and wholesome ordinances, such as it is the good custom to make for those who go to sea. Nevertheless he did not entirely declare the voyage which he was going to make, so that his men should not from amazement and fear be unwilling to accompany him on so long a voyage, as he had undertaken in his intention. Considering the great and impetuous storms which are on the ocean sea, where I wished to go; and for another reason also, that is to say that the masters and captains of the other ships of his company did not love him of this I do not know the reason, except by cause of his, the captain-general, being Portuguese, and they were Spaniards or Castilians, who for a long time have been in rivalry and ill will with one another. Notwithstanding this all were obedient to him. He made his ordinances such as those that follow, so that during the storms at sea, which often come on by night and day, his ships should not go away and separate from one another. These ordinances he published and made over in writing to each master of the ships, and commanded them to be observed and inviolably kept, unless there were great and legitimate excuses, and appearance of not having been able to do otherwise.

Firstly, the said captain-general willed that the vessel in which he himself was should go before the other vessels, and that the others should follow it; therefore he carried by night on the poop of his ship a torch or faggot of burning wood, which they called farol, which burned all the night, so that his ships should not lose sight of him. Sometimes he set a lantern, sometimes a thick cord of reeds was lighted, which was called trenche. This is made of reeds well soaked in the water, and much beaten, then they are dried in the sun or in the smoke, and it is a thing very suitable for such a matter. When the captain had made one of his signals to his people, they answered in the same way. In that manner they knew whether the ships were following and keeping together or not. And when he wished to take a tack on account of the change of weather, or if the wind was contrary, or if he wished to make less way, he had two lights shown; and if he wished the others to lower their small sail, which was a part of the sail attached to the great sail, he showed three lights. Also by the three lights, notwithstanding that the wind was fair for going faster, he signalled that the studding sail should be lowered; so that the great sail might be quicker and more easily struck and furled when bad weather should suddenly set in, on account of some squall or otherwise. Likewise when the captain wished the other ships to lower the sail he had four lights shown, which shortly after he had put out and then showed a single one, which was a signal that he wished to stop there and turn, so that the other ships might do as he did. Withal, when he discovered any land, or shoal, that is to say, a rock at sea, he made several lights be shown or had a bombard fired off. If he wished to make sail, he signalled to the other ships with four lights, so that they should do as he did, and follow him. He always carried this said lantern suspended to the poop of his vessel. Also when he wished the studding sail to be replaced with the great sail, he showed three lights. And to know whether all the ships followed him and were coming together, he showed one light only besides the fanol, and then each of the ships showed another light, which was an answering signal.

Besides the above-mentioned ordinances for carrying on seamanship as is fitting, and to avoid the dangers that may come upon those who do not keep watch, the said captain, who was expert in the things required for navigation, ordered that three watches should be kept at night. The first was at the beginning of the night, the second at midnight, and the third towards break of day, which is commonly called La diane, otherwise the star of the break of day. Every night these watches were changed; that is to say, he who had kept the first watch, on the following day kept the second, and he who had kept the second kept the third; and so on they changed continually every night. The said captain commanded that his regulations both for the signals and the watches should be well observed, so that their voyage should be made with greater security. The crews of this fleet were divided into three companies; the first belonged to the captain, the second to the pilot or nochier, and the third to the master. These regulations having been made; the captain-general deliberated on sailing, as follows.

Monday, the day of St. Laurence, the 10th of August, in the year above mentioned, the fleet, provided with what was necessary for it, and carrying crews of different nations, to the number of two hundred and thirty-seven men in all the five ships, was ready to set sail from the mole of Seville; and firing all the artillery, we made sail only on the foremast, and came to the end of a river named Betis, which is now called Guadalcavir. In going along this river we passed by a place named Gioan de Farax, where there was a large population of Moors, and there was a bridge over the river by which one went to Seville. This bridge was ruined, however there had remained two columns which are at the bottom of the water, on which account it is necessary to have people of the country of experience and knowledge to point out the convenient spot for safely passing between these two columns, from fear of striking against them. Besides that, it is necessary in order to pass safely by this bridge and by other places on this river, that the water should be rather high. After having passed the two columns we came to another place named Coria, and passing by many little villages lying along the said river, at last we arrived at a castle, which belongs to the Duke of Medina Sidonia, named St. Lucar, where there is a port from which to enter the ocean sea. It is entered by the east wind and you go out by the west wind. Near there is the cape of St. Vincent, which, according to cosmography, is in thirty-seven degrees of latitude, at twenty miles distance from the said port; and from the aforesaid town to this port by the river there are thirty-five or forty miles. A few days afterwards the captain-general came along the said river with his boat, and the masters of the other ships with him, and we remained some days in this port to supply the fleet with some necessary things. We went every day to hear mass on shore, at a church named Our Lady of Barrameda, towards St. Lucar. There the captain commanded that all the men of the fleet should confess before going on any further, in which he himself showed the way to the others. Besides he did not choose that anyone should bring any married woman, or others to the ships, for several good considerations.

Tuesday, the 20th September of the said year, we set sail from St. Lucar, making the course of the south-west otherwise named Labeiche; and on the twenty-sixth of the said month we arrived at an island of great Canaria, named Teneriphe, which is in twenty-eight degrees latitude; there we, remained three days and a half to take in provisions and other things which were wanted. After that we set sail thence and came to a port named Monterose, where we sojourned two days to supply ourselves with pitch, which is a thing necessary for ships. It is to be known that among the other isles which are at the said great Canaria, there is one, where not a drop of water is to be found proceeding from a fountain or a river, only once a day at the hour of midday, there descends a cloud from the sky which envelops a large tree which is in this island, and it falls upon the leaves of the tree, and a great abundance of water distils from these leaves, so that at the foot of the tree there is so large a quantity of water that it seems as if there was an ever-running fountain. The men who inhabit this place are satisfied with this water; also the animals, both domestic and wild, drink of it.

Monday, the third of October of the said year, at the hour of midnight, we set sail, making the course auster, which the levantine mariners call Siroc, entering into the ocean sea. We passed the Cape Verd and the neighbouring islands in fourteen-and-a-half degrees, and we navigated for several days by the coast of Guinea or Ethiopia; where there is a mountain called Sierra Leona, which is in eight degrees latitude according to the art and science of cosmography and astrology.

Sometimes we had the wind contrary and at other times sufficiently good, and rains without wind. In this manner we navigated with rain for the space of sixty days until the equinoctial line, which was a thing very strange and unaccustomed to be seen, according to the saying of some old men and those who had navigated here several times. Nevertheless, before reaching this equinoctial line we had in fourteen degrees a variety of weather and bad winds, as much on account of squalls as for the head winds and currents which came in such a manner that we could no longer advance. In order that our ships might not perish nor broach to (as it often happens when the squalls come together), we struck our sails, and in that manner we went about the sea hither and thither until the fair weather came. During the calm there came large fishes near the ships which they called Tiburoni (sharks), which have teeth of a terrible kind, and eat people when they find them in the sea either alive or dead. These fishes are caught with a device which the mariners call hams, which is a hook of iron. Of these, some were caught by our men. However, they are worth nothing to eat when they are large; and even the small ones are worth but little. During these storms the body of St. Anselme appeared to us several times; amongst others, one night that it was very dark on account of the bad weather, the said saint appeared in the form of a fire lighted at the summit of the mainmast, and remained there near two hours and a half, which comforted us greatly, for we were in tears, only expecting the hour of perishing; and when that holy light was going away from us it gave out so great a brilliancy in the eyes of each, that we were near a quarter-of-an-hour like people blinded, and calling out for mercy. For without any doubt nobody hoped to escape from that storm. It is to be noted that all and as many times as that light which represents the said St. Anselme shows itself and descends upon a vessel that is in a storm at sea, that vessel never is lost. Immediately that this light had departed the sea grew calmer, and then we saw divers sorts of birds, amongst others there were some which had no fundament. There is also another kind of bird of such a nature that when the female wishes to lay her eggs she goes and lays them on the back of the male, and there it is that the eggs are hatched. This last kind have no feet and are always in the sea. There is another kind of bird that only lives on the droppings of the other birds, this is a true thing, and they are named Cagaselo, for I have seen them follow the other birds until they had done what nature ordered them to do; and after it has eat this dirty diet it does not follow any other bird until hunger returns to it; it always does the same thing. There are also fish which fly, and we saw a great quantity of them together, so many that it seemed that it was an island in the sea.

After that we had passed the equinoctial line, towards the south, we lost the star of the tramontana, and we navigated between the south and Garbin, which is the collateral wind [or point] between south and west; and we crossed as far as a country named Verzin, which is in twenty-four degrees and a half of the Antarctic sky. This country is from the cape St. Augustine, which is in eight degrees in the Antarctic sky. At this place we had refreshments of victuals, like fowls and meat of calves, also a variety of fruits, called battate, pigne (pineapples), sweet, of singular goodness, and many other things, which I have omitted mentioning, not to be too long. The people of the said place gave in order to have a knife or a hook for catching fish, fire or six fowls and for a comb they gave two geese, and for a small mirror, or a pair of scissors, they gave so much fish that ten men could have eaten of it. And for a bell (or hawk's-bell) they gave a full basket of the fruit named battate; this has the taste of a chestnut, and is of the length of a shuttle. For a king of cards, of that kind which they used to play with in Italy, they gave me five fowls, and thought they had cheated me. We entered into this port the day of Saint Lucy (13th December), before Christmas, on which day we had the sun on the zenith, which is a term of astrology. This zenith is a point in the sky, according to astrologers, and only in imagination, and it answers to over our head in a straight line, as may be seen by the treatise of the sphere, and by Aristotle, in the first book, De Caelo et Mondo. On the day that we had the sun in the zenith we felt greater heat, as much as when we were on the equinoctial line.

The said country of Verzin is very abundant in all good things, and is larger than France, Spain, and Italy together. It is one of the countries that the King of Portugal has conquered (acquired). Its inhabitants are not Christians, and adore nothing, but live according to the usage of nature, rather bestially than otherwise. Some of these people live a hundred, or a hundred and twenty, or a hundred and forty years, and more; they go naked, both men and women. Their dwellings are houses that are rather long, and that they call "boy"; they sleep upon cotton nets, that they call, in their language, "amache". These nets are fastened to large timbers from one end of their house to the other. They make the fire to warm themselves right under their bed. It is to be known that in each of these houses, which they call "boy", there dwells a family of a hundred persons, who make a great noise. In this place they have boats, which are made of a tree, all in one piece, which they call "canoo". These are not made with iron instruments, for they have not got any, but with stones, like pebbles, and with these they plane and dig out these boats. Into these thirty or forty men enter, and their oars are made like iron shovels : and those who row these oars are black people, quite naked and shaven, and look like enemies of hell. The men and women of this said place are well made in their bodies. They eat the flesh of their enemies, not as good meat, but because they have adopted this custom. Now this custom arose as follows : an old woman of this place of Verzim had an only son, who was killed by his enemies, and, some days afterwards, the friends of this woman captured one of the said enemies who had put her son to death, and brought him to where she was. Immediately the said old woman, seeing the man who was captured, and recollecting the death of her child, rushed upon him like a mad dog, and bit him on the shoulder. However, this man who had been taken prisoner found means to run away, and told how they had wished to eat him, showing the bite that the said old woman had made in his shoulder. After that, those who were caught on one side or other were eaten. Through that arose this custom in this place of eating the enemies of each other. However, they do not eat up the whole body of the man whom they take prisoner; they eat him bit by bit, and for fear that he should be spoiled, they cut him up into pieces, which they set to dry in the chimney, and every day they cut a small piece, and eat it with their ordinary victuals in memory of their enemies. I was assured that this custom was true by a pilot, named John Carvagio, who was in our company, and had remained four years in this place; it is also to be observed that the inhabitants of this place, both men and women, are accustomed to paint themselves with fire, all over the body, and also the face. The men are shaven, and wear no beard, because they pluck it out themselves, and for all clothing they wear a circle surrounded with the largest feathers of parrots, and they only cover their posterior parts, which is a cause of laughter and mockery. The people of this place, almost all, excepting women and children, have three holes in the lower lip, and carry, hanging in them, small round stones, about a finger in length. These kind of people, both men and women, are not very black, but rather brown, and they openly show their shame, and have no hair on the whole of their bodies. The king of this country is called Cacich, and there are here an infinite number of parrots, of which they give eight or ten for a looking-glass; there are also some little cat-monkeys having almost the appearance of a lion; they are yellow, and handsome, and agreeable to look at. The people of this place make bread, which is of a round shape, and they take the marrow of certain trees which are there, between the bark and the tree, but it is not at all good, and resembles fresh cheese. There are also some pigs which have their navel on the back, and large birds which have their beak like a spoon, and they have no tongue. For a hatchet or for a knife they used to give us one or two of their daughters as slaves, but their wives they would not give up for anything in the world. According to what they say the women of this place never render duty to their husbands by day, but only at night; they attend to business out of doors, and carry all that they require for their husband's victuals inside small baskets on their heads, or fastened to their heads. Their husbands go with them, and carry a bow of vergin, or of black palm, with a handful of arrows of cane. They do this because they are very jealous of their wives. These carry their children fastened to their neck, and they are inside a thing made of cotton in the manner of a net. I omit relating many other strange things, not to be too prolix; however, I will not forget to say that mass was said twice on shore, where there were many people of the said country, who remained on their knees, and their hands joined in great reverence, during the mass, so that it was a pleasure and a subject of compassion to see them. In a short time they built a house for us, as they imagined that we should remain a long time with them, and, at our departure thence, they gave us a large quantity of verzin. It is a colour which proceeds from the trees which are in this country, and they are in such quantity that the country is called from it Verzin.

It is to be known that it happened that it had not rained for two months before we came there, and the day that we arrived it began to rain, on which account the people of the said place said that we came from heaven, and had brought the rain with us, which was great simplicity, and these people were easily converted to the Christian faith. Besides the above-mentioned things which were rather simple, the people of this country showed us another, very simple; for they imagined that the small ships' boats were the children of the ships, and that the said ships brought them forth when the boats were hoisted out to send the men hither and thither; and when the boats, were alongside the ship they thought that the ships were giving them suck.

A beautiful young girl came, one day inside the ship of our captain, where I was, and did not come except to seek for her luck : however, she directed her looks to the cabin of the master, and saw a nail of a finger's length, and went and took it as something valuable and new, and hid it in her hair, for otherwise she would not have been able to conceal it, because she was naked, and, bending forwards, she went away; and the captain and I saw this mystery.

Some words of this people of Verzin

Millet - Au mil (Maize)
Flour - Farine (Huy)
A hook - Ung haim (Pinda)
A knife - Ung coutteau (Taesse, Tarse)
A comb - Ung peigne (Chignap, Chipag)
A fork - Une forcette (Pirame)
A bell - Une sonnette (Itemnaraca, Hanmaraca)
Good, more than good - Bon, plus que bon tam maraghatom

We remained thirteen days in this country of Verzin, and, departing from it and following our course, we went as far as $34\frac{1}{3}°$ towards the Antarctic pole; there we found, near a river, men whom they call cannibals, who eat human flesh, and one of these men, great as a giant, came to the captain's ship to ascertain and ask if the others might come. This man had a voice like a bull, and whilst this man was at the ship his companions carried off all their goods that they had to a castle further off, from fear of us. Seeing that, we landed a hundred men from the ships, and went after them to try to catch some others; however they gained in running away. This kind of people did more with one step than we could do at a bound. In this same river there were seven little islands, and in the largest of them precious stones are found. This place was formerly called the Cape of St. Mary, and it was thought there that from thence there was a passage to the Sea of Sur; that is to say, the South Sea. And it is not found that any ship has ever discovered anything more, having passed beyond the said cape. And now it is no longer a cape, but it is a river that has a mouth seventeen leagues in width, by which it enters into the sea. In past time, in this river, these great men named Canibali ate a Spanish captain, named John de Sola, and sixty men who had gone to discover land, as we were doing, and trusted too much to them.

Afterwards following the same course towards the Antarctic pole, going along the land, we found two islands full of geese and goslings, and sea wolves, of which geese the large number could not be reckoned; for we loaded all the five ships with them in an hour. These geese are black, and have their feathers all over the body of the same size and shape, and they do not fly, and live upon fish; and they were so fat that they did not pluck them, but skinned them. They have beaks like that of a crow. The sea wolves of these two islands are of many colours, and of the size and thickness of a calf, and have a head like that of a calf, and the ears small and round. They have large teeth, and have no legs, but feet joining close on to the body, which resemble a human hand; they have small nails to their feet, and skin between the fingers like geese. If these animals could run they would be very bad and cruel, but they do not stir from the water, and swim and live upon fish. In this place we endured a great storm, and thought we should have been lost, but the three holy bodies, that is to say, St. Anselmo, St. Nicolas, and Sta. Clara, appeared to us, and immediately the storm ceased.

Departing thence as far as forty nine degrees and a half in the Antarctic heavens (as we were in the winter), we entered into a port to pass the winter, and remained there two whole months without ever seeing anybody. However, one day, without anyone expecting it, we saw a giant, who was on the shore of the sea, quite naked, and was dancing and leaping, and singing, and whilst singing he put the sand and dust on his head. Our captain sent one of his men towards him, whom he charged to sing and leap like the other to reassure him, and show him friendship. This he did, and immediately the sailor led this giant to a little island where the captain was waiting for him; and when he was before us he began to be astonished, and to be afraid, and he raised one finger on high, thinking that we came from heaven. He was so tall that the tallest of us only came up to his waist; however he was well built. He had a large face, painted red all round, and his eyes also were painted yellow around them, and he had two hearts painted on his cheeks; he had but little hair on his head, and it was painted white. When he was brought before the captain he was clothed with the skin of a certain beast, which skin was very skilfully sewed. This beast has its head and ears of the size of a mule, and the neck and body of the fashion of a camel, the legs of a deer, and the tail like that of a horse, and it neighs like a horse. There is a great quantity of these animals in this same place. This giant had his feet covered with the skin of this animal in the form of shoes, and he carried in his hand a short and thick bow, with a thick cord made of the gut of the said beast, with a bundle of cane arrows, which were not very long, and were feathered like ours, but they had no iron at the end, though they had at the end some small white and black cut stones, and these arrows were like those which the Turks use. The captain caused food and drink to be given to this giant, then they showed him some things, amongst others, a steel mirror. When the giant saw his likeness in it, he was greatly terrified, leaping backwards, and made three or four of our men fall down.

After that the captain gave him two bells, a mirror, a comb, and a chaplet of beads, and sent him back on shore, having him accompanied by four armed men. One of the companions of this giant, who would never come to the ship, on seeing the other coming back with our people, came forward and ran to where the other giants dwelled. These came one after the other all naked, and began to leap and sing, raising one finger to heaven, and showing to our people a certain white powder made of the roots of herbs, which they kept in earthen pots, and they made signs that they lived on that, and that they had nothing else to eat than this powder. Therefore our people made them signs to come to the ship and that they would help them to carry their bundles. Then these men came, who carried only their bows in their hands; but their wives came after them laden like donkeys, and carried their goods. These women are not as tall as the men, but they are very sufficiently large.

When we saw them we were all amazed and astonished, for they had the breasts half an eel long, and had their faces painted, and were dressed like the men. However, they wore a small skin before them to cover themselves. They brought with them four of those little beasts of which they make their clothing, and they led them with a cord in the manner of dogs coupled together. When these people wish to catch these animals with which they clothe themselves, they fasten one of the young ones to a bush, and afterwards the large ones come to play with the little one, and the giants are hid behind some hedge, and by shooting their arrows they kill the large ones. Our men brought eighteen of these giants, both men and women, whom they placed in two divisions, half on one side of the port, and the other half at the other, to hunt the said animals. Six days after, our people on going to cut wood, saw another giant, with his face painted and clothed like the above mentioned, he had in his hand a bow and arrows, and approaching our people he made some touches on his head and then on his body, and afterwards did the same to our people. And this being done he raised both his hands to heaven. When the captain-general knew all this, he sent to fetch him with his ship's boat, and brought him to one of the little islands that are in the port, where the ships were. In this island the captain had caused a house to be made for putting some of the ships' things in whilst he remained there. This giant was of a still better disposition than the others, and was a gracious and amiable person, who liked to dance and leap. When he leapt he caused the earth to sink in a palm depth at the place where his feet touched. He was a long time with us, and at the end we baptised him, and gave him the name of John. This giant pronounced the name of Jesus, the Pater noster, Ave Maria, and his name as clearly as we did : but he had a terribly strong and loud voice. The captain gave him a shirt and a tunic of cloth, and seaman's breeches, a cap, a comb, some bells, and other things, and sent him back to where he had come from. He went away very joyous and satisfied. The next day this giant returned, and brought one of those large animals before mentioned, for which the captain gave him some other, things, so that he should bring more. However, afterwards he did not return, and it is to be presumed that the other giants killed him because he had come to us.

Fifteen days later we saw four other giants, who carried no arrows, for they had hid them in the bushes, as two of them showed us, for we took them all four, and each of them was painted in a different way. The captain retained the two younger ones to take them to Spain on his return; but it was done by gentle and cunning means, for otherwise they would have done a hurt to some of our men. The manner in which he retained them was that he gave them, many knives, forks, mirrors, bells, and glass, and they held all these things in their hands. Then the captain had some irons brought, such as are put on the feet of malefactors these giants took pleasure in seeing the irons, but they did not know where to put them, and it grieved them that they could not take them with their hands, because they were hindered by the other things which they held in them. The other two giants were there, and were desirous of helping the other two, but the captain would not let them, and made a sign to the two whom he wished to detain that they would put those irons on their feet, and then they would go away : at this they made a sign with their heads that they were content. Immediately the captain had the irons put on the feet of both of them, and when they saw that they were striking with a hammer on the bolt which crosses the said irons to rivet them, and prevent them from being opened, these giants were afraid, but the captain made them a sign not to doubt of anything. Nevertheless when they saw the trick that had been played them, they began to be enraged, and to foam like bulls, crying out very loud Setebos, that is to say, the great devil, that he should help them. The hands of the other two giants were bound, but it was with great difficulty; then the captain sent them back on shore, with nine of his men to conduct them, and to bring the wife of one of those who had remained in irons, because he regretted her greatly, as we saw by signs. However, in going away one of those two who were sent away, untied his hands and escaped, running with such lightness that our men lost sight of him, and he went away where his companions were staying; but he found nobody of those that he had left with the women because they had gone to hunt. However he went to look for them, and found them, and related to them all that had been done to them. The other giant whose hands were tied struggled as much as he could to unfasten himself, and to prevent his doing so, one of our men struck him, and hurt him on the head, at which he got very angry; however he led our people there where their wives were.

Then John Cavagio, the pilot who was the chief conductor of these two giants, would not bring away the wife of one of the giants who had remained in irons on that evening, but was of opinion that they should sleep there, because it was almost night. During this time the one of the giants who had untied his hands came back from where he had been, with another giant, and they seeing their companion wounded on the head, said nothing at that moment, but next morning they spoke in their language to the women, and immediately all ran away together, and the smallest ran faster than the biggest, and they left all their chattels. Two of these giants being rather a long way off shot arrows at our men, and fighting thus, one of the giants pierced with an arrow the thigh of one of our men, of which he died immediately. Then seeing that he was dead, all ran away. Our men had crossbows and guns, but they never could hit one of these giants, because they did not stand still in one place, but leaped hither and thither. After that, our men buried the man who had been killed, and set fire to the place where those giants had left their chattels. Certainly these giants run faster than a horse, and they are very jealous of their wives.

When these giants have a stomach-ache, instead of taking medicine they put down their throats an arrow about two feet long; then they vomit a green bile mixed with blood and the reason why they throw up this green matter is because they sometimes eat thistles. When they have headaches they make a cut across the forehead, and also on the arms and legs, to draw blood from several parts of their bodies. One of the two we had taken, and who was in our ship, said that the blood did not choose to remain in the place and spot of the body where pain was felt. These people have their hair cut short and clipped in the manner of monks with a tonsure : they wear a cord of cotton round their head, to this they hang their arrows when they go a-hunting....

When one of them dies, ten or twelve devils appear and dance all round the dead man. It seems that these are painted, and one of these enemies is taller than the others, and makes a greater noise, and more mirth than the others : that is whence these people have taken the custom of painting their faces and bodies, as has been said. The greatest of these devils is called in their language Setebos, and the others Cheleule. Besides the above-mentioned things, this one who was in the ship with us, told us by signs that he had seen devils with two horns on their heads, and long hair down to their feet, and who threw out fire from their mouths and rumps. The captain named this kind of people Pataghom, who have no houses, but have huts made of the skins of the animals with which they clothe themselves, and go hither and thither with these huts of theirs, as the gypsies do; they live on raw meat, and eat a certain sweet root, which they call Capac. These two giants that we had in the ship ate a large basketful of biscuit, and rats without skinning them, and they drank half a bucket of water at each time.

We remained in this port, which was called the port of St. Julian, about five months, during which there happened to us many strange things, of which I will tell a part. One was, that immediately that we entered into this port, the masters of the other four ships plotted treason against the captain-general, in order to put him to death. These were thus named : John of Carthagine, conductor of the fleet; the treasurer, Loys de Mendoza; the conductor, Anthony Cocha; and Gaspar de Casada. However, the treason was discovered, for which the treasurer was killed with stabs of a dagger, and then quartered. This Gaspar de Casada had his head cut off, and afterwards was cut into quarters; and the conductor having a few days later attempted another treason, was banished with a priest, and was put in that country called Pattagonia. The captain-general would not put this conductor to death, because the Emperor Charles had made him captain of one of the ships. One of our ships, named St. James, was lost in going to discover the coast; all the men, however, were saved by a miracle, for they were hardly wet at all. Two men of these, who were saved, came to us and told us all that had passed and happened, on which the captain at once sent some men with sacks full of biscuit for two months. So, each day we found something of the ship of the other men who had escaped from the ship which was lost, and the place where these men were was twenty-five leagues from us, and the road bad and full of thorns, and it required four days to go there, and no water to drink was to be found on the road, but only ice, and of that little. In this port of St. Julian there were a great quantity of long capres, called Missiglione; these had pearls in the midst. In this place they found incense, and ostriches, foxes, sparrows, and rabbits a good deal smaller than ours. We set up at the top of the highest mountain which was there a very large cross, as a sign that this country belonged to the King of Spain; and we gave to this mountain the name of Mount of Christ.

Departing thence, we found in 51° less ⅓ (50° 40' S.), in the Antarctic, a river of fresh water, which was near causing us to be lost, from the great winds that it sent out; but God, of his favour, aided us. We were about two months in this river, as it supplied fresh water and a kind of fish an ell long, and very scaly, which is good to eat. Before going away, the captain chose that all should confess and receive the body of our Lord like good Christians.

CHAPTER

After going and taking the course to the fifty-second degree of the said Antarctic sky, on the day of the Eleven Thousand Virgins (October 2)], we found, by a miracle, a strait which we called the Cape of the Eleven Thousand Virgins, this strait is a hundred and ten leagues long, which are four hundred and forty miles, and almost as wide as less than half a league, and it issues in another sea, which is called the peaceful sea; it is surrounded by very great and high mountains covered with snow. In this place it was not possible to anchor with the anchors, because no bottom was found, on which account they were forced to put the moorings of twenty-five or thirty fathoms length on shore. This strait was a round place surrounded by mountains, as I have said, and the greater number of the sailors thought that there was no place by which to go out thence to enter into the peaceful sea. However, the captain- -general said that there was another strait for going out, and said that he knew it well, because he bad seen it by a marine chart of the King of Portugal, which map had been made by a great pilot and mariner named Martin of Bohemia. The captain sent on before two of his ships, one named St. Anthony and the other the Conception, to seek for and discover the outlet of this strait, which was called the Cape de la Baya. And we, with the other two ships, that is to say, the flagship named Trinitate, and the other the Victory, remained waiting for them within the Bay, where in the night we had a great storm, which lasted till the next day at midday, and during which we were forced to weigh the anchors and let the ships go hither and thither about the bay. The other two ships met with such a head wind that they could not weather a cape which the bay made almost at its extremity; wishing to come to us, they were near being driven to beach the ships. However, on approaching the extremity of the bay, and whilst expecting to be lost, they saw a small mouth, which did not resemble a mouth but a corner, and (like people giving up hope) they threw themselves into it, so that by force they discovered the strait. Seeing that it was not a corner, but a strait of land, they went further on and found a bay, then going still further they found another strait and another bay larger than the first two, at which, being very joyous, they suddenly returned backwards to tell it to the captain-general. Amongst us we thought that they had perished : first, because of the great storm; next, because two days had passed that we had not seen them. And being thus in doubt we saw the two ships under all sail, with ensigns spread, come towards us : these, when near us, suddenly discharged much artillery, at which we, very joyous, saluted them with artillery and shouts. Afterwards, all together, thanking God and the Virgin Mary, we went to seek further on.

After having entered inside this strait we found that there were two mouths, of which one trended to the Sirocco (S.E.), and the other to the Garbin (S.W.). On that account the captain again sent the two ships, St. Anthony and Conception, to see if the mouth which was towards Sirocco had an outlet beyond into the said peaceful sea. One of these two ships, named St. Anthony, would not wait for the other ship, because those who were inside wished to return to Spain : this they did, and the principal reason was on account, of the pilot of the said ship being previously discontented with the said captain-general, because that before this armament was made, this pilot had gone to the Emperor to talk about having some ships to discover countries. However, on account of the arrival of the captain-general, the Emperor did not give them to this pilot, on account of which he agreed with some Spaniards, and the following night they took prisoner the captain of their ship, who was a brother of the captain-general, and who was named Alvar de Meschite; they wounded him, and put him in irons. So they carried him off to Spain. And in this ship, which went away and returned, was one of the two above-mentioned giants whom we had taken, and when he felt the heat he died.

Pigafetta's map of Magellan's Strait

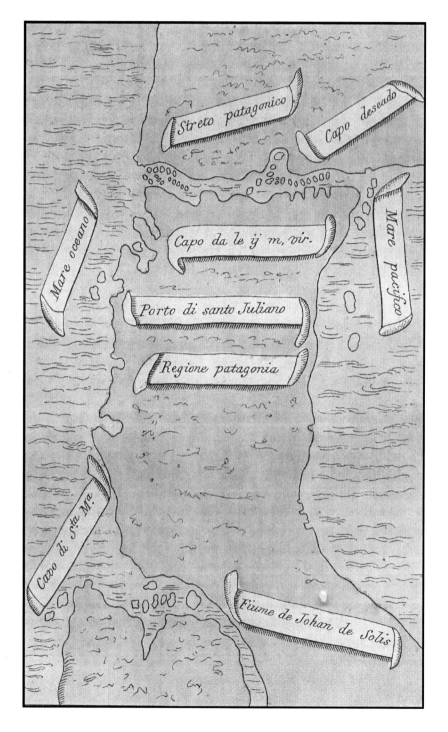

The other ship, named the Conception, not being able to follow that one, was always waiting for it, and fluttered hither and thither. However, it lost its time, for the other took the road by night for returning. When this happened, at night the ship of the captain and the other ship went together to discover the other mouth to Garbin (S.W.), where, on always holding on our course, we found the same strait. However, at the end we arrived at a river which we named the River of Sardines, because we found a great quantity of them. So we remained there four days to wait for the other two ships. A short time after we sent a boat well supplied with men and provisions to discover the cape of the other sea : these remained three days in going and coming. They told us that they had found the cape, and the sea great and wide. At the joy which the captain-general had at this he began to cry, and he gave the name of Cape of Desire to this cape, as a thing which had been much desired for a long time. Having done that we turned back to find the two ships that were at the other side, but we only found the Conception, of which ship we asked what had become of her companion. To this the captain of the said ship, named John Serrano (who was pilot of the first ship that was lost as has been related), replied that he knew nothing of her, and that he had never seen her since she entered the mouth. However, we sought for her through all the strait, as far as the said mouth, by which she had taken her course to return. Besides that, the Captain-General sent back the ship named the Victory as far as the entrance of the strait to see if the ship was there, and he told the people of this ship that if they did not find the ship they were looking for, they were to place an ensign on the summit of a small hill, with a letter inside a pot placed in the ground near the ensign, so that if the ship should by chance return, it might see that ensign, and also find the letter which would give information of the course which the captain was holding. This manner of acting had been ordained by the captain from the commencement, in order to effect the junction of any ship which might be separated from the others. So the people of the said ship did what the captain had commanded them, and more, for they set two ensigns with letters; one of the ensigns was placed on a small hill at the first bay, the other on an islet in the third bay, where there were many sea wolves and large birds. The captain-general waited for them with the other ship near the river named Isles : and he caused a cross to be set upon a small island in front of that river, which was between high mountains covered with snow. This river comes and falls into the sea near the other river of the Sardines.

If we had not found this strait the captain-general had made up his mind to go as far as seventy-five degrees towards the Antarctic pole; where at that height in the summer time there is no night, or very little : in a similar manner in the winter there is no daylight, or very little, and so that every one may believe this, when we were in this strait the night lasted only three hours, and this was in the month of October.

The land of this strait on the left hand side looked towards the Sirocco wind, which is the wind collateral to the Levant and South; we called this strait Pathagonico. In it we found at every half league a good port and place for anchoring, good waters, wood all of cedar, and fish like sardines, missiglioni, and a very sweet herb named appio (celery). There is also some of the same kind, which is bitter. This herb grows near the springs, and from not finding anything else we ate of it for several days. I think that there is not in the world a more beautiful country, or better strait than this one.

In this ocean, sea one sees a very amusing chase of fish, that are of three sorts, of an ell or more in length, and they call these fish Dorades, Albacores, and Bonitos; these follow and pursue another sort of fish which flies, which they call Colondriny, which are a foot long or more, and are very good to eat. When these three sorts of fish find in the water any of these flying fish, immediately they make them come out of the water, and they fly more than a cross bowshot, as long as their wings are wet; and whilst these fishes fly the other three ran after them under the water, seeing the shadow of those that fly : and the moment they fall into the water they are seized upon and eaten by the others which pursue them, which is a thing marvellous and agreeable to see.

VOCABULARY OF THE PATAGONIAN GIANTS

Le chef - Her.. Idem
Les oreilles - Sane.. id.
Yeulx - Ather.. Oter
Les esselles - Salischin.. id.

Le nez - Or.. id.
La mamelle - Othen.. oton
Les silz - Occhechl.. id.
La poitrine - Ochy.. ochii
Paupieres des yeulx - Sechechiel.. id.
Le corps - Gechel
Aux deux narines - Orescho.. id.
Le vit - Scachet.. sachet
La bouche - Xiam.. chian
Le couillons - Scancos.. sachancos
Les leures - Schiane.. schiaine
Le con - Isle.. id.
Les dentz - Phor.. for
Le foutre - Johoi
La langue - Schial.. id.
Les cuisses - Chiaue.. id.
Le menton - Sechen.. Secheri
Le genouil - Tepin.. id.
Les cheueulx - Ajchir.. archiz
Le cul - Schiachen.. schiaguen
Le visaige - Cogechel
Les fesses - Hoy.. hoii
La gorge - Ohumer.. Ohumez
Le braz - Mar.. riaz
La copa (le cou) - Schialeschin
Le poulse - Ohoy.. holion
Les epaulles - Peles
Les jambes - Choss.. id.
Le coude - Cotel
Les piedz - Teche.. ti
La main - Chene
Alcalcagno - There.. tire
La paulme de la main - Canneghin
La cheuille du pied - Perchi.. id.
Le doit - Cori.. id.
La plante ou sole du pied - Cartschem.. caotschoni
Les ongles - Colim.. colmi
Nous - Chen

Le cueur - Chol.. tol
Si ou ouy - Rei
Le grater - Ghecare.. Id.
L'or - Pelpeli.. id.
Homo sguerzo - Calischen.. id.
Petre lazure - Secheghi.. sechey
Au jeune - Calemi.. id.
Le soleil - Calexchem.. id.
L'eau - Oli.. holi
Les estoilles - Settere.. id.
Le feu - Ghialeme.. gialeme
La mer - Aro.. id.
La fumée - Jaiche.. giache
Le vent - Om.. oni.
La fortune (storm) - Ohone.. id.
A la pignate - Aschame.. id.
Le poisson - Hoi.. id.
A demander - Ghelhe.. gheglie
Le manger - Mecchiere.. id.
Vien icy - Haisi.. hai.
Une escuelle - Elo.. etlo
Au regarder - Conne.. id.
A combatre - Oamaghei.. Ohomagse
A aller - Rhei.. id.
Alle frezze - Sethe.. Seche
A la nef - Theu.. id.
Ung chien - Holl.. id.
A courir - Hiam.. tiam
Ung loup - Ani.. id.
Al struzzo vcelo - Hoihoi
A aller loing - Schien
A ses oeufs - Jan
A la guide - Anti
La pouldre d'herbe - Qui
Aladorer - Os.. id.
Mangent - Capac.. id.
Ung papegault - Cheche
Le bonnet - Aichel.. id.

La caige doyseau - Cleo.. id.
Coulernoire - Amet.. oinel
Al missiglion (oyster) - Siameni.. id.
Rouge - Theiche.. faiche
Drap rouge - Terechai.. id.
Jaulne - Peperi.. id.
Al cocinare - Ixecoles.. irocoles
Le diable grand - Setebos.. id.
La ceincture - Cathechin.. id.
Les petitz diables - Cheleule.. id.
Une oye - Chache.. cache

All these words are pronounced in the throat, because they pronounce them thus.

These words were given me by that giant whom we had in the ship, because he asked me for capac, that is to say bread, since they thus name that root which they use for bread, and oli that is to say water. When he saw me write these names after him, and ask for others he understood (what I was doing) with my pen in my hand. Another time I made a cross and kissed it in showing it to him; but suddenly he exclaimed Setebos ! and made signs to me that if I again made the cross it would enter into my stomach and make me die. When this giant was unwell he asked for the cross, and embraced and kissed it much, and he wished to become a Christian before his death, and we named him Paul. When these people wish to light a fire they take a pointed stick and rub it with another until they make a fire in the pith of a tree that is placed between these sticks.

Wednesday, the twenty-eighth of November, 1520, we came forth out of the said strait, and entered into the Pacific sea, where we remained three months and twenty days without taking in provisions or other refreshments, and we only ate old biscuit reduced to powder, and full of grubs, and stinking from the dirt which the rats had made on it when eating the good biscuit, and we drank water that was yellow and stinking. We also ate the ox hides which were under the main-yard, so that the yard should not break the rigging : they were very hard on account of the sun, rain, and wind, and we left them for four or five

days in the sea, and then we put them a little on the embers, and so ate
them; also the sawdust of wood, and rats, which cost half-a-crown
each, moreover enough of them were not to be got. Besides the
above-named evils, this misfortune that I will mention was the worst, it
was that the upper and lower gums of most of our men grew so much
that they could not eat, and in this way so many suffered, that nineteen
died, and the other giant, and an Indian from the county of Verzin.
Besides those who died, twenty-five or thirty fell ill of divers
sicknesses, both in the arms and legs, and other places, in such manner
that very few remained healthy. However, thanks be to the Lord, I had
no sickness. During those three months and twenty days we went in an
open sea, while, we ran fully four thousand leagues in the Pacific sea.
This was well named Pacific, for during this same time we met with no
storm, and saw no land except two small uninhabited islands, in which
we found only birds and trees. We named them the Unfortunate
Islands; they are two hundred leagues apart from one another, and there
is no place to anchor, as there is no bottom. There we saw many sharks,
which are a kind of large fish which they call Tiburoni. The first isle is
in fifteen degrees of austral latitude, and the other island is in nine
degrees. With the said wind we ran each day fifty or sixty leagues or
more; now with the wind astern, sometimes on a wind or otherwise.
And if our Lord and his Mother had not aided us in giving us good
weather to refresh ourselves with provisions and other things, we
should all have died of hunger in this very vast sea, and I think that
never man will undertake to Perform such a voyage.

When we had gone out of this strait, if we had always navigated to the
west we should have gone without finding any land except the Cape of
the Eleven Thousand Virgins, which is the eastern head of the strait in
the ocean sea, with the Cape of Desire at the west in the Pacific sea
These two capes are exactly in fifty-two degrees of latitude of the
Antarctic pole.

The Antarctic pole is not so covered with stars as the arctic, for there
are to be seen there many small stars congregated together, which are
like to two clouds a little separated from one another, and a little
dimmed, in the midst of which are two stars, not very large, nor very
brilliant, and they move but little : these two stars are the Antarctic

pole. Our compass needle still pointed a little to its arctic pole; nevertheless it had not as much power as on its own side and region. Yet when we were in the open sea, the captain-generals asked of all the pilots, whilst still going under sail, in what direction they were navigating and pointing the charts. They all replied, by the course he had given, punctually (pricked in); then he answered, that they were pointing falsely (which was so), and that it was fitting to arrange the needle of navigation, because it did not receive so much force as in its own quarter. When we were in the middle of this open sea we saw a cross of five stars, very bright, straight, in the west, and they are straight one with another.

During this time of two months and twelve days we navigated between west and north-west (maestral), and a quarter west of north-west, and also north-west, until we came to the equinoctial line, which was at [a point] one hundred and twenty-two degrees distant from the line of repartition. This line of delimitation is thirty degrees distant from the meridian, and the meridian is three degrees distant from the Cape Verd towards the east. In going by this course we passed near two very rich islands; one is in twenty degrees latitude in the Antarctic pole, and is called Cipanghu; the other, in fifteen degrees of the same pole, is named Sumbdit Pradit. After we had passed the equinoctial line we navigated between west, and north-west and a quarter west, by north-west. Afterwards we made two hundred leagues to westwards, then changed the course to a quarter of south-west, until in thirteen degrees north latitude, in order to approach the land of Cape Gaticara, which cape (under correction of those who have made cosmography), (for they have never seen it), is not placed where they think, but is towards the north, in twelve degrees or thereabouts.

After having navigated sixty leagues by the said course, in twelve degrees latitude, and a hundred and forty-six of longitude, on Wednesday, the 6th of March, we discovered a small island in the north-west direction, and two others lying to the south-west. One of these islands was larger and higher than the other two. The captain-general wished to touch at the largest of these three islands to get refreshments of provisions; but it was not possible because the people of these islands entered into the ships and robbed us, in such a way that it was impossible to preserve oneself from them. Whilst we were striking and lowering the sails to go ashore, they stole away with much address and diligence the small boat called the skiff, which was made fast to the poop of the captain's ship, at which he was much irritated, and went on shore with forty armed men, burned forty or fifty houses, with several small boats, and killed seven men of the island; they recovered their skiff. After this we set sail suddenly, following the same course. Before we went ashore some of our sick men begged us that if we killed man or woman, that we should bring them their entrails, as they would see themselves suddenly cured.

CHAPTER

It must be known that when we wounded any of this kind of people with our arrows, which entered inside their bodies, they looked at the arrow, and then drew it forth with much astonishment, and immediately afterwards they died. Immediately after we sailed from that island, following our course, and those people seeing that we were going away followed us for a league, with a hundred small boats, or more, and they approached our ships, showing to us fish, and feigning to give it to us. However, they threw stones at us, and then ran away, and in their flight they passed with their little boats between the boat which is towed at the poop and the ship going under full sail; but they did this so quickly, and with such skill that it was a wonder. And we saw some of these women, who cried out and tore their hair, and I believe that it was for the love of those whom we had killed.

CHAPTER

These people live in liberty and according to their will, for they have no lord or superior; they go quite naked, and some of them wear beards, and have their hair down to the waist. They wear small hats, after the fashion of the Albanians; these hats are made of palm leaves. The people are as tall as us, and well made : they adore nothing, and when they are born they are white, later they become brown, and have their teeth black and red. The women also go naked, except that they cover their nature with a thin bark; pliable like paper, which grows between the tree and the bark of the palm. They are beautiful and delicate, and whiter than the men, and have their hair loose and flowing, very black and long, down to the earth. They do not go to work in the fields, nor stir from their houses, making cloth and baskets of palm leaves. Their provisions are certain fruits named Cochi, Battate; there are birds, figs a palm long [bananas or plantains], sweet canes, and flying fish. The women anoint their bodies and their hair with oil of cocho and giongioli (sesame). Their houses are constructed of wood, covered with planks, with fig leaves, which are two ells in length : they have only one floor : their rooms and beds are furnished with mats, which we call matting, which are made of palm leaves, and are very beautiful, and they lie down on palm straw, which is soft and fine. These people have no arms, but use sticks, which have a fish bone at the end. They are poor, but ingenious, and great thieves, and for the sake of that we called these three islands the Ladrone Islands. The pastime of the men and the women of this place, and their diversion, is to go with their little boats to catch those fish which fly, with hooks made of fish bones. The pattern of their small boats is painted here-after, they are like the fuseleres, but narrower. Some of them black and white, and others red. On the opposite side to the sail, they have a large piece of wood, pointed above, with poles across, which are in the water, in order to go more securely under sail : their sails are of palm leaves, sewed together, and of the shape of a lateen sail, fore and aft. They have certain shovels like hearth shovels, and there is no difference between the poop and the prow in these boats, and they are like dolphins bounding from wave to wave. These thieves thought, according to the signs they made, that there were no other men in the world besides them.

Saturday, the 16th of March, 1521, we arrived at daybreak in sight of a high island, three hundred leagues distant from the before mentioned Thieves' island. This isle is named Zamal. The next day the captain-general wished to land at another uninhabited island near the first, to be in greater security and to take water; also to repose there a few days. He set up there two tents on shore for the sick, and had a sow killed for them. Monday the 18th of March, after dinner, we saw a boat come towards us with nine men in it : upon which the captain-general ordered that no one should move or speak without his permission. When these people had come into this island towards us, immediately the principals one amongst them went towards the captain-general with demonstrations of being very joyous at our arrival. Five of the most showy of them remained with us, the others who remained with the boat went to call some men who were fishing, and afterwards all of them came together. The captain seeing that these people were reasonable ordered food and drink to be given them, and he gave them some red caps, looking glasses, combs, bells, ivory, and other things. When these people saw the politeness of the captain, they presented some fish, and a vessel of palm wine, which they call in their language Uraca; figs more than a foot long; and others smaller and of a better savour, and two cochos. At that time they had nothing to give him, and they made signs to us with their hands that in four days they would bring us Umai, which is rice, cocos, and many other victuals.

To explain the kind of fruits above-named it must be known that the one that they call cochi, is the fruit that the palm trees bear. And as we have bread, wine, oil, and vinegar, proceeding from different kinds, so these people have those things proceeding from these palm trees only. It must be said that wine proceeds from the said palm trees in the following manner. They make a hole at the summit of the tree as far as its heart, which is named palmito, from which a liquor comes out in drops down the tree, like white must, which is sweet, but with somewhat of bitter. They have canes as thick as the leg, in which they draw off this liquor, and they fasten them to the tree from the evening till next morning, and from the morning to the evening, because this liquor comes little by little. This palm produces a fruit named cocho, which is as large as the head, or thereabouts : its first husk is green, and two fingers in thickness, in it they find certain threads, with which they make the cords for fastening their boats. Under this husk there is another very hard, and thicker than that of a walnut. They burn this second rind, and make with it a powder which is useful to them. Under this rind there is a white marrow of a finger's thickness, which they eat fresh with meat and fish, as we do bread, and it has the taste of an almond, and if anyone dried it he might make bread of it. From the middle of this marrow there comes out a clear sweet water and very cordial, which, when it has rested a little, and settled, congeals and becomes like an apple. When they wish to make oil they take this fruit, the coco, and let it get rotten, and they corrupt this marrow in the water, then they boil it, and it becomes oil in the manner of butter. When they want to make vinegar, they let the water in the coconut get bad, and they put it in the sun, when it turns to vinegar like white wine. From this fruit milk also can be made, as we experienced, for we scraped this marrow and then put it with its water, and passed it through a cloth, and thus it was milk like that of goats. This kind of palm tree is like the date-palm, but not so rugged. Two of these trees can maintain a family of ten persons : but they do not draw wine as above-mentioned always from one tree, but draw from one for eight days, and from the other as long. For if they did not, otherwise the trees would dry up. In this manner they last a hundred years.

These people became very familiar and friendly with us, and explained many things to us in their language, and told us the names of some islands that we saw with our eyes before us. The island where they dwelt is called Zuluam, and it is not large. As they were sufficiently agreeable and conversible we had great pleasure with them. The captain seeing that they were of this good condition, to do them greater honour conducted them to the ship, and showed them all his goods, that is to say, cloves, cinnamon, pepper, ginger, nutmeg, mace, gold, and all that was in the ship. He also had some shots fired with his artillery, at which they were so much afraid that they wished to jump from the ship into the sea. They made signs that the things that the captain had shown them grew there where we were going. When they wished to leave us they took leave of the captain and of us with very good manners and gracefulness, promising us to come back to see us. The island we were at was named Humunu; nevertheless because we found there two springs of very fresh water we named it the Watering Place of good signs, and because we found here the first signs of gold. There is much white coral to be found here, and large trees which bear fruit smaller than an almond, and which are like pines. There were also many palm trees both good and bad. In this place there were many circumjacent islands, on which account we named them the archipelago of St. Lazarus, because we stayed there on the day and feast of St. Lazarus. This region and archipelago is in ten degrees north latitude, and a hundred and sixty-one degrees longitude from the line of demarcation.

Friday, the 22nd of March, the above-mentioned people, who had promised us to return, came about midday, with two boats laden with the said fruit cochi, sweet oranges, a vessel of palm wine, and a cock, to give us to understand that they had poultry in their country, so that we bought all that they brought. The lord of these people was old, and had his face painted, and had gold rings suspended to his ears, which they name Schione, and the others had many bracelets and rings of gold on their arms, with a wrapper of linen round their head. We remained at this place eight days : the captain went there every day to see his sick men, whom he had placed on this island to refresh them : and he gave them himself every day the water of this said fruit the cocho, which comforted them much. Near this isle is another where there are a kind of people who wear holes in their ears so large that they can pass their arms through them; these people are Caphre, that is to say, Gentiles, and they go naked, except that round their middles they wear cloth made of the bark of trees. However, there are some of the more remarkable of them who wear cotton stuff, and at the end of it there is some work of silk done with a needle. These people are tawny, fat, and painted, and they anoint themselves with the oil of coco nuts and sesame, to preserve them from the sun and the wind. Their hair is very black and long, reaching to the waist, and they carry small daggers and knives, ornamented with gold, and many other things, such as darts, harpoons, and nets to fish, like....., and their boats are like ours.

The Monday of Passion week, the 25th of March, and feast of our Lady, in the afternoon, and being ready to depart from this place, I went to the side of our ship to fish, and putting my feet on a spar to go down to the store room, my feet slipped, because it had rained, and I fell into the sea without any one seeing me, and being near drowning by luck I found at my left hand the sheet of the large sail which was in the sea, I caught hold of it and began to cry out till they came to help and pick me up with the boat. I was assisted not by my merits, but by the mercy and grace of the fountain of pity. That same day we took the course between west and southwest, and passed amidst four small islands, that is to say, Cenalo, Huinanghar, Ibusson, and Abarien.

Thursday, the 28th of March, having seen the night before fire upon an island, at the morning we came to anchor at this island; where we saw a small boat which they call Boloto, with eight men inside, which approached the ship of the captain-general. Then a slave of the captain's, who was from Sumatra, otherwise named Traprobana, spoke from afar to these people, who understood his talk, and, came near to the side of the ship, but they withdrew immediately, and would not enter the ship from fear of us. So the captain seeing that they would not trust to us showed them a red cap, and other things, that he had tied and placed on a little plank, and the people in the boat took them immediately and joyously, and then returned to advise their king. Two hours afterwards, or thereabouts, we saw come two long boats, which they call Ballanghai, full of men. In the largest of them was their king sitting under an awning of mats; when they were near the ship of the captain-general, the said slave spoke to the king, who, understood him well, because in these countries the kings know more languages than the common people. Then the king ordered some of his people to go to the captain's ship, whilst he would not move from his boat, which was near enough to us. This was done, and when his people returned to the boat, he went away at once. The captain gave good entertainment to the men who came to his ship, and gave them all sorts of things, on which account the king wished to give the captain a rather large bar of solid gold, and a chest full of ginger. However, the captain thanked him very much but would not accept the present. After that, when it was late, we went with the ships near to the houses and abode of the king.

The next day which was Good Friday, the captain sent on shore the before-mentioned slave, who was our interpreter, to the king to beg him to give him for money some provisions for his ships, sending him word that he had not come to his country as an enemy, but as a friend. The king on hearing this came with seven or eight men in a boat, and entered the ship, and embraced the captain, and gave him three china dishes covered with leaves full of rice, and two dorades, which are rather large fish, and of the sort above-mentioned, and he gave him several other things. The captain gave this king a robe of red and yellow cloth, made in the Turkish fashion, and a very fine red cap, and to his people be gave to some of them knives, and to others mirrors. After that refreshments were served up to them. The captain told the king, through the said interpreter, that he wished to be with him, cassi, that is to say, brothers. To which the king answered that he desired to be the same towards him. After that the captain showed him cloths of different colours, linen, coral, and much other merchandise, and all the artillery, of which he had some pieces fired before him, at which the king was much astonished; after that the captain had one of his soldiers armed with white armour, and placed him in the midst of three comrades, who struck him with swords and daggers. The king thought this very strange, and the captain told him, through the interpreter, that a man thus in white armour was worth a hundred of his men; he answered that it was true; he was further informed that there were in each ship two hundred like that man. After that the captain showed him a great number of swords, cuirasses, and helmets, and made two of the men play with their swords before the king; he then showed him the sea chart and the ship compass, and informed him how he had found the strait to come there, and of the time which he had spent in coming; also of the time he had been without seeing any land, at which the king was astonished. At the end the captain asked if he would be pleased that two of his people should go with him to the places where they lived, to see some of the things of his country. This the king granted, and I went with another.

When I had landed, the king raised his hands to the sky, and turned to us two, and we did the same as he did; after that he took me by the hand, and one of his principal people took my companion, and led us under a place covered with canes, where there was a ballanghai, that is to say, a boat, eighty feet long or thereabouts, resembling a fusta. We sat with the king upon its poop, always conversing with him by signs, and his people stood up around us, with their swords, spears, and bucklers. Then the king ordered to be brought a dish of pig's flesh and wine. Their fashion of drinking is in this wise, they first raise their hands to heaven, then take the drinking vessel in their right hand, and extend the left hand closed towards the people. This the king did, and presented to me his fist, so that I thought that he wanted to strike me; I did the same thing towards him; so with this ceremony, and other signs of friendship, we banqueted, and afterwards supped with him.

I ate flesh on Good Friday, not being able to do otherwise; and before the hour of supper, I gave several things to the king, that I had brought. There I wrote down several things as they name them in their language, and when the king and the others saw me write, and I told them their manner of speech, they were all astonished. When the hour for supper had come, they brought two large china dishes, of which one was full of rice, and the other of pig's flesh, with its broth and sauce. We supped with the same signs and ceremonies, and then went to the king's palace, which was made and built like a hay grange, covered with fig and palm leaves. It was built on great timbers high above the ground, and it was necessary to go up steps and ladders to it. Then the king made us sit on a cane mat, with our legs doubled as was the custom; after half an hour there was brought a dish of fish roast in pieces, and ginger fresh gathered that moment, and some wine. The eldest son of the king, who was the prince, came where we were, and the king told him to sit down near us, which he did; then two dishes were brought, one of fish, with its sauce, and the other of rice, and this was done for us to eat with the prince. My companion enjoyed the food and drink so much that he got drunk. They use for candles or torches the gum of a tree which is named Animé, wrapped up in leaves of palms or fig trees. The king made a sign that he wished to go to rest, and left with us the prince, with whom we slept on a cane mat, with some cushions and pillows of leaves. Next morning the king came and took me by the hand, and so we went to the place where we had supped, to breakfast, but the boat came to fetch us. The king, before we went away, was very happy, and kissed our hands, and we kissed his. There came with us a brother of his, the king of another island, accompanied by three men. The captain-general detained him to dine with us, and we gave him several things.

In the island belonging to the king who came to the ship there are mines of gold, which they find in pieces as big as a walnut or an egg, by seeking in the ground. All the vessels that he makes use of are made of it, and also some parts of his house, which was well fitted up according to the custom of the country, and he was the handsomest man that we saw among these nations. He had very black hair coming down to his shoulders, with a silk cloth on his head, and two large gold rings hanging from his ears, he had a cloth of cotton worked with silk, which covered him from the waist to the knees, at his side he wore a dagger, with a long handle which was all of gold, its sheath was of carved wood. Besides he carried upon him scents of storax and benzoin. He was tawny and painted all over. The island of this king is named

Zuluan and Calagan, and when these two kings wish to visit one another they come to hunt in this island where we were. Of these kings the painted king is called Raia Calambu, and the other Raia Siani.

On Sunday, the last day of March, and feast of Easter, the captain sent the chaplain ashore early to say mass, and the interpreter went with him to tell the king that they were not coming on shore to dine with him, but only to hear the mass. The king hearing that sent two dead pigs. When it was time for saying mass the captain went ashore with fifty men, not with their arms, but only with their swords, and dressed as well as each one was able to dress, and before the boats reached the shore our ships fired six cannon shots as a sign of peace. At our landing the two kings were there, and received our captain in a friendly manner, and placed him between them, and then we went to the place prepared for saying mass, which was not far from the shore. Before the mass began the captain threw a quantity of musk rose water on those two kings, and when the offertory of the mass came, the two kings went to kiss the cross like us, but they offered nothing, and at the elevation of the body of our Lord they were kneeling like us, and adored our Lord with joined hands. The ships fired all their artillery at the elevation of the body of our Lord. After mass had been said each one did the duty of a Christian, receiving our Lord. After that the captain had some sword-play by his people, which gave great pleasure to the kings. Then he had a cross brought, with the nails and crown, to which the kings made reverence, and the captain had them told that these things that he showed them were the sign of the emperor his lord and master, from whom he had charge and commandment to place it in all places where he might go or pass by. He told them that he wished to place it in their country for their profit, because if there came afterwards any ships from Spain to those islands, on seeing this cross, they would know that we had been there, and therefore they would not cause them any displeasure to their persons nor their goods; and if they took any of their people, on showing them this sign, they would at, once let them go. Besides this, the captain told them that it was necessary that this cross should be placed on the summit of the highest mountain in their country, so that seeing it every day they might adore it, and that if they did thus, neither thunder, lightning, nor the tempest could do them hurt. The kings thanked the captain, and said they would do it willingly.

Then he asked whether they were Moors or Gentiles, and in what they believed. They answered that they did not perform any other adoration, but only joined their hands, looking up to heaven, and that they called their God, Aba. Hearing this, the captain was very joyful, on seeing that, the first king raised his hands to the sky and said that he wished it were possible for him to be able to show the affection which he felt towards him. The interpreter asked him for what reason there was so little to eat in that place, to which the king replied that he did not reside in that place except when he came to hunt and to see his brother, but that he lived in another island where he had all his family. Then the captain asked him if he had any enemies who made war upon him, and that if he had any he would go and defeat them with his men and ships, to put them under his obedience. The king thanked him, and answered that there were two islands the inhabitants of which were his enemies; however, that for the present it was not the time to attack them. The captain therefore said to him that if God permitted him to return another time to this country, he would bring so many men that he would put them by force under his obedience. Then he bade the interpreter tell them that he was going away to dine, and after that he would return to place the cross on the summit of the mountain. The two kings said they were content, and on that they embraced the captain, and he separated from them.

After dinner we all returned in our dress coats, and we went together with the two kings to the middle of the highest mountain we could find, and there the cross was planted. After that the two kings and the captain rested themselves; and, while conversing, I asked where was the best port for obtaining victuals. They replied that there were three, that is to say, Ceylon, Zzubu, and Calaghan, but that Zzubu was the largest and of the most traffic. Then the kings offered to give him pilots to go to those ports, for which he thanked them, and deliberated to go there, for his ill-fortunes would have it so. After the cross had been planted on that mountain, each one said the Paternoster and Ave Maria, and adored it, and the kings did the like. Then we went down below to where their boats were. There the kings had brought some of the fruit called cocos and other things to make a collation and to refresh us. The captain, being desirous to depart the next day in the morning, asked the king for the pilots to conduct us to the above-mentioned ports, promising him to treat them like themselves, and that he would leave one of his own men as a hostage. The first king said that he would go himself and conduct him to this port, and be his pilot, but that he should wait two days, until he had had his rice gathered in and done other things which he had to do, begging him to lend him some of his men so as to get done sooner. This the captain agreed to.

This kind of people are gentle, and go naked, and are painted. They wear a piece of cloth made from a tree, like a linen cloth, round their body to cover their natural parts : they are great drinkers. The women are dressed in tree cloth from their waists downwards; their hair is black, and reaches down to the ground; they wear certain gold rings in their ears. These people chew most of their time a fruit which they call areca, which is something of the shape of a pear; they cut it in four quarters, and after they have chewed it for a long time they spit it out, from which afterwards they have their mouths very red. They find themselves the better from the use of this fruit because it refreshes them much, for this country is very hot, so that they could not live without it. In this island there is a great quantity of dogs, cats, pigs, fowls, and goats, rice, ginger, cocoa, figs, oranges, lemons, millet, wax, and gold mines. This island is in $9^{2}/_{3}°$ north latitude, and one hundred and sixty-two longitude from the line of demarcation : it is twenty-five leagues distant from the other island where we found the two fountains of fresh water. This island is named Mazzava.

We remained seven days in this place; then we took the tack of Maestral, passing through the midst of five isles, that is to say, Ceylon, Bohol, Canighan, Baibai, and Satighan. In this island of Satighan is a kind of bird called Barbastigly, which are as large as eagles. Of these we killed only one, because it was late. We ate it, and it had the taste of a fowl. There are also in this island doves, tortoises, parrots, and certain black birds as large as a fowl, with a long tail. They lay eggs as large as those of a goose. These they put a good arm's length under the sand in the sun, where they are hatched by the great heat which the heated sand gives out; and when these birds are hatched they push up the sand and come out. These eggs are good to eat. From this island of Mazzabua to that of Satighan there are twenty leagues, and on leaving Satighan we went by the west; but the King of Mazzabua could not follow us;

therefore we waited for him near three islands, that is to say, Polo, Ticobon, and Pozzon. When the king arrived he was much astonished at our navigation, the captain-general bade him come on board his ship with some of his principal people, at which they were much pleased. Thus we went to Zzubu, which is fifteen leagues off from Satighan.

Sunday, the 7th of April, about midday, we entered the port of Zzubu, having passed by many villages. There we saw many houses that were built on trees. On approaching the principal town the captain-general commanded all his ships to hang out their flags. Then we lowered the sails in the fashion in which they are struck when going to fight, and he had all the artillery fired, at which the people of this place were greatly frightened. The captain sent a young man whom he had brought up, with the interpreter to the king of this island Zzubu. These having come to the town, found a great number of people and their king with them, all alarmed by the artillery that had been fired. However, the interpreter reassured them, saying that it was the fashion and custom to, fire artillery when they arrived at ports, to show signs of peace and friendship; and also, to do more honour to the king of the country, they had fired all the artillery. The king and all his people were reassured. He then bade one of his principal men ask what we were seeking. The interpreter answered him that his master was captain of the greatest king in the world, and that he was going by the command of the said sovereign to discover the Molucca islands. However, on account of what he had heard where he had passed, and especially from the King of Mazzava, of his courtesy and good fame, he had wished to pass by his country to visit him, and also to obtain some refreshment of victuals for his merchandise. The king answered him that he was welcome, but that the custom was that all ships that arrived at his country or port paid tribute, and it was only four days since that a ship called the Junk of Ciama, laden with gold and slaves, had paid him his tribute, and, to verify what he said, he showed them a merchant of the said Ciama, who had remained there to trade with the gold and slaves. The interpreter said to him that this captain, on account of being captain of so great a king as his was, would not pay tribute to any sovereign in the world; and that if he wished for peace he would have peace, and if he wished for war he would have war. Then the merchant above-mentioned replied to the king in his own language, "Look well, oh king, what you will do, for these people are of those who have conquered Calicut, Malacca, and all greater India; if you entertain them well and treat them well you will find yourself the better for it, and if ill, it will be so much the worse for you, as they have done at Calicut and Malacca." The interpreter, who understood all this discourse, said to them that the king, his master, was a good deal more powerful in ships and by land than the King of Portugal, and declared to him that he was the King of Spain and Emperor of all Christendom, wherefore, if he would not be his friend and treat his subjects well, he would another time send against him so many men as to destroy him. Then the king answered that he would speak to his council, and give an answer the next day. Afterwards the king ordered a collation to be brought of several viands, all of meat, in porcelain dishes, with a great many vessels of wine. When the repast was over, our people returned, and related all to the captain; and the King of Mazzabua, who was on board the captain's ship, and who was the first king after him of Zzubu, and the lord of several isles, wished to go on shore to relate to the king the politeness and courtesy of our captain.

Monday morning our clerk went with the interpreter to the town of Zzubu, and the king, accompanied by the principal men of his kingdom, came to the open space, where we made our people sit down near him, and he asked whether there was more than one captain in all those ships, and whether he wished that the king should pay tribute to the emperor, his master, to which our people answered, no, but that the captain only wished to trade with the things that he had brought with the people of his country, and not with others. Then the king said that he was content, and as a greater sign of affection he sent him a little of his blood from his right arm, and wished he should do the like. Our people answered. that he would do it. Besides that, he said that all the captains who came to his country had been accustomed to make a present to him, and he to them, and therefore they should ask their captain if he would observe the custom. Our people answered that he would; but as the king wished to keep up the custom, let him begin and make a present, and then the captain would do his duty.

Tuesday morning following the King of Mazzava, with the Moor, came to the ship, and saluted the captain on behalf of the King of Zzubu, and said that the king was preparing a quantity of provisions, as much as he could, to make a present of to him, and that after dinner he would send two of his nephews, with others of his principal people, to make peace with him. Then the captain had one of his men armed with his own armour, and told him that all of us would fight armed in that manner, at which the Moorish merchant was rather astonished; but the captain told him not to be afraid, and that our arms were soft to our friends and rough to our enemies; and that as a cloth wipes away the sweat from a man, so our arms destroy the enemies of our faith. The captain said this to the Moor, because he was more intelligent than the others, and for him to relate it all to the King of Zzubu.

After dinner, the nephew of this king, who was a prince, with the King of Mazzava, the Moor, the governor, and the chief of police, and eight of the principal men, came to the ship to make peace with us. The captain-general was sitting in a chair of red velvet, and near him were the principal men of the ships sitting in leather chairs, and the others on the ground on mats. Then the captain. bade the interpreter ask the above-mentioned persons if it was their custom to speak in secret or in public, and whether the prince who was come with them had power to conclude peace. They answered yes, that they would speak in public, and that they had the power to conclude peace. The captain spoke at length on the subject of peace, and prayed God to confirm it in heaven. These people replied that they had never heard such words as these that the captain had spoken to them, and they took great pleasure in hearing them. The captain, seeing then that those people listened willingly to what was said to them, and that they gave good answers, began to say a great many more good things to induce them to become Christians. After many other subjects, the captain asked them who would succeed the king in their country after his death. They answered that the king had no son, but several daughters, and that this prince was his nephew, and had for a wife the king's eldest daughter, and for the sake of that they called him prince. They also said that when the father and mother were old they took no further account of them, but their children commanded them. Upon which the captain told them how God had made heaven and earth and all other things in the world, and that He had commanded that everyone should render honour and obedience to his father and mother, and that whoever did otherwise was condemned to eternal fire. He then pointed out to them many other things concerning our faith. The people heard these things willingly, and besought the captain to leave them two men to teach and show them the Christian faith, and they would entertain them well with great honour. To this the captain answered that for the moment he could not leave them any of his people, but that if they wished to be Christians that his priest would baptise them, and that another time he would bring priests and preachers to teach them the faith. They then answered that they wished first to speak to their king, and then would become Christians. Each of us wept for the joy which we felt at the goodwill of these people, and the captain told them not to become Christians from fear of us, or to please us, but that if they wished to become Christian they must do it willingly, and for the love of God, for even though they should not become Christian, no displeasure would be done them, but those who became Christian would be more loved and better treated than the others. Then they all cried out with one voice, that they did not wish to become Christians from fear, nor from complaisance, but of their free will. The captain then said that if they became Christians he would leave them the arms that the Christians use, and that his king had commanded him so to do. At last they said they did not know what more to answer to so many good and beautiful words which he spoke to them, but that they placed themselves in his hands, and that he should do with them as with his own servants. Then the captain, with tears in his eyes, embraced them, and, taking the hand of the prince and that of the king, said to him that by the faith he had in God, and to his master the emperor, and by the habit of St. James, which he wore, he promised them to cause them to have perpetual peace with the King of Spain, at which the prince and the others promised him the same. After peace had been concluded, the captain had refreshments served to them. The prince and the King of Mazzava, who was with him, presented to the captain on behalf of his king large baskets full of rice, pigs, goats, and fowls, and desired the captain to be told he should pardon them that their present was not as fine as was fitting for him. The captain gave to the prince some very, fine cloth and a red cap, and a quantity of glass and a cup of gilt glass. Glasses are much prized in this country. To the other people belonging to the Prince he gave various things. Then he sent by me and another person to the King of Zzubu a robe of yellow and violet silk in the fashion of a Turkish jubbeh, a red cap, very fine, and certain pieces of glass, and had all of them put in a silver dish, and two gilt glasses.

When we came to the town we found the King of Zzubu at his palace, sitting on the ground on a mat made of palm, with many people about him. He was quite naked, except that he had a cloth round his middle, and a loose wrapper round his head, worked with silk by the needle. He had a very heavy chain round his neck, and two gold rings hung in his ears with precious stones. He was a small and fat man, and his face was painted with fire in different ways. He was eating on the ground on another palm mat, and was then eating tortoise eggs in two china dishes, and he had four vessels full of palm wine, which he drank with a cane pipe. We made our obeisance, and presented to him what the captain had sent him, and told him through the interpreter that it was not as a return for his present which he had sent to the captain, but for the affection which he bore him. That done, his people told him all the good words and explanations of peace and religion which he had spoken to them. The king wished to detain us to supper, but we made our excuses and took leave of him. The prince, nephew of the king, conducted us to his house, and showed us four girls who played on four instruments, which were strange and very soft, and their manner of playing is rather musical. Afterwards he made us dance with them. These girls were naked except from the waist to the knees, where they wore a wrap made of the palm tree cloth, which covered their middles, and some were quite naked. There we made a repast, and then returned to the ships.

Wednesday morning, because the night before one of our men had died, the interpreter and I, by order of the captain, went to ask the king for a place where we might bury the deceased. We found the king accompanied by a good many people, and, after paying him due honour, we told him of the death of our man, and that the captain prayed him that he might be put into the ground. He replied that if he and his people were ready to obey our master, still more reason was there for his land and country being subject to him. After that we said we wished to consecrate the grave in our fashion and place a cross on it. The sovereign said that he was content, and that he would worship that cross as we did. The deceased was buried in the middle of the open

Page 267

space of the town, as decently as possible, and performing the above mentioned ceremonies to set them a good example, and in the evening we buried another. This done, we brought a good quantity of merchandise into the town of this king, and placed it in a house, and he took it under his charge and promised that no one would do harm or injury to the king. Four of our men were chosen to despatch and sell this merchandise. These people live with justice, and good weight and measure, loving peace, and are people who love ease and pleasure. They have wooden scales, after the fashion of those of north of the Loire, for weighing their merchandise. Their houses are made of wood and beams and canes, founded on piles, and are very high, and must be entered by means of ladders; their rooms are like ours, and underneath they keep their cattle, such as pigs, goats, and fowls. The young people sound bagpipes, made like ours, and call them Subin.

In this island of the king's there is a kind of animal carrying a shell called carniolle, fine to look at, which cause the whale to die. For the whale swallows them alive then, when they are inside its body, they come out of their shell and go and eat the whale's heart : and the people of this country find this animal alive inside the whale. These animals, the carniolles, have the teeth and skin black, and their shell is white. Their flesh is good to eat, and they call them Laghan [a large sea snail].

The following Friday we showed them a shop full of our merchandise, which was of various strange sorts, at which they were surprised. For metal, iron, and other big goods they gave us gold, and for the other small and sundry goods they gave us rice, pigs, goats, and other provisions. They gave us ten weights of gold for fourteen pounds of iron each weight is a ducat and a half. The captain-general would not allow a large quantity of gold to be taken, so that the sailors should not sell what belonged to them too cheap from thirst for gold, and lest by that means he might be constrained to do likewise with his merchandise, for he wished to sell it better.

Saturday following a scaffolding was made in the open space, fitted with tapestry and palm branches, because the king had promised our captain to become Christian on Sunday. He told him not to be afraid when our artillery fired on that day, for it was the custom to load it on those feasts without firing stones or other balls.

Sunday morning, the fourteenth day of April, we went on shore, forty men, of whom two were armed, who marched before us, following the standard of our king emperor. When we landed, the ships discharged all their artillery, and from fear of it the people ran away in all directions. The captain and the king embraced one another, and then joyously we went near the scaffolding, where the captain and the king sat on two chairs, one covered with red, the other with violet velvet. The principal men sat on cushions, and the others on mats, after the fashion of the country. Then the captain began to speak to the king through the interpreter to incite him to the faith of Jesus Christ, and told him that if he wished to be a good Christian, as he had said the day before, that he must burn all the idols of his country, and, instead of them, place a cross, and that everyone should worship it every day on their knees, and their hands joined to heaven : and he showed him how he ought every day to make the sign of the cross. To that the king and all his people answered that they would obey the commands of the captain and do all that he told them. The captain took the king by the hand, and they walked about on the scaffolding, and when he was baptised he said that he would name him Don Charles, as the emperor his sovereign was named; and he named the prince Don Fernand, after the brother of the emperor, and the King of Mazzava Jehan : to the Moor he gave the name of Christopher, and to the others each a name of his fancy. Thus, before mass, there were fifty men baptised. After mass had been heard the captain invited the king and his other principal men to dine with him, but he would not. He accompanied the captain, however, to the beach, and on his arrival there the ships fired all their artillery. Then, embracing one another, they took leave.

After dinner our chaplain and some of us went on shore to baptise the queen. She came with forty ladies, and we conducted them on to the scaffolding; then made her sit down on a cushion, and her women around her, until the priest was ready. During that time they showed her an image of our Lady, of wood, holding her little child, which was very well made, and a cross. When she saw it, she had a greater desire to be a Christian, and, asking for baptism, she was baptised and named

Jehanne, like the mother of the emperor. The wife of the prince, daughter of this queen, had the name of Catherine, the Queen of Mazzava Isabella, and the others each their name. That day we baptised eight hundred persons of men, women, and children. The Queen was young and handsome, covered with a black and white sheet; she had the mouth and nails very red, and wore on her head a large hat made of leaves of palm, with a crown over it made of the same leaves, like that of the Pope. After that she begged us to give her the little wooden boy to put in the place of the idols. This we did, and she went away. In the evening the king and queen, with several of their people, came to the sea beach, where the captain had some of the large artillery fired, in which they took great pleasure. The captain and the king called one another brother.

At last, in eight days, all the inhabitants of this island were baptised, and some belonging to the neighbouring islands. In one of these we burned a village because the inhabitants would not obey either the king or us. There we planted a cross because the people were Gentiles : if they had been Moors, we should have erected a column, as a sign of their hardness of heart, because the Moors are more difficult to convert than the Gentiles. The captain-general went ashore every day to hear mass, to which there came many of the new Christians, to whom he explained various points of our religion. One day the queen came with all her state. She was preceded by three damsels, who carried in their hands three of her hats : she was dressed in black and white, with a large silk veil with gold stripes, which covered her head and shoulders. Very many women followed her, with their heads covered with a small veil, and a hat above that : the rest of their bodies and feet were naked, except a small wrapper of palm cloth which covered their natural parts. Their hair fell flowing over their shoulders. The queen, after making a bow to the altar, sat upon a cushion of embroidered silk, and the captain sprinkled over her and over some of her ladies rose water and musk, a perfume which pleases the ladies of this country very much. The captain on that occasion approved of the gift which I had made to the queen of the image of the Infant Jesus, and recommended her to put it in the place of her idols, because it was a remembrancer of the Son of God. She promised to do all this, and to keep it with much care.

In order that the king might be more respected and obeyed, the captain-general got him to come one day at the hour of mass with his silk robe, and summoned his two brothers, one named Bondara, who was the father of the prince, and the other named Cadaro, and some of his chief men, whose names were Simiut, Sibuaia, Sisacai, Magalibe, and others whom it is unnecessary to name separately; and he made them all swear to be obedient to their king, whose hand they all of them kissed. He then asked the king to swear that he would always be obedient and faithful to the King of Spain, and he took the oath. Then the captain drew a sword before the image of the Virgin Mary, and said to the king that when such an oath had been taken by anyone, he should rather die than be wanting to his oath. After that he himself promised to be always faithful to him, swearing by the image of our Lady, by the life of the emperor his sovereign, and by the habit which he wore. He then made a present to the king of a velvet chair, and told him that wherever he went he should always have it carried before him by some of his attendants, and showed him the way in which it should be carried. The king told the captain that he would do all this on account of the affection which he bore him, of which he wished to give him a token, preparing for that purpose some jewels to present to him; these were two rather large gold rings for the ears, two others for the arms, and two for the ankles, all of them adorned with precious stones. The finest ornaments of the kings of these countries consist in these rings, for otherwise they go naked and barefooted, with only a piece, of cloth from the waist to the knees.

The captain-general, who had informed the king and all those who had been baptised of the obligation they were under of burning their idols, which they had promised to do, seeing that they retained them and made them offerings of meat, reproved them severely for it. They thought to excuse themselves sufficiently by saying that they did not do that now on their own account, but for a sick person, for the idols to restore him his health. This sick man was a brother of the prince, and was reputed to be the most valiant and wise man in the island, and his illness was so severe that for four days he had not spoken. Having heard this, the captain, seized with zeal for religion, said that if they had a true faith in Jesus Christ, they should burn all the idols, and the sick man should be baptised, and he would be immediately cured, of which he was so certain that he consented to lose his head if the miracle did not take place. The king promised that all this should be done, because he truly believed in Jesus Christ. Then we arranged, with all the pomp that was possible, a procession from the place to the house of the sick man. We went there, and indeed found him unable to speak or to move. We baptised him, with two of his wives and ten girls. The captain then asked him how he felt, and he at once spoke, and said that by the grace of Our Lord he was well enough. This great miracle was done under our eyes. The captain, on hearing him speak, gave great thanks to God. He gave him a refreshing drink to take, and afterwards sent to his house a mattress, two sheets, a covering of yellow wool, and a cushion, and he continued to send him, until he was quite well, refreshing drinks of almonds, rosewater, rosoglio, and some sweet preserves.

On the fifth day the convalescent rose from his bed, and as soon as he could walk, he had, burned, in the presence of the king and of all the people, an idol which some old women bad concealed in his house. He also caused to be destroyed several temples constructed on the sea shore, in which people were accustomed to eat the meat offered to the idols. The inhabitants applauded this, and, shouting "Castile, Castile", helped to throw them down, and declared that if God gave them life they would burn all the idols they could find, even if they were in the king's own house.

These idols are made of wood, they are concave or hollowed out behind, they have the arms and legs spread out, and the feet turned upwards; they have a large face, with four very large teeth like those of a wild boar, and they are all painted.

Since I have spoken of the idols, it may, please your illustrious Highness to have an account of the ceremony with which, in this island, they bless the pig. They begin by sounding some great drums (tamburi), they then bring three large dishes, two are filled with cakes of rice and cooked millet rolled up in leaves, and roast fish, in the third are Cambay clothes, and two strips of palm cloth. A cloth of Cambay is spread out on the ground : then two old women come, each of whom has in her hand a reed trumpet. They step upon the cloth and make an obeisance to the Sun : they then clothe themselves with the above mentioned cloths. The first of these puts on her head a handkerchief which she ties on, her forehead so as to make two horns, and taking another handkerchief in her hand, dances and sounds her trumpet, and invokes the Sun. The second old woman takes one of the strips of palm cloth, and dances, and also sounds her trumpet; thus they dance and sound their trumpets for a short space of time, saying several things to the sun. The first old woman then drops the handkerchief she has in her hand, and takes the other strip of cloth, and both together sounding their trumpets, dance for a long time round the pig which is bound on the ground. The first one always speaks in a low tone to the sun, and the second answers her. The second old woman then presents a cup of wine to the first, who, whilst they both continue their address to the sun, brings the cup four or five times near her mouth as though going to drink, and meanwhile sprinkles the wine on the heart of the pig. She then gives up the cup, and receives a lance which she brandishes, whilst still dancing and reciting, and four or five times directs the lance at the pig's heart, at last with a sudden and well aimed blow she pierces, it through and through. She withdraws the lance from the wound, which is then closed and dressed with herbs. During the ceremony a torch is always burning, and the old woman who pierced the pig takes and puts it out with her mouth, the other old woman dips the end of her trumpet in the pig's blood, and with it marks with blood the forehead of her husband, and of her companion, and then of the rest of the people. However, they did not come and do this to us. That done the old women took off their robes, and ate what was in the two dishes, inviting only women to join them. After that they get the hair off the pig with fire. Only old women are able to consecrate the boar in this manner, and this animal is never eaten unless it is killed in this manner.

When our people went on shore by day or by night, they always met with some one who invited them to eat and drink. They only half cook their victuals, and salt them very much, which makes them drink a great deal; and they drink much with reeds, sucking the wine from the vessels. Their repasts always last from five to six hours.

When one of their chiefs dies they always use the following funeral ceremonies, of which I was witness. The most respected women of the country came to the house of the deceased, in the midst of which lay the corpse in a chest; round which were stretched cords after the manner of an enclosure, and many branches of trees were tied to these cords : a strip of cotton was fastened to each of these branches like a pennant. Under these the women I have mentioned sat down covered with white cotton cloth. Each of them had a damsel who fanned her with a palm fan. The other women sat sadly round the room. Meanwhile a woman cut off by degrees the hair of the dead man with a knife : another who had been his principal wife, lay extended on him, with her mouth, hands and feet on the mouth, hands and feet of the dead man. When the first woman cut off the hair, she wept, and when she stopped cutting, she sung.

Round the room there were many vases of porcelain, with embers in them, on which, from time to time, they threw myrrh, storax, and benzoin, which gave out a good and strong smell in the room. These ceremonies last for five or six days, during which the corpse is kept in the house, and I believe that they anoint it with oil of camphor to preserve it. They afterwards put it in a chest, closed with wooden bolts, and place it in an enclosed place covered with logs of wood.

The islanders told us that every evening towards midnight, there used to come to the city, a black bird of the size of a crow, which perching on the houses whistled, and caused all the dogs to howl, and these double-cries, lasted four or five hours. They would, never tell us the cause of that phenomenon, of which we also were witnesses.

Friday, the 26th of April, Zula, who was one of the principal men or chiefs of the island of Matan, sent to the captain a son of his with two goats to make a present of them, and to say that if he did not do all that he had promised, the cause of that was another chief named Silapulapu, who would not in any way obey the King of Spain, and had prevented him from doing so : but that if the captain would send him the following night one boat full of men to give him assistance, he would fight and subdue his rival. On the receipt of this message, the captain decided to go himself with three boats. We entreated him much not to go to this enterprise in person, but he as a good shepherd would not abandon his flock.

We set out from Zubu at midnight, we were sixty men armed with corslets and helmets; there were with us the Christian king, the prince, and some of the chief men; and many others divided among twenty or thirty balangai. We arrived at Matan three hours before daylight. The captain before attacking wished to attempt gentle means, and, sent on shore the Moorish merchant to tell those islanders who were of the party of Cilapulapu, that if they would recognise the Christian king as their sovereign, and obey the King of Spain, and pay us the tribute which had been asked, the captain would become their friend, otherwise we should prove how our lances wounded. The islanders were not terrified, they replied that if we had lances, so also had they, although only of reeds, and wood hardened with fire. They asked however that we should not attack them by night, but wait for daylight, because they were expecting reinforcements, and would be in greater number. This they said with cunning, to excite us to attack them by night, supposing that we were ready; but they wished this because they had dug ditches between their houses and the beach, and they hoped that we should fall into them.

We however waited for daylight; we then leaped into the water up to our thighs, for on account of the shallow water and the rocks the boats could not come close to the beach, and we had to cross two good crossbow shots through the water before reaching it. We were forty-nine in number, the other eleven remained in charge of the boats. When we reached land we found the islanders fifteen hundred in number, drawn up in three squadrons; they came down upon us with terrible shouts, two squadrons attacking us on the flanks, and the third in front. The captain then divided his men in two bands. Our musketeers and crossbow-men fired for half an hour from a distance, but did nothing, since the bullets and arrows, though they passed through their shields made of thin wood, and perhaps wounded their arms, yet did not stop them. The captain shouted not to fire, but he was not listened to. The islanders seeing that the shots of our guns did them little or no harm would not retire, but shouted more loudly, and springing from one side to the other to avoid our shots, they at the same time drew nearer to us, throwing arrows, javelins, spears hardened in fire, stones, and even mud, so that we could hardly defend ourselves. Some of them cast lances pointed with iron at the captain-general.

He then, in order to disperse this multitude and to terrify them, sent some of our men to set fire to their houses, but this rendered them more ferocious. Some of them ran to the fire, which consumed twenty or thirty houses, and there killed two of our men. The rest came down upon us with greater fury; they perceived that our bodies were defended, but that the legs were exposed, and they aimed at them principally. The captain had his right leg pierced by a poisoned arrow, on which account he gave orders to retreat by degrees; but almost all our men took to precipitate flight, so that there remained hardly six or eight of us with him. We were oppressed by the lances and stones which the enemy hurled at us, and we could make no more resistance. The bombards which we had in the boats were of no assistance to us, for the shoal water kept them too far from the beach. We went thither, retreating little by little, and still fighting, and we had already got to the distance of a crossbow shot from the shore, having the water up to our knees, the islanders following and picking up again the spears which they had already cast, and they threw the same spear five or six times; as they knew the captain they aimed specially at him, and twice they knocked the helmet off his head. He, with a few of us, like a good knight, remained at his post without choosing to retreat further. Thus we fought for more than an hour, until an Indian succeeded in thrusting a cane lance into the captain's face. He then, being irritated, pierced the Indian's breast with his lance, and left it in his body, and trying to draw his sword he was unable to draw it more than half way, on account of a javelin wound which he had received in the right arm. The enemies seeing this all rushed against him, and one of them with a great sword, like a great scimetar gave him a great blow on the left leg, which brought the captain down on his face, then the Indians threw themselves upon him, and ran him through with lances and scimitars, and all the other arms which they had, so that they deprived of life our mirror, light, comfort, and true guide. Whilst the Indians were thus overpowering him, several times he turned round towards us to see if we were all in safety, as though his obstinate fight had no other object than to give an opportunity for the retreat of his men. We who fought to extremity, and who were covered with wounds, seeing that he was dead, proceeded to the boats which were on the point of going away. This fatal battle was fought on the 27th of April of 1521, on a Saturday; a day which the captain had chosen himself, because he had a special devotion to it. There perished with him eight of our men, and four of the Indians, who had become Christians; we had also many wounded, amongst whom I must reckon myself. The enemy lost only fifteen men.

He died; but I hope that your illustrious highness will not allow his memory to be lost, so much the more since I see revived in you the virtue of so great a captain, since one of his principal virtues was constance in the most adverse fortune. In the midst of the sea he was able to endure hunger better than we. Most versed in nautical charts, he knew better than any other the true art of navigation, of which it is a certain proof that he knew by his genius, and his intrepidity, without any one having given him the example, how to attempt the circuit of the globe, which he had almost completed.

The Christian king could indeed have given us aid, and would have done so; but our captain far from forseeing that which happened, when he landed with his men, had charged him not to come out of his balangai, wishing that he should stay there to see how we fought. When he knew how the captain had died he wept bitterly for him.

In the afternoon the king himself, with our consent, sent to tell the inhabitants of Matan, that if they would give up to us the body of our captain, and of our other companions who were killed in this battle, we would give them as much merchandise as they might wish for; but they answered that on no account would they ever give up that man, but they wished to preserve him as a monument of their triumph. When the death of the captain was known, those who were in the city to trade, had all the merchandise at once transported to the ships. We then elected in the place of the captain, Duarte Barbosa, a Portuguese, and a relation of the captain's, and Juan Serrano a Spaniard.

Our interpreter, who was a slave of the captain general, and was named Henry, having been slightly wounded in the battle, would not go ashore any more for the things which we required, but remained all day idle, and wrapped up in his mat (Schiavina). Duarte Barbosa, the commander of the flag ship, found fault with him, and told him that though his master was dead, he had not become free on that account, but that when we returned to Spain he would return him to Doña

Beatrice, the widow of the captain-general; at the same time he
threatened to have him flogged, if he did not go on shore quickly, and
do what was wanted for the service of the ships. The slave rose up, and
did as though he did not care much for these affronts and threats; and
having gone on shore, he informed the Christian king that we were
thinking of going away soon, but that if he would follow his advice, he
might become master of all our goods and of the ships themselves. The
King of Zubu listened favourably to him, and they arranged to betray
us. After that the slave returned on board, and showed more
intelligence and attention than he had done before.

Wednesday morning, the 1st of May, the Christian king sent to tell the
two commanders that the jewels prepared as presents for the King of
Spain were ready, and he invited them to come that same day to dine
with him, with some of his most honoured companions, and he would
give them over to them. The commanders went with twenty-four
others, and amongst them was our astrologer named San Martin of
Seville. I could not go because I was swelled with a wound from a
poisoned arrow in the forehead. Juan Carvalho, with the chief of police,
who also were invited, turned back, and said that they had suspected
some bad business, because they had seen the man who had recovered
from illness by a miracle, leading away the priest to his own house.
They had hardly spoken these words when we heard great lamentations
and cries. We quickly got up the anchors and, coming closer to the
beach, we fired several shots with the cannon at the houses. There then
appeared on the beach Juan Serrano, in his shirt, wounded and bound,
who entreated us, as loudly as he could, not to fire any more, or else he
would be massacred. We asked him what had become of his
companions and the interpreter, and he said that all had been slain
except the interpreter. He then entreated us to ransom him with some
merchandise; but Juan Carvalho, although he was his gossip, joined
with some others, refused to do it, and they would not allow any boat to
go ashore, so that they might remain masters of the ships. Serrano
continued his entreaties and lamentations, saying, that if we departed
and abandoned him there, he would soon be killed; and after that he
saw his lamentations were useless, he added that he prayed God to ask
for an account of his life at the day of Judgment from Juan Carvalho,

his gossip. Notwithstanding, we sailed immediately; and I never heard any more news of him.

In this island of Zubu there are dogs and cats, and other animals, whose flesh is eaten; there is also rice, millet, panicum, and maize; there are also figs, oranges, lemons, sugar-canes, cocos, gourds, ginger, honey, and other such things; they also make palm-wine of many qualities. Gold is abundant. The island is large, and has a good port with two entrances : one to the west, and the other to the east north-east. It is in ten degrees north latitude and 154 east longitude from the line of demarcation.

In this island there are several towns, each of which has its principal men or chiefs. Here are the names of the towns and their chiefs :- Cingapola : its chiefs are Cilaton, Ciguibucan, Cimaninga, Cimaticat, Cicanbul; Mandani : its chief is Aponoaan; Lalan : its chief is Teten; Lalutan : its chief is Japau; Lubucin : its chief is Cilumai. All these countries were in obedience to us, and paid a kind of tribute.

Near to Zubu there is, as we said, the island of Matan, the most considerable town of which is called Matan, and its chiefs are Zula and Cilapulapu. The village, which we burned on the occasion of the fatal battle, is named Bulaia.

In this island, before we lost our captain-general, we had news of Maluco.

DEPARTURE FROM ZUBU

When we were at a distance of eighteen leagues from the island of Zubu, near the head of another island called Bohol, in the midst of that archipelago, seeing that our crews were too much reduced in number, so that they were not sufficient for managing all the three ships, we burned the Conception after transporting into the other two all that it contained that was serviceable. We then took the S.S.W. course, coasting along an island called Panilongon, where the people were black as in Ethiopia.

We then arrived at a large island, the king of which having come on board our ship, in order to show that he made alliance with us and would be friendly, drew blood from his left hand, and stained with it his breast, his face, and the tip of his tongue. We then did likewise, and when the king went away, I alone accompanied him on shore to see the island.

We entered a river where we met many fishermen, who presented some of their fish to the king. He then took off the cloth which covered his middle, and some of his chief men who were with him did the same, they then all began to row and to sing. Passing near many houses, which were on the brink of the river, we arrived at two hours of the night at the house of the king, which was two leagues from the mouth of the river where the ships were.

When we reached the house, people came to meet us with many torches, made of canes and palm leaves, full of the before mentioned gum, called anime. Whilst supper was being got ready, the king, with two of his chiefs, and two rather handsome ladies, drank a large vase full of palm wine, without eating anything. I, excusing myself saying that I had already supped, only drank once. In drinking they use the ceremony which I have already described in speaking of the King of Massava. Then the supper was brought, which consisted of rice and fish, very much salted, in porcelain dishes. Rice with them takes the place of bread. They cook it in the following manner, which is common to all these countries. They place inside an earthen pot like ours, a large leaf which lines it all round internally, then they put in the water and the rice, and cover up the pot. They let it boil until the rice has taken the consistency of bread, and then they take it out in pieces.

When the supper was over the king had brought a cane mat, and a mat of palm leaf, with a cushion of leaves, and this was to be my bed. I slept there with one of his chiefs. The king with the two ladies went to sleep in another place.

When it was day, whilst breakfast was being prepared, I went to take a turn in the island, and entered several houses, constructed like those of the neighbouring islands; I saw there a good many utensils of gold, but very little victuals. I returned to the king's house, and we breakfasted with rice and fish. I succeeded in making the king understand by signs, that I should like to see the queen; and he made a sign to me that he was content, and we set out together to the top of a hill, under which her house was placed. I entered the house and made her an obeisance, she did likewise to me. I sat down by the side of her; she was weaving a palm mat to sleep upon. Throughout her house were seen porcelain vases suspended to the walls, and four metal timbals, of which one was very large, another of middle size, and two small ones, and she amused herself by playing on them. There were many male and female slaves for her service. We asked leave and returned to the king's house, who immediately ordered a refreshment of sugar canes.

After midday, as I wished to return to the ships, the king, with the other chief men of the island, desired to accompany me in the same balangai, going by the same river; on its right bank I saw on an eminence three men hanging to a tree, the branches of which had been cut off. I asked of the king what those unhappy people were, he answered me that they were malefactors and thieves. These people go naked like their neighbours. In this island are found pigs, goats, fowls, rice, ginger, and other things which were common to the islands named before. That which is most abundant is gold. They showed me certain valleys, making signs that there was more gold there than hairs on the head, but that as they had not iron to dig it out, it required great labour to acquire it, and which they did not choose to undergo. The king is named Raja Calanao.

This part of the island called Chipit is the same land as Butuan and Calagan, it passes above Bohol, and borders on Massava. Its port is good enough; it is in 8° N. latitude, and 167° of longitude from the line of demarcation; it is fifty leagues distance from Zubu. Towards the North-west is the island of Lozon, which is at two days distance; a large island, to which come to trade every year six or eight junks of the people called Lequii.

On leaving this place, and taking our course between west and south-west, we touched at an almost uninhabited island, which afterwards we learned was named Cagayan. The few people there are

Moors, who have been banished from an island called Burné. They go naked like the others, and carry blowpipes with small quivers at their sides full of arrows, and a herb with which they poison them. They have daggers, with hilts adorned with gold and precious stones, lances, bucklers, and small cuirasses of buffaloes' hide. These people took us for something Divine or holy. There are some very large trees in this island, but little victuals. It is in 7° 30' North latitude, and forty three leagues from Chipit.

Continuing our voyage we changed our course to between West and North-west, and after running twenty-five leagues, we arrived at a large island, which we found well provided with victuals, and it was great good fortune for us since we were so reduced by hunger and so badly supplied, that we were several times on the point of abandoning the ships, and establishing ourselves on some land, in order to live. In this island, which we learned was named Palaoan, we found pigs, goats, fowls, yams, bananas of various kinds, some of which are half a cubit long, and as thick as the arm, others are only a span long, and others are still smaller, and these are the best; they have coconuts, sugar canes, and certain roots like turnips. They cook rice under the fire in bamboo canes, or wooden vessels, and it keeps longer than that cooked in earthen pots. They draw from the rice with a kind of alembic, a wine that is better and stronger than the palm wine. In short we found this island to be a promised land.

We presented ourselves to the king, who contracted alliance and friendship with us, and to assure us of it, he asked for one of our knives, with which he drew blood from his breast, with which he touched his forehead and tongue. We repeated the same ceremony.

The people of Palaoan go naked like the other islanders, they almost all till their own fields. They have blowpipes, with thick arrows more than a span in length, with a point like that of a harpoon; some have a point made with a fish bone, and others are of reed, poisoned with a certain herb; the arrows are not trimmed with feathers, but with a soft light wood. At the foot of the blowpipe they bind a piece of iron, by means of which, when they have no more arrows, they wield the blowpipe like a lance. They like to adorn themselves with rings and chains of gimp and with little bells, but above all they are fond of brass wire, with which they bind their fish hooks. They have some rather large domestic cocks, which, from some superstition, they do not eat, but they keep them for fighting; on such occasions they make bets and offer prizes, which are acquired by the owner of the conquering cock.

Going from Palaoan towards the South-west, after a run of ten leagues, we reached another island. Whilst coasting it, it seemed in a certain manner to go forward; we coasted it for a distance of fully fifty leagues, until we found a port. We had hardly reached the port when the heavens were darkened, and the lights of St. Elmo appeared on our masts.

The next day the king of that island sent a prahu to the ships; it was very handsome, with its prow and stern ornamented with gold; on the bow fluttered a white and blue flag, with a tuft of peacock's feathers at the top of the staff; there were in the prahu some people playing on pipes and drums, and many other persons. Two almadias followed the prahu; these are fishermen's boats, and a prahu is a kind of fusta. Eight old men of the chiefs of the island came into the ships, and sat down upon a carpet on the poop, and presented a painted wooden vase full of betel and areca (fruits which they constantly chew), with orange and jessamine flowers, and covered over with a cloth of yellow silk. They also gave two cages full of fowls, two goats, three vessels full of wine, distilled from rice, and some bundles of sugar cane. They did the same to the other ship; and embracing us they departed. Their rice wine is clear like water, but so strong that many of our men were intoxicated. They call it arak.

Six days later the king again sent three very ornamented prahus, which came playing pipes and drums and cymbals, and going round the ships, their crews saluted us with their cloth caps, which hardly cover the tops of their heads. We saluted them, firing the bombards without stones. Then they made us a present of various victuals, but all made with rice, either wrapped in leaves in the form of a long cylinder, or in the shape of a sugar loaf, or in the shape of a cake, with eggs and honey. They then said that their king was well pleased that we should make provisions here of wood and water, and that we might traffic at our pleasure with the islanders. Having heard this, seven of us entered one of the prahus, taking with us presents for the king, and for some of his court. The present intended for the king consisted in a Turkish coat of green velvet, a chair of violet coloured velvet, five ells of red cloth, a cap, a gilt goblet, and a vase of glass, with its cover, three packets of paper, and a gilt pen and ink case. We took for the queen three ells of yellow cloth, a pair of slippers, ornamented with silver, and a silver case full of pins. For the king's governor or minister three ells of red cloth, a cap, and a gilt goblet; and for the herald who had come in the prahu, a coat of the Turkish fashion, of red and green colours, a cap and a packet of paper. For the other seven chief men who had come with him, we prepared presents; for one cloth, for another a cap, and for each a packet of paper. Having made these preparations, we entered the prahu, and departed.

When we arrived at the city, we were obliged to wait about two hours in the prahu, until there came thither two elephants covered with silk, and twelve men, each of whom carried a porcelain vase covered with silk, for conveying and wrapping up our presents. We mounted the elephants, and those twelve men preceded us, carrying the vases with our presents. We went as far as the house of the governor, who gave us supper with many sorts of viands. There we slept through the night, on mattresses filled with cotton, and covered with silk, with sheets of Cambay stuff.

On the following day we remained doing nothing in the house till midday, and after that we set out for the king's palace. We were again mounted upon the elephants, and the men with the presents preceded us as before. From the governor's house to that of the king, all the streets were full of men armed with swords, spears, and bucklers, the king having so commanded. We entered the palace still mounted upon the elephants; we then dismounted, and ascended a staircase, accompanied by the governor and some of the chief men, and entered a large room full of courtiers, whom we should call the barons of the kingdom; there we sat upon a carpet, and the vases with the presents were placed near us.

At the end of this hall there was another a little higher, but not so large, all hung with silk stuffs, among which were two curtains of brocade hung up, and leaving, open two windows which gave light to the room.

There were placed three hundred men of the king's guard with naked daggers in their hands, which they held on their thighs. At the end of this second hall was a great opening, covered with a curtain of brocade, and on this being raised we saw the king sitting at a table, with a little child of his, chewing betel. Behind him there were only women.

Then one of the chief men informed us that we could not speak to the king, but that if we wished to convey anything to him, we were to say it to him, and he would say it to a chief or courtier of higher rank, who would lay it before a brother of the governor, who was in the smaller room, and they by means of a blow pipe placed in a fissure in the wall would communicate our thoughts to a man who was near the king, and from him the king would understand them. He taught us meanwhile to make three obeisances to the king, with the hands joined above the head, raising first one then the other foot, and then to kiss the hands to him. This is the royal obeisance.

Then by the mode which had been indicated to us, we gave him to understand that we belonged to the King of Spain, who wished to be in peace with him, and wished for nothing else than to be able to trade with his island. The king caused an answer to be given that he was most pleased that the king of Spain was his friend, and that we could take wood and water in his states, and traffic according to our pleasure. That done we offered the presents, and at each thing that they gave to him, he made a slight inclination with his head. To each of us was then given some brocade, with cloth of gold, and some silk, which they placed upon one of our shoulders, and then took away to take care of them. A collation of cloves and cinnamon was then served to us, and after that the curtains were drawn and the windows closed. All the men who were in the palace had their middles covered with cloth of gold and silk, they carried in their hands daggers with gold hilts, adorned with pearls and precious stones, and they had many rings on their fingers.

We again mounted the elephants, and returned to the house of the governor. Seven men preceded us there, carrying the presents made to us, and when we reached the house they gave to each one of us what was for him, putting it on our left shoulder, as had been done in the king's palace. To each of these seven men we gave a pair of knives in recompense for their trouble.

Afterwards there came nine men to the governor's house, sent by the king, with as many large wooden trays, in each of which were ten or twelve china dishes, with the flesh of various animals, such as veal, capons, fowls, peacocks, and others, with various sorts of fish, so that only of flesh there were thirty or thirty-two different viands. We supped on the ground on a palm mat; at each mouthful we drank a little china cup of the size of an egg full of the distilled liquor of rice : we then ate some rice and some things made of sugar using gold spoons made like ours. In the place in which we passed the two nights there were two candles of white wax always burning, placed on high chandeliers of silver, and two oil lamps with four wicks each. Two men kept watch there to take care of them. The next morning we came upon the same elephants to the sea shore, where there were two prahus ready, in which we were taken back to the ships.

This city is entirely built on foundations in the salt water, except the houses of the king and some of the princes : it contains twenty-five thousand fires or families. The houses are all of wood, placed on great piles to raise them high up. When the tide rises the women go in boats through the city selling provisions and necessaries. In front of the king's house there is a wall made of great bricks, with barbicans like forts, upon which were fifty-six bombards of metal, and six of iron. They fired many shots from them during the two days that we passed in the city.

The king to whom we presented ourselves is a Moor, and is named Raja Siripada : he is about forty years of age, and is rather corpulent. No one serves him except ladies who are the daughters of the chiefs. No one speaks to him except by means of the blowpipe as has been described above. He has ten scribes, who write down his affairs on thin bark of trees; and are called chiritoles. He never goes out of his house except to go hunting.

On Monday, the 29th of July, we saw coming towards us more than a hundred prahus, divided into three squadrons, and as many tungulis, which are their smaller kind of boats. At this sight, and fearing treachery, we hurriedly set sail, and left behind an anchor in the sea. Our suspicions increased when we observed that behind us were certain junks that had come the day before. Our first operation was to free ourselves from the junks, against which we fired, capturing four and killing many people : three or four other junks went aground in escaping. In one of those which we captured was a son of the king of the isle of Luzon, who was captain-general of the King of Burné, and who was coming with the junks from the conquest of a great city named Laoe, situated on a headland of this island opposite Java Major. He had made this expedition and sacked that city because its inhabitants wished rather to obey the King of Java than the Moorish King of Burné. The Moorish king having heard of the ill-treatment by us of his, junks, hastened to send to say, by means of one of our men who was on shore to traffic, that those vessels had not come to do any harm to us, but were going to make war against the Gentiles, in proof of which they showed us some of the heads of those they had slain.

Hearing this, we sent to tell the king that if it was so, that he should allow two of our men who were still on shore, with a son of our pilot, Juan Carvalho, to come to the ships : this son of Carvalho's had been born during his first residence in the country of Brazil : but the king would not consent. Juan Carvalho was thus specially punished, for without communicating the matter to us, in order to obtain a large sum of gold, as we learned later, he had given his liberty to the captain of the junks. If he had detained him, the King Siripada would have given anything to get him back, that captain being exceedingly dreaded by the Gentiles who are most hostile to the Moorish king. And, with respect to that, it is well to know and understand that in that same port where we were, beyond the city of the Moors of which I have spoken, there is another inhabited by Gentiles, larger than this one, and also built in the salt water. So great is the enmity between the two nations that every day there occurs strife. The king of the Gentiles is as powerful as the king of the Moors, but he is not so proud; and it seems that it would not be so difficult to introduce the Christian religion into his country. As we could not get back our men, we retained on board sixteen of the chiefs, and three ladies whom we had taken on board the junks, to take them to Spain. We had destined the ladies for the Queen; but Juan Carvalho kept them for himself.

The Moors of Burné go naked like the other islanders. They esteem quicksilver very much, and swallow it. They pretend that it preserves the health of those who are well, and that it cures the sick. They venerate Mahomed and follow his law. They do not eat pig's flesh... . With their right hand they wash their face, but do not wash their teeth with their fingers. They are circumcised like the Jews. They never kill goats or fowls without first speaking to the suns. They cut off the ends of the wings of fowls and the skin under their feet, and then split them in two. They do not eat any animal that has not been killed by themselves.

In this island is produced camphor, a kind of balsam that exudes from between the bark and the wood of the tree. These drops are small as grains of bran. If it is left exposed by degrees it is consumed : here it is called capor. Here is found also cinnamon, ginger, mirabolans, oranges, lemons, sugarcanes, melons, gourds, cucumbers, cabbage, onions. There are also many animals, such as elephants, horses, buffaloes, pigs, goats, fowls, geese, crows, and others.

They say that the King of Burné has two pearls as large as a hen's eggs, and so perfectly round that if placed on a smooth table they cannot be made to stand still. When we took him the presents I made signs to him that I desired to see them, and he said that he would show them to me, but he did not do so. On the following day some of the chief men told me that they had indeed seen them.

The money which the Moors use in this country is of metal, and pierced for stringing together. On one side only it has four signs, which are four letters of the great King of China : they call it Picis. For one cathil (a weight equal to two of our pounds) of quicksilver they gave us six porcelain dishes, for a cathil of metal they gave one small porcelain vase, and a large vase for three knives. For a hand of paper they gave one hundred picis. A bahar of wax (which is two hundred and three cathils) for one hundred and sixty cathils of bronze : for eighty cathils a bahar of salt : for forty cathils a bahar of anime, a gum which they use to caulk ships, for in these countries they have no pitch. Twenty tabil make a cathil. The merchandise that is most esteemed here is bronze, quicksilver, cinnabar, glass, woollen stuffs, linens; but above all they esteem iron and spectacles.

Since I saw such use made of porcelain, I got some information respecting it, and I learned that it is made with a kind of very white earth, which is left underground for fully fifty years to refine it, so that they are in the habit of saying that the father buries it for his son. It is said that if poison is put into a vessel of fine porcelain it breaks immediately.

The junks mentioned several times above are their largest vessels, and they are constructed in this manner. The lower part of the ships and the sides to a height of two spans above water-line are built of planks joined together with wooden bolts, and they are well enough put together. The upper works are made of very large canes for a counterpoise. One of these junks carries as much cargo as our ships. The masts are of bamboo, and the sails of bark of trees. This island is so large that to sail round it with a prahu would require three months. It is in 5° 15' north latitude and 176° 40' of longitude from the line of demarcation.

On leaving this island we returned backwards to look for a convenient place for caulking our ships, which were leaking, and one of them, through the negligence of the pilot, struck on a shoal near an island named Bibalon; but, by the help of God, we got her off. We also ran another great danger, for a sailor, in snuffing a candle, threw the lighted wick into a chest of gunpowder; but he was so quick in picking it out that the powder did not catch fire.

On our way we saw four prahus. We took one laden with coconuts on its way to Burné; but the crew escaped to a small island, and the other three prahus escaped behind some other small islands.

Between the northern cape of Burné and the island named Gimbonbon, situated in 8° 7' N. latatude, there is a very convenient port for refitting ships, and we entered it; but as we were wanting many things necessary for our work, we had to spend there forty-two days. Each one worked at one thing or another according to the beat of his knowledge or ability; but our greatest labour was going to get wood in the thickets, as the ground was covered with briars and thorny shrubs, and we had no shoes.

In this island there are some very large wild boars. Whilst we were in a boat we killed one which was crossing from one island to another. Its head was two and a half spans long, and its tusks were exceedingly long. Here also are crocodiles; those of the land are larger than those of the seacoast. There are oysters and very large turtles; of these we caught two. The flesh alone of one of them weighed twenty pounds, and of the other forty-four pounds. We caught a kind of fish with a head like that of a pig, and which had two horns; its body was all covered with bone, and on its back it had a kind of saddle : this was a small one. In this island are also found certain trees, the leaves of which, when they fall, are animated, and walk. They are like the leaves of the mulberry tree, but not so long; they have the leaf stalk short and pointed, and near the leaf stalk they have on each side two feet. If they are touched they escape, but if crushed they do not give out blood. I kept one for nine days in a box. When I opened it the leaf went round the box. I believe they live upon air. The island in which we were is called Pulaoan.

On leaving this island - that is to say, the port that is at the extremity of it - we met a junk that was coming from Borneo. We made signals to it to strike its sails; but as it would not obey we overtook it, captured and pillaged it. It had on board the Governor of Pulaoan, with a son and a brother of his. We made them all prisoners, and put them to ransom to give within seven days four hundred measures of rice, twenty pigs, as many goats, and four hundred and fifty fowls. They caused all this to be given us, and besides added spontaneously coconuts, figs, sugarcanes, and vessels full of palm wine. We, in consequence of his generosity, restored to him some of his daggers and arquebuses; we also gave him a flag, a garment of yellow damask, and fifteen ells of linen. We gave to his son a cloak of blue cloth, and to his brother a garment of green cloth, and to the others other things, and we parted good friends.

We turned backwards, passing between the island of Cagayan and the port of Cipit, taking a course east and a quarter south-east, to seek the islands of Maluco. We passed between certain little mountains, around which we found many weeds, although there was there a great depth. Passing between these islets it seemed that we were in another sea.

Having left Cipit to the east, we saw to the west two islands called Zolo and Taghima, near which islands pearls are found. The two pearls of the King of Burné, of which I have spoken, were found there, and this is the manner in which he obtained them, according to the account which was given me of it. The King of Burné married a daughter of the King of Zolo, who told him that her father had these two big pearls. He desired to have them, and decided on getting them by any means, and one night he set out with five hundred prahus full of armed men, and went to Zolo, and took the king with his two sons, and brought them to Burné, and did not restore them to liberty until they gave him the two pearls.

Continuing our course east and a quarter north-east we passed near two inhabited places called Cavit and Subanin, and passed near an island called Monoripa, ten leagues distant from the before-mentioned islets. The inhabitants of this island always live in their vessels, and have no houses on shore. In these two districts of Cavit and Subanin, which are situated in the same island as that in which are Butuan and Calagan, the best cinnamon of any grows. If we could have remained here only two days, we could have laden the ships with it; but we did not wish to lose time, but to profit by the favourable wind, for we had to double a cape and some islets which were around it. Wherefore, remaining under sail, we made a little barter, and obtained seventeen pounds of cinnamon for two big knives, which we had taken from the Governor of Pulaoan.

Having seen the cinnamon tree, I can give some description of it. It is a small tree, not more than three or four cubits high, and of the thickness of a man's finger, and it has not got more than three or four little branches. Its leaf is like that of the laurel. The cinnamon for use which comes to us, is its bark, which is gathered twice in the year. Its wood and leaves when they are green have the taste and force of the bar itself. Here it is called Cainmana, since cain means wood and mana sweet.

Having set the head of the ship to north-east, we made for a large city called Maingdanao, situated in the same island in which are Butuan and Calagan, in order to get precise information of the position of Maluco. Following this course we took possession of a bignaday, a vessel similar to a prahu, and being obliged to have recourse to force and violence, we killed seven out of eighteen men who formed the crew. These men were better made and more robust than all those we had seen hitherto, and they were all chief men of Mindanao. There was among them a brother of the king who said that he well knew where Maluco was. Afterwards, following his indications, we left the north-east course which we held, and took a south-east course. We were then in 6° 7' N. Latitude and thirty leagues distant from Cavit.

We were told that at a cape of this island near to a river there are men who are rather hairy, great warriors, and good archers, armed with swords a span broad. When they make an enemy prisoner they eat his heart only, and they eat it raw with the juice of oranges or lemons. This cape is called Benaian.

Making for the south-east we found four islands, named Ciboco, Birabam, Batolac, Sarangani, and Candigar. Saturday, the 26th of October, about nightfall, whilst coasting the island of Birabam Batolac, we met with a very great storm, before which we lowered all our sails, and betook ourselves to prayer. Then our three saints appeared upon the masts and dispersed the darkness. St. Elmo stood for more than two hours at the mainmast head like a flame. St. Nicholas at the head of the foremast, and St. Clara on the mizenmast. In gratitude for their assistance we promised a slave to each of the saints, and we gave to each an offering.

Continuing our voyage we entered a port between the two islands Sarangani and Candigar, and cast anchor to the east, near a village of Sarangani, where pearls and gold are found. This port is in 5° 9' N. latitude, and fifty leagues from Cavit. The inhabitants are Gentiles and go naked like the others.

Having remained here a day we compelled by force two pilots to come with us to show us the way to Maluco. We were directed to take a south-south-west course, and passed between eight islands partly inhabited, partly uninhabited, which formed a kind of street. These were named Cheava, Caviao, Cabiao, Camanuca, Cabaluzao, Cheai, Lipan, and Nuza. At the end of these we reached an island which was very beautiful, named Sanghir. However, having a contrary wind, which did not allow us to double the cape, we tacked about backwards and forwards near it.

On this occasion, profiting by the darkness of the night, one of the pilots whom we had caught at Sarangani, and with him the brother of the king of Mindanao with his little son, escaped by swimming and reached that island; but we learned later that the son not being able to hold on well to his father's shoulders, was drowned.

Seeing that it was impossible to double the head of this island we passed below it, where we saw many small islands. This large island has four kings whose names are Raja Matandatu, Raja Laga, Raja Bapti, and Raja Parabu. These are Gentiles. It is in 3° 30' N. latitude and twenty seven leagues from Sarangani.

Continuing our course in the same direction we passed near five islands named Cheoma, Carachita, Para, Zangalura, and Cian. This last is ten leagues distant from Sanghir. In this island there is a rather high mountain, but not one of great extent. Its king is named Raja Ponto. We came next to the island Paghinzara, which has three high mountains, and in it the king is Raja Babintan. We saw at twelve leagues to the east of Paghinzara another island, Talent, and also two islands, not large but inhabited, called Zoar and Mean.

Wednesday, the 6th of November, having passed beyond these two islands, we discovered four other rather high islands at a distance of fourteen leagues towards the east. The pilot who had remained with us told us those were the Maluco islands, for which we gave thanks to God, and to comfort ourselves we discharged all our artillery. It need not cause wonder that we were so much rejoiced, since we had passed twenty-seven months less two days always in search of Maluco, wandering for that object among the immense number of islands. However, I must say that near all these islands the least depth that we found was one hundred fathoms, for which reason attention is not to be given to all that the Portuguese have spread, according to whom the islands of Maluco are situated in seas which cannot be navigated on account of the shoals, and the dark and foggy atmosphere.

Friday, the 8th November of 1521, three hours before sunset, we entered a port of the island called Tadore, and having gone near the shore, we cast anchor in twenty fathoms, aid discharged all our artillery. Next day the king came to the ships in a prahu, and went round them. We went to meet him with a boat to show him honour, and he made us enter his prahu, and sit near him. He was sitting under a silk umbrella, which sheltered him. In front of him was his son with the royal sceptre, there were also two men with gold vases to give, him water for his hands, and two others with gilt caskets full of betel.

The king gave us a welcome, and said that a long time back he had dreamed that some ships were coming to Maluco from distant countries, and that to assure himself with respect to this, he had examined the moon, and he had seen that they were really coming, and that indeed they were our ships. After that he came on board our ships, and we all kissed his hand : we then conducted him to the poop, but he, in order to avoid stooping, would not enter the cabin except by the upper opening. We made him sit down on a chair of red velvet, and placed on him a Turkish robe of yellow velvet. In order to do him more honour we sat down before him on the ground. When he had heard who we were, and what was the object of our voyage, he said that he and all his people were well content to be the most faithful friends and vassals of the King of Spain; that he received us in this island as his own sons; that we might go on shore and remain there as in our own houses; and that his island for the future should not be named Tadore, but Castile, in proof of the great love he bore to the king our master. Then we presented to him the chair on which, he sat, and the robe which we had put on him, a piece of fine linen, four ells of scarlet cloth, a robe of brocade, a cloth of yellow damask, a piece of the whitest Cambay linen, two caps, six strings of glass beads, twelve knives, three large mirrors, six scissors, six combs, some gilt goblets, and other things. We gave to his son an Indian cloth of gold and silk, a large mirror, a cap and two knives. To each of the nine chief men of his suite we made a present of a piece of silk, a cap and two knives; and to many others of his suite we made a present, to one of a cap, to another of a knife, until the king told us not to give any more presents. He then said that he had got nothing worthy to be sent as a present to our king, unless he sent himself, now that be considered him as his lord. He invited us to come closer to the city, and if any one attempted to come on board the ships at night, he told us to fire upon him with our guns. He came out of the stern cabin by the same way by which he had entered it, without ever bending his head. At his departure we fired all the cannon.

This king is a Moor, of about forty-five years of age, rather well made, and of a handsome presence. He is a very great astrologer. His dress consisted of a shirt of very fine white stuff, with the ends of the sleeves embroidered with gold, and a wrapper which came down from his waist almost to the ground. He was barefooted; round his head he had a silk veil, and over that a garland of flowers. He is named Raja Sultan Manzor.

On the 10th of November - a Sunday - we had another conversation with the king, who wished to know how long a time we had been absent from Spain, and what pay and what rations the king gave to each of us; and we told him all this. He asked us for a signature of the king and a royal standard, since he desired that both his island of Tadore, and also that of Tarenate (where he intended to have his nephew named Calanogapi, crowned king) should become subject to the King of Spain, for whose honour he would fight to the death; and if it should happen that he should be compelled to give way, he would take refuge in Spain with all his family, in a new junk which he was having constructed, and would take with him the royal signature and standard.

He begged us to leave with him some of our men, who would always keep alive his recollection of us and of our king, as he would more esteem having some of us with him than our merchandise, which would not last him a long time. Seeing our eagerness to take cloves on board, he said that for that purpose he would go to an island called Bachian, where he hoped to find as much of them as were wanted, since in his island there was not a quantity sufficient of dry cloves to load the two ships. On that day there was no traffic because it was Sunday. The holiday of these people is on Friday.

It may please your illustrious lordship to have some description of the islands where the cloves grow. They are five - Tarenate, Tador, Mutir, Machian, and Bachian. Tarenate is the principal island. Its king, whilst he lived, had almost entire dominion over the other four. Tadore, the island in which we were, has its own king. Mutir and Machian have no king, but are governed by the people; and when the kings of Tarenate and Tidore are at war, they furnish them with combatants. The last is Bachian, and it has a king. All this province in which the cloves grow is called Maluco.

When we arrived here, eight months had not elapsed since a certain Portuguese, Francisco Serrano, had died in Tarenate. He was captain-general of the King of Tarenate when he was making war on the King of Tadore; and be acted so strenuously that this king was compelled to give his daughter in marriage to the King of Tarenate, who also received as hostages almost all the sons of the chief men of Tadore. Peace was then made, and from that daughter was born the nephew Calanopagi, of whom I have spoken. However, the King of Tadore never forgave Serrano in his heart; and he having come several years later to Tadore to traffic in cloves, the king had him poisoned with some betel leaves, so that he survived hardly four days. The King of Tarenate wished to have him buried according to their own usage, but three Christian servants that Serrano had with him did not consent to it. In dying he left a little son and a little girl that he had of a lady he had taken in Java major, and two hundred bahars of cloves.

Francisco Serrano was a great friend and a relation of our unfortunate captain-general, and he it was who induced him to undertake that voyage, for when Magellan was at Malacca, he had several times learned by letters from Serrano that he was here. Therefore, when D. Manuel, King of Portugal, refused to increase his pension by a single testoon per month, an increase which he thought he had well deserved, he came to Spain and made the proposal to his Sacred Majesty to come here by way of the west and he obtained all that he asked for.

Ten days after the death of Serrano, the King of Tarenate, named Raja Abuleis, drove out from his kingdom his son-in-law the King of Bachian, whose wife, the daughter of the King of Tarenate, came to Tarenate under the pretext of concluding peace, and gave him (her father) such a poison that he only survived two days, and dying left nine sons, whose names were told to me as follows : Chechili-Momuli, Jadore Vunghi, Chechilideroix, Cilimanzur, Cilipagi, Chialinchechilin, Cataravajecu, Serich, and Calanopagi.

Monday, the 11th of November, Chechilideroix, one of the above mentioned sons of the King of Tarenate, came with two prahus to the ships sounding drums : he was dressed in red velvet. We learned that he had near him the widow and sons of Francisco Serrano. When we knew him, being aware that he was an enemy of the King of Tadore, we sent to ask him whether we might receive him in the ships, which, as we were in his port, we would not do without his consent. The king sent us word to do whatever we pleased. However, meantime Chechilideroix, seeing our hesitation, had some suspicion, and moved further off from the ships. We then went to him in a boat, and made him a present of an Indian cloth of gold and silk, with some looking-glasses, knives, scissors, etc : these things he accepted but disdainfully, and soon after departed. He had with him an Indian who had become a Christian, named Manuel, the servant of a certain Pedro Alfonzo de Lorosa, a Portuguese, who, after the death of Serrano, had come from Bandan to Tarenate. Manuel being able to speak Portuguese, came on board the ships, and told us that although the sons of the King of Tarenate were enemies to the King of Tadore, yet they were disposed towards the service of Spain. Then, by means of him, we wrote to De Lorosa to come to our ships without any suspicion or fear.

These kings have as many ladies as they please, but one only is the principal wife, and all the others are subject to her. The King of Tadore had a large house outside the city, where there were two hundred of the ladies he was most fond of, and as many more to serve them. The king eats alone, or with his principal wife, on a kind of raised dais, from which he can see all the others sitting round, and he decides upon the one who most pleases him to come to him. When the king's dinner is finished, the ladies all eat together if he permits it, or else each one goes to eat in her own room. No one without special permission from the king can see those ladies, and if anybody by day or by night were found near their house he would be killed immediately. Each family is bound to give one or two daughters to the king. Rajah Sultan Manzour had twenty-six children, of whom eight were boys and eighteen girls. In the island of Tadore there is a kind of bishop, and the one that was there in our time had forty ladies and very many children.

On Tuesday, the 12th of November, the king had a house built in the city for our merchandise, and it was built in one day. Thither we carried all that we had to barter, and placed it in the custody of three of our men, and the trade began at once. It was carried out in this manner. For ten ells of red cloth of pretty good quality they gave a bahar of cloves. A bahar is four quintals and six pounds. For fifteen ells of middling quality a bahar, for fifteen hatchets a bahar, for thirty-five glass cups a bahar; and the king in this manner had from us almost all our goblets : for seventeen cathils of cinnabar a bahar; the same for as much quicksilver. For twenty-six ells of common linen a bahar, and the same for twenty-five ells of finer linen; for a hundred and fifty knives a bahar; for fifty scissors a bahar; for forty caps a bahar; for ten Guzerat cloths a bahar; for three of their cymbals two bahars : for a quintal of bronze a bahar. Almost all our mirrors were broken, and the few that remained entire the king wished to have. Many of the above-mentioned goods had been obtained by us by the capture of the junks, which I have related; and the haste we were in to return to Spain caused us to sell our goods at a lower price than we should have done had we not been in a hurry.

Every day there came to the ships many boats laden with goats, fowls, plantains, coconuts, and other victuals, that it was a wonder to see. We supplied the ships with good water taken from a spring whence it issued hot, but if it remains only one hour in the open air it becomes very cold. They say that it comes out like that because it issues from the mountain of the cloves. It may be seen from this how those lied who said that fresh water had to be brought to Maluco from distant countries.

The next day the king sent his son named Mossahap to the island of the

Mutir for cloves with which to freight our ships. We had spoken to the king that day of some Indians whom we had captured, and he entreated us to make a present of them to him, as he had the intention of sending them back to their native country, accompanied by five men of Tadore, who, on restoring them to their country, would praise and commend the King of Spain and make a good name for the Spaniards. We gave him the three ladies whom we had destined for the queen, as has been said above, and all the men except those of Burné : he very much appreciated this gift.

The king then asked another favour - that was, that we should kill all the pigs we had on board, for which he would give an ample compensation in fowls and goats. We gave him satisfaction in this, cutting their throats and hanging them up under the deck, so that the Moors should not have occasion to see them, since if by accident they see any pig they covered their faces not to see it or perceive its smell.

In the evening of the same day Pedro Alfonso, the Portuguese, came in a prahu, but before he came on board the ships the king sent to call him, and said to him, that although he belonged to Tarenate he should take good care not to answer falsely to the questions we were going to ask him. He indeed, after coming on board, told us that he had come to India sixteen years ago, and of these years he had passed ten in Maluco; and it was just ten years since those islands had been discovered by the Portuguese, who kept the discovery secret from us. He then related to us that a year, less fifteen days, had elapsed since a large ship had come hither proceeding from Malacca, and had gone away laden with cloves; but that, on account of, the bad weather she had been obliged to remain some months at Bandam. He added that her captain was Tristan de Menses, a Portuguese, from whom, on asking what news there was in Europe, he had heard that a squadron of five ships had sailed from Seville to discover Maluco in the name of the King of Spain, and that the captain of this squadron was Ferdinand Magellan, a Portuguese, for which reason the King of Portugal, being angry that a subject of his should attempt to do a thing so opposed to him, had sent some ships to the cape of Good Hope, and others to the Cape Sta. Maria, where the cannibals are, to impede their passage, but they had not fallen in with them. Having learned later that Magellan had passed by another sea, and was making for Maluco by way of the west, he had written to his Captain-Major of the Indies, named Diogo Lopez de Sequeira, to send six ships to Maluco against the Spanish squadron. However, the Captain-Major, having at that time received information that the Grand Turk was planning an expedition against Malacca, was obliged to send against him sixty sail to the Straits of Mekkah, in the country of Jiddah, where, however, they only found a few galleys which had grounded near the beautiful and strong city of Aden, and they set fire to them.

This enterprise, added De Lorosa, had prevented the Captain-Major from immediately sending an expedition against Magellan; but a little later he had sent to Maluco a great galleon with two rows of cannon, commanded by Francisco Faria, a Portuguese : but neither did this one come, for on account of the shoals and currents which are near Malacca, and the contrary winds, it was unable to pass that promontory, and was compelled to turn back.

He also related that a few days before a caravel with two junks had come to these parts to get news of us. The junks had sailed to Bachian to load cloves, with seven Portuguese on board. These men, who did not respect the wives of the inhabitants, nor even those of the king, notwithstanding the warning they had received from the king himself, were all killed. The men of the caravel, on hearing of this, returned in haste to Malacca, abandoning the junks with four hundred bahars of cloves and as much merchandise as would have purchased another hundred bahars. He also related that every year many junks go from Malacca to Bandan to buy mace and nutmeg, and go thence to Maluco to purchase cloves. They make the voyage from Bandan to Maluco in three days, and employ fifteen in the voyage from Bandan to Malacca. He said, lastly, that since ten years back the King of Portugal had derived great profit from these islands, and he took especial care to keep these countries concealed from and unknown to the Spaniards. He related many other similar things, passing several hours in conversation with us : and we said and did so much, offering him a large salary, that we made him determine on coming with us to Spain.

Friday, the 15th of November, the king told us that he thought of going himself to Bachian to get the cloves which the Portuguese had left there, and asked us for presents to give to the two governors of Mutir in the name of the King of Spain. Meanwhile, having come close to our ships, he wished to see how we shot with the crossbow, with guns, and with a swivel gun, which is a weapon larger than an arquebuse. He himself fired three times with a crossbow, but he did not care to fire with a gun.

Opposite Tadore there is another very large island, called Giailolo, and it is so large that a prahu can with difficulty go round it in four months. It is inhabited by Moors and Gentiles. The Moors have two kings, one of whom, according to what the King of Tadore related to us, has had six hundred children, and the other has had five hundred and twenty-five. The Gentiles have not got so many, women as the Moors, and are less superstitious. The first thing they meet in the morning when they go out of their houses is the object which they worship throughout that day. The king of these Gentiles is named Rajah Papua. He is very rich in gold, and inhabits the interior of the island. There grow here among the rocks bamboos as thick as a man's leg, full of water, which is very good to drink. We purchased many of them.

On Saturday the Moorish King of Giailolo came to the ships with many prahus, and we made him a present of a green damask robe, two ells of red cloth, some looking-glasses, scissors, knives, combs, and two gilt goblets, which things pleased him very much, and he said to us that, as we were friends of the King of Tadore, we were also his friends, since he loved that king like one of his own sons. He invited us to come to his country, promising to do us great honour. This king is powerful, and held in sufficient respect throughout all these islands. He is very old, and his name is Raja Jussu.

Sunday morning this same king came on board the ships and wished to see how we fought, and how we discharged the bombards, at which he was greatly pleased, for in his youth he had been a great warrior. The same day I went on shore to see how the cloves grow, and this is what I observed. The tree from which they are gathered is high, and its trunk is as thick as a man's body, more or less, according to the age of the plant. Its branches spread out somewhat in the middle of the tree, but near the top they form a pyramid. The bark is of an olive colour, and the leaves very like those of the laurel. The cloves grow at the end of little branches in bunches of ten or twenty. These trees always bear more fruit on one side than on the other, according to the seasons. The cloves are white when they first sprout, they get red as they ripen, and blacken when dry. They are gathered twice in the year, once about Christmas and the other time about St. John's day, when the air in these countries is milder, and it is still more so in December. When the year is rather hot, and there is little rain, they gather in each of these islands from three to four hundred bahars of cloves. The clove tree does not live except in the mountains, and if it is transferred to the plain it dies there. The leaf, the bark, and the wood, as long as they are green, have the strength and fragrance of the fruit itself. If these are not gathered when just ripe they get so large and hard that nothing of them remains good except the rind. It is said that the mist renders them perfect, and indeed we saw almost every day a mist descend and surround one or other of the above mentioned mountains. Among these people everyone possesses some of these trees, and each man watches over his own trees and gathers their fruit, but does not do any work round them to cultivate them. This tree does not grow except in the five mountains of the five Maluco islands. There are, however, a few trees in Giailolo and in a small island between Tadore and Mutir named Mare, but they are not good.

There are in this island of Giailolo some trees of nutmegs. These are like our walnuts, and the leaves also are similar. The nutmeg, when gathered, is like the quince in form and colour, and the down that covers it, but it is smaller. The outside rind is as thick as the green rind of our walnuts, beneath which is a thin web, or rather cartilage, under which is the mace, of a very bright red, which covers and surrounds the rind of the nuts, inside which is the nutmeg properly so called.

There also grows in Tadore the ginger, which we used to eat green, instead of bread. Ginger is not a tree, but a shrub, which sends out of the earth shoots a span long like the shoots of canes, which they also resemble in the shape of the leaves, only those of the ginger are narrower. The shoots are good for nothing; that which makes ginger is the root. When green, it is not so strong as when it is dry, and to dry it they use lime, or else it would not keep.

The houses of these people are built like those already described, but are not so high above the ground, and are surrounded with canes after the fashion of a hedge. The women here are ugly, and go naked like the others, having only their middles covered with cloth made of bark. The men also are naked, and notwithstanding that their women are ugly, they are exceedingly jealous; and amongst other things that displeased them, was that we came ashore without cloaks, because they imagined that might cause temptation to their wives. Both men and women always go barefoot.

Since I have spoken of cloth, I will relate how they make it. They take a piece of bark and leave it in water until it has grown soft; they then beat it with wooden clubs to extend it in length and breadth, as much as they please; thus it becomes like a veil of raw silk with filaments enlaced within it, so that it appears as if it was woven.

Their bread is made with the wood of a tree like a palm tree, and they make it in this way. They take a piece of this wood, and extract from it certain long black thorns which are situated there; then they pound it, and make bread of it which they call sagu. They make provisions of this bread for their sea voyages.

Every day there came from Tarenate many boats laden with cloves, but we, because we were waiting for the king, would not traffic for those goods, but only for victuals : and the men of Tarenate complained much of this.

On Sunday night, the 24th of November, the king arrived, and on entering the port had his drums sounded, and passed between our ships. We fired many bombards to do him honour. He told us that for four days we should be continually supplied with cloves.

In effect, on Monday he sent seven hundred and ninety one catils, without taking tare. To take tare means to take spice for less than what it weighs, and the reason of this is because when they are fresh, every day they diminish in weight. As these were the first cloves that we took on board, and the principal object of our voyage, we fired our bombards for joy. Cloves are, called Gomode in this place; in

Sarangani where we took the two pilots they are called Bonglavan, and in Malacca Chianche.

Tuesday the 26th November the King came to tell us that for us he had done what a King never does here, that was to leave his own island; but he had gone to show the affection he had for the King of Castile, and because when we had got our cargo, we could sooner return to Spain, and afterwards return with greater forces to avenge the death of his father, who had been killed in an island called Buru, and his body had been thrown into the sea.

He afterwards added that it was the custom in Tadore, when the first cloves were embarked in a vessel, or in junks, that the king gave a feast to their crews and merchants, and they made prayers to God to bring them in safety to their port. He wished to do the same for us, and at the same time the feast would serve for the King of Bachian, who was coming with a brother of his to pay him a visit, and on that account he had the streets cleaned. Hearing this, some of us began to suspect some treachery; all the more because we learned that, not long before, three Portuguese of the companions of Francisco Serrano had been assassinated at the place where we got water, by some of the islanders concealed in the thickets; also we often saw them. whispering with the Indians whom we had made prisoners. Therefore, although some of us were inclined to accept the invitation, we concluded not to betake ourselves thither, recollecting the unfortunate feast given to our men in the island of Zubu, and we decided on a speedy departure.

Meantime a message was sent to the king to thank him, and to ask him to come soon to the ships, where we would deliver to him the four men we had promised him, with the goods which we had destined for him. The King came soon, and on entering the ship, as though he had observed that we had doubts, said that he entered with as much confidence and security as into his own house. He made us feel how much he was displeased by our unexpected haste to depart, since ships used to employ thirty days in taking in their cargo; and that if he had made a journey out of the island, he certainly had not done it to injure us but to assist us, so that we might more speedily obtain the cloves which we required, and a part of which we were still expecting. He added that it was not then a fit season for navigating in those seas, on account of the many shoals near Bandan, and besides it would be a likely thing that we should fall in with some Portuguese ships. When, in spite of what he had said, he saw we were still determined on going away, he said that we must take back all that we had given him, since the Kings, his neighbours, would consider him as a man without reputation for receiving so many presents in the name of so great a king as the King of Spain, and he had given nothing in return, and perhaps they would suspect that the Spaniards had gone away in such haste for fear of some treachery, so that they would fix upon him the name of traitor. Then, in order that no suspicion might remain in our minds of his honesty and good faith, he ordered his Koran to be brought, and kissing it devoutly he placed it four or five times on his head whilst whispering certain words to himself, with a rite which they call Zambehan, and he said in the presence of us all, that he swore by Allah and by the Koran, which he held in his hand, that he would ever be faithful and a friend to the King of Spain. He said all this almost weeping and with so great an appearance of sincerity and cordiality, that we promised to prolong our sojourn at Tadore for another fortnight. We then gave him the Royal signature and standard. We learned later, by a sure and certain channel, that some of the chiefs of those islands had indeed counselled him to kill all of us, by which thing he would have acquired for himself great merit with the Portuguese, who would have given him good assistance to avenge himself on the King of Bachian, but he, loyal and constant to the King of Spain, with whom he had sworn a peace, had answered that he would never do such an act on any account whatever.

Wednesday, the 27th November, the king issued a proclamation that whoever had cloves might freely sell them to us. For which reason all that and the following day, we bought cloves like mad.

Friday, in the afternoon, the governor of Machian came with many prahus, but he would not come on shore, because his father and his brother, who had been banished from Machian, had taken refuge here.

The following day the King of Tadore, with his nephew, the governor, named Humai, a man of twenty-five years of age, came on board the ships, and the king, on hearing that we had no more cloth, sent to fetch from his house six ells of red cloth, and gave them to us in order that we might, by adding other objects, make a fitting present to the governor. We made him the present, and he thanked us much, and said that soon he would send us plenty of cloves. At his departure from the ship we fired several bombards.

Sunday the 1st day of December, the above-mentioned governor departed from Tadore; and we were told that the king had made him a present of some silk cloths and drums, for him to send us the cloves sooner. On Monday, the king himself went again out of the island for the same object. Wednesday morning, as it was the day of St. Barbara, and on account of the King's arrival all the artillery was discharged. The king came to the beach to see how we fired rockets and fire balls, and took great pleasure in them.

Thursday and Friday we purchased a good many cloves both in the city and at the ships at a much lower price, as the time of our departure grew nearer. For four ells of riband they gave a bahar of cloves, for two little chains of brass which were worth a marcello, they gave us a hundred pounds; and at last each man being desirous of having his portion of the cargo, and as there were no more goods to give in exchange for cloves, one gave his cloak, another his coat, and another a shirt or other clothes to obtain them.

On Saturday three sons of the King of Tarenate, with their wives, who were daughters of our King of Tadore, and afterwards Pedro Alfonso, the Portuguese, came to the ships. We gave a gilt glass goblet to each of the brothers, and to the three wives scissors and other things; and when they went away we fired several bombards in their honour. We afterwards sent on shore a present of several things to the widow of the King of Tarenate, daughter of the King Tadore, who had not ventured to come on board the ships.

Sunday the 8th December, we fired many bombards, rockets, and fireballs to celebrate the Conception of our Lady. Monday in the afternoon, the King came to the ships with three women who carried his betel. It is to be observed that no one can take women about with him except the king. Afterwards the King of Giailolo came to see again our gun exercise.

Some days later, as the, day of our departure grew near, the king showed us a sincere affection, and among other obliging things; said to us that it seemed to him that he was a sucking child whom its mother was about to leave, and that he remained disconsolate all the more now that he had become acquainted with us and liked several things of Spain, for which reason he entreated us not to delay our return thence to Tadore. Meantime, he begged us to leave him some of our swivel guns for his own defence. He warned us at the same time not to navigate except by daylight, on account of the shoals and reefs which exist in these seas; but we answered him that because of our need to arrive in Spain as soon as possible, we were obliged, to navigate night and day : he then added that, being unable to do anything else, he would pray God every day to firing us home in safety.

During this time, Pedro Alfonso de Lorosa had come to the ships with his wife and property to return with us. Two days after, Kechilideroix, son of the King of Tarenate, came with a prahu well filled with men, and approaching the ships requested Lorosa to come into his prahu; but Lorosa, who suspected him, refused to do so, and told him he had determined on going away with those ships to Spain. For the same suspicion he advised us not to receive him in the ships; and we did not choose that he should come on board when he asked to do so. It was known later that Kechili was a great friend of the Portuguese captain of Malacca, and had the intention of seizing Lorosa and of conducting him thither; and on that account, he severely reprimanded those persons with whom this Portuguese lived, for having let him depart without his permission.

The king had informed us that the King of Bachian would soon arrive, with a brother of his who was going to marry one of his daughters, and had asked us to do him honour by firing bombards on his arrival. He arrived on Sunday the 15th of December, in the afternoon, and we did him honour as the king had desired; we did not, however, discharge the heavier cannon, as we were heavily laden. The king and his brother came in a prahu with three banks of rowers on each side, a hundred and twenty in number. The prahu was adorned with many streamers made of white, yellow and red parrot's feathers. They were sounding many cymbals, and that sound served to give the measure to the rowers to keep time. In two other prahus were the damsels who were to be presented to the bride. They returned us the salute by going round the ships and round the port.

As it is the custom that no king disembarks on the land of another king, the King of Tadore came to visit him of Bachian in his own prahu : this one, seeing the other coming, rose from the carpet on which he was sitting, and placed himself on one side to make way for the king of the country : but he, out of ceremony, would not sit on the carpet, but sat on the other side of it, leaving the carpet between them. Then the King of Bachian gave to him of Tadore five hundred patol, as if in payment of the daughter he was giving as a wife to his brother. Patols are cloths of gold and silk worked in China, and are very much prized in these islands. Each of these cloths is paid for with three bahars of cloves more or less, according as they are more or less rich in gold and embroidery. Whenever one of the chief men die, his relations put on these cloths to do him honour.

Monday, the King of Tadore sent a dinner to the king of Bachian, carried by fifty women - clothed with silk from their waists to their knees. They went two and two with a man between in the midst of them. Each one carried a large dish upon which were small dishes with various viands; ten of the oldest of these women were the mace bearers. They proceeded in this way to the prahu, and presented everything to the king who was sitting on a carpet under a red and yellow canopy. As they were returning, they caught some of our men who had come out of curiosity and who were obliged to make them presents of some trifle to get free. After that the king sent also to us a present of goats, coconuts, wine, and other things.

This day we bent on the ships new sails, upon which was the cross of St. James, of Gallicia, with letters which said : "This is the figure of our good fortune."

Tuesday, we presented to the king some pieces of artillery; that is some arquebuses which we had taken as prizes in the Indies, and some of our swivel-guns with four barrels of powder. We took on board each ship eighty barrels of water. Wood we were to find at the island of Mare, where the king had already five days ago sent a hundred men to prepare it, and near which we were to pass.

This day, the King of Bachian, with the consent of the King of Tadore, came on shore, preceded by four men holding up daggers in their hands, to make alliance with us : he said, in the presence of the King of Tadore and of all his suite, that he would always be ready for the service of the King of Spain, that he would keep in his name the cloves left in his island by the Portuguese, until another Spanish squadron arrived there, and he would not give them up without his consent. He sent through us to the King of Spain a present of a slave and two bahars of cloves. He would have wished to have sent ten bahars, but our ships were so heavily laden, that we could not receive any more.

He also gave us for the King of Spain two most beautiful dead birds. These birds are as large as thrushes; they have small heads, long beaks, legs slender like a writing pen, and a span in length; they have no wings, but instead of them long feathers of different colours, like plumes : their tail is like that of the thrush. All the feathers, except those of the wings, are of a dark colour; they never fly, except when the wind blows. They told us that these birds come from the terrestrial Paradise, and they call them "bolon dinata" that is divine birds.

The King of Bachian was a man of about seventy years of age. Not only did the King of Bachian recognise the King of Spain as his Sovereign; but every king of Maluco wrote to him that he desired always to be his faithful subject.

One day the King of Tadore sent to tell our men, who dwelt in the magazine for the merchandise, that they should take care not to go out of the house by night, since there were certain men, natives of the country, who by anointing themselves, walk by night in the shape of men without heads and if they meet anyone to whom they wish ill, they touch his hand and anoint his palm, and that ointment causes him soon to grow ill, and die at the end of three or four days. However, if they meet three or four persons together they do not touch them, but make them giddy. He added that he had a watch kept to discover them, and he had already had several executed.

When they build a new house, before going to inhabit it, they make a fire round it, and give many feasts there. Then they fasten to the roof of the house a pattern or sample of everything that is to be found in the island, persuaded that by that means none of those things will be ever wanting to whoever inhabits the house.

Wednesday morning everything was prepared for our departure from Maluco. The Kings of Tadore, of Giailolo, and of Bachian, and a son of the King of Tarenate had come to accompany us as far as the island of Mare. The ship "Victoria" made sail and stood out a little, waiting for the ship "Trinity"; but she had much difficulty in getting up the anchor, and meanwhile the sailors perceived that she was leaking very much in the hold. Then the "Victoria" returned to anchor in her former position. They began to discharge the cargo of the "Trinity" to see if the leak could be stopped, for it was perceived that the water came in with force as through a pipe, but we were never able to find out at what part it came in. All that day and the next we did nothing else but work at the pumps, but without any advantage.

Hearing this, the King of Tadore came at once to the ships, and occupied himself with us in searching for the leak. For this purpose he sent into the sea five of his men, who were accustomed to remain a long time under the water, and although they remained more than half-an-hour they could not find the fissure. As the water inside the ship continually increased, the king, who was as much affected by it as we were, and lamenting this misfortune, sent to the end of the island for three other men, more skilful than the first at remaining under water.

He came with them early the next morning. These men dived under water with their hair loose, thinking that their hair, attracted by the water which penetrated into the ship, would indicate to them the leak, but though they remained more than an hour in the water, they did not find it. The king, seeing that there was no remedy for it, said with lamentation, "Who will go to Spain to take news of me to the king our lord ?" We answered him that the "Victoria" would go there, and would sail at once to take advantage of the east winds, which had already commenced. The "Trinity," meanwhile, would be refitted and would wait for the west winds and go to Darien, which is on the other side of the sea, in the country of Diucatan. The king approved our thoughts, and said that he had in his service two hundred and twenty-five carpenters who would do all the work under the direction of our men, and that those who should remain there would be treated as his own children, and he said this with so much emotion that he moved us all to tears.

We, who were on board the "Victoria", fearing that she might open, on account of the heavy cargo and the long voyage, lightened her by discharging sixty hundred weight of cloves, which we had carried to the house where the crew of the "Trinity" were lodged. Some of our own crew preferred to remain at Maluco rather than go with us to Spain, because they feared that the ship could not endure so long a voyage, and because, mindful of how much they had suffered, they feared to die of hunger in mid-ocean.

Saturday, the 21st December, day of St. Thomas the Apostle, the King of Tadore came to the ships and brought us the two pilots, whom we had already paid, to conduct us out of these islands. They said that the weather was then good for sailing at once, but, having to wait for the letters of our companions who remained behind, and who wished to write to Spain, we could not sail till midday. Then the ships took leave of one another by a mutual discharge of bombards. Our men accompanied us for some distance with their boat, and then with tears and embraces we separated. Juan Carvalho remained at Tadore with fifty-three of our men : we were forty-seven Europeans and thirteen Indians.

The king's governor came with us as far as the island of Mare : we had hardly arrived there when four prahus laden with wood came up, which in less than an hour we got on board. We then took the south-west course.

In all the above-mentioned islands of Maluco are to be found cloves, ginger, sagu, which is their bread made of wood, rice, coconuts, plantains, almonds larger than ours, sweet and bitter pomegranates, sugar-canes, oil of cocoa and of sesame, melons, cucumbers, pumpkins, comilicai, which is a refreshing fruit the size of a watermelon, another fruit like a peach called guave, and other eatable vegetables. They also have goats and fowls, honey produced by bees not larger than ants, which make their hives in trunks of trees. There are also parrots of many kinds, and amongst them there are white ones called Catara, and red ones called Nori, which are the most sought after, not so much for the beauty of their plumage, as because they talk more clearly. One of these is sold for a bahar of cloves.

It is hardly fifty years since the Moors conquered Maluco and dwelt there. Before that, these islands were inhabited only by Gentiles, who did not care for the cloves. There are still some families of them who have taken refuge in the mountains, where the cloves grow.

The island of Tadore is in 0 deg. 27 min. North latitude, and 161 deg. west of the line of demarcation; it is 9 deg. 30 min. distant from the first island of this archipelago, named Zamal, to the south-east and a quarter south. The island of Tarenate is in 0 deg. 40 min. of N. latitude. Mutir is exactly under the equinoctial line. Machian is in 0 deg. 15 min. S. latitude, and Bachian in 1 deg. of the same latitude. Tarenate, Tadore, Mutir, and Machian, are like four high and pointed mountains, upon which the clove trees grow. Bachian is not visible from these four islands, but it is a larger island than any of those. Its clove mountain is not so high nor so pointed as those of the other islands, but it has a larger base.

RETURN FROM THE MOLUCCAS TO SPAIN

Pursuing our voyage, after having taken in wood at the islet of Mare, we passed between the following islands Caioan, Laigoma, Sico, Giogi, Cafi, Laboan, Toliman, Titameti, Bachian, Latalata, Jabobi, Mata, and Batutiga. They told us that in the island of Cafi the people were small and dwarfed like the Pigmies; they have been subjected by force by the King of Tadore. We passed outside of Batutiga to the west, and we steered between west and southwest, and we discovered some islets to the south, on which account the pilots of Maluco said it would be better to cast anchor so as not to drift at night among many islets and shoals. We, therefore, altered our course to south-east, and went to an island situated in 2 deg. S. latitude, and fifty-three leagues from Maluco.

This island is named Sulach; its inhabitants are Gentiles, and have not got a king. They eat human flesh; both men and women go naked, except a piece of the bark of a tree of two fingers breath before their natural parts. There are many other islands around here inhabited by anthropophagi. These are the names of some of them :- Silan, Noselao, Biga, Atulabaon, Leitimor, Tenetum, Gonda, Kailaruru, Mandan and Benaia. We left to the east the islands named Lamatola and Tenetum.

Having run ten leagues from Sulach in the same direction, we went to a rather large island named Buru, in which we found plenty of victuals, such as pigs, goats, fowls, sugarcanes, coconuts, sagu, a certain food of theirs made of bananas called kanali, and chiacare, which here they call Nanga. The chiacare are fruit like watermelons, but knotty on the outside; inside they have some small red fruit like plums, they have not got a stone in the middle, but instead of that have a certain pith like a white bean, but larger, they are tender to eat like chestnuts. We found here another fruit which externally is like a pine cone, and it is yellow, but white inside; on cutting, it is something like a pear, but much softer and better tasted. Here it is called comilicai. The inhabitants of this island are Gentiles, and have no king : they go naked like those of Sulach. The island of Buru is in 3 deg. 30 min. S. latitude, and seventy-five leagues from Maluco.

To the east of this island, at a distance of ten leagues, there is another one larger, and which borders on Giailolo, and it is named Ambon. It is inhabited by Moors and Gentiles, but the former are on the sea shore, and the others in the interior; these are also anthropophagi. The products of this island are the same as those of Buru. Between Buru and Ambon, there are three islands surrounded by reefs named Vudia, Kailaruru and Benaia. To the south of Buru, at a distance of four leagues, is another small island named Ambalao.

At thirty-five leagues from Buru, south and a quarter south-west, is

Bandon, with thirteen other islands. In six of them grow mace and nutmeg. Zoroboa is the largest of them, Chelicel, Saniananpi, Pulai, Puluru, and Rasoghin, the other six are Unuveru, Pulanbaracan, Lailaca, Mamica, Man, and Meut. In these islands nutmegs are not found, but only sagu, rice, coconuts, bananas, and other fruits, and they are near one another. The inhabitants of these are Moors, and have no king. Bandan is in 6 deg. of S. latitude, and 163 deg. 30 min. longitude from the line of demarcation. As this island was a little out of our course, we did not go to it.

Leaving the island of Buru in the direction south-west and a quarter west, about eight degrees of latitude, we arrived at three other islands near each other named Zolot, Nocemamor, and Galian. Whilst we sailed amidst these islands, a great storm fell upon us, for which we made a vow of a pilgrimage to our Lady della Guida. We put the ship before the storm and made for a rather high island, which afterwards we learned was named Mallua, but before we could reach it, we had to struggle much with the squalls of wind which descended from the mountains and with the currents. The inhabitants of this island are savages, and more beasts than men; they eat human flesh; they go naked, except the usual piece of bark to cover their natural parts. However, when they go to fight they wear on the back, the breast, and the flanks, pieces of buffalo hide, ornamented with shells, and boars tusks, and tails of goat skins, hanging before and behind. They wear the hair raised high up by means of cane combs with long teeth, which go through it. They wrap up their beards with leaves, and enclose them in cases or tubes of reed, a thing which seemed to us very ridiculous. In one word these were the ugliest men we had seen in these Indies. Both their bows and arrows are made of reeds, and they carry their food in bags made of leaves. When their women saw us they came towards us with their bows drawn, but when we had given them some presents we soon became friends.

We passed fifteen days in this island in caulking the ship whose sides had suffered. We found here goats, fowls, wax, coconuts, and pepper. For a pound of old iron they gave fifteen pounds of wax or of pepper.

There are two kinds of pepper here, the long and the round. The long pepper is like the flower of the hazel tree in winter; its plant is like ivy, and like it clings to trees; its leaves are like those of the mulberry tree; it is called luli. The round pepper grows like the other, but its fruit is in ears like Indian corn, and the grains are pulled off in the same manner; it is called lada. The fields here are full of pepper plants.

Here we took a man to conduct us to some island where we could find plenty of victuals.

The island of Mallua is in 8 deg. 30 min. S. latitude, and 169 deg. 40 min. longitude from the line of demarcation.

The old pilot from Maluco related to us, whilst sailing, that in this neighbourhood there was an island named Aruchete, the inhabitants of which, men and women, are not more than one cubit high, and they have ears as large and as long as themselves, so that when they lie down one serves them for a mattress, and with the other they cover themselves. They are shorn and naked, their voices are shrill, and they run very swiftly. They dwell under ground, live on fish and a certain substance which grows between the bark and the wood of a tree, which is white and round like coriander comfits, and which is named ambulon. We would have gone there willingly, but the shoals and currents did not allow of it.

Saturday the 25th of January, (1522), at 22 o'clock we left the island of Mallua; and the following day, having run five leagues to the south-south-east, we arrived at a large island called Timor. I went ashore alone to speak to the head man of a village named Amaban, about his providing us with victuals. He offered me buffaloes, pigs, and goats, but when it was a question of the goods which he wanted in exchange, we could not come to an agreement, because he asked a great deal, and we had got very little to give. Then as we were constrained by hunger, we took the measure of detaining on board the ship the chief of another village named Balibo, who had come there in good faith with a son of his; and we imposed upon him as a ransom for recovering his liberty, to give six buffaloes, ten pigs, and ten goats. He, being much afraid that we should kill him, quickly gave orders to have all this brought to us; and as there were only five goats and two pigs, they gave us instead an additional buffalo. We then sent him ashore with his son, and he was well pleased when we not only left him free, but also gave him some linen, some Indian cloths of silk and cotton, some hatchets, some Indian knives, scissors, looking-glasses, and some of our knives.

The chief man, whom I went to speak to first, has only women in his service; all were naked like those of the neighbouring islands, and wear in their ears small gold rings with tufts of silk hanging from them; on their arms they wear many rings of gold and copper, which often cover them up to the elbow. The men are naked like the women, and wear attached to their necks round plates of gold, and on their heads reed combs ornamented with gold rings. Some of them, instead of gold rings, wore in their ears dried necks of gourds.

In this island there are buffaloes, pigs, and goats, as has been said; there are also fowls and parrots of various colours. There is also rice, bananas, ginger, sugar canes, oranges, lemons, beans and almonds.

We had approached that part of the island where there were some villages with their chiefs or head men. On the other side of the island are the dwellings of four kings, and their districts are named Oibich, Lichsana, Suai, and Cabanaza. Oibich is the largest place. We were told that in a mountain near Cabanaza, very much gold is found, and its inhabitants buy whatever they want with small pieces of gold. All the trade in sandal wood and wax, carried on by the people of Malacca and Java, is done here; and indeed, we found here a junk which had come from Lozon to trade in sandal wood; for white sandal wood only grows in this country.

These people are Gentiles; we were told that when they go to cut sandal wood, the devil appears to them in various forms, and tells them that if they want anything they should ask him for it; but this apparition frightens them so much, that they are ill of it for some days. The sandal wood is cut at a certain phase of the moon, and it is asserted that if cut at another time it would not be good. The merchandise most fitting for bartering here for sandal wood is red cloth, linen, hatchets, iron, and nails.

This island is entirely inhabited. It extends a long way from east to west, and little from north to south. Its south latitude is in 10 deg., and the longitude 174 deg. 30 min. from the line of demarcation.

In all these islands that we visited in this archipelago, the evil of Saint Job prevailed, and more here than in any other place, where they call it "for franki", that is to say, Portuguese illness.

We were told that at a day's voyage, west-north-west from Timor, there was an island in which much cinnamon grows, called Ende; its inhabitants are Gentiles, and have no king. Near this are many others forming a series of islands as far as Java Major, and the Cape of Malacca. The names of these islands are Ende, Tanabuton, Crenochile, Bimacore, Azanaran, Main, Zubava, Lombok, Chorum, and Java Major, which by the inhabitants is not called Java but Jaoa.

In this island of Java are the largest towns; the principal of them is Magepaher, the king of which, when he lived, was the greatest of all the kings of the neighbouring islands, and he was named Raja Patiunus Sunda. Much pepper grows there. The other towns are Dahadama, Gagiamada, Minutarangam, Ciparafidain, Tuban, Cressi, and Cirubaya. At half a league from Java Major are the islands of Bali, called Java Minor, and Madura, these are of equal size.

They told us that in Java Major, it was the custom when one of the chief men died, to burn his body; and then his principal wife, adorned with garlands of flowers, has herself carried in a chair by four men throughout the town, with a tranquil and smiling countenance, whilst comforting her relations, who are afflicted because she is going to burn herself with the corpse of her husband, and encouraging them not to lament, saying to them, "I am going this evening to sup with my dear husband, and to sleep with him this night." Afterwards, when close to the place of the pyre, she again turns towards the relations, and after again consoling them, casts herself into the fire and is burned. If she did not do this she would not be looked upon as an honourable woman, nor as a faithful wife.

Our old pilot related to us other extravagant things. He told us that the young men of Java... and that in an island called Ocoloro, below Java Major, there are only women who become pregnant with the wind, and when they bring it forth, if the child is a male, they kill it, and if a female, they bring it up; and if any man visits their island, whenever they are able to kill him, they do so.

They also related to us that beyond Java Major, towards the north in the Gulf of China, which the ancients named Sinus Magnus, there is an enormous tree named Campanganghi, in which dwell certain birds named Garuda, so large that they take with their claws, and carry away flying, a buffalo, and even an elephant, to the place of the tree, which place is named Puzathaer. The fruit of this tree is called Buapanganghi, and is larger than a water melon. The Moors of Burné, whom we had with us in the ships, told us they had seen two of these birds, which had been sent to their king from the kingdom of Siam. No junk, or other vessel, can approach this tree within three or four leagues, on account of the great whirlpools which the water makes there. They related to us, moreover, how in a wonderful manner what is related of this tree became known, for a junk, having been carried there by the whirlpools, was broken up, and all the seamen perished, except a child who attached himself to a plank and was miraculously borne near the tree, upon which he mounted. There he placed himself under the wing of one of these birds, which was asleep, without its perceiving him, and next day the bird having taken flight carried him with it, and having seen a buffalo on the land, descended to take it; the child took advantage of the opportunity to come out from under its wing, and remained on the ground. In this manner the story of these birds and of the tree became known, and it was understood that those fruits which are frequently found in the sea came from that place.

We were told that there were in that kingdom, on the banks of the rivers, certain birds which feed on carrion, but which will not touch it unless another bird has first eaten its heart.

The Cape of Malacca is in 1 deg. 30 min. of S. latitude. To the east of that Cape are many cities and towns, of a few of which I will note the names - Singapola, which is at the Cape, Pahan, Kalantan, Patani, Bradlini, Benan, Lagon, Cheregigharan, Trombon, Joran, Ciu, Brabri,

Banga, India, Jandibum, Laun, Langonpifa. All these cities are constructed like ours, and are subject to the King of Siam who is named Siri Zacabedera, and who inhabits India.

Beyond Siam is situated Camogia; its king is named Saret Zacabedera; next Chiempa, the king of which is named Raja Brahami Martu. There grows the rhubarb, and it is found in this manner : men go together in companies of twenty or twenty-five, to the woods, and at night ascend the trees, both to get out of the way of the lions, the elephants, and other wild beasts, and also to be able better to smell the odour of the rhubarb borne to them by the wind. In the morning they go to that quarter whence they have perceived that the odour comes, and seek for the rhubarb till they find it. This is the rotten wood of a large tree, which acquires its odour by putrefaction. The best part of the tree is the root, but the trunk is also good, which is called Calama.

The kingdom of Cocchi lies next, its sovereign is named Raja Seri Bummipala. After that follows Great China, the king, of which is the greatest sovereign of the world, and is called Santoa raja. He has seventy crowned kings under his dependence; and some of these kings have ten or fifteen lesser kings dependent on them. The port of this kingdom is named Guantan, and among the many cities of this empire, two are the most important, namely Nankin and Comlaha, where the king usually resides.

He has four of his principal ministers close to his palace, at the four sides looking to the four cardinal winds, that is, one to the west, one to the east, to the south, and to the north. Each of these gives audience to those that come from his quarter. All the kings and lords of India major and superior obey this king, and in token of their vassalage, each is obliged to have in the middle of the principal place of his city the marble figure of a certain animal named Chinga, an animal more valiant than the lion; the figure of this animal is also engraved on the king's seal, and all who wish to enter his port must carry the same emblem in wax or ivory.

If any lord is disobedient to him, he is flayed, and his skin, dried in the sun, salted, and stuffed, is placed in an eminent part of the public place, with the head inclined and the hands on the head in the attitude of doing zongu, that is obeisance to the king.

He is never visible to anybody; and if he wishes to see his people, he is carried about the palace on a peacock most skilfully manufactured, and very richly adorned, with six ladies dressed exactly like himself, so that he cannot be distinguished from them. He afterwards passes into a richly-adorned figure of a serpent called Naga, which has a large glass in the breast, through which he and the ladies are seen, but it is not possible to distinguish which is the king. He marries his sisters in order that his blood should not mix with that of others.

His palace has seven walls round it, and in each circle there are daily ten thousand men on guard, who are changed every twelve hours at the sound of a bell. Each wall has its gate, with a guard at each gate. At the first stands a man with a great scourge in his hand, named Satuhoran with Satubagan; at the second a dog called Satuhain; at the third, a man with an iron mace, called Satuhoran with pocumbecin; at the fourth, a man with a bow in his hand, called Satuhoran with anatpanan; at the fifth, a man with a lance, called Satuhoran, with tumach; at the sixth, a lion called Satuhorimau; at the seventh, two white elephants called Gagiapute.

The palace contains seventy-nine halls, in which dwell only the ladies destined to serve the king; there are always torches burning there. It is not possible to go round the palace in less than a day. In the upper part of it are four halls where the ministers go to speak to the king : one is ornamented with metal, both the pavement and the walls; another is all of silver, another all of gold, and the other is set with pearls and precious stones. The gold and other valuable things which are brought as tribute to the king are placed in these rooms; and when they are there deposited, they say, Let this be for the honour and glory of our Santoa Raja. All these things and many others relating to this king, were narrated to us by a Moor, who said that he had seen them.

The Chinese are white, and are clothed; they eat on tables like us. They have crosses, but it is not known why they have them. It is from China that musk comes; the animal that produces it is a kind of cat, like the civet cat; it eats nothing but a certain soft wood, slender as a finger, named chamaru. To extract the musk from this animal they attach a leech to it, and leave it till it is full of blood, and when they see that it is well filled, they crush it, and collect the blood in a plate, and put it in the sun for four or five days, moistening it every day with urine. In this way it becomes perfect musk. Whoever keeps one of these cats pays a tribute to the king. The grains of musk which come to Europe as musk, are only small pieces of kid's flesh soaked in real musk, and not the blood, since though it can be made into grains, it easily evaporates. The cat that produces musk is called castor, and the leech is called Linta.

Continuing along the coast of China, many nations are met with, and they are these : the Chienchi, who inhabit the islands in which they fish for pearls, and where the cinnamon grows. The Lecchii inhabit the mainland : the entrance to their port is traversed by a large rock, for which reason all the junks and vessels which wish to enter must take down their masts. The king of this country is called Moni. He has on the mainland twenty kings under him, and he is subject to the King of China : his capital is Baranaci, and here is situated Oriental Cathay. Han is a high and cold island, where there is copper, silver, pearls, and silk; its king is named Raja Zotra. There is also Miliaula, the king of which is named Raja Quetischeniga, and Guio, the king of which is Raja Sudacali. These places are cold and on the mainland. Friagonba and Trianga are two islands which also produce copper, silver, pearls, and silk; their king is Raja Ruzon. Bassi is a low land on the continent. There come afterwards Sumbdit and Pradit, two islands very rich in gold, where the men wear a large ring of gold round the ankle. In the neighbouring mountains dwell people who kill their parents when they are old, so that they may cease from travail. All the people of these countries are Gentiles.

Tuesday night (between it and Wednesday) on the 11th of February of 1522, we left the island of Timor, and entered upon the great sea named Laut Chidol, and taking a west-south-west course, we left to the right and to the North, from fear of the Portuguese, the island of Zumatra, anciently named Taprobana; also Pegu, Bengala, Urizza, Chelim, where are the Malabars, subjects of the King of Narsinga : Calicut which is under the same king; Cambaya in which are the Guzeratis; Cananor, Goa, Armus, and all the other coast of India major.

In this kingdom dwell six classes of persons, that is to say : Nairs, Panicals, Franas, Pangelins, Macuas, and Poleas. The Nairs are the chiefs; the Panicals are the townspeople; these two classes live and converse together. The Franas collect the wine from the palm trees and the bananas. The Macuas are fishermen; and the Poleas sow and harvest the rice; these last always dwell in the fields, and never enter the city, and when it is desired to give them anything, it is placed on the ground and they take it. When they go along the roads they always cry out, po, po, po, that is take care of yourself; and we were told that a Nair who had been accidentally touched by a Polea, not to survive such a disgrace, had himself killed.

In order to double the Cape of Good Hope, we went as far as 42° South latitude, and we remained off that cape for nine weeks, with the sails struck on account of the Western and North-western gales which beat against our bows with fierce squalls. The Cape of Good Hope is in 34° 30' South latitude, 1600 leagues distant from the Cape of Malacca, and it is the largest and most dangerous cape in the world.

Some of our men, and among them the sick, would have liked to land at a place belonging to the Portuguese called Mozambique, both because the ship made much water, and because of the great cold which we suffered; and much more because we had nothing but rice and water for food and drink, all the meat of which we had made provision having putrified, for the want of salt had not permitted us to salt it. However, the greater number of us, prizing honour more than life itself, decided on attempting at any risk to return to Spain.

At length, by the aid of God, on the 6th of May, we passed that terrible cape, but we were obliged to approach it within only five leagues distance, or else we should never have passed it. We then sailed towards the north-west for two whole months without ever taking rest; and in this short time we lost twenty-one men between Christians and Indians. We made then a curious observation on throwing them into the sea, that was that the Christians remained with the face turned to the sky, and the Indians with the face turned to the sea. If God had not granted us favourable weather, we should all have perished of hunger.

Constrained by extreme necessity, we decided on touching at the Cape Verde Islands, and on Wednesday the 9th of July, we touched at one of those islands named St. James's. Knowing that we were in an enemy's country, and amongst suspicious persons, on sending the boat ashore to get provision of victuals, we charged, the seamen to say to the Portuguese that we had sprung our foremast under the equinoctial line (although this misfortune had happened at the Cape of Good Hope), and that our ship was alone, because whilst we tried to repair it, our captain-general had gone with the other two ships to Spain. With these good words, and giving some of our merchandise in exchange, we obtained two boatloads of rice.

In order to see whether we had kept an exact account of the days, we charged those who went ashore to ask what day of the week it was, and they were told by the Portuguese inhabitants of the island that it was Thursday, which was a great cause of wondering to us, since with us it was only Wednesday. We could not persuade ourselves that we were mistaken; and I was more surprised than the others, since having always been in good health, I had every day, without intermission, written down the day that was current. However, we were afterwards advised that there was no error on our part, since as we had always sailed towards the west, following the course of the sun, and had returned to the same place, we must have gained twenty-four hours, as is clear to any one who reflects upon it.

The boat, having returned for rice a second time to the shore, was detained, with thirteen men who were in it. As we saw that, and, from the movement in certain caravels, suspected that they might wish to capture us and our ship, we at once set sail. We afterwards learned, some time after our return, that our boat and men had been arrested, because one of our men had discovered the deception, and said that the captain-general was dead, and that our ship was the only one remaining of Magellan's fleet.

At last, when it pleased Heaven, on Saturday the 6th of September of the year 1522, we entered the bay of San Lucar; and of sixty men who composed our crew when we left Maluco, we were reduced to only eighteen, and these for the most part sick. Of the others, some died of hunger, some had run away at the island of Timor, and some had been condemned to death for their crimes.

From the day when we left this bay of San Lucar until our return thither, we reckoned that we had run more than fourteen thousand four hundred and sixty leagues, and we had completed going round the earth from East to West.

Monday the 8th of September, we cast anchor near the mole of Seville, and discharged all the artillery.

Tuesday, we all went in shirts and barefoot, with a taper in our hands to visit the shrine of St. Maria of Victory, and of St. Maria de Antigua.

Then, leaving Seville, I went to Valladolid, where I presented to his Sacred Majesty Don Carlos, neither gold nor silver, but things much more precious in the eyes of so great a Sovereign. I presented to him among other things, a book written by my hand of all the things that had occurred day by day in our voyage. I departed thence as I was best able, and went to Portugal, and related to King John the things which I had seen. Returning through Spain, I came to France, where I presented a few things from the other hemisphere to Madam the Regent, mother of the most Christian King Don Francis. Afterwards, I turned towards Italy, where I established for ever my abode, and devoted my leisure and vigils to the very illustrious and noble lord, Philip de Villiers Lisleadam, the very worthy grand master of Rhodes.

The Chevalier,

ANTHOYNE PIGAPHETE.

CHAPTER 21

PIGAFETTA'S TREATISE OF NAVIGATION

Besides writing a journal of Magellan's voyage around the world, the Italian navigator Antonio Pigafetta wrote a treatise of navigation detailing the navigation methods he used.

****

Treatise of Navigation of the Chevalier Antony Pigafetta

The armillary sphere, of which the author gives a drawing, serves to explain the system of the world according to Ptolemy, and could also serve as an astrolabe, for one sees at the top of it a kind of handle or ring, by which to hold it suspended, as is seen in the above-mentioned drawing. He begins his treatise by giving us an idea of that system, as have done all those after him, who have written of the elements of the nautical art and of pilotage.

"The earth is round," he says, "and remains suspended and immovable in the midst of all the celestial bodies. The first index fixed on two poles, the arctic and Antarctic, which are supposed to correspond with the poles of the earth. It runs from East to West, and transports with itself all the planets and stars. Besides this there is the eighth sphere, the poles of which are at 23 deg. 33 min., it runs from West to East."

"It is supposed that all the circumference of the earth is divided into 360 degrees; and each degree is of 17 leagues and a half, consequently the circumference of the earth is 6,300 leagues. Land leagues are of three miles and sea leagues of four miles."

"The ten circles of the armillary sphere, of which the six major pass through the centre of the earth, serve to determine the situation of countries and climates. The Ecliptic determines the movement of the sun and the planets : the two Tropics indicate the point to which the sun declines from the equator towards the North in summer, and towards the South in winter. The Meridian, always variable, because it passes through all points of the equator, cutting it perpendicularly, designates the longitude, and it is on it that the latitudes are marked."

OF LATITUDE

After having well explained the armillary sphere with all its parts, and their use according to the system of Ptolemy, the author goes on to teach the method of taking the altitude of the pole, on which the latitude is calculated; fixing the pole at 0° and the equator at 90°.

"The Polar star," he says, "is not precisely on the point corresponding to the axis of the earth; but it turns round it, as do all the other stars. In order to know its true position with regard to the pole, it must be observed where the Guard stars stand. If these are on the western arm, the polar star stands one degree above the pole : if they are on the line the pole star stands 3 deg. 30 min. below the pole : if they are on the eastern arm the pole star is one degree below the pole. When one wishes to take the altitude of the pole star, in whichever of the above-mentioned four places the Guard stars may be, the degrees which the pole star has above the pole will be subtracted from its altitude, or those which it has below the pole will be added to it. I have spoken in the account of the voyage of the stars of the Antarctic Pole."

"The latitude of the place may also be ascertained by the sun's altitude. 1. If you find yourself between the equinoctial and the arctic pole and the shadow falls towards that pole, look how many degrees and minutes meridianal declination the sun has that day; and this you will subtract from the altitude of the sun which you have taken : afterwards, deducting the remaining degrees from 90 deg., you will have in the residue the number of degrees of North latitude, that is your distance from the equator. 2. If the sun has a boreal declination, in such a manner that the shadow falls towards the south, take the sun's declination on that day, and add it to the sun's altitude which you have taken, from that sum subtract 90 degs., and the remaining degrees will indicate your boreal latitude. 3. If the sun is between the equinoctial and the Antarctic, and the shadow falls towards the Antarctic, observe the sun's declination for that day, subtract it from the altitude taken, according to the first rule, and you will have the degrees of south latitude. 4. If, when you and the sun are between the equinoctial and the Antarctic pole, the shadow falls towards the north, you will add the altitude you have taken to the sun's declination that day, and act according to the second rule. 5. When you have an altitude of 90 deg., you will be so many degrees distant from the equator as there are degrees of the sun's declination, and if the sun has no declination you will be under the equator. 6. If you are to the north of the equator, and the sun is in the southern signs you will look what is its declination, you will add these degrees of declination to those of the altitude observed, and as many degrees as are wanting from 90 deg., so many will you be distant from the equinoctial. 7. You will do the same when you find yourself to the south of the equinoctial, whilst the sun is in the northern signs."

OF LONGITUDE

"Longitude indicates the degrees from east to west : I have considered many methods or means for ascertaining it, and I have found three methods fitting for that object. The last is the most convenient for those who do not know astrology. At the present time the pilots content themselves with knowing the latitude; and are so proud that they will not hear speak of longitude."

"I. From the latitude of the moon the longitude is calculated of the place in which the observation is made. The distance of the moon from the ecliptic is called its latitude : the ecliptic is the path of the sun. The moon, in its movement, always increases its distance until it reaches the furthest point of its distance : and thence it returns back, to diminish, so to say, its latitude, until it is with the head or tail of the dragon there it cuts the ecliptic. And since the moon, whilst it lengthens its distance from the ecliptic, has more degrees towards the west than towards the east, it must necessarily have more latitude on one side (of the globe) than on the other : and when the latitude is known, by measuring the degrees and minutes with the astrolabe, it will be known whether it is found, and how far it is found towards the east or the west. However, in order to ascertain the longitude, you must know in what latitude the moon ought to be at that same moment in the place from which you sailed, for instance, in Seville. By knowing the latitude and longitude of the moon at Seville in degrees and minutes, and seeing also the latitude and longitude which it has in the place where you are, you will know how many hours and minutes you are distant from Seville; and afterwards you will calculate the distance in east or west longitude."

"II. The moon furnishes another method for ascertaining the longitude, but that is when I knew the precise hour in which the moon observed at Seville ought to be in conjunction with a given star or planet, or ought to be in a certain opposition to the sun, of which the degrees are determined : and this I can know by means of an almanac. And since that happens in the east before it happens in the west, as many as may be the hours and minutes that may elapse from the time when the conjunction took place at Seville, till the time in which I observe it to take place, so much will be my longitude west of Seville. However, if I should see the conjunction take place before the hour in which it ought to happen with respect to Seville, then my distance in longitude will be east. For each hour, fifteen degrees of longitude are calculated."

"To understand this does not require any great genius. It should be borne in mind that the moon has a motion opposed to the general motion of the heavens; that is, it goes from west to east, and in every two hours it progresses a degree and a few minutes; and since it is in the first heaven, and the stars are in the eighth, it certainly never enters in conjunction with them; but sometimes it interposes itself before the rays which come from them to our eye : but this does not happen at the same time to those who are at Seville, and to those who are at Valencia. The annexed figure will give an idea of this, from which it is seen that the ray of the star D is intercepted by the moon c for those who are at A, and not for those who are at B, for whom it was intercepted when the moon was at E."

"III. The compass can also supply a method, still easier, for finding the longitude of the place in which you are. It is known that the compass, or the magnetised needle which is in it, directs itself to a given point, because of the tendency that the loadstone has towards the pole. The reason of this tendency is because the loadstone does not find in the heavens any other spot in repose except the pole, and on that account directs itself towards it. This is an explanation of the phenomenon which I propose; and I believe it to be true, so long as experience does not inform us of some better explanation."

"In order to know, by means of the needle, the degrees of longitude, form a large circle, in which place the compass, and divide it into 360 deg. : and having placed the needle at 360 deg., where it indicates the arctic pole; when the needle is in repose, draw a thread, which should pass from the arctic pole, pointed out by the needle to the Antarctic pole, and let this thread be longer than the diameter. After that take the south, which you will know by the greatest altitude of the sun. Turn the compass, until the thread which traverses it coincides with the direction of the meridian shade; then, from the Antarctic pole of the needle, with the thread which remained over, draw another thread to the arctic pole, that is, to the flower; and you will thus find how many degrees the needle of the compass is distant from the meridian line, that is, from the true pole. So many will be the degrees of longitude, which you will have from the place where the compass begins to set itself in motion. Therefore, with the more accuracy you take the true meridian so much the more exactly will you be able to ascertain the degrees of longitude. And from this it may be seen that the meridian should never be taken with the compass, because it north-easts or north-wests, as soon as it goes out of the true meridian; but take an observation of the south with the astrolabe, and judge that it is midday when the sun is at its greatest height."

"If it is not possible to take the sun's altitude at midday, that can be determined with an hour-glass of sand, taking the hours of the night from sunset till the moment of its rising. Having learned the hours of the night, you will know how many are wanting of the twenty-four, and these you will divide into two equal parts. When half of this has elapsed, be sure that it is midday, and that the shadow indicates to you the true meridian. However, since the sand clock may often be inexact, it will be better to take the sun's altitude with the astrolabe by means of its mediclino."

"The true meridian may also be ascertained, or rather the equinoctial line, which cuts the meridian at right angles, by observing the points where the sun rises and sets, and by observing how much they are distant from the equinoctial either to the north or to the south. For this purpose an astrolabe is formed with the globe; that is a circle is made representing the earth's circumference, divided into 360 deg.. At sunrise fix two pins in the circumference, in such a manner that a line drawn from one to the other should pass through the centre, and place the pins so that both should be in a line opposite the sun's center. Place two other pins in the same way in the circumference when the sun sets. You will thus see how much the sun declines from the equinoctial line, either to the north or to the south. And as many degrees as the pins are distant from the equinoctial, so many degrees are the sun's declination. Having found the sun's rising and setting, you will also find the medium distance; that is, the meridian line, and afterwards you will see how much the compass or magnetic needle north-easts or north-wests. You will infer from this how far you are from the Fortunate islands; that is, from Tenerife towards the east or the west. This method has been tried by experience."

DIRECTION OF THE SHIP

"If you wish to navigate to any place, you must first know its position; that is, its latitude and longitude. Then, by means of the compass you will point directly to that place. And since the compass varies to east and west, you must, by the methods above described, ascertain its variation, and subtract or add that which is necessary, so that the ship's head, regulated by the compass, may have the required direction."

"Should the compass be lost, or if its variation east or west is not known, you may regulate yourself by the sun at midday. When you have fixed the meridian in such a manner that it cuts the ship in its width, it will be easy to direct the prow wherever you wish. Here is an example : suppose you wish to go from north-east to south-west, place the chart in such manner that the ship should have her head to west and the poop to the east; then on the circle of the winds, divided into 360, or in four times 90, fix two pins, one at 45 degrees between east and north, the other at 45 degrees between west and south; bring the two pins on the line of the meridian by turning the ship's head for that purpose, and the prow will be directed to the place to which you are going. If the pins do not come in a line with the meridian, it is a sign that you are navigating in a false direction, and you must rectify the course. When you reach land, you will see that what I have said is true."

"With an astrolabe made with plates, observations may be taken of the meridian line, the poles, and the equinoctial line, at any hour of the day or night, looking at the moon or any star; and for these, place in the middle of the astrolabe instead of the verghezita or sight, two straight bars between which you will observe the star."

"Thus the method being known by which the required direction is given to the ship, the author teaches the method for determining the point or degree on the chart of the winds, to which the ship on leaving a place to go to a given country should be directed. For clearness, he gives some examples of this. "Do you wish," he says, "to go from south to north, or vice versa, on the same longitude ? always proceed on the same meridian. Do you wish to go from east to west, or vice versa, in the same latitude ? always proceed on the same parallel. Do you wish to go from one place to another as many degrees distant in longitude as it is different in latitude ? Then take the course of 45 degrees either to the south-west or south-east, or northwest or north-east. If the latitude is greater than the longitude, then add to the 45 degrees as many degrees towards the nearest pole, as the number of degrees by which the latitude exceeds the longitude. For instance, if I wish to go from Cape St. Vincent to Cape Bojador, I reckon the degrees of longitude and those of latitude to know the difference between these two capes. I find that the degrees of longitude are five and a half, and those of latitude are eleven, from which I subtract the degrees of longitude and there remain 5 deg. 30 min.. Then, instead of going in the direction of from north-east to south-west (as I should do if the longitude were equal to the latitude), I go from 5 deg. 30 min. above north-east towards north, to 5 deg. 30 min. below south-west towards south. If the longitude is greater than the latitude, the lesser number is still subtracted from the greater; and the direction will be 45 deg. after deducting the residue. For instance, do you want to go from the island of Ferro to Guadeloupe; you know that the first is in 27 deg. latitude and the second in 15 deg.; then take their difference, which is 12 deg. : look at the map for their longitude, and you see that Ferro is in 1 deg.

and Guadeloupe in 45 deg., whence their difference is 44 deg. : subtract from these the 12 deg. residue of latitude, and there remain 32 deg. Then you must subtract these 32 deg. from 45 deg., and there will remain 13 deg. Therefore your course will be from north-east 13 deg. north to south-west 13 deg. south."

DIRECTION OF THE WINDS.

"The rose of the winds, divided into 360 deg., will give a clearer idea of what has been here said; it being well understood that the pilot must place the center of the winds on the point from which he starts, or from which he takes the course, and he must fix the pole to the true pole observed from the sun, and not trusting to the compass, which north-easts or north-wests."

"Then, to ascertain whence comes the wind, place a little stick with a little sail in the centre of your rose or circle of winds, divided into 360 deg., and placed in such a manner that north and south stand on the true Solar meridian. The direction of the vane moved by the wind will indicate exactly which wind blows : on the equinoctial is east and west; at 45 deg. there is north-east, south-west, north-west, and south-east; at 22½ deg. towards north you have northnorth-east, and so on with the others."

CHAPTER 22

ALBO'S LOG BOOK OF THE VOYAGE

Francisco Albo (or Alvaro or Calvo), the contramaestre of the Trinidad, kept a log book of the voyage, largely consisting of nautical observations that provide data for the actual course sailed by the vessels of the fleet.

****

Tuesday, 29th day of November, I began to take the altitude of the sun whilst following the said voyage; and whilst in the vicinity of Cape St. Augustine, and in 7° altitude on the S. side, and at a distance from the said cape a matter of 27 leagues to S.W..

Wednesday, 30th of said month, I took the sun in 76°, and its declination was 22° 59', and its polar altitude was 8° 59', and the course was S.S.W..

On the 1st December, Thursday, the sun had 78° meridian altitude, and 23° 4' declination, and our distance (from the equator) 11° 4', and the course was S.S.W..

Friday, the 2nd of the said month, I took the sun in barely 80°, and its declination was 23° 3', the altitude was just 13°, and the course S.S.W..

Saturday, the 3rd of the said month, I took the sun in 82° 15', which had 23° 13' declination, and our distance was 14° 58', and the course was S.S.W..

Sunday, the 4th of the said month, the sun had 83° altitude, and 23° 17' declination; and our distance came to be 16° 17', and the course was S.S.W..

Monday, 5th of the said month, I took the sun in barely 84°, and it had 23° 21' declination; and our distance to the South came to be 17° 13', and the course was S.S.W. ¼W..

Tuesday, 6th of the said month, the sun had 85° meridian altitude, and 23° 25' declination; and the height to the S. Pole came to be 18° 25'; the course was S.W. ¼S..

Wednesday, 7th of the said month, I took the sun in 86° 30', and it had 23° 29' declination; our distance from the line came 18° 57', and the course was to W.S.W..

Thursday, 8th of the said month, I took the sun in 86° 30', and it had 23° 29' declination; and so our altitude came to be 19° 59', and the course was S.W., and we sounded here, and found bottom at 10 fathoms; and this day we saw land, flat beaches, and it was the day of the Conception of our Lady.

Friday, 9th of the said month (December), I took the sun in 88°, and its declination was 23° 31'; and our distance from the equinoctial line towards the South part came to be 21° 31', and the course was S.S.W., and we arose in the morning to the right of St. Thomas, on a great mountain, and south slopes along the coast in the S.S.W. direction; and on this coast, at 4 leagues to sea, we found bottom at 25 fathoms, free from shoals; and the mountains are separated one from another, and have many reefs round them; and in Brazil and St.Thomas there are many rivers and ports; and going along the coast 6 leagues there are many shoals 2 leagues out to sea, and there is a depth of 12 fathoms on them, and 10, and 8; but the coast runs N.E. and S.W. to Cape Frio, and there are many islands and rivers.

At Cape Frio there is a very large river, and to the N.E., at three leagues distance, there is the peak of a high mountain and three islands; and the cape is in 23°, and at the said cape there are three islands, and you leave them outside. Passing the said cape there is a large bay, and at its entrance there is a low island, and the bay within is very large, with many ports; it extends two leagues from the mouth, and it is called Bay of St. Lucy; and if you wish to pass the island, you leave it on the left hand, and (the entrance) is narrow; but there is a depth of 7 fathoms, and a foul bottom; but outside there is a depth of 20 to 25 fathoms, and within, where there is anchorage, there are 18 fathoms. In this bay there are good people, and plenty of them, and they go naked, and barter with

Page 334

fish-hooks, and looking-glasses, and little bells, for victuals. There is a good deal of brazil wood, and this bay is in 23°, and we entered here the day of St. Lucy, and remained till the day of St. John, which is the 27th of the month of December; and we set sail the same day, and went to W.S.W., and found seven islets, and to the right of them there is a bay, and it is called the Bay of Kings; it has a good entrance, and in this neighbourhood, on the 31st of the month, I took the sun in 86° 45', and its declination was 22° 8', and our latitude came to be 25° 23'.

Sunday, 1st of January of the year 1520, I took the sun in 84°, and it had 21° 23' declination and the altitude from the pole came to be 27° 29'; and on the days after the first day we went to S.W., and the other to W., and the fourth day to S.W.¼S..

Thursday, the 5th, the sun was in 85° 30' of altitude, and 23° 19' of declination; so that our distance from the line came to be 29° 49', and the course was S.W. ¼S..

On the 6th, the day of the Kings, the sun was in barely 80°, and had 21° 8' of declination; and the altitude from the pole came to be 31°, and the course was S.W.¼W..

Saturday, the 7th, I took the sun in 78°; it had 20° 56' of declination, and our parallel was 32° 56'; the course was to S.W.¼S., and we went along the coast.

On the 8th I did not take the sun, but we went to S.W. ¼ S., and at night we sounded and found 50 fathoms; and we altered the course, and went on the 9th of the said month to W.S.W.; and in the morning we sounded, and found 15 fathoms, and we went till midday, and saw land, and there I took the sun in 76°, and it had 20° 31' of declination; and at night we anchored in a bottom of 12 fathoms 34° 31'.

Tuesday, 10th January (1520), I took the sun in 75°; it had a declination of 20°, and our latitude came to 35°. We were to the right of the Cape of Sta. Maria. Thence forward the coast runs East and West, and the land is sandy; we gave it the name of Montevidi (now they call it correctly Santovidio), and between it and the Cape Sta Maria there is a river which is called (de los Patos) Duck River. From thence we went on forward through fresh water, and the coast runs E.S.E. and W.N.W. for ten leagues distance; after that it trends N.E. and S.W. as far as 34½°, with a depth of 5, 4 and 3 fathoms; there we anchored, and sent the ship Santiago along the coast to see if there was a roadstead, and the river is in 33½°. To the N.E. we found some islets, and the mouth of a very large river (it was the river of Solis), and it went to the N.. Here they turned back to the ships, and the said ship was away from us a matter of 25 leagues, and they were 15 days in coming; and during this time two other of our ships went in a southerly direction to see if there was a roadstead for staying at; and those went in the space of two days, and the Captain General went thither, and they found land to the S.S.W., 20 leagues distance from us, and they were four days in coming; and on returning we took in water and wood, and we went away from there, tacking from one tack to the other with contrary winds, until we came in sight of Montevidi; and this was on the 2nd day of the month of February, the day of our Lady of the Candlemas; and at night we anchored at 5 leagues from the mountain, and it lay to the S.E. and ¼°S. of us. Afterwards, on the morning of the 3rd, we set sail for the South, and we sounded, and found 4, 5, 6, and 7 fathoms, always increasing in depth; and this day we took the sun in 68° 30'; it had 13° 35' declination, and our latitude came to 35°.

Saturday, 4th February, we anchored in a depth of seven fathoms, the ship San Antonio having got leaky, and we were there till the 5th, and afterwards we weighed on the 6th, and stood on the south course, and at night we anchored in eight fathoms, and remained there till next day. The 7th we set sail to reconnoitre better the coast, and we saw that it trended S.E. ¼S.; after that we took another tack and anchored in 8 fathoms, and there we took the sun in 66° 30', and it had 12° 15' declination, with which our distance from the equinoctial line to the south came to be 35¾°; after that we sailed the same day, and at night we anchored in 9 fathoms, and stood for Cape Santanton [Cabo Blanco] it was to the south in 36°, and this was Tuesday, the 7th.

On the 8th we set sail from the said point, and it is north and south with Montevidi, and 27 leagues distant from it this coast runs N. and S. [the width of the Rio de la Plata is 27 leagues]; from that place forward we went along the coast round the cape of St. Polonia; after that the coast trends from N.E. to S.W.. The said cape is in 37°, and the land sandy and very low, it has sea of shallow depth for a distance of two leagues from land, of 8, 9, and 10 fathoms; so we ran all this day to the S.W., and the night and day.

Thursday, 9th of February, I took the sun in 631¼°; it had 11½° declination, and the altitude came to be 38° 30'; the coast can be sounded, and not very high nor mountainous, and we made out many smokes along the coast; this coast runs E.W. ¼N.W. S.E., and the point is called Punta de las Arenas.

On the 10th I took the sun in 62 ⅓°, and it had 11° 8' declination, out-distance from the equinoctial came to be 38° 48', and the coast runs E. W., and it is a very pretty coast for running in one or other direction.

On the 11th of the said month, I took the sun in 62°, it had 10^0 47' declination, and the altitude came to be 38° 47', and the course was W. ¼ N.W., and the coast ran east and west from the Point de las Arenas; to this place there is a very good coast, with soundings, with many little green hills and low land.

Sunday the 12th, we did not take the sun, but from the day before till midday we began to run to S.W. and to S.W. and ¼ W., and to W.S.W., and W. ¼ S.W., but I calculate that the whole course was W.S.W., and this run was from midday of the 11th, till nightfall of the 12th, and at that hour we anchored in 9 fathoms, and further on in 13 fathoms, and after that we had anchored we saw land, and we set sail to the N., and this was on the 13th, and in the morning we were alongside of some shoals, where the Victoria bumped several times.

Item, the same day we were at anchor, and we did not take the sun's altitude, and we were in soundings of 7 fathoms, and we remained there till the 14th, and the said day I took the sun in 60½°, and it had 9° 41' declination, and our altitude came to 39° 11'.

On the 15th of the said month I took the sun in 60 °, and it had 9° 13' declination, and our distance came to be 39° 19', and we sailed a south course.

Thursday the 16th, we could not take the sun until the 18th, and on that day we were in 39¼°; and the next day, the 19th, we were in 39¹/₃°, and this day we went to S.W., and we went by this course, and could not take the sun until the 20th of the month.

On the 20th I took the sun in 57°, it had 7° 27' declination, and our distance to the south came to 40° 17'.

On the 21st, I took the sun in 55°, it had 7° 4' declination, our altitude came to 42° 4', the course was S.W. ¼W., and we sounded and found bottom at 55 fathoms.

Wednesday the 22nd, I took the sun in 53°, it had 6° 41' declination, and our distance came to 43° 26', the course was S.W.¼W.; at night we sounded and found bottom at 55 fathoms.

On the 23rd I took the sun in 53¼°, it had 6° 18' declination, our distance from the line came to be 43° 3', the course was W.N.W..

On the 24th I took the sun in 53°, it had 5° 54' declination, our altitude from the pole came to 42° 54', and our course was W.N.W., and we were to the right of a very large bay, to which we gave the name of Bay of St. Matthew, because we found it on his day; we entered well in, and could not find bottom until we were entirely inside, and we found 80 fathoms, and it has a circuit of 50 leagues, and the mouth is to the N.W., and it is in the latitude of 42½°.

On the 25th I did not take the sun, but I took it on the 26th, in 51²/₃°, and it had 5° 7' declination, by which we found ourselves in 43° 27' to the south of the line, and the coast runs N.W. S.E. ¼N.S..

On the 27th I took the sun in 50¼°, and it had 4¾° declination, and so our altitude came to be 44°; and here to the right hand we found a bay, and three leagues before it there are two rocks, and they lie East and West with the said bay, and further on we found another (bay), and there were in it many sea wolves, of which we caught eight, and on this land there are no people, but it is very good land, with pretty plains without trees, and very flat country.

Tuesday, 28th, I took the sun in 48½°, and it had 4° 21' declination, and so we found ourselves in 44° 21', and the course was to the south, and at night we saw land to W.N.W..

On the 29th I took the sun in 48½°, and this day it had 4° declination, by which we found ourselves in 45½°, and the course was to S.S.W. and to W.S.W. and to W.N.W., and I give the whole of the run as to W.S.W. until I took the sun, and afterwards we were two days that we could not take it.

On Friday, 2nd of March, I took the sun in 43° 50', it had 3° 10' declination, with which our distance came to be 47°; and after that we did not take the sun again until we entered a port called St. Julian, and we entered there on the last day of March, and remained there till the day of St. Bartholomew, which is the 24th of August, and the said port is in 49⅔° and there we caulked the ships, and many Indians came there, who go covered with skins of antas, which are like camels without humps, and they carry some bows of canes very small like the Turkish, and the arrows are like theirs, and at the point they have a flint tip for iron, and they are very swift runners, and well made men, and well fashioned. We sailed thence on the 24th of the said month of August, and went along the coast to S.W.¼W., a matter of 30 leagues, and found a river called Santa Cruz, and we entered there on the 26th of August, and remained till the day of S. Lucas, which is the 18th of the month of October, and there we caught much fish, and we took in water and wood, and this coast is well defined and with good marks.

Thursday, the 18th of October, we sailed from the said river of Santa Cruz, with contrary winds, we went for two days tacking about, and then we had a fair wind, and went to the S.S.W. for two days, and in that time we took the sun in 50⅔°, and it was on the 20th.

On the 21st of the said month, I took the sun in exactly 52°, at five leagues from the land, and there we saw an opening like a bay, and it has at the entrance, on the right hand a very long spit of sand, and the cape which we discovered before this spit, is called the Cape of the Virgins, and the spit of sand is in 52° latitude, and 52½° longitude, and from the spit of sand to the other part, there may be a matter of 5 leagues, and within this bay we found a strait which may be a league in width, and from this mouth to the spit you look East and West, and on the left hand side of the bay there is a great elbow, within which are many shoals, but when you enter the strait, keep to the North side, and when you are in the strait go to the S.W., in the middle of the channel, and when you are in the strait, take care of some shallows less than three leagues from the entrance of the straits, and after them you will find two islets of sand, and then you will find the channel open, proceed in it at your pleasure without hesitation; and passing this strait we found another small bay, and then, we found another strait of the same kind as the first, and from one mouth to the other runs East and West, and the narrow part runs N.E. and S.W., and after we had come out of the two straits or narrows, we found a very large bay, and we found some islands, and we anchored, at one of them; and took the sun, and found ourselves in 52⅓°, and thence we came in S.S.E. direction, and found a spit on the left hand, and from thence to the first mouth there will be a matter of 30 leagues after that we went to S.W. a matter of 20 leagues, and there we took the sun, and we were in 53⅔°, and from there we returned to N.W., a matter of 15 leagues, and there anchored in 53° latitude. In this strait there are a great many elbows, and the chains of mountains are very high and covered with snow, with much forest. After that we went to N.W. and ¼ W., and in this course there are many islets; and issuing from this strait the coast turns to the north, and on the left hand we saw a cape with an island, and we gave them the name of Cape Fermoso and Cape Deseado, and it is in the same latitude as the Cape of the Virgins, which is at the beginning of the straits, and from the said Cape Fermoso we afterwards went to N.W. and to N., and to N.N.E., and we went in this course two days and three nights, and in the morning we saw land of pointed hills, and it runs North and South (thus runs the coast of the South sea) and from this land to Cape Fermoso there is a matter of 20 leagues, and we saw this land the 1st December.

Now I will commence the course and latitude of this voyage after this land, and the 1st day of December, when we were opposite to it; it is in latitude 48°.

December

On the 2nd of December we did not take the sun, but we went to the N.N.E., and were in 47¼°, and this day we found ourselves that much ahead, as all this country is in the same altitude.

On the 3rd, we went N.W., and found ourselves in 46° 30'
On the 4th, to N.W., and found ourselves in 45½°
On the 5th, to N.¼N.W., and found ourselves in 44¼°
On the 6th, to N.E.¼E., and found ourselves in 44°
On the 7th, to N.E.¼E., and found ourselves in 43²/₃°
On the 8th, to N.E.¼N., and found ourselves in 43¼°
On the 9th, to N.N.E., and found ourselves in 42²/₃°
On the 10th, to N.E.¼E., and found ourselves in 42° 12'
On the 11th, to N.E.¼E., and found ourselves in 41²/₃°
On the 12th, to N.E.¼E., and found ourselves in 41¼°
On the 13th, to N.E.¼N., and found ourselves in 40°
On the 14th, to N., and found ourselves in 38¾°
On the 15th, to N.¼N.E., and found ourselves in 38°
On the 16th, to N.¼° N.W., and found ourselves in 36½°
On the 17th, to N.W.¼° N., and found ourselves in 34½°
On the 18th, to N.¼N.W., and found ourselves in 33½°
On the 19th, to N.W., and found ourselves in 32¾°
On the 20th, to N.W., and found ourselves in 31¾°
On the 21st, to N.W., and found ourselves in 30²/₃°
On the 22nd, to W.¼S.W., and found ourselves in 30²/₃°
On the 23rd, to W.N.W., and found ourselves in 30°
On the 24th, to W.N.W., and found ourselves in 29¾°
On the 25th, to W.N.W., and found ourselves in 29½°
On the 26th, to N.W.¼W., and found ourselves in 28¾°
On the 27th, to N.W.¼W., and found ourselves in 27²/₃°
On the 28th, to N.W.¼W., and found ourselves in 26²/₃°
On the 29th, to W.N.W., and found ourselves in 26¹/₃°
On the 30th, to W. 12 leagues
On the 31st, to N.W., and found ourselves in 25½°

Year 1521
January

On the 1st, to W.¼N.W., and found ourselves in 25°
On the 2nd, to W.N.W., and found ourselves in 24°
On the 3rd, to N.W.¼W., and found ourselves in 23½°
On the 4th, to W.N.W., and found ourselves in 22°
On the 5th, to W.¼S.W., and found ourselves in 23°
On the 6th, to W.¼N.W., and found ourselves in 22°
On the 7th, to W. 25 leagues
On the 8th, to W. 23 leagues
On the 9th, to W.¼N.W., and found ourselves in 22¼°
On the 10th, to W.¼N.W., and found ourselves in 22°
On the 11th, to W.¼N.W., and found ourselves in 21¾°
On the 12th, to W.¼N.W., and found ourselves in 21⅓°
On the 13th, to W.¼N.W., and found ourselves in 21°
On the 14th, to N.W.¼W., and found ourselves in 20½°
On the 15th, to W.N.W., and found ourselves in 19½°
On the 16th, to W.N.W., and found ourselves in 19°
On the 17th, to W.N.W., and found ourselves in 18¼°
On the 18th, to W.N.W., and found ourselves in 17½°
On the 19th, to N.W.¼W., and found ourselves in 16¼°
On the 20th, to N.W.¼W., and found ourselves in 15°
On the 21st, to S.W., and found ourselves in 15⅔°
On the 22nd, to S.W., and found ourselves in 16¾°
On the 23rd, to W.¼N.W., and found ourselves in 16½°
On the 24th, to W.¼N.W., and found ourselves in 16¼°
And in this neighbourhood we found an islet with trees on it. It is uninhabited; and we took soundings at it, and found no bottom, and so we went on our course. We called this islet San Pablo, having discovered it on the day of his conversion, and it is 9 leagues from that of Tiburones.
On the 25th of the said month, to N.W.¼W., in 15¾°
On the 26th of the said month, to N.W.¼W., in 15⅓°
On the 27th of the said month, to N.W.¼W., in 15°
On the 28th of the said month, to W.N.W., in 14½°
On the 29th of the said month, to W.N.W., in 13¾°
On the 30th of the said month, to W.¼N.W., in 13½°

On the 31st of the said month, to W.¼N.W., in 13⅓°

February

On the 1st of the said month, to N.W., in 13°
On the 2nd of the said month, to N.W., in 12½°
On the 3rd of the said month, to N.W., in 11¾°
On the 4th of the said month, to N.W., in 11¾°
In this latitude we found an uninhabited island, where we caught many sharks, and therefore we gave it the name of Isle of Tiburones, and it is with the Strait N.W. and S.E.¼E. and W., and it is in 10⅔° S. latitude, and is distant ..... leagues from the Ladrone Islands.
On the 5th Feb., to N.W., in 10°
On the 6th Feb., to N.W., in 9¼°
On the 7th Feb., to N.W., in 8⅔°
On the 8th Feb., to N.W., in 7⅔°
On the 9th Feb., to N.W.¼W., in 6½°
On the 10th Feb., to N.W., in 5°
On the 11th Feb., to N.W., in 2½°
On the 12th Feb., to N.W., in 1°
On the 13th Feb., to N.W., in 30' N. of the line
On the 14th Feb., to N.W., in N. latitude
On the 15th Feb., to N.W., in 1¾°
On the 16th Feb., to W.N.W., in 2½°
On the 17th Feb., to W.N.W., in 3½°
On the 18th Feb., to W.N.W., in 5°
On the 19th Feb., to W.N.W., in 5¾°
On the 20th Feb., to W.N.W., in 6½°
On the 21st Feb., to W.N.W., in 8°
On the 22nd Feb., to W.N.W., in 9½°
On the 23rd Feb., to W.N.W., in 11½°
On the 24th Feb., to W.N.W., in 12°
On the 25th Feb., to W.¼N.W., in 12⅓°
On the 26th Feb., to W., in 12°
On the 27th Feb., to W., in 12°
On the 28th Feb., to W.¼N.W., in 13°

March, 1521

On the 1st March, to W., in 13 °
On the 2nd March, to W., in 13 °
On the 3rd March, to W., in 13 °
On the 4th March, to W., in 13 °
On the 5th March, to W., in 13 °
On the 6th March, to W., in 13°.

This day we saw land, and went to it, and there were two islands, which were not very large; and when we came between them, we turned to the S.W., and left one to the N.W., and then we saw a quantity of small sails coming to us, and they ran so, that they seemed to fly, and they had mat sails of a triangular shape, and they went both ways, for they made of the poop the prow, and of the prow the poop, as they wished, and they came many times to us and sought us to steal whatever they could; and so they stole the skiff of the flag-ship, and next day we recovered it; and there I took the sun, and one of these islands is in $12^2/_3°$ and the other in 13° and more (N. latitude); and this island of 12° is with that of Tiburones W.N.W. and E.S.E. (and it appears to be 20 leagues broad at the N. end), from the island of 12° we sailed on the 9th of March, in the morning, and went W.¼S.W. The islands of Ladrones are 300 leagues from Gilolo.

On the 9th of March, to W.¼S.W., in 12°
On the 10th of March, to W.¼S.W., in $12^1/_3$ °
On the 11th of March, to W.¼S.W., in $11½$°
On the 12th of March, to W.¼S.W., in 11°
On the 14th of March, to W.¼S.W., in $10^2/_3$°
On the 15th of March, to W.¼S.W., in 10°

On the 16th (March) we saw land, and went towards it to the N.W., and we saw that the land trended north, and that there were many shoals near it, and we took another tack to the south, and we fell in with another small island, and there we anchored : and this was the same day, and this island is called Suluano, and the first one is named Yunuguan; and here we saw some canoes, and we went to them, and they fled; and this island is in $9^2/_3$° N. latitude and in 189° longitude from the meridian. To these first islands, from the archipelago of St. Lazarus....

Ytem. From the Strait of All Saints and Cape Fermoso to these two islands, there will be 106° 30' longitude, which strait is with these islands in a straight course W.N.W. and E.S.E., which brings you straight to them. From here we went on our course.

Leaving these islands, we sailed W., and fell in with the island of Gada, which is uninhabited, and there we provided ourselves with water and wood. This island is very free from shoals.

From here we departed and sailed W., and fell in with a large island called Seilani, which is inhabited, and contains gold; we coasted it, and went to W.S.W., to a small inhabited island called Mazaba. The people are very good, and there we placed a cross upon a mountain; and from thence they showed us three islands in the W.S.W. direction, and they say there is much gold there, and they showed us how they gather it, and they found small pieces like beans and like lentils; and this island is in $9^1/_3$° N. latitude.

We departed from Mazaba and went N., making for the island of Seilani, and afterwards coasted the said island to the N.W. as far as 10°, and there we saw three islets; and we went to the W., a matter of 10 leagues, and then we fell in with two islets, and at night we stopped; and on the morrow we went S.W. and ¼S., a matter of 12 leagues, as far as $10^1/_3$°, and there we entered a channel between two islands, one called Matan, and the other Subo; and Subo, with the isle of Mazaba and Suluan, are E.W.¼N.W.S.E.; and between Subo and Seilani we saw a very high land to the north, which is called Baibai, and they say that there is in it much gold and provisions, and much extent of land, that the end of it is not known.

From Mazaba and Seilani and Subo, by the course which we came, towards the south part, take care; for there are many shoals, and they are very bad; for this a canoe would not stop which met us in this course.

From the mouth of the channel of Subo and Matan we went west in mid-channel, and met with the town of Subu, at which we anchored, and, made peace, and there they gave us rice and millet and flesh; and we remained there many days; and the king and the queen, with many people, became Christians of their free will.

We sailed from Subu, and went S.W. till 9¾° between the head of Subu and an island called Bohol; and on the W. side of the head of Subu there is another, which is named Panilongo, and it belongs to black men; and this island and Subu contain much gold and much ginger, and it is in 9¹/₃°, and Subu in 10¹/₃°; and so we came out of the channel, and came ten leagues to the S., and anchored off the island of Bohol, and there of the three ships we made two, and burned the other, not having crews enough; and this island is in 9½°.

We sailed from Bohol to Quipit to the S.W., and came to anchor at the same anchorage to the right of a river; and in the offing to the N.W. part there are two islets, which are in 8½°, and there we could not get provisions, for there were none, but we made peace with them; and this island of Quipit has much gold, ginger, and cinnamon, and so we decided on going to seek provisions; and from this head of Quipit to the first islands there will be a course of 112 leagues; it lies with them E.W. ¼N.E. S.W., and this island lies due East and West.

From thence we sailed and went to W.S.W., and to S.W. and W., until we fell in with an island in which there were very few people, and it was named Cuagayan; and here we anchored on the N. side of it, and we asked where the island of Poluan was, to get provisions of rice, for there is much of it in that island, and they load many ships for other parts; and so they showed us where it was, and so we went to the W.N.W., and fell in with the head of the island of Poluan. Then we went to N.¼N.E., coasting along it until the town Saocao, and there we made peace, and they were Moors; and we went to another town, which is of Cafres; and there we bought much rice, and so we provisioned ourselves very well; and this coast runs N.E. S.W., and the cape of the N.E. part is in 9¹/₃°, and the part of S.W. is in 8¹/₃°; and so we returned to S.W. as far as the head of this island, and there we found an island, and near it there is a shoal, and in this course, and along Poluan, there are many shoals, and this head lies E.W. with Quipit, and N.W. S.E. ¼E.W. with Cuagayan.

From Poluan we sailed for Borney, and we coasted the above-named island, and went to its S.W. head, and near there found an island which has a shoal on the E.; and in 7½° we had to change the course to W., until running 15 leagues; after that we ran S.W., coasting the island of Bornei until the city itself; and you must know that it is necessary to go close to land, because outside there are many shoals, and it is necessary to go with the sounding lead in your hand, because it is a very vile coast, and Bornei is a large city, and has a very large bay, and inside it and without it there are many shoals; it is, therefore, necessary to have a pilot of the country. So we remained here several days, and began to trade, and we made good agreements of peace; and after that they armed many canoes to take us, which were 260 in number, and they were coming to us, and as we saw them we sailed in great haste, and we went outside and we saw some junks coming, and we went to them, and we captured one, in which was a son of the King of Luzon, which is a very large island, and also the captain let him go without the counsel of anyone.

Borney is a large island, and there is also in it cinnamon, mirabolams, and camphor, which is worth much in these countries; and they say that when they die they embalm themselves with it. Borney is in 5° 25' latitude - that is, the port itself - and 201° 5' of longitude from the line of demarcation, and from here we sailed and returned by the same road; and this port of Borney lies E.N.E. W.S.W. with the isle of Mazaba, and in this course there are many islands; and from the cape at the N.E. of Bornei to Quipit is E.W. ¼N.E. S.W..

We sailed from Borney, and returned by the same course which we had come, and so we passed between the head of the isle of Bornei and Poluan; and we went to the W., to fall in with the isle of Cuagayan; and so we went by the same course to make for the island of Quipit on the S. side, and in this course, between Quipit and Cuagayan, we saw to the S. an island which they call Solo, in which there are many pearls, very large - they say that the king of this island has a pearl like an egg. This island is in 6° latitude; and so, going on this course, we fell in with three small islands; and further on we met with an island named Tagima, and they say there are many pearls there; and this island lies with Solo N.E. S.W. ¼E.W., and Tagima is in 6⅚°. It is opposite the

Cape of Quipit, and the said cape is in 7¼°, and lies with Paluan E.S.E. W.N.W..

From here we coasted the island of Quipit on the south side, and we went to E.¼S.E. as far as some islets; and along the coast there are many villages, and there is much good cinnamon in this island, and we bought some of it; and there is much ginger on this coast; and so we went to E.N.E., until we saw a gulf; then we went to S.E. until we saw a large island, and thence to the cape at the east of the island of Quipit, and at the cape of this island there is a very large village, which collects much gold from a very large river, and this cape is 191½° of the meridian.

We sailed from Quipit to go to Maluco, and went to S.E., sighting an island called Sibuco; after that we went to S.S.E., and saw another island, called Virano Batolague; and we went by the same course as far as the cape of this island, and after that we saw another, which they call Candicar; and we went to the E. between the two, until we went ahead of it; and there we entered a channel between Candicar and another, which they call Sarangani; and at this island we anchored and took a pilot for Maluco; and these two islands are in 4⅔°, and the cape of Quipit in 7¼°, and the Cape of Sibuco, on the south side, is in 6°, and the Cape of Viranu Batologue in 5°, and from the Cape of Quipit and Candicar the run is from N.N.W. to S.S.E., without touching any cape.

We sailed from Sarangani, and went S.¼S.E., until we came opposite an island called Sanguin, and between the two are many islets, and they are on the West side, and this island is in 3⅔°. From Sangui we went S.¼S.E. to an island called Sian; between them there are many islets, and this island is in just 3°. From Sian we went to S.¼S.W., as far as an island called Paginsara, it is in 1⅙°; and from this island to Sarangani the run is N.S ¼N.E. S.W. in sight of all these islands.

From Paginsara we went to S.¼ S.E., until we came between two islets, which lie together, N.E. and S.W., and that one to the N.E. is named Suar, and the other is named Atean, and one is in 1°45'. and the other in 1½°.

From Atean we went S.S.E. until we sighted the Molucos, and then we went to East, and entered between Mare and Tedori, at which we anchored, and there we were very well received, and made very good arrangements for peace, and made a house on shore for trading with the people, and so we remained many days, until we had taken in cargo.

The islands of the Malucos are these : Terrenate, Tidori, Mare, Motil, Maquian, Bachian, and Gilolo, these are all those which contain cloves and nutmeg; and there are also several others among them, the names of which I will mention, and in what altitude they are, and the first is Terrenate, which is on the side of the equinoctial line.

Terrenate is in altitude of 1° 0'
Tidori is in altitude of 0° 30'
Mare is in altitude of 0° 15'
Motil is on the line 0°
Maquian is to the south 0° 15'
Cayoan is to the south 0° 20
Bachian is to the south 1°
La Talata is to the south 1° ¼
La Talata (Lata-lata) lies north of Terrenate N.N.E. and S.S.W., and that which is on the equinoctial line is 190° 30' of longitude from the line itself, and the island of Motil itself with Cagayan lies N.W. and S.E., and with Tagima, which is opposite the island of Quipit, it lies N.E. And S.W. ¼N.S., but in these courses one cannot venture to pass, for they say there are many shoals, and so we came by another course, coasting the said islands. From the islands of Maluco we sailed Saturday, 21st December, of the said year 1521, and we went to the island of Mare, and there took in wood to burn, and the same day we sailed and went to S.S.W., making for Motil, and thence we went by the same course, making for Maquian, and thence we went to S.W., running by all these islands, and others, which are these : Cuayoan, Laboan, Agchian, Latalata, and other small islands, which remain in the N.W. quarter, and now I will say in what latitude and longitude are each one separately, and which are those which contain cloves and other spices. The first to the North is Terrenate, which is in 1° North, and Tidore 40' and Mare 15', and Motil on the equinoctial line, and these lie North and South. The others to the South are these : Maqui is

in 20', Cuayoan in 40', and Laboan in 1° and Latalata in 1° 15', and Bachian lies with Terrenate E.N.E. and W.S.W.; and to the S.E. of all these islands there is a very large island called Gilolo, and there are cloves in it, but very few; therefore there are seven islands which contain cloves, and those which have a large quantity are these Terrenate, Tidore, Motil, Maqui, and Bachian, which are the five principal ones, and some of them contain nutmeg and mace. Motil is on the line, and is in longitude of the meridian of 191° 45'.

From Latalata we went to S.W.¼W., and fell in with an island which is called Lumutola, it is in 1¾°, and on the W. side there is another island called Sulan, and at these islands there are many shoals, and from hence we took the course to the South, towards an island named Buro, and between these three, there is another island which is named Fenado, it is in 2½°, and Buro is in 3½°, and it lies with Bachian N.E. and S.W. ¼N.S. in longitude 194°; and to the East of Buro there is a very large island called Ambon, in which they make much cotton cloths, and between it and Buro there are some islets; take care of them, for this it is necessary to coast the island of Buro to the East, and to the South of it. I took the sun in 70⁰ 24', it had 22° 36' declination, and so the latitude came to be 3°. I was in the Southern part of the island, and this was on the 27th of December, on Friday. On the 28th of the said month, I did not take the sun, but we were in the neighbourhood of the said isle of Buro, and Bidia, which lies to the eastward.

Sunday, 29th, I took the sun in 71½°, it had 22° 21' declination, and our distance came to be 3° 51', and we were opposite the isle of Ambon.

On the 30th I took the sun in the altitude of the day before, in calm, it was Monday.

On the 31st I did not, take the sun, we were a matter of 12 leagues from the Isle of Ambon E.N.E. and W.S.W., the day was Tuesday.

1522

The 1st day of January 1522, I took the sun in barely 73°, it had 21° 54' declination, the altitude came to be 4° 45'.

On the 2nd of the month, I took the sun in 73¾°, it had 21¼° declination, our distance came to be 5½°, the course was to S.W., and it was Thursday.

Friday, 3rd, I did not take the sun, but the ship made the course of S.S.W., in latitude of 6½°, after that we took the course to N.W.

On the 4th of the month I did not take the sun, but we were in 5¾°, the course was to N.W., and the day Saturday.

Sunday, the 5th, I took the sun in 75° it had 21° 14' declination, the latitude came to 6° 14'.

On the 6th, Monday, I took the sun in 76°, it had 21° 2' declination, the latitude came to be 7° 2'.

On the 7th, I took the sun in 76⅔°, it had 20° 50' declination, the latitude came to be 7½°, and the course was to S.W. Tuesday.

On the 8th of the month, I took the sun in 77½°, it had 30° 37' declination, and the latitude came to be 8° 7', the course was to S.W., and the day Wednesday, and this day we saw some islands, which lie East and West, and this day we entered between two of them, which are these, Lamaluco and Aliguom; between them are two little ones which you will leave on the right hand after entering the channel, they are inhabited; this channel lies N.E. S.W. ¼E.W., with Buro, and all these islands are ten in number, and they lie E.W. ¼N.E. S.W., and they have of longitude a matter of 50 leagues; we ran along them, with very bad weather from the South; we coasted them and anchored off the last, which is called Malua, which is in 8⅓°, the others are named Liaman, Maumana, Cui, Aliguim, Bona, Lamaluco, Ponon, Vera. We sailed from Malua and went to the South, and found the island of Timor, and we coasted the coast from east to west, on the north side of this island, which is in the latitude of 9°, and the nearest land on the north side, and this land will have 10 leagues journey, and this coast lies with Buro N.E. S.W. ¼N.S., in longitude of 197° 45', and of this island of Timor we coasted all the coast from east to west, as far as the village of Manvai; and first we came near the village of Queru, and from Queru to Manvai, the coast runs N.E. S.W. ¼N.S., and here I took the sun on the 5th day of February, in $86^{2}/_{3}°$, and it had 12° 44' declination, so that the latitude came to be 9° 24', and this island is very large and populous, and all the island has much sandal wood, and there are many towns in it.

On the 8th of February I took the sun in 87½°, and it had 11° 42' of declination, with which our distance came to be $9^{1}/_{6}°$, and we were at the head of the island of Timor, at the West end, and from here to the Eastern cape the coast runs E.N.E. to W.S.W., and it was Saturday.

Sunday, 9th of the said month, I took the sun in $88^{1}/_{6}°$, and it had $11/_{3}°$ declination. Our latitude came to be 9° 35', and we were at the most salient cape of all the island, and from there it goes falling off to the S.W. and S.

On the 10th of the same month I took the sun in 88¼°, it had 10° 58' declination; our latitude came to be 9° 28', and the head of the island lay to the south, and the day was Monday.

On the 11th, Tuesday, I took the sun in 88¼°, it had $9^{1}/_{3}°$ declination; the latitude came to 9° 35', and we were in calm.

Wednesday, the 12th, I did not take the sun, but we were becalmed in the neighbourhood of where we were the day before, or a little more.

On the 13th I took the sun in $89^{2}/_{3}°$; it had 9° 52' declination; the latitude came to 10° 32', and we were in the neighbourhood of islands of which we do not know the names, nor whether they are inhabited. They lie E.S.E. and W.N.W. with the west cape of Timor, and from here we took our course to the Cape of Good Hope, and went to W.S.W.

After this the course was W.S.W. for several days, and there is nothing worthy of note till Tuesday, the 18th of March, when the Victoria discovered Amsterdam Island.

On the 18th of the said month (March), I took the sun in 49½°, it had 2°

55' declination, the latitude came to be 37° 35', and whilst taking the sun we saw a very high island, and we went towards it to anchor, and we could not fetch it; and we struck the sails and lay to until next day, and the wind was W.; and we made another tack to the north under storm sails; and this was on the 19th, and we could not take the sun; we were east and west with the island, and it is in 38° to the south, and it appears that it is uninhabited, and it has no trees at all, and it has a circumference of a matter of six leagues.

On the 20th of the said month, Thursday, I did not take the sun, but we were east and west with the island, and we went to N.W. and to N.N.W. and ¼N.W., and for the whole course I put down a matter of 15 leagues to the N.N.W., and in the latitude of 35½°.

On the 22nd of the said month I took the sun in 50¼° : it had 4° 27' declination; the latitude came to 36° 18'. The day before we had struck the sails until the morning of the said Saturday, and this day we set sail and went to the N.W..

On the 8th of the said month (May) I did not take the sun; but, according to the run we had made, we thought we were ahead of the Cape, and on this day we saw land, and the coast runs N.E. and S.W. and a quarter east and west; and so we saw that we were behind the Cape a matter of 160 leagues, and opposite the river Del Infante, eight leagues distant from it in the offing; and this day we were lying to with winds from the west and west-northwest, and it was Thursday.

On the 9th I did not take the sun, but we made land and anchored, and the coast was very wild, and we remained thus till next day; and the wind shifted to W.S.W., and upon that we set sail, and we went along the coast to find some port for anchoring and taking refreshments for the people who were most suffering, which we did not find. And we stood out to sea, to be at our ease ; and we saw many smokes along the coast, and the coast was very bare, without any trees, and this coast runs N.E. and S.W. : it is in 33° latitude, and it was Saturday, 10th of May.

Friday, the 16th (May), I took the sun in 33¼°; it had 21° 6' declination;

the latitude came to 35⁰ 39', and we were E.S.E. and W.N.W., with the Cape of Good Hope twenty leagues off from it; and this day we sprung our foremast and fore-yard, and we were all day hove to, and the wind was W..

[The Victoria doubled the Cape of Good Hope between the 18th and the 19th of May, and arrived] on the 9th of the month of July, and anchored in the port of Rio Grande in Santiago [of the Cape Verde Islands], and they received us very well, and gave us what provisions we wanted; and this day was Wednesday, and they reckoned this day as Thursday, and so I believe that we had made a mistake of a day; and we remained there till Sunday in the night, and we set sail for fear of bad weather and the difficulty of the port; and on the morrow we sent our boat on shore to get more rice, which we wanted, and we were standing off and on till it came.

On the 14th of July, Monday, we sent our boat on shore for more rice, and it came at midday, and returned for more, and we were waiting for it till night, and it did not come; and we waited till next day, and it never came; then we went near the port to see what the matter was, and a boat came and told us to give ourselves up, and that they would send us with a ship which was coming from the Indies, and that they would put some of their people in our ship, and that the gentlemen had so ordered. We required them to send us our boat and men, and they said that they would bring an answer from the gentlemen; and we said we would take another tack, and would wait: and so we took another tack, and we made all sail, and went away with twenty-two men, sick and sound, and this was Tuesday, the 15th of the month of July. On the 14th I took the sun. This town is in 15° 10'.

September, 1522

On the 4th of the said month, in the morning, we saw land, and it was Cape St. Vincent, and it was to the northeast of us, and so we changed our course to the S.E., to get away from that Cape.

CHAPTER 23

ACCOUNT BY AN UNKNOWN PORTUGUESE

In Ramusio's Navigationi et Viaggi occurs a brief account of the voyage by an unknown Portuguese, who was a companion of Odoardo Barbosa, on board the ship Victoria.

****

In the name of God and of good salvation. We departed from Seville with five ships on the tenth of August, in the year 1519, to go and discover the Molucca Islands. We commenced our voyage from San Lucar for the Canary Islands, and sailed south-west 960 miles, where we found our selves at the island of Tenerife, in which is the harbour of Santa Cruz in twenty-eight degrees of north latitude.

And from the island of Tenerife we sailed southwards 1680 miles, when we found ourselves in four degrees of north latitude. From these four degrees of north latitude we sailed south-west, until we found ourselves at the Cape of Saint Augustin, which is in eight degrees of south latitude, having accomplished 1200 miles. And from Cape Saint Augustin we sailed south and by south-west 864 miles, where we found ourselves in twenty degrees of south latitude. From twenty degrees of south latitude, being at sea, we sailed 1500 miles south-west, when we found ourselves near the river, whose mouth is 108 miles wide, and lies in thirty-five degrees of the said south latitude. We named it the river of Saint Christopher.

From this river we sailed 1638 miles south-west by west, where we found ourselves at the point of the Lupi Marini, which is in forty-eight degrees of south latitude. And from the point of the Lupi Marini we sailed south-west 350 miles, where we found ourselves in the harbour of Saint Julian, and stayed there five months waiting for the sun to return towards us, because in June and July it appeared for only four hours each day.

From this harbour of Saint Julian, which is in fifty degrees, we departed on the 24th of August, 1520, and sailed westward a hundred miles, where we found a river to which we gave the name of River of Santa Cruz, and there we remained until the 18th of October. This river is in fifty degrees.

We departed thence on the 18th of October, and sailed along the coast 378 miles south-west by west, where we found ourselves in a strait, to which we gave the name Strait of Victoria, because the ship Victoria was the first that had seen it : some called it the Strait of Magalhaens, because our captain was named Fernando de Magalhaens. The mouth of this strait is in fifty-three degrees and a half, and we sailed through it 400 miles to the other mouth, which is in the same latitude of fifty-three degrees and a half.

We emerged from this strait on the 27th of November, 1520, and sailed between west and north-west 9858 miles, until we found ourselves upon the equinoctial line. In this course we found two uninhabited islands, the one of which was distant from the other 800 miles. To the first we gave the name of Saint Peter, and to the other the island of the Tiburones. Saint Peter is in eighteen degrees, the island of the Tiburones in fourteen degrees of south latitude.

From the equinoctial line we sailed between west and north-west 2046 miles, and discovered several islands between ten and twelve degrees of north latitude. In these islands there were many naked people as well men as women. We gave the islands the name of the Ladrones, because the people had robbed our ship : but it cost them very dear.

I shall not relate further the course that we made, because we lengthened it not a little. However, I will tell you that to go direct from these islands of the Ladrones to the Moluccas it is necessary to sail south-west a 1000 miles, and there occur many islands, to which we gave the name of the Archipelago of Saint Lazarus. A little further there are the islands of the Moluccas, of which there are five, namely, Ternate, Tidor, Molir, Machiam, Bachian. In Ternate, the Portuguese had built a very strong castle before I left. From the Molucca Islands to the islands of Banda, there are three hundred miles, and one goes thither by different courses, because there are many islands in between, and one must sail by sight. In these islands until you reach the islands of Banda, which are in four degrees and a half of south latitude, there are collected from thirty to forty thousand cantaros of nutmegs annually, and there is likewise collected much mastic; and if you wish to go to Calicut you must always sail amidst the islands as far as Malacca, which is distant from the Moluccas 2000 miles, and from Malacca to Calicut are 2000 miles more. From Calicut to Portugal there are 14,000 miles.

If from the islands of Banda you wish to round the Cape of Good Hope, you must sail between west and south-west until you find yourself in thirty four degrees and a half of south latitude, and from there you sail westward, always keeping a good look-out at the prow not to run aground on the said Cape of Good Hope or its neighbourhood. From this Cape of Good Hope one sails north-west by west 2400 miles, and there finds the island of Saint Helena, where Portuguese ships go to take in water and wood, and other things. This island is in sixteen degrees south latitude, and there is no habitation except that of a Portuguese man, who has but one hand and one foot, no nose, and no ears, and is called Fornam-lopem.

Sailing 1600 miles north-west from this island of Saint Helena you will find yourself upon the equinoctial line from which line you will sail 3534 miles north-west by north, until you find yourself in thirty-nine degrees north latitude. And if you wish to go from these thirty-nine degrees to Lisbon you will sail 950 miles eastward, where you will find the islands of the Azores, of which there are seven, namely, Terceira, San Jorge, Pico, Fayal, Graciosa, on the east, the island of Saint Michael, and the island of Saint Mary, all are between thirty-seven and forty degrees of north latitude. From the island of Terceira you will then sail eastward 1100 miles, where you will find yourself on the land of Lisbon.

CHAPTER 24

GASPAR CORREA'S ACCOUNT

The historian, Gaspar Correa gave descriptions in his "Lendas da India" of the voyage that bear evidence of a degree of first-hand information.

****

Ferdinand Magellan went to Castile to the port of Seville, where he married the daughter of a man of importance, with the design of navigating on the sea, because he was very learned in the art of pilots, which is that of the sphere. The emperor kept the House of Commerce in Seville, with the overseers of the treasury, with great powers, and much sea-faring traffic, and fleets for abroad.

Magellan, bold with his knowledge, and with the readiness which he had to annoy the King of Portugal, spoke to the overseers of this House of Commerce, and told them that Malacca, and Maluco, the islands in which cloves grew, belonged to the emperor on account of the demarcation drawn between them both [the Kings of Spain and Portugal] : for which reason the King of Portugal wrongfully possessed these lands : and that he would make this certain before all the doctors who might contradict him, and would pledge his head for it. The overseers replied to him, that they well knew that he was speaking truth, and that the emperor also knew it, but that the emperor had no navigation to that part, because he could not navigate through the sea within the demarcation of the King of Portugal. Magellan said to them : "If you would give me ships and men, I would show you navigation to those parts, without touching any sea or land of the King of Portugal; and if not, they might cut off his head." The overseers, much pleased at this, wrote it to the emperor, who answered them that he had pleasure in the speech, and would have much more with the deed; and that they were to do everything to carry out his service, and the affairs of the King of Portugal, which were not to be meddled with; rather than that everything should be lost. With this answer from the emperor, they spoke with Magellan, and became much more convinced by what he said, that he would navigate and show a course outside of the seas of the King of Portugal; and that if they gave him the ships he asked for, and men and artillery, he would fulfil what he had, said, and, would discover new lands which were in the demarcation of the emperor, from which he would bring gold, cloves, cinnamon, and other riches. The overseers hearing this, with a great desire to, render so great a service to the emperor as the discovery of this navigation, and to make this matter more certain, brought together pilots and men learned in the sphere, to dispute upon the matter with Magellan, who gave such reasons to all, that they agreed with what he said, and affirmed that he was a very learned man.

So the overseers at once made agreements with him, and arrangements, and powers, and regulations, which they sent to the emperor, who confirmed everything, reserving specially the navigation of the King of Portugal; thus he commanded and prohibited, and ordered that everything which Magellan asked for should be given him. On this account, Magellan went to Burgos, where the emperor was, and kissed his hand, and the emperor gave him a thousand cruzados alimony for the expenses of his wife whilst he was on his voyage, set down in the rolls of Seville, and he gave him power of life and death over all persons who went in the fleet, of which he should be Captain-Major, with regard to which he assigned him large powers.

So, on his return to Seville, they equipped for him five small ships, such as he asked for, equipped and armed as he chose, with four hundred men-at-arms, and they were laden with the merchandise which he asked for. The overseers told him to give the captaincies, with regard to which he excused himself, saying that he was new in the country and did not know the men; and that they should seek out men who would be good and faithful in the emperor's service, and who would rejoice to endure hardships in his service, and the bad life which they would have to go through in the voyage. The overseers were obliged to him for this, and held it to be good advice, and decided to inform the captains they might make, and the crews they might take, of the powers which he had received from the emperor. This they did, and they sought in Seville for trustworthy men for captains, who were Juan de Cartagena, Luis de Mendoça, Juan Serrano, Pero de Quesada. This fleet having been fitted out, and the crews paid for six months, he sailed from San Lucar de Barrameda in August of the year 1519. So he navigated to the Canary Islands, and took in water; whilst he was there a vessel arrived with letters from his father-in-law, in which he warned him to keep a good watch for his personal safety, because he had learned that the captains whom he took with him had said to their friends and relations, that if he annoyed them they would kill him, and would rise up against him. To this he replied, that he would do them no injuries so that they should have reason to act thus; and on that account he had not appointed them, but the overseers, who knew them, had given them; and whether they were good or bad, he would labour to do the service of the emperor, and for that they had offered their lives. The father-in-law showed this answer to the overseers, who greatly praised the good heart of Magellan.

He sailed from the Canaries of Tanarife, and made the Cape Verde, whence he crossed over to the coast of Brazil, and there entered a river which is named Janeiro. There went, as chief pilot, a Portuguese named Joan Lopes Carvalhinho, who had already been in this river, and took with him a son whom he had gotten there of a woman of the country. From this place they went on sailing until they reached the Cape of Santa Maria, which Joan of Lisbon had discovered in the year 1514; thence they went to the river San Julian. While they were there taking in water and wood, Juan de Cartagena, who was sub-Captain-Major, agreed with the other captains to rise up, saying that Magellan had got them betrayed and entrapped. As they understood that Gaspar de Quesada was a friend of Magellan's, Juan de Cartagena got into his boat at night, with twenty men, and went to the ship of Gaspar Quesada, and went in to speak to him, and took him prisoner, and made a relation of his captain of the ship, in order that all three might go at once to board Magellan and kill him, and after that they would reduce the other ship of Joan Serrano, and would take the money and goods, which they would hide, and would return to the emperor, and would tell him that Magellan had got them entrapped and deceived, having broken faith with his instructions, since he was navigating in seas, and countries of the King of Portugal : for which deed they would get first a safe conduct from the emperor. So they arranged matters for their treason, which turned out ill for them.

Magellan had some suspicion of this matter, and before this should happen, he sent his skiff to the ships to tell the captains that the masters were to arrange their ships for beaching them to careen them; and with this pretext he warned a servant of his to notice what the captains answered. When this skiff came to the revolted ships they did not let it come alongside, saying that they would not execute any orders except those of Juan de Cartagena, who was their Captain-Major. The skiff having returned with this answer, Magellan spoke to Ambrosio Fernandes, his chief constable, a valiant man, and gave him orders what he was to do, and to go secretly armed; and he sent a letter to Luis de Mendoça by him with six men in the skiff, whom the chief constable selected.

And the current set towards the ships, and Magellan ordered his master to bend a long hawser, with which he might drop down to the ships if it suited him. All being thus arranged, the skiff went, and coming alongside of Luiz de Mendoça, they would not let him come on board. So the chief constable said to the captain that it was weakness not to bid him enter, as he was one man alone who was bringing a letter. Upon which the captain bade him enter. He came on board, and giving him the letter, took him in his arms, shouting : "On behalf of the emperor, you, are arrested !" At this the men of the skiff came on board with their swords drawn; then the chief constable cut the throat of Luis de Mendoça with a dagger, for he held him thrown down under him, for so Magellan had given him orders. Upon this a tumult arose, and Magellan, hearing it; ordered the hawser to be paid out, and with his ship dropped down upon the other ships, with his men under arms, and the artillery in readiness.

On reaching the ship of Mendoça, he ordered six men to be hung at the yard-arms, who had risen up against the chief constable, and these were seized upon by the sailors of the ship, of which he at once made captain, Duarte Barbosa, a Portuguese, and a friend of his : and he ordered the corpse of Mendoça to be hung up by the feet, that they might see him from the other ships. He then ordered Barbosa to prepare the men for going and boarding one of the other ships; and to avoid doing the harm which it was in its power to have done, and since he was a Portuguese, and the crews belonged to the emperor, he used a stratagem, and spoke secretly to a sailor, whom he trusted, who fled to the, ship of Cartagena, where, at night when the current set for Magellan's ship, which was astern, the sailor seeing his opportunity, cut the cable or loosed the ship of Cartagena, so that it drifted upon that of Magellan, who came up, shouting : "Treason ! Treason !" Upon which he entered the ship of Cartagena, and took him and his men prisoners, and made captain of the ship one Alvaro de Mesquita, whom Cartagena had arrested and put in irons, because he found fault with him for the mutiny which he was making. Seeing this, the other ship at once surrendered. He ordered Cartagena to be quartered, having him publicly cried as a traitor; and the body of Luis de Mendoça also was quartered; and he ordered the quarters and the executed men to be set on shore, spitted on poles. So the Castilians had great fear of him, for he kept the mutineers prisoners in irons, and set to the pumps, during three months that he remained in this river, in which he careened and refitted his ships very well.

When he was about to set sail, he ordered the prisoners to be set at liberty, and pardoned them, and he sent them to go along the shore, following the bank of the river until they found the headland from which they could see the sea on the other side; and whoever returned to him with this news he would give him a hundred ducats as a reward for good news. These men went for more than forty leagues, and returned without news; and they brought back two men, fifteen spans high, from a village that they found. He then sent Serrano, because his vessel was the smallest, to go along the river to discover its extremity; and he went with a strong current, which carried him without wind. And, going along thus, his ship grounded on some rocks, on which it was lost, and the boat returned laden with the crew. Magellan sent the boats thither, and they saved everything, so that only the hull was lost. Then he ordered two priests, who had taken part in the mutiny, to be set on shore, and a brother of Cartagena, whom he pardoned at he petition of Mesquita, and he left them thus banished.

Then he sailed from the river and ran along the coast until he reached a river, to which they gave the name of Victoria, and which had high land on either side. From this river Mesquita's ship ran away, and it was not known whether they had killed him, or if he had gone of his own accord; but an astrologer and diviner told him that the captain was a prisoner, and that they were returning to Castile, but that the emperor would do them an injury.

Then Magellan, with the three ships which he had, entered the river, through which he ran for more than a hundred leagues, and came out on the other side into the open sea, where he had a stern wind from the east, with which they ran for more than five months without lowering their sails, and they fetched some uninhabited islands, in one of which they found some savages, who lived in huts underground. They went to another island where they gave them gold for its weight of iron, by which means they collected much gold : the people also were of a good disposition, and had a king. They were well governed people, who were at war with other neighbours who were more powerful than themselves; for which reason the king became Christian, with all his people, in order that Magellan might assist him against his enemies. This, Magellan offered to do, and with his armed men, and the people of the country, he went against the enemy, of whom he killed many, and burned a village. The enemy got assistance from others, and many came to fight with Magellan, who defeated them, and the struggle was a severe one. They acted with cunning, for they had placed ambuscades of men hidden in the bush, who, seeing the Castilians wearied, came out against them and killed many, and another ambuscade came out of the bush to seize the boats, which were on the beach without men : then the king came out, and fought with them, and defended the boats, and brought-off the men.

The king who had fled, seeing himself defeated, plotted treachery with the Christian king, and made an agreement with him to give him his daughter in marriage, and plighted his troth to him, that when he died, for he was already old, all would remain to him, and they would always live as friends; because the Castilians would depart, and if he did not act thus he would always make war on him : and this was with the condition that he was to find him means for killing the Castilians. And the Christian king, like a brutal man, consented to the treachery, and prepared a great feast and banquet for carrying it out, to which he invited Magellan, who went to the banquet with thirty men, of the most honourable and well dressed : while they were enjoying themselves at the banquet, the armed enemies entered, and killed Magellan, and all the Castilians, and none of them escaped, and they stripped Serrano, and dragging him along, brought him to the beach, where they executed him, and killed him thrown down on the ground.

Those who were in the ships, seeing the misfortune on shore, which the sailors who had gone in the boats related to them, raised up from among them as captain, Carvalhinho, the pilot of the flag-ship, whom all obeyed. He ordered one of the ships, which was very leaky, to be stripped, and set fire to it in the midst of the sea, so that the people on shore should not profit by the iron, and he made captain of the ship of Serrano one Gonzalo Gomez d'Espinosa, who was a relation of the astrologer, who also died with Magellan, and did not divine the evil that befel him.

The two ships departed thence, running between many islands, and they went to one which had much very fine cinnamon. From this place they went running through many islands to the island of Borneo, where they found in the port many merchant junks from all the parts of Malacca, which made frequent visits to Borneo. Here Carvalhinho sent a present to the king of scarlet cloth, and coloured silks, and other things, with which the king was much pleased, and he did him, great honour, and gave him leave and safe conduct to remain on shore for twenty days, for such was their custom to give to new people, the first time that they came to their port, in which they could buy and sell freely as much as they pleased. However, the king, knowing how much goods the ships contained, got up a plot to kill them, and take the ships. This treachery was concerted by the king with the Javanese who were in the port in large junks; and for this object the king showed great honour to those who went on shore, and sent refreshments to the ships, and leave to remain in the port as long as they pleased. Carvalhinho became suspicious at this, and ordered good watch to be kept day and night, and did not allow more than one or two men to go ashore. The king perceiving this sent to beg Carvalhinho to send him his son who had brought the present, because his little children who had seen him, were crying to see him. He sent him, very well dressed, with four men, who, on arriving where the king was, were ordered by him to be arrested. When Carvalhinho knew this he raised his moorings, and with armed men went to board a junk which was filled with many people and ready to sail. They entered this junk and plundered much gold and rich stuffs, and captured, a son of the King of Luzon, who was captain of the junk and of three others which were in the port, and who had come in them to marry a daughter of this King of Borneo. They found in this junk valuable things of gold and jewellery which he had brought for his wedding; and they found there three girls of extreme beauty, whom Carvalhinho took care of, saying that he would take them to the emperor : at which all rejoiced. However, he did not act thus, but slept with them, so that the Castilians were near killing him; but he divided with the Castilians so liberally that they became friends; for he agreed with the bridegroom, that he and his people should escape by night, and for that should give him much wealth of precious stones, and by night they got away by swimming; and Carvalhinho pretended to have been asleep, and woke up complaining of the watch. However, the Castilians understood the deceit, and took Carvalhinho and put him in irons, and took from him all he had, and raised up as captain one Juan Bautista, master of the ship, because he understood pilot's work.

Thence they sailed and went to Maluco, Ternate, and Tidore, where they took to the kings the presents which Magellan had set apart for them. They paid them great honour, and received them hospitably, for they also gave to their ministers; and to the kings they gave an embassage on the part of the emperor, relating to them his magnificence, so that both soon obeyed him, and did homage as vassals for ever; and they established trade and prices for buying and selling, and established factories on shore, and began to collect cloves, and very much was brought to them, because the Castilians gave what they asked, for they had a superfluity of merchandise; thus they became lords of the land. As the ships were much injured, they patched them up a little, the best they could, and hastened to fill both ships with cargo, which they did in one month. When they were about to sail there came to the Castilians a Portuguese, named Juan de la Rosa, who had come to Ternate, saying he was a pilot, and would take them to Castile, upon which they agreed with him to give him fifty quintals of cloves in each ship, because he said he would take them to the island of Banda, which had more riches than Maluco. So the Castilians rejoiced greatly at taking this man back to the emperor, for the greater certainty as to their discovery. This Juan de la Rosa warned the Castilians that they would come from India and seek for them, and kill the all, for this was spoken of in India. To this the Castilians gave much credit, and on that account did him great honour. They settled with the King of Tidore to leave with him a factor with the merchandise, which they had, because many ships would soon come, sent by the emperor; for which reason they should have much cloves collected together. They then set sail, making de la Rosa captain of the ship of Carvalhinho.

When they were at sea they freed him from his irons, from the need they felt for his navigation, and they went to the island of Banda, where they restored to Carvalhinho his captaincy, and they went to Banda, where they took samples of nutmeg and mace, as they had nowhere to take in cargo of it. All having been consulted, they set sail to make for the Cape of Good Hope, and navigate thence to Castile, for they did not dare take any other course. Setting sail with this design, they met with hard weather, with which the ship of Carvalhinho put into port, and that of la Rosa continued her course. Carvalhinho put into Maluco, where he discharged half the ship's cargo, and heeled her over, and repaired her as well as possible; this he did in twenty days, and again set to taking in cargo and departing; but he fell ill with the labour, and died on setting sail. They made Gonzalo Gomez d'Espinosa captain of the ship again, and he, by the instructions of Carvalhinho, took a course to search for the river through which they had come; but when at sea, the ship again took in so much water, that they ran before the wind to beach her on the first land they made, which was in Batochina, where they beached the ship, and saved from her no great quantity of goods.

Whilst they were at this juncture D. Gracia Anriques arrived at Maluco, with a ship to take in cloves, which came from Malaca, and learning how these Castilians were there be sent to call them under his safe conduct, that they should all come, because if they did not he would hold them as enemies, and would go at once and fetch them. The Castilians therefore, constrained by fortune, went to where D. Gracia was, like as men who were lost, so that D. Gracia had compassion upon them, and gave them a good reception, and supplied them with necessaries, and having laden his ship, he embarked them all with him, and they were more than thirty, and he took them to Malaca, where

Jorge d'Albuquerque was captain, who ordered the factor to give them provisions for their maintenance, and in the monsoon to send them to India, where D. Duarte [de Meneses] was governor. He commanded those who chose to be written down in the rolls for pay, and he forbade the ships of the kingdom to take them, that they might not return to Castile; and in fact all died, only Gonzalo Gomes d'Espinosa passed to Portugal in the year 1525, and he was made a prisoner in Lisbon, and set at liberty by a letter which the empress sent to the king.

The other ship followed its course, so that la Rosa made the Cape of Good Hope, and while she was going near the land Pero Coresma, who was going to India in a small ship, met her, and spoke her; and he was told she belonged to the emperor, and came from Maluco, and it did not come into his understanding to send her to the bottom, that she might not return to Castile, and the ship entered the watering place of Saldanha, and thence fetched Cape Verde, where they went ashore to get wood and water; there some Portuguese, learning that the ship came from Maluco, took the boat when it came ashore, with twenty Castilians; and as there was no ship in the port they got into a boat to go and capture the ship but the ship seeing the boat come with armed men, for the arms glittered, weighed and set sail for Cape St. Vincent, and thence entered San Lucar with thirteen men, for now there were no more, and it arrived in the year 1521. From Cape Verde they wrote to the king about the Castilians, who remained there; the king ordered that they should let them go till they died, but never to allow them to embark for any port; and so it was done.

CHAPTER 25

ACCOUNT OF THE "GENOESE PILOT"

A first hand account of the voyage was written by the "Genoese pilot", who almost certainly was neither Genoese nor a pilot because the manuscript is written in remarkably pure Portuguese and bears no evidence of having been written by a pilot, and because no Genoese sailed as pilot in the fleet.

****

Navigation and voyage that Fernando De Magalhães made from Seville to Maluco in the year 1519. (By a Genoese pilot)

He sailed from Seville on the 10th day of August of the said year, and remained at the bar until the 21st day of September, and as soon as he got outside, he steered to the south west to make the island of Tenerife, and they reached the said island on the day of St. Michael, which was the 29th of September. Thence he made his course to fetch the Cape Verde islands, and they passed between the islands and the Cape without sighting either the one or the other. Having got as far as this neighbourhood, he shaped his course so as to make for Brazil, and as soon as they sighted the other coast of Brazil, he steered to the south-east along the coast as far as Cabo-frio, which is in twenty-three degrees south latitude; and from this cape he steered to the west, a matter of thirty leagues, to make the Rio de Janeiro, which is in the same latitude as Cabo-frio, and they entered the said Rio on the day of St. Lucia, which was the 13th December, in which place they took in wood, and they remained there until the first octave of Christmas, which was the 26th of December of the same year.

They sailed from this Rio de Janeiro on the 26th December, and navigated along the coast to make the Cape of St. Maria, which is in thirty-four and two thirds degrees; as soon as they sighted it, they made their course west-northwest, thinking they would find a passage for their voyage, and they found that they had got into a great river of fresh water, to which they gave the name of river of St. Christopher, and it is in this thirty-four degrees, and they remained in it till the 2nd of February, 1520.

He sailed from this river of St. Christopher on the 2nd of the said month of February; they navigated along the said coast, and further on to the south they discovered a point which is in the same river more to the south, to which they gave the name of Point St. Antony; it is in thirty-six degrees, hence they ran to the south-west, a matter of twenty-five leagues, and made another cape that they named Cape St. Apelonia, which is in thirty-six degrees; thence they navigated to the west-south-west to some shoals, which they named Shoals of the Currents, which are in thirty-nine degrees; and thence they navigated out to sea, and lost sight of land for a matter of two or three days, when they again made for the land, and they came to a bay, which they entered, and ran within it the whole day, thinking that there was an outlet for Maluco, and when night came they found that it was quite closed up, and in the same night they again stood out by the way that they had come in. This bay is in thirty-four degrees; they name it the island of St. Matthew.

They navigated from this island of St.Matthew along the coast until they reached another bay, where they caught many sea-wolves and birds; to this they gave the name of "Bay of Labours"; it is in thirty-seven degrees; here they were near losing the flag-ship in a storm. Thence they navigated along the said coast, and arrived on the last day of March of the year 1520 at the Port of St. Julian, which is in forty-nine and one-third degrees, and here they wintered, and found the day a little more or less than seven hours.

In this port three of the ships rose up against the Captain-Major, their captains saying that they intended to take him to Castile in arrest, as he was taking them all to destruction. Here, through the exertions of the said Captain-Major, and the assistance and favour of the foreigners whom he carried with him, the Captain-Major went to the said three ships which were-already mentioned, and there the captain of one of them was killed, who was treasurer of the whole fleet, and named Luis de Mendoça; he was killed in his own ship by stabs with a dagger by the chief constable of the fleet, who was sent to do this by Fernando de

Magalhães in a boat with certain men. The said three ships having thus been recovered, five days later Fernando de Magalhães ordered Gaspar de Queixada to be decapitated and quartered; he was captain of one of the ships, and was one of those who had mutinied.

In this port they refitted the ship. Here the Captain-Major made Alvaro de Mesquita, a Portuguese, captain of one of the ships the captain of which had been killed. There sailed from this port on the 24th of August four ships, for the smallest of the ships had been already lost; he had sent it to reconnoitre, and the weather had been heavy, and had cast it ashore, where all the crew had been recovered along with the merchandise, artillery and fittings of the ship. They remained in this port, in which they wintered, five months and twenty-four days, and they were seventy degrees less ten minutes to the southward.

They sailed on the 24th day of the month of August of the said year from this port of St. Julian and navigated a matter of twenty leagues along the coast, and so they entered a river which was called Santa Cruz, which is in fifty degrees, where they took in goods and as much as they could obtain : the crew of the lost ship were already distributed among the other ships, for they had returned by land to where Fernando de Magalhães was, and they continued collecting the goods which had remained there during August and up to the 18th September, and there they took in water and much fish which they caught in this river; and in the other, where they wintered, there were people like savages, and the men are from nine to ten spans in height, very well made; they have not got houses, they only go about from one place to another with their flocks, and eat meat nearly raw : they are all of them archers and kill many animals with arrows, and with the skins they make clothes, that is to say, they make the skins very supple, and fashion them after the shape of the body, as well as they can, then they cover themselves with them, and fasten them by a belt round the waist. When they do not wish to be clothed from the waist upwards, they let that half fall which is above the waist, and the garment remains hanging down from the belt which they have girt round them. They wear shoes which cover them four inches above the ankle, full of straw inside to keep their feet warm. They do not possess any iron, nor any other ingenuity of weapons, only they make the points of their arrows with flints, and so also the knives with which they cut, and the adze and awls with which they cut and stitch their shoes and clothes. They are very agile people, and do no harm, and thus they follow their flocks : wherever night finds them there they sleep; they carry their wives along with them with all the chattels which they possess. The women are very small and carry heavy burdens on their backs; they wear shoes and clothes just like the men. Of these men they obtained three or four and brought them in the ships, and they all died except one, who went to Castile in a ship which went thither .

They sailed from this river of Santa Cruz on the 18th of October : they continued navigating along the coast until the 21st day of the same month, October, when they discovered a cape, to which they gave the name of Cape of the Virgins, because they sighted it on the day of the eleven thousand virgins; it is in fifty-two degrees, a little more or less, and from this cape a matter of two or three leagues distance, we found ourselves at the mouth of a strait. We sailed along the said coast within that strait which they had reached the mouth of : they entered in it a little and anchored. Fernando de Magalhães sent to discover what there was further in, and they found three channels, that is to say, two more in a southerly direction, and one traversing the country in the direction of Maluco, but at that time this was not yet known, only the three mouths were seen. The boats went thither, and brought back word, and they set sail and anchored at these mouths of the channels, and Fernando de Magalhães sent two ships to learn what there was within, and these ships went : one returned to the Captain-Major, and the other, of which Alvaro de Mesquita was captain, entered into one of the bays which was to the south, and did not return any more.

Fernan de Magalhães seeing that it did not come back, set sail, and the next day he did not choose to make for the bays, and went to the south, and took another which runs north-west and south-east, and a quarter west and east. He left letters in the place from which he sailed, so that if the other ship returned, it might make the course which he left prescribed. After this they entered into the channel, which at some places has a width of three leagues, and two, and one, and in some places half a league, and he went through it as long as it was daylight, and anchored when it was night : and he sent the boats, and the ships went after the boats, and they brought news that there was an outlet, for they already saw the great sea on the other side; on which account Fernando de Magalhães ordered much artillery to be fired for rejoicing; and before they went forth from this strait they found two islands, the first one larger, and the other nearer towards the outlet is the smaller one : and they went out between these islands and the coast on the southern side, as it was deeper than on the other side. This strait is a hundred leagues in length to the outlet; that outlet and the entrance are in fifty-two degrees latitude. They made a stay in this strait from the 21st October to the 26th of November, which makes thirty-six days of the said year of 1520, and as soon as they went out from the strait to sea, they made their course, for the most part, to west-north-west, when they found that their needles varied to the north-west almost two-fourths, and after they had navigated thus for many days, they found an island in a little more or less than eighteen degrees, or nineteen degrees, and also another, which was in from thirteen to fourteen degrees, and this in south latitude; they are uninhabited.

They ran on until they reached the line, when Fernan de Magalhães said that now they were in the neighbourhood of Maluco, as he had information that there were no provisions at Maluco, he said that he would go in a northerly direction as far as ten or twelve degrees, and they reached to as far as thirteen degrees north, and in this latitude they navigated to the west, and ¼ south-west, a matter of a hundred leagues, where on the 6th of March, 1521, they fetched two islands inhabited by many people, and they anchored at one of them, which is in twelve degrees north; and the inhabitants are people of little truth, and they did not take precautions against them until they saw that they were taking away the skiff of the flagship, and they cut the rope with which it was made fast, and took it ashore without their being able to prevent it. They gave this island the name of Thieves' Island (dos ladrões).

Fernando de Magalhães seeing that the skiff was lost, set sail, as it was already night, tacking about until the next day; as soon as it was morning they anchored at the place where they had seen the skiff carried off to, and he ordered two boats to be got ready with a matter of fifty or sixty men, and he went ashore in person, and burned the whole village, and they killed seven or eight persons, between men and women, and recovered the skiff, and returned to the ships; and while they were there they saw forty or fifty paros come, which came from the same land, and brought much refreshments.

Fernan de Magalhães would not make any further stay, and at once set sail, and ordered the course to be steered west, and a quarter south-west; and so they made land, which is in barely eleven degrees. This land is an island, but he would not touch at this one, and they went to touch at another further on which appeared first. Fernando de Magalhães sent a boat ashore to observe the nature of the island; when the boat reached land, they saw from the ships two paráos come out from behind the point; then they called back their boat. The people of the paraos seeing that the boat was returning to the ships, turned back the paraos, and the boat reached the ships, which at once set sail for another island very near to this island, which is in ten degrees, and they gave it the name of the island of Good Signs, because they found some gold in it.

Whilst they were thus anchored at this island, there came to them two paráos, and brought them fowls and coconuts, and told them that they had already seen there other men like them, from which they presumed that these might be Lequios or Mogores; a nation of people who have this name, or Chiis; and thence they set sail, and navigated further on amongst many islands, to which they gave the name of the Valley Without Peril, and also St. Lazarus, and they ran on to another island twenty leagues from that from which they sailed, which is in ten degrees, and came to anchor at another island, which is named Macangor, which is in nine degrees; and in this island they were very well received, and they placed a cross in it.

This king conducted them thence a matter of thirty leagues to another island named Cabo, which is in ten degrees, and in this island Fernando de Magalhães did what he pleased with the consent of the country, and in one day eight hundred people became Christian, on which account Fernan de Magalhães desired that the other kings, neighbours to this one, should become subject to this who had become Christian : and these did not choose to yield such obedience. Fernan de Magalhães seeing that, got ready one night with his boats, and burned the villages of those who would not yield the said obedience; and a matter of ten or twelve days after this was done he sent to a village about half a league from that which he had burned, which is named Matam, and which is also an island, and ordered them to send him at once three goats, three pigs, three loads of rice, and three loads of millet for provisions for the ships; they replied that of each article which he sent to ask them three of, they would send to him by twos, and if he was satisfied with this they would at once comply, if not, it might be as he pleased, but that they would not give it. Because they did not choose to grant what he demanded of them, Fernan de Magalhães ordered three boats to be equipped with a matter of fifty or sixty men, and went against the said place, which was on the 28th day of April, in the morning; there they found many people, who might well be as many as three thousand or four thousand men, who fought with such a good will that the said Fernan de Magalhães was killed there, with six of his men, in the year 1521.

When Fernan de Magalhães was dead the Christians got back to the ships, where they thought fit to make two captains and governors whom they should obey; and having done this, they took counsel [and decided] that the two captains should go ashore where the people had turned Christians to ask for pilots to take them to Borneo, and this was on the first day of May of the said year; when the two captains went, being agreed upon what had been said, the same people of the country who had become Christians, armed themselves against them, and whilst they reached the shore let them land insecurity as they had done before. Then they attacked them, and killed the two captains and twenty-six gentlemen, and the other people who remained got back to the boats, and returned to the ships, and finding themselves again without captains they agreed, in as much as the principal persons were killed, that one Joam Lopez, who was the chief treasurer, should be Captain-Major of the fleet, and the chief constable of the fleet should be captain of one of the ships; he was named Gonzalo Vaz Despinosa.

Having done this they set sail, and ran about twenty-five leagues with three ships, which they still possessed; they then mustered, and found that they were altogether one hundred and eight men in all these three ships, and many of them were wounded and sick, on which account they did not venture to navigate the three ships, and thought it would be well to burn one of them - the one that should be most suitable for that purposes - and to take into the two ships those that remained : this they did out at sea, out of sight of any land. While they did this many paraos came to speak to them; and navigating amongst the islands, for in that neighbourhood there are a great many, they did not understand one another, for they had no interpreter, for he had been killed with Fernan de Magalhães. Sailing further on amongst islets they came to anchor at an island which is named Carpyam, where there is gold enough, and this island is in fully eight degrees.

Whilst at anchor in this port of Capyam, they had speech with the inhabitants of the island, and made peace with them; and Carvalho, who was Captain-Major, gave them the boat of the ship which had been burnt : this island has threes islets in the offing; here they took in some refreshments, and sailed further on to west south-west, and fell in with another island, which is named Caram, and is in eleven degrees; from this they went on further to west south-west, and fell in with a large island, and ran along the coast of this island to the north-east, and reached as far as nine degrees and a half, where they went ashore one day, with the boats equipped to seek for provisions, for in the ships there was now not more than for eight days. On reaching shore the inhabitants would not suffer them to land, and shot at them with arrows of cane hardened in the fire, so that they returned to the ships.

Seeing this, they agreed to go to another island, where they had had some dealings, to see if they could get some provisions. Then they met with a contrary wind, and going about a league in the direction in which they wished to go, they anchored, and whilst at anchor they saw that people on shore were hailing them to go thither; they went there with the boats, and as they were speaking to those people by signs, for they did not understand each other otherwise, a man at arms, named Joam de Campos, told them to let him go on shore, since there were no provisions in the ships, and it might be that they would obtain some means of getting provisions; and that if the people killed him, they would not lose much with him, for God would take thought of his soul; and also if he found provisions, and if they did not kill him, he would find means for bringing them to the ships and they thought well of this.

So he went on shore, and as soon as he reached it, the inhabitants received him, and took him into the interior the distance of a league, and when he was in the village all the people came to see him, and they gave him food, and entertained him well, especially when they saw that he ate pig's flesh; because in this island they had dealings with the Moors of Borneo, and because the country and people were greedy, they made them neither eat pigs nor bring them up in the country. This country is called Dyguasam, and is in nine degrees.

The said Christian seeing that he was favoured and well treated by the inhabitants, gave them to understand by his signs that they should carry provisions to the ships, which would be well paid for. In the country there was nothing except rice not pounded. Then the people set to pounding rice all the night, and when it was morning they took the rice and the said Christian, and came to the ships, where they did them great honour, and took in the rice and paid them, and they returned on shore. This man being already set on shore, inhabitants of another village, a little further on, came to the ships and told them to go to their village, and that they would give them much provisions for their money; and as soon as the said man whom they had sent arrived, they set sail and went to anchor at the village of those who had come to call them, which was named Vay Palay Cucara Canbam, where Carvalho made peace with the king of the country, and they settled the price of the rice, and they gave them two measures of rice which weighed one hundred and fourteen pounds for three fathoms of linen stuff of Britanny; they took there as much rice as they wanted, and goats and pigs, and whilst they were at this place there came a Moor, who had been in the village of Dyguaçam, which belongs to the Moors of Borneo, as has been said above, and after that he went to his country.

While they were at anchor near this village of Diguaçam, there came to them a parao in which there was a negro named Bastiam, who asked for a flag and a passport for the governor of Diguaçam, and they gave him all this and other things as a present. They asked the said Bastiam, who spoke Portuguesa sufficiently well, since he had been in Maluco, where he became a Christian, if he would go with them and show them Borneo; he said he would very willingly, and when the departure arrived he hid himself, and seeing that he did not come, they set sail from this port of Diguaçam on the 21st day of July to seek for Borneo. As they set sail there came to them a parao, which was coming to the port of Diguaçam, and they took it, and in it they took three Moors, who said they were pilots, and that they would take them to Borneo.

Having got these Moors, they steered along this island to the south-west, and, fell in with two islands at its extremity, and passed between them; that on the north side is named Bolyna, and that on the south Bamdym. Sailing to the west south-west a matter of fourteen leagues, they fell in with a white bottom, which was a shoal below the water, and the black men they carried with them told them to draw near to the coast of the island, as it was deeper there, and that was more in the direction of Borneo, for from that neighbourhood the island of Borneo could already be sighted. This same day they reached and anchored at some islands, to which they gave the name of islets of St. Paul, which was a matter of two and a half or three leagues from the great island of Borneo, and they were in about seven degrees at the south side of these islands. In the island of Borneo there is an exceedingly great mountain, to which they gave the name of Mount St. Paul; and from thence they navigated along the coast of Borneo to the south-west, between an island and the island of Borneo itself; and they went forward on the same course and reached the neighbourhood of Borneo, and the Moors whom they had with them told them that there was Borneo, and the wind did not suffer them to arrive thither, as it was contrary. They anchored at an island which is there, and which may be eight leagues from Borneo.

Close to this island is another which has many myrobolans, and the next day they set sail for the other island, which is nearer to the port of Borneo; and going along thus they saw so many shoals that they anchored, and sent the boats ashore in Borneo, and they took the aforesaid Moorish pilots on shore, and there went a Christian with them; and the boats went to set them on land, from whence they had to go to the city of Borneo, which was three leagues off, and there they were taken before the Shahbender of Borneo, and he asked what people they were, and for what they came in the ships; and they were presented to the King of Borneo with the Christian. As soon as the boats had set the said men on shore, they sounded in order to see if the ships could come in closer : and during this they saw three junks which were coming from the port of Borneo from the said city out to sea, and as soon as they saw the ships they returned inshore : continuing to sound, they found the channel by which the port is entered; they then set sail, and entered this channel, and being within the channel they anchored, and would not go further in until they received a message from the shore, which arrived next day with two paraos : these carried certain swivel guns of metal, and a hundred men in each parao, and they brought goats and fowls, and two cows, and figs, and other-fruit, and told them to enter further in opposite the islands which were near there, which was the true berth; and from this position to the city there might be three or four leagues. Whilst thus at anchor they established peace, and settled that they should trade in what there was in the country, especially wax, to which they answered that they would willingly sell all that there was in the country for their money. This port of Borneo is in eight degrees.

For the answer thus received from the King they sent him a present by Gonzalo Mendes Despinosa, captain of the ship Victoria, and, the King accepted the present, and gave to all of them China stuffs : and when there had passed twenty or twenty-three days that they were there trading with the people of the island, and had got five men on shore in the city itself, there came to anchor at the bar, close to them, five junks, at the hour of vespers, and they remained there that evening and the night until next day in the morning, when they saw coming from the city two hundred paraos, some under sail, others rowing. Seeing in this manner the five junks and the paraos, it seemed to them that there might be treachery, and they set sail for the junks, and as soon as the crews of the junks saw them under sail, they also set sail and made off where the wind best served them; and they overhauled one of the junks with the boats, and took it with twenty-seven men; and the ships went and anchored abreast of the island of the Myrololans, with the junk made fast to the poop of the flagship, and the paraos returned to shore, and when night came there came on a squall from the west in which the said junk went to the bottom alongside the flagship, without being able to receive any assistance from it.

Next day in the morning they saw a sail, and went to it and took it; this was a great junk in which the son of the King of Lucam came as captain, and had with him ninety men, and as soon as they took them they sent some of them to the King of Borneo; and they sent him word by these men to send the Christians whom they had got there, who were seven men, and they would give him all the people whom they had taken in the junk; on which account the King sent two men of the seven whom he had got there in a parao, and they again sent him word to send the five men who still remained, and they would send all the people whom they had got from the junk. They waited two days for the answer, and there came no message; then they took thirty men from the junk, and put them into a parao belonging to the junk, and sent them to the King of Borneo, and set sail with fourteen men of those they had taken and three women; and they steered along the coast of the said island to the north-east, returning backwards; and they again passed between the islands and the great island of Borneo, where the flagship grounded on a point of the island, and so remained more than four hours, and the tide turned and it got off, by which it was seen clearly that the tide was of twenty-four hours .

Whilst making the aforesaid course the wind shifted to north-east, and they stood out to sea, and they saw a sail coming, and the ships anchored, and the boats went to it and took it; it was a small junk and carried nothing but coconuts; and they took in water and wood, and set sail along the coast of the island to the north-east, until they reached the extremity of the said island, and met with another small island, where they overhauled the ships. They arrived at this island on the day of our Lady of August, and in it they found a very good point for beaching the ships, and they gave it the name of Port St. Mary of August, and it is in fully seven degrees.

As soon as they had taken these precautions they set sail and steered to the south-west until they sighted the island which is named Fagajam, and this is a course of thirty-eight to forty leagues : and as soon as they sighted this island they steered to the south-west, and again made an island which is called Seloque, and they had information that there were many pearls there : and when they had already sighted that island the wind shifted to a headwind, and they could not fetch it by the course they were sailing, and it seemed to them that it might be in six degrees. This same night they arrived at the island of Quipe, and ran along it to the south-east, and passed between it and another island called Tamgym, and always running along the coast of the said island, and going thus, they fell in with a parao laden with sago in loaves, which is bread made of a tree which is named cajare, which the people of that country eat as bread. This parao carried twenty-one men, and the chief of them had been in Maluco in the house of Francisco Serram, and having gone further along this island they arrived in sight of some islands which are named Semrryn; they are in five degrees, a little more or less. The inhabitants of this land came to see the ships, and so they had speech of one another, and an old man of these people told them that he would conduct them to Maluco.

In this manner, having fixed a time with the old man, an agreement was made with him, and they gave him a certain price for this; and when the next day came, and they were to depart, the old man intended to escape, and they understood it, and took him and others who were with him, and who also said that they knew pilot's work, and they set sail; and as soon as the inhabitants saw them go they fitted out to go after them : and of these paraos there did not reach the ships more than two, and these reached so near that they shot arrows into the ships, and the wind was fresh and they could not come up with them. At midnight of that day they sighted some islands, and they steered more towards them; and next day they saw land, which was an island; and at night following that day they found themselves very close to it, and when night fell the wind calmed and the currents drew them very much inshore; there the old pilot cast himself into the sea, and betook himself to land.

Sailing thus forward, after one of the pilots had fled, they sighted another island and arrived close to it, and another Moorish pilot said that Maluco was still further on, and navigating thus, the next day in the morning they sighted three high mountains, which belonged to a nation of people whom they called the Salabos; and then they saw a small island where they anchored to take in some water, and because they feared that in Maluco they would not be allowed to take it in; and they omitted doing so, because the Moorish pilot told them that there were some four hundred men in that island, and that they were all very bad, and might do them some injury, as they were men of little faith; and that he would give them no such advice as to go to that island; and also because Maluco, which they were seeking, was now near, and that its kings were good men, who gave a good reception to all sorts of men in their country; and while still in this neighbourhood they saw the islands themselves of Maluco, and for rejoicing they fired all the artillery, and they arrived at the island on the 8th of November of 1521, so that they spent from Seville to Maluco two years, two months and twenty-eight days, for they sailed on the 10th of August of 1519.

As soon as they arrived at the island of Tydor, which is in half a degree, the King thereof did them great honour, which could not be exceeded : there they treated with the King for their cargo, and the King engaged to give them a cargo and whatever there was in the country for their money, and they settled to give for the bahar of cloves fourteen ells of yellow cloth of twenty-seven tem, which are worth in Castile a ducat the ell; of red cloth of the same kind ten ells; they also gave thirty ells of Brittany linen cloth, and for each of these quantities they received a bahar of cloves, likewise for thirty knives eight bahars : having thus settled all the above mentioned prices, the inhabitants of the country gave them information that further on, in another island near, there was a Portuguese man. This island might be two leagues distant, and it was named Targatell; this man was the chief person of Maluco; there we now have got a fortress. They then wrote letters to the said Portuguese, to come and speak with them, to which he answered that he did not dare, because the King of the country forbade it; that if they obtained permission from the King he would come at once; this permission they soon got, and the Portuguese came to speak with them. They gave him an account of the prices which they had settled, at which he was amazed, and said that on that account the King had ordered him not to come, as they did not know the truth about the prices of the country; and whilst they were thus taking in cargo there arrived the King of Baraham, which is near there, and said that he wished to be a vassal of the King of Castile, and also that he had got four hundred bahars of cloves, and that he had sold it to the King of Portugal, and that they had bought it, but that he had not yet delivered it, and if they wished for it, he would give it all to them; to which the captains answered that if he brought it to them, and came with it, they would buy it, but otherwise not. The King, seeing that they did not wish to take the cloves, asked them for a flag and a letter of safe conduct, which they gave him, signed by the captains of the ships.

While they were thus waiting for the cargo, it seemed to them, from the delay in the delivery, that the King was preparing some treachery against them, and the greater part of the ships' crews made an uproar and told the captains to go, as the delays which the King made were for nothing else than treachery : as it seemed to them all that it might be so, they were abandoning everything, and were intending to depart; and being about to unfurl the sails, the King, who had made the agreement with them, came to the flagship and asked the captain why he wanted to go, because that which he had agreed upon with him he intended to fulfil it as had been settled. The captain replied that the ships' crews said they should go and not remain any longer, as it was only treachery that was being prepared against them. To this the King answered that it was not so, and on that account he at once sent for his Koran, upon which he wished to make oath that nothing such should be done to them. They at once brought him this Koran, and upon it he made oath, and told them to rest at ease with that. At this the crews were set at rest, and he promised them that he would give them their cargo by the 15th December 1521, which he fulfilled within the said time without being-wanting in anything.

When the two ships were already laden and about to unfurl their sails, the flagship sprung a large leak, and the King of the country learning this, he sent them twenty-five divers to stop the leak, which they were unable to do. They settled that the other ship should depart, and that this one should again discharge all its cargo, and unload it; and as they could not stop the leak, that they [the people of the country] should give them all that they might be in need of. This was done, and they discharged the cargo of the flagship; and when the said ship was repaired, they took in her cargo, and decided on making for the country of the Antilles, and the course from Maluco to it was 2,000 leagues a little more or less. The other ship, which set sail first, left on the 21st of December of the said year, and went out to sea for Timor, and made its course behind Java, 2,055 leagues to the Cape of Good Hope.

They refitted the ship, and took in the cargo in four months and sixteen days : they sailed on the 6th of April of the year 1522, and took their course for the mainland of the Antilles by the strait through which they had come; and at first they navigated to the North, until they came out from the islands of Ternate and Tymor; afterwards they navigated along the island of Betachina, ten or eleven leagues to the North-east; after that they steered about twenty leagues to the North-east, and so arrived at an island, which is named Doyz, and is in three and a half degrees South latitude at its South-eastern side : from this place they navigated three or four leagues eastwards, and sighted two islands, one large and the other small; the large one was named Porquenampello, and passed between it and Batechina, which lay on their starboard side. They reached a cape, to which they gave the name Cape of Palms, because they sighted it on the vigil of Palms. This cape is in two and a half degrees : thence they steered to the South to make Quimar, which is land belonging to the King of Tydor, and the said King had ordered that they should receive whatever there was in the country for their money, and there they took pigs and goats, and fowls and coconuts and hava : they remained in this port eight or nine days. This port of Camarfya is in one and a quarter degree.

They sailed from this port on the 20th of April, and steered for about seventeen leagues, and came out of the channel of the island of Batechina and the island Charam, and as soon as they were outside, they saw that the said island of Charam ran to the South-east a good eighteen or twenty leagues, and it was not their course, for their direction was to the East and a quarter North-east; and they navigated in the said course some days, and always found the winds very contrary for their course. On the 3rd of May they made two small islands, which might be in five degrees more or less, to which they gave the name of islands of St. Antony. Thence they navigated further on to the North-east, and arrived at an island which is named Cyco, which is in fully nineteen degrees, and they made this island on the 11th of July. From this island they took a man, whom they carried away with them, and they navigated further on, tacking about with contrary winds, until they reached forty-two degrees North latitude.

When they were in this neighbourhood, they were short of bread, wine, meat, and oil; they had nothing to eat only water and rice, without other provisions; and the cold was great, and they had not sufficient covering, the crews began to die, and seeing themselves in this state, they decided on putting back in the direction of Maluco, which they at once carried into effect. When at a distance of five hundred leagues from it, they desired to make the island which is named Quamgragam, and as they sighted it at night, they did not choose to make it; they waited thus till it dawned next day, and they were unable to fetch the said island; and the man whom they carried with them, and whom before they had taken from that island, told them to go further on, and they would make three islands, where there was a good port, and this which the black man said, was in order to run away at them, as indeed he did run away. On arriving at these three islands, they fetched them with some danger, and anchored in the middle of them in fifteen fathoms. Of these islands, the largest was inhabited by twenty persons between men and women : this island is named Pamo; it is in twenty degrees more or less : here they took in rainwater, as there was no other in the country. In this island the black man ran away. Thence they sailed to make the land of Camafo, and as soon as they sighted it they had calms, and the currents carried them away from the land; and afterwards they had a little wind, and they made for the land, but could not fetch it; they then went to anchor between the islands of Domi and Batechina, and while at anchor, a parao passed by them with some men who belonged to the King of an island named Geilôlo, and they gave, them news that the Portuguese were in Maluco making a fortress. Learning this, they at once sent the clerk of the ship with certain men to the Captain-Major of those Portuguese, who was named Antonio de Bryto, to ask him to come and bring the ship to the place where they were; because the crew of the ship had mostly died, and the rest were sick, and could not navigate the ship. As soon as Antonio de Bryto saw the letter and message, he sent down Dom Gonzalo Amriquiz, captain of the ship Sam Jorge, and also a fusta with some country paraos, and they went thus in search of the ship, and having found it, they brought it to the fortress, and whilst they were discharging its cargo, there came a squall from the north, which cast it on shore. Where this ship turned to put back to Maluco was a little more or less than 1050 or 1100 leagues from the island.

This was transcribed from the paper-book of a Genoese pilot, who came in the said ship, who wrote all the voyage as it is here. He went to Portugal in the year 1524 with Dom Amriqui de Menezes. Thanks be to God.

CHAPTER 26

LETTER OF MAXIMILIAN TRANSYLVANUS

Maximilian Transylvanus, an under-secretary at the court of Charles V was at Valladolid when El Cano arrived. Maximilian interrogated him and his two companions, Albo and Bustamante. He wrote his description of the voyage in a letter to his father Cardinal Archbishop Lang of Salzburg.

****

Most Reverend and Illustrious Lord, my only Lord, to you I most humbly commend myself.

One of those five ships has lately returned that Caesar sent in former years, when he was living at Saragossa, to a strange, and for so many ages, an unknown world, in order to search for the islands where spices grow. For though the Portuguese bring a great quantity of them from the Golden Chersonesus, which we now suppose to be Malacca, yet their own Indies produce nothing but pepper. Other spices, such as cinnamon, cloves, and the nutmeg, which we call muscat, and its covering (mace), which we call muscat flower, are brought to their own Indies from distant islands till now only known by name, and in ships which are fastened together not by iron but by palm leaves. The sails of these ships are round and woven, too, of the palm fibre. This sort of ships they call junks, and they only use them with a wind directly fore and aft.

It is no wonder that these islands should be unknown to any human beings almost up to our time. For whatever we read concerning the native soil of the spices has been told us by ancient authors, and is partly, certainly, fabulous; and, partly, so far from the truth, that even the very countries in which they said that they grew naturally, are but little less distant from those where it is now known that they grow, than we are. For to omit others, Herodotus, in other respects a most famed author, has said that cinnamon is found in birds' nests, to which the birds have brought it from most distant regions, and specially the

Phoenix, and I know not who has seen his nest. However, Pliny, who thought himself able to give more certain information, because, before his time, many things had been made clear by the voyages of the fleets of Alexander the Great and of others, relates that cinnamon, grows in Aethiopia on the borders of the land of the Troglodytae, whilst now it is known that cinnamon is produced very far from any part of Aethiopia, and specially from the Troglodytae (that is, the dwellers in subterranean caverns). However, our men, who have now returned, and who were perfectly acquainted with Aethiopia, have been obliged to make a complete circuit of the world, and that a very wide one, before they could find the islands and return. As this voyage may be considered marvellous, and not only unaccomplished, but even unattempted either in our age or in any previous one, I have resolved to write as truly as possible to your Reverence the course (of the expedition) and the sequence of the whole matter. I have taken care to have everything related to me most exactly by the captain and by the individual sailors who have returned with him. They have also related each separate event to Caesar and to others with such good faith and sincerity, that they seemed not only to tell nothing fabulous themselves, but by their relation to disprove and refute all the fabulous stories which had been told by old authors. For who can believe that these were Monosceli, Scyopodae, Syritae, Spitamei, Pygmies, and many others, rather monsters than men.

And as so many places beyond the Tropic of Capricorn have been sought, found, and carefully examined, both by the Spaniards in the south-west and by the Portuguese sailing eastwards, and as the remainder of the whole world has now been sailed over by our countrymen, and yet nothing trustworthy has been heard concerning these man-monsters, it must be believed that the accounts of them are fabulous, lying, and old women's tales, handed down to us in some way by no credible author. However, lest I, who have to travel over the whole world, should seem too diffuse in my introduction, I return to my story.

When, nearly thirty years ago, the Spaniards in the west, and the Portuguese in the east, began to search for new and unknown lands, their two kings, lest one should be a hindrance to the other, divided the whole globe between them by the authority, most likely, of Pope Alexander the Sixth, in this manner : that a straight line should be drawn 360 miles, which they call leucae, west of the islands of the Hesperides, which are now called the islands of Cape Verd; towards the north, and another towards the south Pole, till they should meet again, and so divide the world into two equal parts. And whatever strange land should be discovered eastwards (of this line) should be ceded to the Portuguese, and whatever west of it to the Spaniards. In this manner it happened that the Spaniards always sailed southwest, and there they discovered a very large continent and very great and innumerable islands, rich in gold and pearls and in other wealth, and now, quite lately, have they discovered the vast Mediterranean city, Tenostica, situated in a lake, like Venice. About this city Peter Martyr, an author more careful about his facts than the elegance of his style, has written many wonderful, and yet true, things. However, the Portuguese, passing southwards by the shores of the Hesperides and of the ichthyophagous Aethiopians, and crossing the equinoctial line and the Tropic of Capricorn, sailed eastward, and discovered many great and unknown islands, and afterwards the sources of the Nile and the land of the Troglodytae. Thence they sailed past the Arabian and Persian Gulfs to the shores of India, within the Ganges, where there is now the mighty emporium and kingdom of Calicut. Thence they sailed to Taprobanes, which they now call Zamatara. For there is now no island which either can be, or can be supposed to be, Taprobanes, in the position in which Ptolemy, Pliny, and the other cosmographers placed it. Going thence, they arrived at the Golden Chersonesus, where now is situated that most famous city of Malacca, the greatest emporium of the East.

After this they entered the Great Gulf, which reaches as far as the country of the Sinae, which they now call Schinae, where they found a white and tolerably civilised people, like our Germans. They believe that the Seres and the Asiatic Scythians extend as far as there. And though there was a certain rumour afloat that the Portuguese had progressed so far to the east as to cross their own limits and enter the territory of the Spaniards, and that Malacca and the Great Bay were within our limits, still all these things were said rather than believed, until four years ago Ferdinand Magellan, a distinguished Portuguese, who, for many years had explored the coasts of the whole of the East as Admiral, took a great hatred to his king, whom he complained of as being most ungrateful to him, and came to Caesar. Christopher Haro, too, my own father-in-law's brother, who had traded for many years in the East by means of his agents, he himself staying in Ulyssipone, commonly called Lisbon, and who had lastly traded with the Chinese, so that he has great practice in such things, having also been unjustly treated by the King of Portugal, came also home to Spain. And they both showed Caesar that though it was not yet quite sure whether Malacca was within the confines of the Spaniards or the Portuguese, because, as yet, nothing of the longitude had been clearly proved, yet that it was quite plain that the Great Gulf and the people of Sinae lay within the Spanish boundary. This, too, was held to be most certain, that the islands which they call the Moluccas, in which all the spices are produced, and are thence exported to Malacca, lay within the Spanish western division, and that it was possible to sail there; and that spices could be brought thence to Spain more easily, and at less expense and cheaper, as they came direct from their native place.

Their course would be this, to sail westward, coasting the southern hemisphere (till they came) to the East. The thing seemed almost impossible and useless, not because it was thought a difficult thing to go from the west right to the east under the hemisphere, but because it was uncertain whether ingenious nature, which has done nothing without the greatest foresight, had not so dissevered the east from the west, partly by sea and partly by land, as to make it impossible to arrive there by either land or sea travelling. For it had not then been discovered whether that great region which is called Terra Firma did separate the western sea from the eastern; it was clear enough that that continent, in its southern part, trended southwards and afterwards westwards. It was clear, also, that two regions had been discovered in the North, one of which they called Regio Bacalearum (Cod-fish Land), from a new kind of fish; and the other Terra Florida. And if these two were united to that Terra Firma, it was impossible to get to the east by going from the west, as nothing had ever been discovered of any channel through this land, though it had been sought for most diligently and with great labour. And they considered it a very doubtful and most dangerous enterprise to go through the limits of the Portuguese, and so to the east. For which reason it seemed to Caesar and to his counsellors that these men were promising a thing from which much was to be hoped, but still of great difficulty. When they were both brought to an audience on a certain day, Magellan offered to go himself, but Christopher offered to fit out a fleet at his own expense and that of his friends, but only if it were allowed to sail under the authority and protection of Caesar.

Whilst they both persisted rather obstinately in their offers, Caesar himself equipped a fleet of five ships, and appointed Magellan its admiral. Their orders were, to sail southwards along the coast of Terra Firma till they found either its termination or some channel through which they might reach the spice-bearing Moluccas. So Magellan set sail on the 10th of August, 1519, with five ships from Seville. A few days after he reached the Fortunate Islands, which are now sometimes called the Canaries. Thence they arrived at the Islands of the, Hesperides, from which they took a south-western course towards that continent which we mentioned before; and after some days' fair sailing they sighted a promontory, to which the name of Santa Maria has been given. Here Juan Ruy Diaz Solis had been eaten, with some of his companions, by the anthropophagi, whom the Indians call cannibals, whilst, by order of Ferdinand the Catholic, he was exploring the coast of this continent with a fleet.

Sailing thence, our men coasted in an unbroken course along the coasts of this continent, which extend a very long way south, and tend a little west, so that they crossed the Tropic of Capricorn by many degrees. I think that this continent should be called that of the Southern Pole. However, it was not so easy as I have said; for not till the last day of March of the following year did they reach a bay, to which they gave the name of Saint Julian. Here they found the Antarctic Pole star 49 and a fifth degrees above their horizon, both by the altitude and declination of the sun from the Equinoctial, and also by the altitude of the Antarctic (Pole star) itself. This star our sailors generally make use of more than of any other. They state also that the longitude was 56 deg. west of the Fortunate Isles. For, as the ancient cosmographers, and specially Ptolemy, reckoned the longitude from the Fortunate Islands eastward to Catigara at 180 deg., so our men, sailing as far as they could westward also, began to reckon another 180 deg. westward to Catigara, as was right. Yet our sailors seem to me rather to be mistaken in the calculation of the longitudes (of distances ?) than to have fixed them with any certainty, because in so long a voyage, and being so distant from the land, they cannot fix and determine any marks or signs for the longitude. Still I think that these accounts, whatever they be, should not be cast aside, but rather accepted till more certain information be discovered.

This Gulf of Saint Julian seemed very great, and had the appearance of a channel. Wherefore, Admiral Magellan ordered two ships to explore the Gulf and anchored the rest outside. After two days, information was brought to him that the Gulf was full of shoals, and did not extend far inland. Our men, on their way back, saw some Indians picking up shell-fish on the shore; for they call the natives of all unknown lands Indians. They were of extraordinary height, that is to say, about ten spans, were clothed in the skins of wild beasts, and seemed darker than would be expected from the situation of the country. When some of our men went on shore to them and showed them bells and pictures painted on paper, they began a hoarse chant and an unintelligible song, dancing round our men, and, in order to astonish them, they passed arrows a cubit and a half long down their throats to the bottom of their stomachs, and without being sick. And forthwith drawing them out again, they seemed to rejoice greatly, as having shown their bravery by this exploit.

At last three came as ambassadors, and prayed our men, by certain signs, to go further inland with them, as if they, would receive them with all hospitality. Magellan sent seven men, well armed, with them, to investigate as carefully as possible both country and people. When they had gone with them about seven miles inland, they came to a thick and pathless wood.

Here was a rather low hut, covered with skins of wild beasts. There were two apartments in it; in one lived the women with their children, in the other the men. There were thirteen women and children, and five men. These received their guests with a (ferali apparatu) barbarous pomp, which seemed to them a royal one. An animal was slaughtered, which seemed to differ little from the onager, and they served it up half roasted to our men, without any other food or drink. Our men were obliged, contrary to their custom, to sleep under skins, on account of the severity of the snow and wind. Wherefore, before they slept, they set watch. The Indians did the same, and lay down near our men, snoring horribly.

When the day had broken, our men asked them to return with them to the ships, with the whole family. When the Indians had refused for a considerable time, and our men had insisted upon it rather imperiously, the men entered the den-like women's apartment. The Spaniards thought that they were consulting with their wives concerning this expedition; but they returned covered, from the sole of their feet to the crown of their heads, with different horrible skins, and with their faces painted in different colours, and equipped in this terrible and horrible garb with bows and arrows for battle, and (seemingly ?) of much greater stature than before. The Spaniards, who thought that it would come to a fight, ordered (a shot) to be fired. Though this shot was harmless, still the giants, who looked just before fit to contend with Jove, were so frightened by this sound, that they began forthwith to speak of peace. The upshot was, that three men returned with our fellows to the ships, having sent away the rest of the family. So they started for the ships. However, as our men could not only not keep up with these almost giants when the latter were running, but could not, even by running, keep up with them walking, two of them escaped upon the march, on the pretext of pursuing an onager, which they saw feeding at a distance upon a mountain. The third was brought to the ship, but died, within a few days, of fasting, which he had imposed upon himself, according to the habit of the Indians, through home-sickness.

And though the admiral sent again to that hut, in order to catch some one of these giants to take to Caesar on account of their novelty, yet no one was found there, but all had gone elsewhere with the hut. Whence it seems clear that that race is a wandering one, nor did our men ever see another Indian on that coast, though they remained in that bay for many days, as we shall mention farther on. They did not think that there was anything in that region of sufficient importance to justify their exploring it and the interior any farther. Though Magellan perceived that any longer stay there was useless, yet, as the sea for several days was stormy and the sky threatening, and the land stretched continuously southwards, so that the farther they went the colder they would find that region, his departure was necessarily put off from day to day, till the month of May was close upon them, from which time the winter there begins to be most severe, so that it became necessary to winter at the very time when we have our summer.

Magellan foreseeing that the voyage would be a long one, ordered provisions to be served out more sparingly among his crews, so that the stock might last longer. When the Spaniards had borne this patiently for some days, fearing the severity of the winter and the barrenness of the country, they at last petitioned their admiral, Magellan, that, as he saw that the land stretched uninterruptedly to the south, and that no hope remained of its terminating or of the discovery of a strait through it, and that a severe winter was imminent, and that many of them were dead of starvation and hardships; and declared that they could no longer bear the rule which he had made about the allowance of provisions (leg sumptuaria), and begged that he would increase the allowance of provisions, and think about going home; that Caesar never intended that they should too obstinately attempt what nature itself and other obstacles opposed; that their exertions were already sufficiently known and approved of, for they had gone farther than either the boldness or rashness of mortals had ever dared to go as yet; and that they could easily reach some milder shore, if they were to sail south (north?) for a few days, a south wind being then blowing. However, in reply, Magellan, who had already made up his mind either to die or to complete his enterprise, said that his course had been laid down for him by Caesar himself, and that he neither could nor would depart from it in any degree, and that he would in consequence sail till he found either the end of the land or some strait (through it).

That though they could not at present succeed whilst winter was against them, yet that it would be easy in the summer of that region. However, that, if they would continue towards the Antarctic portion of this country, the whole of its summer would be one perpetual day. That there were means if they would only try them, by which they might avoid famine and the rigour of the winter, in as much as there was abundance of wood, and the sea provided shellfish and many sorts of the very best fish. The springs there were wholesome, and bird fowling and hunting would supply many wants; and neither bread nor wine had as yet been lacking, nor would they lack in future if they would only bear that they should be served out when needed, or for health's sake, and not for pleasure or for luxury. They had done nothing as yet worthy of admiration, or which could serve as an excuse for their return, in as much as the Portuguese crossed the tropic of Capricorn by as much as 12 deg. not only every year, but almost every day, when they were sailing eastwards. They would be thought worthy of very little praise who had gone only 4 deg. southwards. He had certainly made up his mind to endure the worst rather than return ignominiously to Spain, and he trusted that all his comrades, or at least those in whom the noble Spanish spirit was not yet dead, would be of the same mind.

He advised them to bear at least the remainder of the winter patiently, and said that their rewards would be the more abundant the more difficulties and dangers they had endured in opening to Caesar a new unknown world, rich in spices and gold. Magellan thought that the minds of his crews were soothed and cheered by this harangue, but within a few days was harassed by a shameful and foul conspiracy. For talking began amongst the crews about the old eternal hatred between the Portuguese and the Spaniards, and about Magellan's being a Portuguese. He, they said, could do nothing more glorious for his own country than to cast away this fleet, with so many men. Nor was it credible that he should wish to discover the Moluccas, even if he were able; but he would think it sufficient if he could lure Caesar on for some years with a vain hope, and meanwhile something new would turn up, by which the Spaniards would for the future be diverted from the search for spices. Nor even had their course begun to turn towards those happy Moluccas, but rather to distant snows and ice, and to perpetual storms.

Magellan, very much enraged by these sayings, punished the men, but rather more harshly than was proper for a foreigner, especially when commanding in a distant country. So, having planned a conspiracy, they seize upon a ship, and make ready to return to Spain. However, he, with the rest whom he had still obedient to his commands, attacked that ship, and put to death the head man and the other ringleaders, those even who could not lawfully be so treated sharing the same fate. For these were certain servants of the king, upon whom no one but Caesar and his Council could lawfully pronounce a sentence of death. Nevertheless, no one from that time dared to disparage the power of the commander. Still, there were not wanting some who whispered that Magellan would, in the same manner, murder all the Spaniards to the last man, until he, having got rid of them all, might return with the few Portuguese with the fleet to his own country. And so this hatred settled more deeply in the hearts of the Spaniards.

As soon as ever Magellan saw the storminess of the sea and the rigour of the winter mitigated, he set sail from the gulf of St. Julian on the 24th of August. And, as before, he followed the course of the coast southwards for many days. A promontory was at last sighted, which they called Santa Cruz, when a severe storm, springing front the east, suddenly caught them, and one of the five ships was cast on shore, the men being all saved, with the merchandise and equipment, except one Ethiopian slave, who was caught and drowned by the waves. After this the land seemed to bear a little east and south, and this they began to coast along as usual, and on the 26th of November certain inlets of the sea were discovered, which had the appearance of a strait. Magellan entered them forthwith with the whole fleet, and when he saw other and again other bays, he gave orders that they should be all carefully examined from the ships, to see if anywhere a passage might be discovered; and said that he would himself wait at the mouth of the strait till the fifth day, to hear what might happen.

One of the ships, which Alvarus Meschito, his nephew, commanded, was carried back by the tide to the sea, to the very place where they entered the gulf. However, when the Spaniards perceived that they were far away from the other ships, they made a plot to return home, put Alvarus, their captain, in irons, bent their course northwards, and were at last carried to the coast of Aethiopia (Guinea), and, having victualled there, they reached Spain eight months after they had deserted the rest. There they compel Alvarus to stand his trial in chains (causam ex vinculis dicere faciunt quasi), for having, by his counsel and advice, induced his uncle Magellan to practice such harshness on the Spaniards.

However, when Magellan had waited for this ship some days longer than the time fixed, another returned, which had discovered nothing but a bay full of shoals and shingle, and very lofty cliffs. The third ship, however, reported that the largest bay had the appearance of a strait, as in three days' sail they had found no way out; but the farther they had gone the narrower the sea was, and they had not been able to sound the depth of it in many places by any length of line, and that they had also noticed that the tide was rather stronger than the ebb, and that so they were persuaded that a passage was open in that, direction to some other sea. He made up his mind to sail through it. This channel, which they did not then know to be a channel, was at one place three Italian miles wide, at another two, sometimes ten, and sometimes five, and pointed a little westward. The altitude of the southern pole was found to be 52 deg., and the longitude to be the same, as at St. Julian's Bay. The month of November was upon them (Aderat jam mensis Novembris), the night was rather more than five hours long, and they had never seen any human beings on the shore.

However, one night a great number of fires were seen, mostly on their left hand, from which they guessed that they had been seen by the natives of the region. However, Magellan, seeing that the country was rocky, and also stark with eternal cold, thought it useless to waste many days in examining it; and so, with only three ships, he continued on his course along the channel, until, on the twenty-second day after he had entered it, he sailed out upon another wide and vast sea. The length of the channel they attest to be nearly a hundred Spanish miles.

There is no doubt that the land which they had upon their right was the continent of which we have spoken, but they think that the land on the left was not a mainland, but islands, because sometimes on that side they heard on a still farther coast the beating and roaring of the sea.

Magellan saw that the continent stretched northwards again in a straight line; wherefore, leaving that huge continent on the right hand, he ordered them to sail through that vast and mighty sea (which I do not think had ever seen either our or any one else's ships) in the direction whence the wind called Corus generally blows - that is, 'twixt north and west - so that he might, by going through west to east, again arrive at the torrid zone; for he thought that it was proved sufficiently clearly that the Moluccas were in the most remote east, and could not be far from the equator. They kept this course uninterruptedly, nor did they ever depart from it, except when rough weather or violent winds compelled them to diverge; and when they had in this manner been carried for forty days by a strong and generally favourable wind, and had seen nothing but sea, and everywhere sea - when they had almost reached the tropic of Capricorn once more, two islands were sighted, but small and barren. These they found uninhabited when they tried to land; still, they stopped there two days for their health's sake, and general recruiting of their bodies, for there was very fair fishing there. They named these the Unfortunate Islands by common consent.

Then they again set sail thence, following their original course and direction of sailing. And when, for three months and twenty days, they had been sailing over this ocean with great good fortune, and had traversed an immense part of the sea - more vast than mind of man can conceive, for they had been driven almost continuously by a very strong wind - they were now at last arrived on this side of the equinoctial line, and at last they saw an island, called, as they learnt afterwards, Inuagana by the natives. When they had approached nearer, they discovered the altitude of the Arctic pole to be 11 deg.. The longitude they thought to be 158 deg. west of Gades. Then they saw other and still more islands, so that they knew they had arrived at some vast archipelago. When they reached Inuagana, the island was discovered to be uninhabited. They then approached a rather small island, where they saw two Indian canoes - for that is the name by which this strange kind of boat is called by the Indians. The canoes are cut and hollowed out of a single trunk of a tree, and hold one, or, at most, two men; and they usually speak by gestures and signs, as if the dumb were talking with the dumb.

They asked the Indians the names of the islands, and where they could get provisions, of which they were in great want. They understood that the island in which they had been was called Inuagana, and that the one where they now were was Acaca, but both of them uninhabited. They said that there was an island not far off, which was called Selani, and which they almost showed with their finger, and that it was inhabited, and that an abundance of everything necessary for life was to be found there.

Our men, having taken in water in Acaca, sailed towards Selani; here a storm took them, so that they could not bring the ships to that island, but were driven to another island called Massaua, where lives a king of (the?) three islands, after that they arrived at Subuth. This is an excellent and large island, and, having made a treaty with its chieftain, they landed immediately to perform divine service, according to the manner of Christians, for it was the feast of the resurrection of Him who was our salvation. Wherefore, they built a small chapel of the sails of the ships, and of boughs, and in that they built an altar according to the Christian rites, and performed service after their home fashion. The chieftain came up with a great number of Indians, who seemed in every way delighted by this worship of the gods. They led the admiral and some of the officers to the chief's hut, and put before them whatever food they had. Their bread, which they call sago, was made of the trunk or wood of a tree, rather like a palm. This, when cut in pieces, and fried in oil in a pan, supplies them with bread, a small piece of which I send to your reverence. Their drink was a liquor which flows and trickles from the boughs of the palm-trees when cut. Fowling, too, supplied the feast, and the rest was the fruit of that region.

Magellan beheld, in the chief's hut, one sick, and almost at the last gasp. He asked who he was, and what illness he was suffering from. He learnt that he was the chief's grandson, and had now suffered for two years from a raging fever. However, he told him to be of good cheer, and that he would immediately recover his health and former strength, if he would only become a Christian. The Indian accepted the condition, and, having adored the Cross, he received baptism, and the next day declared that he was well, rose from his bed, walked, and took food like the rest. He told I know not what visions to the Indians. What need I say more ? The chief himself, with two thousand two hundred Indians, was baptized, and professed the name and religion of Christ. However, Magellan, judging this island to abound in gold and ginger, and, besides, to be convenient from its position with respect to the neighbouring islands, for exploring with ease their wealth and produce of the earth, goes to the Chief of Subuth, and persuades him that as he had abandoned that vain and impious worship of the gods, and had turned to the religion of Christ, it was only fair that the kings of the neighbouring isles should be subject to his rule and command; and he said that he had resolved to send ambassadors concerning this, and compel by arms those who did not listen to his command.

This proposition pleased the savage, and the ambassadors were sent. The chiefs came in one by one, and did homage. The nearest island was called Mauthan, the king of which excelled the others in number of soldiers and in arms, and he refused to do homage to one whom he had been accustomed for so long to command.

Magellan, who desired to finish what he had once begun, gave orders that forty of his men, whose bravery and prowess he had proved, should arm, and he crossed over to Mauthan in boats, for the island was very near. The Chief of Subuth added some of his own men to show him the situation of the island, and to fight, if matters came to that.

The King of Mauthan, seeing our men coming, draws up about three thousand of his subjects in the field, and Magellan draws up his on the shore, with their guns and warlike engines, though only a few; and though he saw that he was far inferior to the enemy in number, yet he thought it better to fight this warlike race, which made use of lances and other long weapons, than either to return or to use the soldiers from Subuth. So he orders his men to be of good cheer and brave hearts, and not to be alarmed at the number of the enemy, for they had often seen, as formerly, so in quite recent times, two hundred Spaniards in the island of Yucatan put sometimes two or three hundred thousand men to flight. However, he pointed out to the Subuth islanders that he had brought them, not to fight, but to watch their bravery and fighting power (robur in acie). So, having charged the enemy, both sides fought valiantly but, as the enemy were more numerous, and used longer weapons, with which they did our men much damage, Magellan himself was at last thrust through and slain. However, the rest of our men, though they did not seem quite conquered, yet retreated, having lost their leader. And the enemy dared not follow them, as they were retreating in good order.

So the Spaniards, having lost their admiral, Magellan, and seven of their comrades, returned to Subuth, where they chose another commander, John Serrano, a man not to be despised. He immediately renewed with fresh gifts the alliance that had been made with the King of Subuth, and promised to subdue the King of Mauthan.

Magellan had a slave, born in the Moluccas, whom he had bought in Malacca some time back; this man was a perfect master of the Spanish language, and, with the assistance of one of the islanders of Subuth as interpreter, who knew the language of the Moluccas, our men managed all their communications. This slave had been present at the battle of Mauthan, and had received some slight wounds in it. For which reason he lay all day long nursing himself. Serrano, who could manage nothing without him, spoke to him very harshly, and told him that he had not ceased to be a slave and bondsman because Magellan was dead, but that the yoke of slavery would be heavier, and that he would be severely flogged unless he did the services required of him more zealously.

This slave conceived an intense hatred of us from these words; but, concealing his anger, he went a few days after to the Chief of Subuth, and told him that the greed of the Spaniards was insatiable, that they had resolved and determined, after they had conquered the King of Mauthan, to make a quarrel with him and take him away prisoner, and there was no other remedy possible than to anticipate their treachery by treachery. The savage believed it all. He made peace secretly with the King of Mauthan and the others, and they plotted our destruction. Serrano, the commander, with all the rest of his officers, who were about twenty-seven in number, were invited to a solemn banquet. They, suspecting no evil - for the savages had cunningly dissimulated in everything - land, careless and unsuspecting, as men who were going to dine with the chief would do. Whilst they were feasting they were set upon by those who had been placed in ambush. Shouts were raised on all sides, and news flew to the ships that our men were murdered, and that everything on the island was hostile to us. Our men see from the ships that the beautiful cross, which they had hoisted on a tree was hurled to the ground, and kicked to pieces by the savages with great fury. However, the remaining Spaniards, who had stopped on board, when they knew of their comrades' murder, feared some still greater treachery. Wherefore, when they had weighed anchor, they begin to set sail quickly. Shortly after, Serrano was brought down to the shore bound most cruelly, and he begged them to redeem him from so harsh a captivity. He said be had prevailed upon them to permit his being ransomed, if our men would only do it.

Though our men thought it shameful to leave their commander in this way, yet, fearing fraud and treachery, they put out to sea, leaving Serrano on the shore, weeping bitterly, and imploring the help and assistance of his fellow countrymen with great and grievous lamentation. The Spaniards sailed along, sad and anxious, having lost their commander and their shipmates, not only alarmed by their loss and by the slaughter of their mates, but because their number was reduced so low that it was quite insufficient for the management of three ships. Wherefore, they hold a council, and, having taken the votes, they agree that there was nothing better to do than to burn some one of the three ships, and keep only two.

So they go to an island near, Cohol by name, and transfer the equipment to the other two ships, and burn the third. Then they sailed to the island called Gibeth. Though they found that it was rich in gold and ginger and many other things, yet they thought it better not to stay there long, because they could not, by any kindness, attract the Indians to them. And their scantiness of number prevented their fighting. Thence they went to the island Porne (Borneo). There are two great and rich islands in this archipelago, one of which was called Siloli, the king of which had six hundred children; and the other Porne.

Siloli was greater than the one called Porne. For it takes nearly six months to sail round it, but Porne only three. However, just so much as the former is larger, so much is the latter better situated as regards fertility of soil, and more famed also for the size of a city of the same name as itself. And, as Porne must be considered of more importance than any of the other islands which they had examined, and seemed to be the source whence the others received their good customs and civilization (cultum vitae), I have resolved to touch, in a few words, upon the customs and laws of these peoples. All these islanders are Caphrae, that is, heathen, and worship the sun and moon. They ascribe the rule of the day to the sun, but that of the night to the moon; the former they call male, and the latter female; and them, too, they call the parents of the stars, which they deem to be all gods, though small ones. They salute the rising sun with certain hymns before they worship it. This they do also to the moon, when it shines at night, to whom they pray for children, and fruitful increase of cattle, and abundant fruits of the earth, and other things of that sort.

However, they practice justice and piety, and specially do they love peace and quiet, but war they greatly detest, and they honour their king as a god whilst he is bent upon peace. However, if he be too desirous of war, they rest not till be has fallen by the hand of the enemy in battle. Whenever he has determined to wage war, which is rarely done, he is placed by his subjects in the vanguard, where he is compelled to bear the whole onslaught of the enemy. Nor do they fight against the enemy with any spirit until they know that their king is dead; then, first do they begin to fight for their liberty and for their future king, nor has there ever been seen among them a king who began a war who has not died in battle. Wherefore, they rarely wage war, and think it unjust to extend their territories; but the special care of all is not wantonly to attack either the neighbouring or the distant peoples. However, if at any time they are attacked, they meet force by force (par pari re ferunt). However, lest the mischief should spread farther they look immediately to making peace. There can be nothing more honourable among them than to be the first to ask for peace, nor more disgraceful than to be anticipated in asking for it, and they think it shameful and hateful to refuse it to anyone, even if he had attacked them without provocation. And all the neighbouring people unite against the one (who refuses peace) for his destruction, as against a cruel and impious man. Whence it happens that they almost always enjoy quiet and repose. There is no robbery among them, and no murder. No one but his wives and children may speak to the king, except by means of canes, which they, place to his ear from a distance, and whisper what they wish through them. They say that man, after his death, has no feeling, as he had none before his birth. They have small houses, built of logs and of earth, partly roofed with, rubble, and partly with palm leaves. [Aedes habent exiles ex lignis & terra constructas, partim rudere, partim palmatis frondibus coopertas.] It is, though, quite certain that in Porne there are twenty thousand houses. They marry as many wives as they can afford, and live on food, which bird-fowling or fishing supplies them with. They make bread of rice, and a drink which drops from the severed branches of the palm, as we said before.

Some carry on traffic in the neighbouring islands, to which they go in junks; some devote themselves to hunting; some to fishing; and others to agriculture. They have dresses of cotton, and almost all the animals that we have, except the sheep, the ox, and the ass; but their horses are very small and feeble. The produce of camphor, of, ginger, and of cinnamon, is great among them. Thence our men, having saluted this king, and heaped him with presents, directed their course to the Moluccas, which had been pointed out to them by the same king. They came to the shores of the island of Solo, where they heard that there were pearls as big as dove's eggs, and sometimes as hen's eggs, but which can only be fished up from the very deepest sea. Our men brought no large pearl, because the season of the year did not allow of the fishery. However, they testify that they had taken an oyster in that region, the flesh of which weighed forty-seven pounds. For which reason I could easily believe that pearls of that great size are found there; for it is clearly proved that pearls are the product of shell-fish. And to omit nothing, our men constantly affirm that the islanders of Porne told them that the king wore in his crown two pearls of the size of a goose's egg.

Hence they went to the island of Gilo, where they saw men with ears so long and pendulous, that they reached to their shoulders. When our men were mightily astonished at this, they learnt from the natives that there was another island not far off where the men had ears not only pendulous, but so long and broad, that one of them would cover the whole head, if they wanted it (cum ex usu esset). However, our men, who sought not monsters but spices, neglecting this nonsense, went straight to the Moluccas, and they discovered them eight months after their admiral, Magellan, had fallen in Mauthan. The islands are five in number, and are called Tarante, Muthil, Thidore, Mare, and Matthien: some on this side, some on the other, and some upon the equinoctial line.

One produces cloves, another nutmegs, and another cinnamon. All are near to each other, but small and rather narrow.

The kings (of ?) Marmin began to believe that souls were immortal a few years ago, induced by no other argument than that they saw that a certain most beautiful small bird never rested upon the ground nor upon anything that grew upon it; but they sometimes saw it fall dead upon the ground from the sky. And as the Mahometans, who travelled to those parts for commercial purposes, told them that this bird was born in Paradise, and that Paradise was the abode of the souls of those who had died, these kings (reguli) embraced the sect of Mahomet, because it promised wonderful things concerning this abode of souls. However, they call the bird Mamuco Diata, and they hold it in such reverence and religious esteem, that they believe that by it their kings are safe in war, even though they, according to custom, are placed in the fore front of battle. The common folk are Caphrae, and of almost the same manners and laws as the islanders of Porne; they are rather poor, as would be likely with people in whose land nothing grows except spices. These they willingly barter for poisons, namely, arsenic and what is commonly called sublimate of mercury, and for linens, in which they generally are dressed; but for what purpose they use these poisons, we have not yet found out. They live on sago bread and fish, and sometimes on parrots, and they shelter in low huts. What need of many words. Everything there is humble, and of no value, but peace, quiet, and spices. The best and noblest of which, and the greatest good possible, namely, peace, seems to have been driven by men's wickedness from our world to theirs. However, avarice and the insatiable greed of the belly, have driven us to seek for spices in their unknown world. (Adeo hominum protervia salubria quaeque haud longius satis nequet protudere neque quae luxus et libidinis appetere.) However, our men having carefully inspected the position of the Moluccas and of each separate island, and also having inquired about the habits of the kings, went to Thedori, because they learnt that in that island the supply of cloves was far above that of the others, and that its king also surpassed the other kings in wisdom and humanity. So, having prepared their gifts, they land, and salute the king, and they offer the presents as if they had been sent by Caesar. He, having received the presents kindly, looks up to heaven, and says : "I have known now for two years from the course of the stars, that you were coming to seek these lands, sent by the most mighty King of Kings. Wherefore, your coming is the more pleasant and grateful to me, as I had been forewarned of it by the signification of the stars."

And, as I know that nothing ever happens to any man which has not been fixed long before by the decree of fate and the stars, I will not be the one to attempt to withstand either the fates or the signification of the stars, but willingly and of good cheer, will henceforth lay aside the royal pomp and will consider myself as managing the administration of this island only in the name of your king : Wherefore draw your ships into port, and order the rest of your comrades to land; so that now at last, after such a long tossing upon the seas, and so many dangers, you may enjoy the pleasures of the land and refresh your bodies. And think not but that you have arrived at your king's kingdom. Having said this, the king, laying aside his crown, embraced them one by one, and ordered whatever food that land afforded to be brought. Our men being overjoyed at this, returned to their comrades, and told them what had happened. They, pleased above measure with the friendly behaviour and kindness of the king, take possession of the island. And when their health was completely restored, in a few days, by the king's munificence, they send envoys to the other kings, to examine the wealth of the islands, and to conciliate the other kings. Tarante was the nearest, and also the smallest, of the islands; for it has a circumference of a little more than six Italian miles. Mathien is next to it, and it, too, is small. These three produce a great quantity of cloves, but more every fourth year than the other three. These trees only grow on steep rocks, and that so thickly as frequently to form a grove. This tree is very like a laurel (or bay tree) in leaf, closeness of growth, and height; and the gariophile which they call clove from its likeness (to a nail, clavus) grows on the tip of each separate twig. First a bud, and then a flower, just like the orange flower is produced.

The pointed part of the clove is fixed at the extreme end of the branch, and then growing slightly longer, it forms a spike. It is at first red, but soon gets black by the heat of the sun. The natives keep the plantations of these trees separate, as we do our vines. They bury the cloves in pits till they are taken away by the traders. Muthil, the fourth island, is not larger than the rest, and it produces cinnamon. The tree is full of shoots, and in other respects barren; it delights in dryness, and is very like the tree which bears pomegranates. The bark of this splits under the influence of the sun's heat, and is stripped off the wood; and, after drying a little in the sun, it is cinnamon. Near to this is another island, called Bada, larger and more ample than the Moluccas. In this grows the nutmeg, the tree of which is tall and spreading, and is rather like the walnut tree, and its nut, too, grows like the walnut; for it is protected by a double husk, at first like a furry calix, and under this a thin membrane, which embraces the nut like network. This is called the Muscat flower with us, but by the Spaniards mace, and is a noble and wholesome spice. The other covering is a woody shell, like that of hazelnut, and in that, as we have already said, is the nutmeg. Ginger grows here and there in each of the islands of the archipelago. It sometimes grows by sowing, and sometimes spontaneously; but that which is sown is the more valuable. Its grass is like that of the saffron, and its root is almost the same too, and that is ginger.

Our men were kindly treated by the chiefs in turn, and they, too, submitted freely to the rule of Caesar, like the King of Thidori. However, the Spaniards, who had but two ships, resolved to bring some of each (spice) home, but to load the ships with cloves, because the crop of that was most abundant that year, and our ships could contain a greater quantity of this kind of spice. Having, therefore, loaded the ships with cloves, and having received letters and presents for Caesar from the kings, they make ready for their departure. The letters were full of submission and respect. The gifts were Indian swords, and things of that sort. However, best of all, the Mamuco Diata; that is, the Bird of God, by which they believe themselves to be safe and invincible in battle. Of which five were sent, and one I obtained from the captain (con gran prieghi), which I send to your reverence, not that your reverence may think yourself safe from treachery and the sword by means of it, as they profess to do, but that you may be pleased by its rareness and beauty. I send also some cinnamon and nutmeg and, cloves, to show that our spices are not only not worse, but more valuable than those which the Venetians and Portuguese bring, because they are fresher.

When our men had set sail from Thedori, one of the ships, and that the larger one, having sprung a leak, began to make water, so that it became necessary to put back to Thedori. When the Spaniards saw that this mischief could not be remedied without great labour and much time, they agreed that the other ship should sail to the Cape of Cattigara, and afterwards through the deep as far as possible from the coast of India, lest it should be seen by the Portuguese, and until they saw the Promontory of Africa, which projects beyond the Tropic of Capricorn, and to which the Portuguese have given the name of Good Hope; and from that point the passage to Spain would be easy. However, as soon as the other ship was refitted, it should direct its course through the archipelago, and that vast ocean towards the shores of the continent which we mentioned before, till it found that coast which was in the neighbourhood of Darien, and where the southern sea was separated from the western, in which are the Spanish Islands, by a very narrow space of land. So the ship sailed again from Thedori, and, having gone twelve degrees on the other side of the equinoctial line, they did not find the Cape of Cattigara, which Ptolemy supposed to extend even beyond the equinoctial line; but when they had traversed an immense space of sea, they came to the Cape of Good Hope and afterwards to the Islands of the Hesperides.

And, as this ship let in water, being much knocked about by this long voyage, the sailors, many of whom had died by hardships by land and by sea, could not clear the ship of the water. Wherefore, they landed upon one of the islands, which is named after Saint James, to buy slaves. However, as our men had no money, they offered, sailor fashion, cloves for the slaves. This matter having come to the ears of the Portuguese who were in command of the island, thirteen of our men were thrown into prison. The rest were eighteen in number. Frightened by the strangeness of this behaviour, they started straight for Spain, leaving their shipmates behind them. And so, in the sixteenth month after leaving Thedori, they arrived safe and sound on the sixth of September, at the port near Hispalis (Seville). Worthier, indeed, are our sailors of eternal fame than the Argonauts who sailed with Jason to Colchis. And much more worthy was their ship of being placed among the stars than that old Argo; for that only sailed from Greece through Pontus, but ours from Hispalis to the south; and after that, through the whole west and the southern hemisphere, penetrating into the east, and again returned to the west.

I commend myself most humbly to your Reverence.

Given at Vallisoleti, on the 23rd of October, 1522.

Your most Reverend and Illustrious Lordship's Most humble and constant servant, MAXIMILIANUS TRANSYLVANUS

(Printed at) Cologne, in the house of Eucharius Cervicornus, in the year of the Virgin's Child, 1523, in the month of January.

BIBLIOGRAPHY

The following are the principle English language sources of information concerning Magellan. They also contain references to the original sources of information :

Magellan (Francis Guillemard, Antonio Pigafetta, Francisco Albo, Gaspar Correa) [2008] - Biography of Magellan, all of the known contemporary accounts of the voyage by : Antonio Pigafetta (plus his treatise on navigation), Maximilian Transylvanus, Francisco Albo, Gaspar Correa, the Genoese Pilot, the anonymous Portuguese, and additional information concerning the voyage including personnel, stores, equipment, costs and orders;

The life of Ferdinand Magellan and the first circumnavigation of the Globe, 1480-1521 (Francis Guillemard) [1891] - Biography of Magellan, documents concerning Magellan, and additional information concerning the voyage including personnel, stores and equipment.

The first voyage round the world, by Magellan. Translated from the accounts of Pigafetta, and other contemporary writers. (translator : Lord Stanley of Alderney) [1874] - All of the known contemporary accounts of the voyage by : Antonio Pigafetta (plus his treatise on navigation), Maximilian Transylvanus, Francisco Albo, Gaspar Correa, the Genoese Pilot, the anonymous Portuguese, and additional information concerning the voyage including costs, personnel and orders.

http://viartis.net/publishers

FOR MORE BOOKS BY VIARTIS

Printed in the United States
123338LV00001B/209/P